Evolutionary Governance in China

HARVARD CONTEMPORARY CHINA SERIES 20

Evolutionary Governance in China

State–Society Relations under Authoritarianism

Edited by
Szu-chien Hsu, Kellee S. Tsai,
and Chun-chih Chang

Published by the Harvard University Asia Center
Distributed by Harvard University Press
Cambridge (Massachusetts) and London 2021

The Harvard University Asia Center publishes several monograph series and, in coordination with the Fairbank Center for Chinese Studies, the Korea Institute, the Reischauer Institute of Japanese Studies, and other faculties and institutes, administers research projects designed to further scholarly understanding of China, Japan, Vietnam, Korea, and other Asian countries. The Center also sponsors projects addressing multidisciplinary and regional issues in Asia.

Library of Congress Cataloging-in-Publication Data

Names: Xu, Sijian, editor.
Title: Evolutionary governance in China : state-society relations under authoritarianism / edited by Szu-chien Hsu, Kellee S. Tsai, and Chun-chih Chang.
Description: Cambridge (Massachusetts) : Published by the Harvard University Asia Center : Distributed by Harvard University Press Cambridge, [2021] | Series: Harvard contemporary China series; 20 | Includes bibliographical references. | Summary: ""Adopts an evolutionary framework to examine how the Chinese state relates with non-state actors across several fields of governance: community, environment, public health, economics, labor, society, and religion; identifies areas where state-society interactions have shifted over time, ranging from constructive engagement to protracted conflict, thereby providing nuanced insight into the circumstances wherein the party-state exerts its coercive power versus engaging in more flexible responses"— Provided by publisher.
Identifiers: LCCN 2020039192 (print) | LCCN 2020039193 (ebook) | ISBN 9780674251199 (paperback) | ISBN 9781684176472 (adobe pdf)
Subjects: LCSH: China—Politics and government. | China—Social conditions. | Authoritarianism—China.
Classification: LCC JQ1510 .E86 2021 (print) | LCC JQ1510 (ebook) | DDC 320.951—dc23
LC record available at https://lccn.loc.gov/2020039192
LC ebook record available at https://lccn.loc.gov/2020039193

♾ Printed on acid-free paper

Last figure below indicates year of this printing
30 29 28 27 26 25 24 23 22 21

To societal actors who speak up and those who listen

Contents

PART III: ENVIRONMENTAL AND PUBLIC
HEALTH GOVERNANCE

PART IV: ECONOMIC AND LABOR GOVERNANCE

PART V: SOCIAL AND RELIGIOUS GOVERNANCE

Tables and Figures

Tables

Figures

Acknowledgments

The underlying inspiration for this volume dates back to our time as graduate students at Columbia University in the 1990s, when the trauma of 1989 was still raw. It was a defining moment for our generation of students studying China. Although we did not envision organizing such a collaborative project at the time, as we studied for comprehensive exams, conducted extensive fieldwork in China, and wrote our dissertations, we became increasingly perplexed by the dizzying diversity of perspectives on the nature of state–society relations in China. The reason for this ambiguity turned out to be deceptively simple: it's a moving target. The relationship between state and societal actors cannot be reduced to a static description because it is fundamentally dynamic, multidimensional, and interactive. No single snapshot adequately captures its evolving nature and variation across different areas of governance.

The analytical implications of taking a long view emerged two decades later, when Szu-chien was the director of the Center for Contemporary China at National Tsing Hua University and Chun-chih was a postdoctoral fellow at Academia Sinica. Over countless after-lunch strolls along the Si-Fen Creek that cuts across the campus of Academia Sinica, they developed the initial methodological framework that frames this volume. In 2014, following the Sunflower Student Movement in Taiwan and Umbrella Movement in Hong Kong, Szu-chien invited Kellee to join as a coeditor.

With principal investigators in place, we secured funding from several sources to host workshops and hire research assistants to engage in an ambitious quantitative case analysis review of literature on state–society relations in China. We acknowledge generous financial support from the Center for Contemporary China at National Tsing Hua University; Hong Kong University of Science and Technology; Institute of Political Science at Academia Sinica; National Social Science Fund of China (17BZZ033); the Republic of China Ministry of Education (MOE-104-3-3-A014); and especially, the Republic of China Ministry of Science and Technology (MOST 108-2410-H-001-090-MY3, MOST 103-2410-H-007-077, MOST 101-2410-H-007-033-MY2, MOST 95-2420-H-004-058-DR).

Many teams of research assistants trained by Szu-chien and Chun-chih engaged in time-intensive discussion and coding of articles presenting complex cases of state–society relations in China. In Taiwan, we thank Yi-Ru Bai, Hao Feng, Zi-Xiu Guo, Hu-Men Li, Bo-Ting Lin, Peng-Da Shen, Yan-Hua Wang, and Mao-Qi Xie. They were enrolled as graduate students in the Institute of Sociology at National Tsing Hua University. We thank the coding team of graduate students at Hong Kong University of Science and Technology (HKUST): Liuyan Jiang, Warren Wenzhi Lu, Yudi Tang, Qingyan Wang, and Shangsi Zhou. In addition, our authors acknowledge the diligent research assistance of Ya-Hsuan Chou, Bowei Hu, Yi-ling Lin, Warren Wenzhi Lu, Wei-ling Tseng, and Yu-Qi Zeng.

The theoretical framework and its execution in the empirical chapters of this volume resulted from deliberation among the contributors over multiple workshops and meetings. Several institutions hosted these engagements, including the Center for Contemporary China at National Tsing Hua University, the Institute of Political Science and Institute of Sociology at Academia Sinica, and the Taiwan Foundation for Democracy. We thank the administrative staff who supported our meetings and manuscript submission—including Shu-Mei Cheng, Minghao Liu, Doris Su, and Meng-Jie Yang at Academia Sinica; and Clara So, Christine Tang, and Josephine Wong at HKUST. Just as valuable, under the chairmanships of S. Philip Hsu and Yu-tzung Chang, respectively, the Department of Political Science at National Taiwan University hosted Kellee as a visiting scholar in the summers of 2016 to 2019. Special thanks to Yi-feng Tao for generously sharing her office during those precious writing retreats, which were made more memorable by her and Ming-chi Chen hosting exquisite home-cooked Columbia reunion dinners at their home.

Throughout the project, our authors benefited from constructive input from multiple colleagues. We are grateful to Kuei-min Chang, Chih-Jou

Jay Chen, Ming-chi Chen, Titus C. Chen, Bih-Er Chou, Chelsea Chia-chen Chou, Sebastian Heilmann, Shao-Hua Liu, Tse-Kang Leng, Joel Migdal, Ngai Pun, Hsiu-hua Shen, Shawn Shieh, Bennis Wai-Yip So, Wen-Hsuan Tsai, Hans H. Tung, Ray Wang, You-Ren Yang, and two anonymous readers commissioned by the Harvard University Asia Center. They are of course absolved from inadequacies in the volume. Behind every published book is an editor who believed in its potential during earlier stages of the manuscript. Bob Graham offered expert support throughout the review and production process. Finally, we are deeply honored and grateful for Elizabeth Perry's timely epilogue, which complements our insights with a reminder of China's revolutionary heritage.

Edited volumes almost invariably take years to come to fruition, and this one is no exception. Just as China under Xi Jinping's leadership has evolved over the course of this project, our conceptual framing and empirical case studies have coevolved. We are perhaps fortuitous that the effort took us deeper into the Xi era, as that perspective provides confidence in our assessment that greater assertion of party-state power has had adverse consequences on the quality of governance.

Yet societal actors throughout "greater China" continue to engage and at times overtly resist variegated expressions and failings of state power. Final revisions occurred during the tumultuous 2019–20 academic year in Hong Kong—starting with the anti–Extradition Law Amendment Bill protests in the summer and fall, which were unexpectedly overshadowed in the spring semester by the coronavirus pandemic first identified in Wuhan, China, and reignited by Beijing's issuance of a National Security Law for Hong Kong. Although these crises continued as this volume went into production, we bracket alarmist headlines and stand by the evolutionary stance of our analytic framework: 2019–20 may well be remembered as an inflection point, but it is by no means an end point. Indeed, we anticipate learning from scholarship that is currently in gestation. Accumulation of knowledge is an evolutionary process as well.

S.C.H., Taipei

K.S.T., Hong Kong

C.C.C., Xiamen

Contributors

Chun-chih Chang is Assistant Professor in the Department of Political Science at Xiamen University.

Christina Chen is Adjunct Assistant Professor in the Center for General Education at Tunghai University.

Chih-peng Cheng is Associate Professor in the Center for General Education at National Tsing Hua University.

Muyi Chou is a Postdoctoral Research Fellow in the Department of Sociology at National Taiwan University.

Yousun Chung is Associate Professor in the Division of Chinese Foreign Affairs and Commerce at Hankuk University of Foreign Studies.

Szu-chien Hsu is Deputy Minister of Foreign Affairs for the Republic of China and Associate Research Fellow at Academia Sinica.

Ke-hsien Huang is Associate Professor in the Department of Sociology at National Taiwan University.

Ming-chun Ku is Associate Professor in the Institute of Sociology at National Tsing Hua University.

Thung-Hong Lin is a Research Fellow in the Institute of Sociology at Academia Sinica and Director of the Center for Contemporary China at National Tsing Hua University.

Elizabeth J. Perry is Henry Rosovsky Professor of Government at Harvard University and Director of the Harvard-Yenching Institute.

Yi-chun Tao is Lecturer in the Department of Politics at East China Normal University.

Kellee S. Tsai is Dean of Humanities and Social Science and Chair Professor of Social Science at the Hong Kong University of Science and Technology, and Research Professor at Johns Hopkins University.

Chanhsi Wang is Adjunct Assistant Professor in the Institute of Sociology at National Tsing Hua University.

Chin-chih Wang is Adjunct Assistant Professor in the Institute of Sociology at National Tsing Hua University.

Weiting Wu is Associate Professor in the Graduate Institute for Gender Studies at Shih Hsin University.

Abbreviations

ACWF	All-China Women's Federation
AFCTU	All-China Federation of Trade Unions
AWA	authoritarianism with adjectives
BMCUP	Beijing Municipal Commission of Urban Planning
BOCA	Bureau of Civil Affairs
BPFA	Beijing Declaration and Platform for Action
CCIS	China Credit Information Service
CCM	country coordinating mechanism
CCP	Chinese Communist Party
CDC	China Center for Disease Control and Prevention
CHRD	Chinese Human Rights Defenders
CPPCC	Chinese People's Political Consultative Conference
CSO	civil society organization
DPC	District People's Congress
ENGO	Environmental nongovernmental organization
FDI	foreign direct investment
GIPA	Greater involvement of people living with HIV/AIDS
GMCCA	Guangzhou Municipal Commission of City Administration

GONGO	government-organized nongovernmental organization
ICH	Intangible Cultural Heritage
INGO	international nongovernmental organizations
LCL	Labor Contract Law
LDAC	Labor dispute arbitration committees
LGBT	lesbian, gay, bisexual, and transgender
MCOCAE	Municipal Commission of City Administration and Environment
MOH	Ministry of Health
NGO	nongovernmental organization
NPC	National People's Congress
OEM	original equipment manufacturer
PRC	People's Republic of China
PSB	Public Security Bureau
QCS	Quantitative case survey
RAB	Religious Affairs Bureau
RDF	refuse-derived fuel
SARA	State Administration of Religious Affairs
SO	social organization
SOE	state-owned enterprise
SP	special project
SSCA	Shining Stone Community Association
SSO	social service organization
TSPM	Three-Self Patriotic Movement
UFWD	United Front Work Department
UNAIDS	Joint United Nations Programme on HIV and AIDS
UNESCO	United Nations Educational, Scientific, and Cultural Organization
WHO	World Health Organization

PART I

Introduction

CHAPTER I

Evolutionary Governance in China

State–Society Interactions under Authoritarianism

KELLEE S. TSAI

In 2011, thousands of villagers in Wukan, Guangdong, protested the seizure and sale of farmland by local officials, leading to a three-month occupation of the Wukan police station and government offices. To diffuse the protracted standoff between protesters and local authorities, provincial governor Wang Yang allowed Wukan to hold direct elections based on secret ballot voting to select a new village party chief and 107 representatives on the village committee. Protest leader Lin Zuluan won the election, displacing the previous village leader, who had served for 42 years. International media hailed the "Wukan model" as a harbinger of political reform in China: it showcased governmental responsiveness to the concerns of ordinary rural citizens and offered an electoral solution that culminated in the removal of corrupt local authorities. By June 2016, however, Wukan was embroiled in conflict again. Hundreds of riot police were dispatched to lock down Wukan in anticipation of anticorruption protests organized by village leaders. Liu was detained on charges of accepting bribes, which precipitated villagers to take to the streets in his defense.

The Wukan protests were ongoing and blocked from domestic media when the Chinese Communist Party (CCP) marked its 95th anniversary on July 1, 2016. On the occasion, General Secretary Xi Jinping (2016) exhorted fellow comrades to remember that "the Party's strength is in the people; therefore, going forward, the Party must always rely on the people and continuously harness the enthusiasm, initiative, and creativity of the masses." The familiar populist message underscored that the CCP is the longest surviving communist party in the world. By 2020, it had governed the People's Republic of China (PRC) continuously for over seven decades since Chairman Mao Zedong pronounced at the first Political Consultative Congress in September 1949, "the Chinese people have stood up." Having outlasted the vast majority of postwar socialist regimes—and by far the most populous one to have existed—the longevity of China's party-state warrants ongoing analysis.

Given the tremendous structural changes that have occurred in China's economy and society over the course of the reform era, what are the shifting sources of authoritarian durability? Clearly the party-state has demonstrated continued capacity to repress most dissent. Yet its ideological commitment to serving the people should not be cynically dismissed as mere rhetoric. Although the masses need to be managed in the interest of preserving social stability (*weiwen* 维稳), they also need to be served. The country needs to be governed on a daily basis—and it is. But how? The premise of this volume is that analyzing the dynamics of state–society relations through an evolutionary framework provides more nuanced insights into the mechanisms of authoritarian governance than approaches focusing on despotic political institutions and elite power-sharing arrangements. Even in autocracies, societal actors deploy a creative array of strategies in pursuing their interests. The state also relies on diverse, if not always internally consistent ways of dealing with expressions of societal discontent. Interactions between state and societal actors are dynamic rather than static. As seen in the case of Wukan, a conciliatory, liberalizing response on the part of the party-state in 2011 was supplanted by a more conventional authoritarian mode of management five years later—when nine protesters were sentenced to up to 10 years in prison. State responses to land and local governance disputes will continue to evolve. The intermediate effects or "outcomes" of state–societal interactions are mediated by the relative stance of state and societal actors over time and may be expected to vary across issue areas. Ultimately, analyzing patterns of evolutionary governance diachronically across different domains can offer insight into the sources of both regime resilience and fragility.

To explore these claims more systematically, the analytic framework of this volume is designed around three main components: (1) a 2×2 typology of state–society interactions; (2) a set of nine outcome variables that reflect specific dimensions of political power, governance, and policy outcomes; and (3) examination of these interactions and outcome variables across eight issue domains. Each component is defined for analytic clarity, but the volume is premised on an evolutionary ontology. Apparently static phrases such as "strong state," "weak society," and "policy outcomes" are assumed to be in potential flux as state, societal, and indeed, hybridized actors recalibrate their strategies in response to one another and to shifts in contextual conditions.

Our conceptual approach builds on existing scholarship on state–society relations in contemporary China, which has more recently extended into studies of governance and China-specific variants of authoritarianism—or what might be called an emergent "authoritarianism with adjectives" literature. As elaborated below, these research agendas have produced rich empirical studies, many of which have yielded counterintuitive insight into the evolving nature of state–society relations. Relatedly, a growing number of political scientists are engaging in concept formation derived from the study of China's reform era. The fact they have reached divergent conclusions about power relations between the party-state and society reflects incomplete dialogue among scholars who focus on different facets of Chinese society, politics, and economy. The broader framework developed in this volume thus seeks to translate a considerable corpus of empirical research into a more integrated typology of state–society relations. Although the framework includes outcome variables, we privilege what Yuen Yuen Ang (2016) conceptualizes as "co-evolutionary sequences" of state–society interactions over seemingly conclusive outcomes at any given point. Methodologically, this approach entails diachronic process tracing of empirical cases, with the expectation of mutual monitoring, if not adaptation in discourse and practices over the course of state–societal interactions. This evolutionary stance means, as Orion Lewis and Sven Steinmo (2012, 320) explain, that "true equilibrium is impossible . . . because both a system's environment changes and an evolutionary system itself generates continued variation."

The discussion proceeds as follows. To familiarize readers with the reform-era genealogy of social science scholarship on China, the first section reviews now-classic contributions to state–society relations. Although many of the earlier studies adopted either a state- or society-centric lens, they were attentive to the embeddedness of state-in-society as an outgrowth of state socialism. As discussed in the second section, these patterns of interaction have varied across different social groups and regions. Drawing macro-level generalizations about state–society relations based on studies of migrant workers in Guangdong, private entrepreneurs in Zhejiang, or farmers in Anhui could be misleading, though comparative subnational studies have been constructive in identifying the contours of regional variation. As discussed in the third part, more recent scholarship has reflected on the nature of authoritarianism in China and proliferated a host of adjectives to distinguish it from classic, full authoritarianism. These thoughtful studies invite synthesis in a more encompassing framework, which is outlined in the remainder of this chapter and detailed in the next section.

State–Society Relations during the 1980s and 1990s

Reflecting the political reality that liberalizing reforms following Mao's death were initiated by the party-state, much of the first generation of reform-era scholarship on state–society relations was state-centric or "statist." As Dorothy Solinger (1993, 3) points out, the reforms of the 1980s were not ends in themselves, but "a *means*, a set of tools to be manipulated in the service of a few fundamental and overarching statist ends: the modernization, invigoration, and enhanced efficiency of the national economy." Statism was not the object of liberalization. If anything, noneconomic reforms were directed toward revitalizing and fortifying party-state institutions (Remick 2004; Shirk 1993). Coupled with revitalization of the statist approach in comparative politics, China specialists similarly embarked on defining the nature of the reform-era state.

THE NATURE OF CHINA'S
REFORM-ERA STATE

Early analyses of the state highlighted the way socialist-era institutions structured the scope for autonomous social organization. Andrew Walder (1986)'s monograph on the work unit (*danwei* 单位) in state-owned enterprises detailed how public monopoly over resources ensured "organized dependence" of workers on individual unit leaders and incentivized clientelism. In rural areas, Vivienne Shue's (1988) essays in *The Reach of the State* described how collectivization of agriculture, combined with limitations on population mobility imposed by the household registration system, led to "social cellularization" in the countryside, such that social experience became deeply localized and parcelized. This "honeycomb structure" of local interests and solidarities limited the ability of the Maoist state to penetrate rural society as local cadres subverted state policies through underreporting and misrepresenting local agricultural output. Shue (1988, 131) thus interpreted Deng-era reforms as an effort to "smash that very honeycomb pattern of economic organization, the entrenched power pockets, and the conspiracies of misinformation that conditioned performance in the lower state apparatus."

Although Shue (1988)'s elegant essays have been critiqued for overstating the extent of local protectionism during the Mao era (Unger 1989), they were constructive in drawing attention to subnational dynamics, which others have explored through empirical studies of China's reform-era political economy. Jean Oi (1995, 1999)'s argument that decollectivization and fiscal reforms led to the rise of "local state corporatism" was particularly influential in the 1990s. Based on research in Sunan and Shandong, Oi compared the local state to a business corporation with the county serving as the corporate headquarters, township governments acting as regional headquarters, and villages serving as companies within the larger corporation. Under local state corporatism, each level functioned as a "profit center" and was incentivized to maximize economic performance. This mutually beneficial partnership between the local developmental state and business yielded rapid rural industrialization based on township and village enterprises in the 1980s and private-sector development in the 1990s.

Although the concept of local state corporatism gained traction among students of China's political economy, other studies made it clear that local states are not always quite so virtuous or developmental as those depicted in Oi's work. Xiaobo Lü (2000) described China as a "booty socialist state" due to the rise of organizational corruption by public agencies; in his monograph with Thomas Bernstein (2008), *Taxation without Representation in Contemporary Rural China*, they observed that local governments are far more predatory in "agricultural China," as compared with the more developmental conduct of those in "industrial China." A host of competing descriptors for China's reform-era state sprouted: clientelist state, corporatist state, developmental capitalist state, entrepreneurial state, Leninist party-state, strong state, and so on (Baum and Shevchenko 1999). Of these various state types, classifying China as a "regulatory state" (Hsueh 2011; Yang 2004) ascribes it with the highest level of state capacity to implement policies and improve its governance. As discussed in the following section, however, this sanguine interpretation of state capacity has been challenged by alternative observations.

REFORM FROM BELOW?

State-led reforms created substantial space for activity by societal actors, as seen in the flourishing of society-centric studies. During the 1990s, various political scientists traced major economic reforms such as decollectivization, the introduction of the household responsibility system, and private entrepreneurship to the initiative of rural entrepreneurs (e.g., Kelliher 1992; Parris 1993; White 1999; Zhou 1996). These monographs tended to overstate the causal influence of the masses on national reforms. Most studies of rural reforms agree that the impetus for decollectivization did not emerge spontaneously from below throughout China's countryside, but came from political elites (Bianco 2001; Unger 2002; Zweig 1997). As Jonathan Unger (2002, 104) summarizes, "The evidence suggests that a complex and unplanned interplay between the top and bottom levels of the bureaucratic structure, involving ambiguous directives from the top and competitive pressures among politically nervous lower-level officials, had culminated in the countryside's near total abandonment of the collectives." Nonetheless, the idea that major economic reforms could emanate from below served an important function in qualifying oversimplified accounts in Western media, particularly after 1989, about the repressive reach of the central party-state.

"CIVIL SOCIETY," NEW SOCIAL GROUPS, AND CONTENTIOUS POLITICS

In the society-centric literature, there has been a long-standing multidisciplinary debate over whether it makes sense to depict associational life in China as civil society. In a special issue of *Modern China* in 1993, various historians had an influential exchange over the extent to which the 18th-century European concepts of the "public sphere" and "civil society" could be applied to China. While William T. Rowe (1993) observed the rise of a "*de facto* public sphere" during the nineteenth century, Philip Huang (1993) argued that the simple binary oppositions of state and society are not fully applicable to the Qing; and Frederic Wakeman (1993) criticized the mechanical application of Western models of state–society relations to China's historical experience.[1]

Political scientists and sociologists have similarly explored the concept of civil society in relation to the emergence of social organizations (*shetuan* 社团) and nongovernmental organizations (NGOs) in contemporary China (Deng 2011; Ma 2006; Simon 2013; Watson 2008; White, Howell, and Shang 1996). Most concur that in contrast to the oppositional stance of society relative to the state in the West, it would be more accurate to speak of "state-led civil society" in China because of state-imposed limits on associational autonomy (Brook and Frolic 1997). Indeed, until the 2000s, the vast majority of registered social organizations and foundations were government-organized NGOs (personal correspondence with Shawn Shieh, July 13, 2017).

Societal development is not merely a top-down process. Many social organizations in China pursue a strategy of voluntary cooptation or what Kevin O'Brien (1994) refers to as "entwinement," meaning that social groups seek to embed themselves in the political system for greater visibility and legitimacy, rather than distancing themselves from the state. This strategy of voluntary cooptation applies to what Yanqi Tong (1994) identified as the "non-critical realm" of civil society, which does not challenge the state's monopoly of political power. Non-critical components of civil society may even operate in partnership with the state by providing services that enhance public welfare (Newland 2018; Teets 2014; L. Tsai 2007), whereas others strategically opt to circumvent or avoid the state

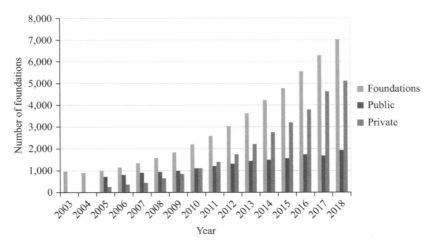

FIGURE 1.1 Growth of foundations in China, 2003–2018
Source: PRC Ministry of Civil Affairs; compiled by Shawn Shieh and Warren Wenzhi Lu.

(Gåsymr 2017; Hsu and Zhang 2015). Indeed, starting in 2010, the number of private foundations and social service providers exceeded public ones (fig. 1.1). Jun Han (2016) interprets the significant increase in private NGOs and foundations as indicating social corporatism because they are initiated by societal rather than state actors. In explaining why private and unofficial NGOs are able to survive in an authoritarian regime, Anthony Spires (2011) contends that the state relates to service-oriented NGOs in a delicate condition of "contingent symbiosis," meaning that local officials permit unregistered grassroots groups to operate when they serve mutual objectives. By contrast, the "critical realm" of civil society is overtly political and threatens the legitimacy of authoritarian regimes. Leninist party-states may tolerate the non-critical realm of civil society as a by-product of economic liberalization, but they predictably repress the critical realm to safeguard political survival.

While few scholars describe China as developing civil society in an unqualified way, since the late 1990s there has been a boom in sectoral analysis of particular groups in society. Besides traditional groups such as state workers, farmers, and intellectuals, China's changing social structure has inspired dedicated studies of migrant workers (Solinger 1999), laid-off workers (Cai 2006; Gold et al. 2009), "leftover women" (Fincher

2014), and the new middle class (Goodman and Chen 2013; Li 2010), including homeowners (Cai 2007; Read 2003), lawyers (Michelson 2007), private entrepreneurs (Pearson 2000; K. S. Tsai 2007), red capitalists (Dickson 2003), and so on. The group-specific analyses have deepened our understanding of the relative winners and losers of reform, although they generally stop short of making deterministic class-based arguments or devolving into pluralist, interest group approaches to politics given the constraints of horizontal organization.[2]

Meanwhile, the growing complexity of Chinese society and its accompanying stresses have produced collaborative volumes focusing on various forms of contentious politics and resistance, ranging from outright protest and legal activism to policy entrepreneurship and more subtle forms of evasion (Goldman and MacFarquar 1999; Gries and Rosen 2010; Perry and Selden 2010). These edited volumes have proven to be helpful for introducing students of Chinese politics to the diversity of societal concerns, organizational resources, and patterns of state–society interactions. They have not attempted to synthesize various observations about state–society relations into a broader framework, a lacuna this volume seeks to address. Analytic efforts have tended to be cast at a lower level of generality or confined to discrete sectors.

Nonetheless, two recurring insights have emerged from studies on contentious politics in particular. First, the persistence of spatial and sectoral variation in protest patterns indicates limited potential for national, class-based collective action. The differences between the concerns of laid-off state workers versus migrant workers, employment conditions in state- versus foreign-invested factories, and local governmental stance toward labor activism are well illustrated in Ching Kwan Lee (2007) and William Hurst (2012)'s studies of labor unrest in different regions. The breadth and depth of their multisite field research serves as a valuable complement to monographs that examine local variation in economic development areas such as the auto sector (Thun 2006), high-technology enterprises (Segal 2003), and informal finance (K. S. Tsai 2002).

A second theme echoed by several studies of state–society relations concerns the variegated structure of the state. As articulated in Kenneth Lieberthal and Michael Oksenburg (1988)'s concept of "fragmented authoritarianism," China's party-state is not a unitary black box, but rather is composed of vertical layers of territorial administration and crosscutting functional bureaucracies. In addition to thwarting policy formation and implementation, this structure has enabled those with grievances to exploit divisions in the state and undermine the authority of lower levels of government by skipping levels (Cai 2010; X. Chen 2012), although the latter has been banned since 2014. Because the state exerts "fragmented control" on a quotidian basis, even labor activists have opportunities to promote their agendas while avoiding repression through strategic self-censorship (Fu 2017). Given this complex terrain, Vivienne Shue and Patricia Thornton (2017) view China's non-monolithic state as deploying a fluid repertoire of governance practices that is "continuously 'in the making,'" and therefore more improvisational than institutionalized. We concur with these empirical observations and propose a framework for evolutionary governance that not only recognizes such dynamism and contingency, but contains it analytically for generating broader insights.

Authoritarianism in China with Adjectives

Analytic sensitivity to different levels and parts of the state has been picked up by a growing number of regime-centric contributions that address post-Mao innovations in governance. Just as the study of third-wave democracies inspired political scientists to identify subtypes of democracies by qualifying them with adjectives such as "neopatrimonial democracy," "illiberal democracy," and "protodemocracy" (Collier and Levitsky 1997), starting in the Hu Jintao era, an "authoritarianism with adjectives" literature has proliferated in the Chinese politics subfield. Table 1.1 presents in chronological order the cornucopia of terms that have been used by scholars to describe the nature of reform-era authoritarianism in China. An indicative measure of their relative influence in the form of Google Scholar citations is also presented.

This intellectual cottage industry of adjectives modifying authoritarianism has been accompanied by a shift away from treating democracy (or its absence) as a dependent variable. Rather than searching for signs of regime change, recent contributions in Chinese politics have focused more on the nature of governance and authoritarian resilience, particu-

Table 1.1
Descriptions of authoritarianism in China with adjectives, 1987–2019

Leadership	Author (Year)	Term	GS Citations[#]
Deng Xiaoping	Harding (1987)	Consultative authoritarianism*	616
	Lieberthal and Oksenberg (1988)	Fragmented authoritarianism*	1,678
Jiang Zemin	Lieberthal and Lampton (1992)	Fragmented authoritarianism	792
Hu Jintao	Nathan (2003)	Resilient authoritarianism	1,174
	Cabestan (2004)	Plutocratic authoritarianism	31
	Baum (2006)	Consultative Leninism*	12
	Lee (2007)	Decentralized legal authoritarianism	1,408
	Perry (2007)	Revolutionary authoritarianism	288
	Brady (2008)	Popular authoritarianism	105
	Weller (2008)	Responsive authoritarianism*	55
	Landry (2008)	Decentralized authoritarianism*	893
	Mertha (2009)	Fragmented authoritarianism 2.0	662
	Tsang (2009)	Consultative Leninism	139
	He and Thøgersen (2010)	Consultative authoritarianism	163
	T. Chen (2010)	Adaptive authoritarianism*	46
	Ahlers and Schubert (2011)	Adaptive authoritarianism	7
	Heilmann and Perry (2011)	Adaptive authoritarianism	322
	He and Warren (2011)	Consultative Leninism	514
	He and Warren (2011)	Deliberative authoritarianism	514
	MacKinnon (2011)	Networked authoritarianism*	394
	Reilly (2011)	Responsive authoritarianism	250
Xi Jinping	X. Chen (2012)	Contentious authoritarianism	423
	Stockmann (2013)	Responsive authoritarianism	445
	C. K. Lee and Zhang (2013)	Bargained authoritarianism	360
	Teets (2013)	Consultative authoritarianism	284
	Tsang (2015)	Consultative Leninism	7
	J. Chen (2016)	Decentralized authoritarianism	12
	J. Chen (2016)	Proactive authoritarianism	12
	Dickson (2016)	Consultative authoritarianism	139
	Tang (2016)	Populist authoritarianism	152
	Lai (2016)	Pragmatic authoritarianism	20
	Heurlin (2016)	Responsive authoritarianism	53
	Yan (2016)	Pre-emptive authoritarianism	14
	W. Tsai (2016)	Networked authoritarianism	27

(continued)

Table 1.1 *(continued)*

Leadership	Author (Year)	Term	GS Citations[#]
	Zhu, Zhang and Liu (2017)	Institutionalized authoritarianism	6
	Marquis and Bird (2018)	Responsive authoritarianism	22
	Robins (2018)	Negotiated authoritarianism	0
	Fuchs, Tse, and Feng (2019)	Coercive authoritarianism	1
	Duckett (2019)	Network authoritarianism	1
	Yue, Wang, and Yang (2019)	Responsive authoritarianism	6

[*]Indicates initial appearance of a term subsequently used by another author at a later date. Subsequent authors do not necessarily use the exact same definition, however. In addition, the first published appearance of the term is not necessarily the most widely cited text.
[#]Number of Google Scholar citations to the publication listed in the second column of this table as of June 26, 2020.

larly since the late 2010s and well into the Xi Jinping era.[3] The effort has yielded at least 20 terms that describe China's regime and different dimensions of state–society relations. Yet it is worth recalling that the adjectives identifying subtypes of authoritarianism in contemporary China have conceptual predecessors in comparative politics. In particular, they provide finer distinctions within the broader category of full authoritarianism, which Juan Linz (1964, 255) described as follows: "Political systems with limited, not responsible political pluralism, without elaborate and guiding ideology, but with distinctive mentalities, without extensive nor intensive political mobilization, except at some points in their development, and in which a leader or occasionally a small group exercises power within formally ill-defined limits but actually quite predictable ones." The defining characteristics were initially cast in negative terms: restrictions on the range of groups permitted to participate in politics, including single-party rule (limited political pluralism); an emotional basis for regime legitimation (non-ideological mentalities); depoliticization of society (limited social mobilization); and informally demarcated executive power.

Linz's classic definition of authoritarianism emerged in the empirical context of describing Spain under Francisco Franco, which was neither democratic nor totalitarian. Authoritarianism represented an additional form of nondemocratic regime that needed to be distinguished from totalitarian ones at the most repressive end of the regime type spectrum. Political scientists have since critiqued authoritarianism as a residual category used to describe all nonliberal democracies. Nonetheless, Linz (1975) did attempt to distinguish among seven subtypes of authoritarianism:

1. bureaucratic-military authoritarian regimes,
2. organic statism,
3. mobilizational authoritarian regimes in postdemocratic societies,
4. post-independence mobilizational authoritarian regimes,
5. racial and ethnic "democracies,"
6. "defective" and "pre-totalitarian" political situations and regimes, and
7. post-totalitarian authoritarian regimes. (273–353)

Few of these subtypes gained traction among comparativists or China scholars. As Wen-Cheng Wu (2015, 240) observes, "Trying to be inclusive, this typology was a little trivial and too complicated. Furthermore, the names of some of these types are quite awkward." Later on, Linz (2000, 174) conceded that it was not "the most fruitful approach to the development of a typology of authoritarian regimes," with the key exception of the last type, renamed "communist post-totalitarian authoritarian regimes."

Gordon Skilling, a specialist of interest group politics in communist systems, further identified subtypes of communist post-totalitarian authoritarian regimes, including "consultative authoritarianism, quasi-pluralistic authoritarianism, democratizing and pluralistic authoritarianism and anarchic authoritarianism" (Linz 2000, 174). Of these, consultative authoritarianism—a term Skilling adopted from Alfred Meyer and Peter Ludz—has been revived and tailored in its application to post-Mao China. The term was originally used to describe the Soviet Union after Khrushchev, when the party continued to monopolize decision-making power but permitted input by bureaucrats in their sectors of expertise. After Mao's passing and the revitalization of party-state institutions, Harry Harding (1987) observed that China had developed into a consultative authoritarian regime, "a significant departure from the totalitarianism of the recent past, but not a truly pluralistic, or even quasi-democratic, political system" (200). To maintain its monopoly of political power, the post-Mao leadership recognized "the need to obtain information, advice, and support from key sectors of the population" (Harding 1987, 200). Nearly two decades later, Richard Baum (2006) proposed that the combination of "consultative Leninism" and economic growth had prolonged the longevity of authoritarian rule in China. Soft authoritarian measures have enabled the CCP to gather "popular *feedback* without encouraging political *pushback*" (Baum 2006, 13; emphasis in original), though Baum questioned the sustainability of consultative Leninism over time.

These themes have been amplified in subsequent studies on consultative authoritarianism/consultative Leninism and other variants of "authoritarianism with adjectives" (AWA) coined to describe contemporary China, albeit with different areas of emphasis. Above all, regardless of the adjective used, none have questioned the CCP's prioritization of regime survival. Steve Tsang (2009) lists "an obsessive focus upon staying in power" as the first defining characteristic of consultative Leninism. Others concur that regime survival is the paramount goal. From this shared premise, there is less consensus over whether enhancing the quality of governance is an additional priority or primarily a strategy for ensuring authoritarian durability. Either way, the AWA literature largely focuses on three modalities of governance: (1) means for conveying and collecting information from society (from the state's perspective), which represent opportunities for providing input to the regime (from society's perspective); (2) mechanisms for holding local officials accountable; and (3) regime responses to information received.

At least half of the AWAs concern the channels for information flows between state and society. Some are more regime-centric, noting the pluralization of elite inputs into the policy-making process, whereas others focus on different types of feedback provided by nonstate actors. Baogang He and Mark Warren (2011)'s concept of deliberative authoritarianism is premised on the observation that a variety of top-down innovations have increased the scope for political participation and public deliberation. These innovations include the introduction of village-level elections, public hearings, deliberative polls, administrative litigation (citizens' right to sue the state), initiatives to disclose government information to the public, and increasing use of People's Congresses to discuss policy. They view these deliberative mechanisms as generating legitimacy through "governance-level participation . . . in the absence of regime-level democ-ratization" (2011, 271). Tsang (2009) similarly defines the second character-istic of consultative Leninism as "continuous governance reform designed to pre-empt public demands for democratization" (1). Expanding on the theme of consultation, Jessica Teets (2014) observes the coexistence of "an autonomous civil society" within state-defined parameters of ser-vice delivery; the resulting expression of consultative authoritarianism is intended "to maximize the benefits of civil society while mitigating its dangers" (24).

A second cluster of AWA studies highlight the media as an important arena for understanding and shaping public opinion. Anne Marie Brady (2008) describes popular authoritarianism as a one-party regime that is highly attentive to public opinion and therefore relies on mass persuasion (propaganda) to maintain its legitimacy. Meanwhile, the commercializa-tion of media has created considerable space for expressing independent opinions about public policy issues. Danielle Stockman (2012) uses the term "responsive authoritarianism" to capture the delicate balance be-tween the regime's tolerance for private expression and the institutional capacity to control information as the need arises. When official messages are disseminated through market-based media, they can shift the senti-ment of "issue publics," meaning groups of people who are highly informed and attentive to a particular issue. Rebecca MacKinnon's (2011) description of China as networked authoritarianism similarly points to the coexis-tence of online activism with party-state censorship and manipulation of digital content. However, increasingly sophisticated cyber-controls cir-cumscribe the possibility for large-scale political dissent. Wen-Hsuan Tsai (2016)'s description of networked authoritarianism outlines the system-atic way data analysts in China's Public Opinion Monitoring Office cal-culate weighted scores of "hot incidents" to rank their sensitivity, which in turn prescribes official responses, ranging from censorship or denial to active manipulation of digital public opinion.

Concurrently, a number of AWA studies have pointed to the para-doxical vibrancy of off-line contentious politics in an otherwise repres-sive authoritarian context. Under contentious authoritarianism (X. Chen 2012), decentralized authoritarianism (J. H. Chen 2016), and responsive authoritarianism (Heurlin 2016), the regime tolerates petitions and pro-tests because they provide information to the center about local conditions, enhance the legitimacy of the central government, and hold local officials accountable. Because of incentives provided by the cadre evaluation system, local officials with political ambitions are pressured to resolve the grievances of their residents through less confrontational means. Two additional terms capture the resulting dialogue and state-societal interaction—bargained authoritarianism (Lee and Zhang 2013) and negotiated authoritarianism (Robins 2018). Sabrina Habich (2015, 2016) observes that "soft coercion, negotiation, and propaganda work" by the local government have been effective for resettling villagers "without causing social unrest" (2016, 1, 2015, 191). To deescalate protests against illegal land grabs, the most expedient solution is often to offer side payments to petitioners (Heurlin 2016).

Some of these studies link the mechanisms for information collection and expression of grievances with policy influence at different levels of government. In *Useful Complaints: How Petitions Assist Decentralized Authoritarianism in China*, Jing Chen (2016) contends that "Petitions contribute to nearly every stage of the policy-making process—such as issue emergence, agenda setting, implementation, evaluation, and feedback" (147). Most are less sanguine about the impact of contentious politics, however. Carl Minzner (2006) regards the petition system as a dysfunctional proxy for formal legal channels that risks escalation of popular discontent. In his discussion of responsive authoritarianism, Heurlin (2016, 15) finds that petitions that signal a "five-alarm fire," literally "burning issues (*redian wenti* 热点问题)," receive more attention than others. Hence, the regime "selectively responds with policy changes when it gauges opposition to be particularly widespread" (Heurlin 2016, 15, 3). Whether issues reach the five-alarm stage or attract higher-level attention can also be a function of the political opportunity structure in a particular issue area. In Xi Chen's (2012) version of contentious authoritarianism, it is apparent that divisions in the party-state structure provide protesters with within-system advocates and protectors. Although the local government is a common target of protest, in other cases local officials may be proactive in allying with nonstate actors to advocate policy changes, as captured in Andrew Mertha's (2009) discussion of fragmented authoritarianism 2.0.

The importance of the local state for effective governance and regime legitimacy is highlighted in another stream of AWA contributions, including decentralized authoritarianism (Landry 2008), decentralized legal authoritarianism (C. K. Lee 2007), and adaptive authoritarianism (Ahlers and Schubert 2011). Pierre Landry (2007) emphasizes how the CCP's personnel management system motivates local officials to promote local development while retaining control over them. Ahlers and Schubert (2011) extend the implications of this by contending that effective state implementation of policies contributes to regime stability and legitimacy. Ching Kwan Lee (2007) notes a significant tension, however, in the expectation that local governments promote economic growth and ensure implementation of labor laws. The dual mandate of accumulation and legitimation means that when local firms violate labor rights, protesting workers blame the local state. This undermines the legitimacy of local governance. Wenfang Tang (2016) concurs that regime stability rests on a fragile foundation even though his surveys found that overall, populist authoritarianism in China generates "a fairly high level of regime support while allowing selective expression of public anger" (117). Indeed, throughout PRC history, protest has been "routine and officially circumscribed" and therefore, "less politically destabilizing," as captured in Elizabeth Perry's (2007, 21) notion of revolutionary authoritarianism.

The final cluster of AWA studies stresses the flexibility and adaptability of governance in China as sources of regime resilience. Some of these studies echo Samuel Huntington's (1970, 24–39) earlier consideration of how revolutionary one-party systems could evolve through transformation, consolidation, and adaptation in a process of adaptive authoritarianism. In particular, Andrew Nathan's (2003) influential discussion of resilient authoritarianism delineated how reform-era Chinese politics had become more institutionalized. Elaborating on this idea, Yongyi Lai (2016) argues that since 1992, China has developed pragmatic authoritarianism. Specifically, its "flexible, practical, and adaptive" approach has significantly improved the quality of economic, social, and political governance—thereby enhancing authoritarian durability. The Color Revolutions of 2005 to 2007 in Eurasia created a sense of urgency at the national level to address simmering sources of domestic discontent, while intensifying control over potentially subversive segments of society, demonstrating adaptive authoritarianism (T. Chen 2010). In this regard, the intensive anticorruption campaign launched under Xi Jinping's leadership has been characterized as institutionalized authoritarianism (Zhu, Zhang, and Liu 2017). At the grassroots level, Xiaojun Yan (2016) uses the term "preemptive authoritarianism" to describe China's elaborate stability maintenance (*weiwen* 维稳) apparatus, which is devoted toward anticipating and managing grievances before they require financial buyouts or coercive action.

Other work on authoritarian resilience has pointed to less institutional aspects of China's governance process. Also using the term "adaptive authoritarianism," Sebastian Heilmann and Elizabeth Perry (2011) contend that "China's governance techniques are marked by a signature Maoist stamp that conceives of policy-making as a process of ceaseless change, tension management, continual adjustment, and ad-hoc adjustment" (3). Rather than institutional rigidity, this guerilla policy style embraces uncertainty and allows for "maximum tinkering" of the sort Nasim Taleb (2007) described as being conducive to innovation. They suggest that the CCP's unorthodox approach to adaptive governance has enabled it to survive recurring crises throughout the reform era (Heilmann 2018; Heilmann and Perry 2011).

Evolutionary Governance under Authoritarianism

Taken together, the AWA contributions are instructive in highlighting the paramount importance of regime survival to the CCP and detailing the modalities of governance intended to support that goal. The shared themes of consultation, participation (within limits), responsiveness, adaptability, and flexibility have been correlated with authoritarian resilience so far. Most of the AWAs further suggest that these attributes serve a legitimizing function. But there is less consensus about the causal mechanisms of authoritarian resilience. The opportunity to provide feedback to the regime does not guarantee a satisfying, stabilizing resolution. We concur that responsiveness, pragmatism, adaptability, and flexibility are helpful for explaining the regime's agility in dealing with crises and broader structural changes in the economy and society. Yet the relative frequency of responsiveness and the domains in which local and nonstate actors may have policy impact remain in question. The dynamics of state–society relations range from highly charged when both sides pursue assertive strategies to less confrontational exchanges, mutual accommodation, or even collaborative partnership. Moreover, the strategies pursued by various stakeholders evolve over the course of these interactions. Under what circumstances does the party-state exert its coercive capacity versus engaging in more flexible responses or policy adaptations?

Introducing yet another term to modify China's authoritarian regime would not be constructive to address these issues. Instead, we propose an analytic framework that traces the dynamics and outcomes of state–society engagements over time. These interactive processes constitute evolutionary governance. We begin by recognizing that when it comes to a particular issue area, state and societal actors start out with different degrees of interest and behavioral assertiveness. For state and societal actors, these initial strategies may be "hard" or "soft," which yields a stylized 2×2 typology of dyadic interactions: hard state/hard society, hard state/soft society, soft state/hard society, and soft state/soft society. What distinguishes our approach from previous studies of state–society relations is that these classifications are assessed diachronically and in interaction. The state–society dyads are mutually evolving, rather than a single data point. An initial hard state strategy and soft societal one could provoke a more assertive societal response later. Conversely, in another sector a strong societal approach might diffuse an apparently recalcitrant state position at a later phase of interaction. Each chapter in this volume explicitly analyzes shifting state and societal strategies and responses across different stages of a problematic issue. In several cases, these phases of interaction span decades. They coevolve over time, as Ang (2016) puts it.

To complete the causal sequence, each author traces those state–society interactions to different types of political outcomes. Whereas "authoritarian resilience" represents the baseline outcome (if not dependent variable) in much of the AWA literature, claiming that China's contemporary regime is resilient risks tautology. To the extent that resilience is indicated by the ability to cope with crises and regime stability, the concept is nearly nonfalsifiable until a regime actually collapses. To address these legitimate concerns, we conceptually disaggregate authoritarian resilience to distinguish between its autocratic and more societally attuned components, such that "authoritarianism" refers to the regime's political power, while "resilience" refers to its governance capacity. Reassembling the first sentence of Samuel Huntington's (1968) book, in our framework "authoritarianism" refers to the degree of government, while "governance" refers to how a regime actually governs. In addition, we include intermediate policy outcomes as a third dimension because they represent the formal institutional context for further evolutionary interaction.[4]

The rationale for conceptual disaggregation—rather than piling more adjectives on to authoritarianism—is to restore the full meaning of authoritarianism while identifying the dimensions of governance that affect its resilience. This resonates with Michael Mann's (1984) distinction between the despotic and infrastructural power of the state. Despotic power is exercised "over society," and infrastructural power is exercised "through society." Following this logic, an authoritarian regime's political power can be depicted in zero-sum terms between state and society. As detailed in chapter 2, we further operationalize political power according to four indicators: political mobilization, agenda setting, political accountability, and political representation. When analyzing a particular issue area, these are all arenas in which the regime may exert its authority at the expense of societal actors. When the latter achieves substantive input in these indicators, authoritarianism is compromised.

In contrast to political power, governance entails a non-zero-sum relationship between state and society. Governance involves sharing information and cooperation between public and private stakeholders. Engagement by both sides is not only mutually beneficial but necessary for effective management of public affairs. As Yongnian Zheng (2011) puts it, a "strong state, strong society" mode of governance is a "win-win" situation. Keping Yu (2012) concurs that "co-governance" between government officials and citizens is key for promoting China's social development. Operationally, we assess governance along the following four dimensions: responsiveness, transparency, input channels, and societal empowerment. When these attributes are observed in the analysis of specific issues or incidents, regime resilience is arguably augmented.

In addition to political power (authoritarianism) and governance (resilience), this volume attends to the policy outcome of state–society interactions as of 2020. Following repeated state–society engagement, does the relevant state policy change in a direction that responds favorably to societal demands? Or does the policy context in which the initial issue emerged remain in place? Although subsequent policy implementation cannot be assumed, the policy impact of state–society interactions remains relevant, particularly in cases where societal actors explicitly target public policy governing their issue domain.

Empirically, the volume combines analysis of an original database of extant literature on state–society relations, followed by case studies of different types of governance issues. All of the chapters present empirical findings derived from in-depth field research in China, in most cases over the course of several years. To operationalize the framework more broadly, in chapter 2, Szu-chien Hsu and Chun-chih Chang present findings from a quantitative case survey project that compiled 125 cases of state–society interactions published between 2005 and 2015 in three of the leading English-language social science journals on China—*China Journal, China Quarterly,* and *Journal of Contemporary China.* Cases that met the selection criteria for inclusion were coded according to their issue area (land/environment/ public health, labor, economic management, community, equality, culture/ religion/ethnicity, and patriotism/nationalism); state strategies (out of 14 possibilities) for up to four phases of interaction; societal strategies (out of seven options) for up to four phases of interaction; and political outcomes. The latter includes the nine indicators of political power, governance, and policy change discussed above. The resulting database enabled the authors to conduct a quantitative assessment of the extent to which different combinations of state and societal strategies generated changes in political power, governance, or public policy.

Although the database does not claim to be a representative sample of state–society interactions, the analysis reveals a number of clear patterns. Not surprisingly, the state continues to wield considerable political power when it chooses a strong strategy of engagement with societal actors. However, societal actors are able to have impact on both governance and policy outcomes when they pursue strong strategies while the state adopts softer ones and when both sides pursue soft strategies. Hsu and Chang observe that this exposes a structural tension in the regime's pursuit of authoritarian resilience. On one hand, repressive strategies enable the state to maintain political power (authoritarianism). On the other hand, the quality of governance (resilience) is enhanced when the state adopts softer modes of engagement with society. This dilemma lies at the core of evolutionary governance under authoritarianism.

These general findings are complemented by the observation that political outcomes vary considerably across issue domains. Overall, disputes regarding local community affairs are most likely to have an effect on political power and governance. The evolutionary dynamics of this pattern can be seen in the chapters on community-based participation. In most of these case studies, state and societal actors eventually pursued soft strategies of engagement, which yielded substantive improvements in key aspects of governance. For example, Szu-chien Hsu and Chin-chih Wang observe that protests against the construction of an incineration plant in Beijing initially provoked a repressive state response. When the affected homeowners shifted their strategy from public opposition to proposing policy alternatives, the municipal government interacted with them in a manner that resulted in a cooperative solution for processing local waste (chapter 7). In another chapter involving Beijing homeowners, Yousun Chung found that the local government similarly demonstrated responsiveness to societal efforts to grant legal status to homeowners assemblies (*yezhu dahui* 业主大会), albeit on an experimental basis (chapter 3). In the anti-incinerator and homeowners' assembly cases, the societal actors are urban middle-class citizens who have the legal knowledge, material resources, and social networks to engage constructively with relevant state entities. They are privileged members of society.

In areas with greater socioeconomic diversity, community governance can be more complicated. Szu-chien Hsu and Muyi Chou examine such a case in a Beijing district where the local residential committee was not providing appropriate public services for migrant workers in its jurisdiction (chapter 4). Both sides were frustrated. The local government hired an NGO, a "civil social organization," specializing in participatory approaches to community affairs to improve communication channels. Although the NGO's mediation empowered residents in managing their public space (resulting in societal empowerment), Hsu and Chou caution against overstating the political implications of NGO involvement in local governance.

Unlike property owners and residents of communities with access to NGOs, industrial workers have fewer state-sanctioned options for defending their interests. The disadvantaged position of labor is reflected in the database of state–society interactions. Out of the eight issue areas, labor–state interactions yielded outcomes that scored well below the mean in political power (political mobilization, political accountability, agenda setting), governance (responsiveness, transparency, input channels), and policy change. Even as the politically dominant actor, the state has not achieved its objectives either. In response to significant escalation in workers' protests during the 1990s and 2000s, the central government enacted a series of labor protections, including the Labor Contract Law in 2007. As Christina Chen observes (chapter 10), the dominant strategy for labor has been contention, while the central state has pursued the soft strategy of legalization to quell labor unrest. The introduction of dispute resolution channels, however, has generated the unintended consequence of fueling an upsurge of strikes and labor disputes. Rather than promoting stability, the availability of institutional channels for mediating labor conflicts has arguably contributed to regime fragility.

In the domain of economic governance, private/foreign capital and the local state are key actors that mediate the course of state–labor interactions. Following the suicides of Foxconn workers in 2010, Thung-Hong Lin contends that the state instrumentally appropriated the attention paid to abusive working conditions in foreign-invested factories as a means to achieve its developmental objective of relocating pollution-producing industry from the coastal south to inland provinces (chapter 9). Protecting labor served as a front for disciplining foreign capital and executing a shift in the state's regional development strategy. A similar approach was pursued when a large-scale strike broke out at the Taiwanese-invested Yue Yuen Group in 2014. Chih-peng Cheng (chapter 8) points out that the strike provided an opportunity for the central state to disrupt collusion between the local government and foreign capital in overlooking labor infractions. Rather than relocating inland, however, Taiwanese investors have been shifting their production to Southeast Asian countries. The departure of foreign capital represents another unintended consequence of central state interventions in labor governance.

In rural and urbanizing areas, land disputes have been a major source of social instability since the early 2000s. As shown in Yi-chun Tao's study of Sanshan village in Guangdong, the local government's illegal appropriation of land triggered a "rights defense" (*weiquan* 维权) movement that went through protracted phases of repression, alliance with non–local rights activists, contention through institutional channels, electoral accommodation, and defeat, respectively (chapter 5). The villagers' initial resistance in 2005 was harshly repressed. The movement regained momentum when an NGO, Chinese Human Rights Defenders (CHRD), assisted the villagers in preparing legal documents, negotiating with Nanhai municipal authorities, and filing petitions with the municipal court. Because of these activities, Chen Qitang, the co-founder of CHRD, was arrested in 2007. Upon his release in 2010, Chen resumed supporting Sanshan's land rights campaign along with villager Guo Houjia. Guo became China's first (democratically elected) rights activist to serve on a local People's Congress. As a legislator, however, Guo encountered continued obstacles in defending villagers' land rights, and key activists were arrested. Out of the eight issue domains, land issues scored the lowest in terms of societal impact on political power.

While community, environmental, labor, and land issues have repeatedly garnered official attention through public forms of collective action, activists promoting other societal concerns have generally engaged in less contentious forms of interaction with the state. This is not to say that they do not pursue "hard" strategies but that their concerns may not be in the public domain during early stages of interaction. Efforts to eradicate domestic violence are a prime example of such an issue. Because of its private and disempowering nature, victims of domestic violence are unlikely to take to the streets to call for protective legislation. Instead, policy advocacy in this domain has been led by the organizations that provide services to abused women. Weiting Wu (chapter 11) examines how three groups involved in the campaign against domestic violence pursued different strategies to expand the political space for their advocacy efforts. The Maple Center has worked in cooperation with the state; the Peking Women's Law Center has been more confrontational; and Common Language, a younger LGBT organization, allied with the antidomestic violence campaign to broaden their networks. In an evolutionary process that started in the late 1980s, the passage of the Domestic Violence Law in 2015 marked their success in agenda setting (1988–2000), political mobilization, responsiveness, and policy change.

In the issue domain of culture/religion/ethnicity, the 12 cases in the literature database scored at the mean for political power (which is low in general) and well below the mean in the governance and policy change indicators. The relationship between the state and religious groups rests on what Ke-hsien Huang refers to as "a micro-level process of pragmatic negotiation between local bureaucrats and religious leaders." Because both experience considerable pressure from hardliners within their group, they "must maintain a shifting distance from each other to keep their legitimacy in their respective organizations" (chapter 13). These micro-level interactions occur in a political context where the state retains control over religious policy, including the determination of "undesirable" versus "desirable" religions. Christianity falls into the undesirable category. Since 2013 there has been a crackdown on unregistered churches, undermining earlier progress on indicators of governance.

By contrast, Ming-chun Ku examines the legitimation of an indigenous folk belief through a process of "heritagization" (chapter 12). Mazu is a sea goddess traditionally worshipped by seafaring communities in Fujian and Taiwan. During the early 1980s, Mazu followers on Meizhou Island rebuilt the Meizhou Ancestral Temple that had been destroyed during the Cultural Revolution. The military objected and threatened to destroy the reconstructed temple because of security concerns: a temple honoring Mazu near their garrison could increase illicit visits by Taiwanese, thereby increasing the military's scope of responsibility. Rather than confronting the military's opposition head on, community leaders galvanized support for the temple's preservation from Chinese People's Political Consultative Conference deputies at the city and provincial levels, cadres handling Taiwan affairs, and even journalists from state-sponsored media outlets. The strategy of building a coalition of official supporters proved to be effective. Meizhou was further developed into a site for cultural tourism, attracting (non-threatening) visitors from Taiwan and Southeast Asian countries. In an extended process involving cooperation between local state and religious leaders, the Mazu ceremony even succeeded in gaining recognition by UNESCO as an Intangible Cultural Heritage. Local activism succeeded in reframing Mazu as an object of local folk religion—that could pose security complications on Meizhou Island—to an internationally certified cultural ritual worthy of protection.

The diachronic sweep of this volume shows that improvements in governance are non-linear, hard won, and reversible. This is evident in the area of HIV/AIDS governance, analyzed by Chanhsi Wang in chapter 6.

Over the span of two decades, the regime has demonstrated both resilience and fragility in its interactions with societal and international actors committed to HIV/AIDS prevention, education, and treatment. During the late 1990s, state and society pursued hard strategies, as seen in the conflict between activists calling attention to the domestic HIV/AIDS crisis and the state concealing the problem, followed by the arrest of activist Wan Yanhai. The state's strategy changed under the Hu Jintao–Wen Jiabao government, however. In the subsequent decade, the state acknowledged the seriousness of HIV/AIDS and accepted international aid, which greatly enhanced the role of the Ministry of Health in fighting the epidemic. One of the unintended consequences of the state's co-governance with international society was tremendous growth in the number of domestic AIDS NGOs, which significantly strengthened the organizational capacity of societal actors. Most of these grassroots NGOs remained unregistered because the state was unwilling to permit meaningful participation by civil society. As Wang explains, the case of HIV/AIDS governance illustrates that the party-state "is willing to share its power for improved governance of public affairs but is unwilling to change the structure of political power." External funding for HIV/AIDS governance declined starting in 2011. Support by international donors retreated because of disappointment over the state's negative stance toward the involvement of autonomous NGOs. This was compounded by expectations that China had developed the economic capacity to take on greater responsibility for its public health expenditures. Under Xi's rule, both domestic and foreign NGOs face heightened repression, which has further restricted the scope for HIV/AIDS outreach, advocacy, and treatment.

On balance, the distribution of outcomes in these chapters mirrors that of the quantitative case studies survey of state–society interactions presented in chapter 2. Over half of the case studies involved assertive societal strategies of engagement, particularly appealing to the state through institutional channels, which eventually yielded a more accommodating state response. Beyond this superficial similarity, the time frame and content of the interactive processes vary considerably among the cases, ranging from phases of coercion, mutual frustration, involvement of new actors, and unexpected turns of events.

Conclusion

Summarizing lessons from the third wave of democratization, Huntington (1991, 174–75) declared that "liberalized authoritarianism is not a stable equilibrium; the halfway house does not stand." Some have suggested that the CCP has been surviving "on borrowed time" (Baum 2006). This can only be confirmed post hoc. In the interim, Beijing has accepted the denouement of spectacular growth rates as "the new normal." Given that economic growth served as a dominant source of performance legitimacy for the party-state in the first four decades of reform, it is especially relevant to examine the non-material indicators of governance—responsiveness, transparency, input channels, and societal empowerment. We contend that these governance indicators in turn serve as metrics for assessing regime resilience in categorical rather than dichotomous terms.

Operationally, the evolutionary framework of this volume examines governance interactively to capture the shifting strategies undertaken by state and societal actors over time. The authors explore several instances in which co-governance has occurred following initial conflict or gridlock. A recurring observation—backed up by the literature database—is that this is most likely to occur when the state adopts soft strategies. As detailed in the empirical chapters, the conditions under which the state pursues softer strategies include interactions involving urban economic elites, community issues, workers in foreign-invested enterprises, and in cases where societal actors persist for decades in demonstrating the normative value of their demands. Soft state strategies include cooperation with societal actors, policy innovation, mediation, consultation, compensation, and acceptance of societal demands.

Ironically, a number of these softer state strategies of engagement with society are echoed in Xi Jinping's prescriptive essays on China's governance. In "Power Must Be Caged by the System" (2014), Xi advises, "He who is good at governing through restriction should first restrict himself, then others." This phrase offers a rationale for the anticorruption campaign under his direction. The piece then appeals to the party's mass line roots by linking its performance with societal feedback: "The people's satisfaction is the standard for measuring progress in changing our way of work. We must extensively solicit public opinions and suggestions, steadily accept public assessment and supervision by the whole of society" (428). Our findings indicate that effective governance and regime resilience are bolstered to the extent that the spirit and substance of this sentiment is implemented.

The party-state has adopted harder strategies in general since 2012. Although the themes of mass consultation and participation represent a normative source of continuity from the preceding Hu-Wen government, on balance there is more evidence of discontinuity in evolutionary governance under Xi's leadership. First, greater centralization of power in most policy areas (S. Lee 2017) has reduced the opportunities for policy entrepreneurship provided by fragmented administration and lack of policy alignment between different levels of government. Second, the aggressive anticorruption campaign and reinvigoration of ideological indoctrination has tempered the norms of pragmatism, adaptability, and flexibility that guided policy making in previous reform-era governments. Chinese politics has arguably shifted to a "crisis mode of governance" such that "decision-making procedures are abruptly centralized and dominated by the personalities of the top individual leaders" (Heilmann 2018). Third, heightened media censorship and repression of social organizations has reduced the state's sources of information and responsiveness to society. Delayed disclosure of the outbreak of COVID-19 and subsequent death of whistle-blower Dr. Li Wenliang in early 2020 were delegitimating expressions of failed governance in public health. Meanwhile, the draconian lockdown of Wuhan, Hubei, and other parts of China demonstrated the robustness of political power in the face of crisis.

These substantive changes in China's political climate have tempered the willingness of local cadres to pursue even soft strategies to improve governance. In turn, this means that societal actors have fewer allies in the party-state. Social organizations in politically sensitive sectors are struggling to survive. Authoritarianism has been enhanced at the expense of interactive governance and regime resilience. Rather than "fragmented authoritarianism 3.0" or other adjective-modified authoritarianism, the CCP-dominated regime in contemporary China is simply authoritarian. The coined adjectives have all been observed empirically in different dimensions of governance, particularly during the Hu Jintao era. Yet attributes such as consultation, negotiation, and responsiveness are ultimately processes that occur unevenly in the course of authoritarian governance. Our evolutionary framework provides a basis for understanding the contingencies of those interactions.

Notes

1. In an August 8, 2013, piece in the *People's Daily*, Wang Shaoguang took the critique further, describing civil society as "a rough fairy tale fabricated by neoliberalism" (*xin ziyou zhuyi bianzao de cucao Shenhua* 新自由主义编造的粗糙神话). http://theory .people.com.cn/n/2013/0808/c40531-22488604.html.

2. A partial exception is Kennedy (2008) who identifies different patterns of lobbying by businesses depending on their ownership type and sector.

3. Note that the works listed in table 1.1 that were published since 2012 are mainly based on research conducted primarily during the pre-Xi period. Studies based on Xi-era fieldwork include Dickson (2016); Fuchs, Tse, and Feng (2019); Robins (2018); Tsang (2015); Zhu, Zhang, and Liu (2017); and parts of Lai (2016) and W.-H. Tsai (2016).

4. As Lewis and Steinmo (2012, 337) contend, "Policy ideas that 'fail' to be adopted at one point are never permanently eliminated. Instead, they ensure continued variation, and by remaining possible courses of action, expand the scope for future rounds of selection."

References

Ahlers, Anna L., and Gunter Schubert. 2011. "'Adaptive Authoritarianism' in Contemporary China: Identifying Zones of Legitimacy Building." In *Reviving Legitimacy: Lessons for and from China*, edited by Deng Zhenglai and Sujian Guo, 61–82. Plymouth: Lexington Books.

Ang, Yuen Yuen. 2016. *How China Escaped the Poverty Trap*. Ithaca, NY: Cornell University Press.

Baum, Richard. 2006. "The Limits of Consultative Leninism." In *China and Democracy: A Contradiction in Terms?*, edited by Mark Mohr, 13–20. Asia Program, Special Report no. 131.

Baum, Richard, and Alexei Shevchenko. 1999. "The State of the State." In *The Paradox of Post-Mao Reforms*, edited by Merle Goldman and Roderick MacFarquar. Cambridge, MA: Harvard University Press.

Bernstein, Thomas P., and Xiaobo Lü. 2008. *Taxation without Representation in Contemporary Rural China*. New York: Cambridge University Press.

Bianco, Lucien. 2001. *Peasants without the Party: Grass-Roots Movements in Twentieth-Century China*. Armonk, NY: M. E. Sharpe.

Brady, Anne-Marie. 2008. *Marketing Dictatorship: Propaganda and Thought Work in Contemporary China*. Lanham, MD: Rowman and Littlefield.

Brook, Timothy, and B. Michael Frolic, eds. 1997. *Civil Society in China*. Armonk, NY: M. E. Sharpe.

Cai, Yongshun. 2006. *State and Laid-Off Workers in Reform China: The Silence and Collective Action of the Retrenched*. New York: Routledge.

———. 2007. "Civil Resistance and Rule of Law in China: The Defense of Homeowners; Rights." In *Grassroots Political Reform in Contemporary China*, edited by Elizabeth J. Perry and Merle Goldman, 174–95. Cambridge, MA: Harvard University Press.

———. 2010. *Collective Resistance in China: Why Popular Protests Succeed or Fail*. Stanford, CA: Stanford University Press.

Chen, Jing. 2016. *Useful Complaints: How Petitions Assist Decentralized Authoritarianism in China*. Lanham, MD: Lexington Books.

Chen, Titus. 2010. "China's Reaction to the Color Revolutions: Adaptive Authoritarianism in Full Swing." *Asian Perspective* 34.2: 5–51.

Chen, Xi. 2012. *Social Protest and Contentious Authoritarianism in China*. New York: Cambridge University Press.

Chung, Jae Ho. 2016. *Centrifugal Empire: Central–Local Relations in China*. New York: Columbia University Press.

Collier, David, and Steven Levitsky. 1997. "Democracy with Adjectives: Conceptual Innovation in Comparative Research." *World Politics* 49.3: 430–51.

Deng, Zhenglai, ed. 2011. *State and Civil Society: The Chinese Perspective*. Singapore: World Scientific Publishing.

Dickson, Bruce J. 2003. *Red Capitalists in China: The Party, Private Entrepreneurs, and Prospects for Political Change*. New York: Cambridge University Press.

———. 2016. *The Dictator's Dilemma: The Chinese Communist Party's Strategy for Survival*. New York: Oxford University Press.

Duckett, Jane. 2019. "International Influences on Policymaking in China: Network Authoritarianism from Jiang Zemin to Hu Jintao." *China Quarterly* 237: 15–37.

Fincher, Leta Hong. 2014. *Leftover Women: The Resurgence of Gender Inequality in China*. London: Zed Books.

Fu, Diana. 2017. "Fragmented Control: Governing Contentious Labor Organizations in China." *Governance* 30: 445–62.

Fuchs, Daniel, Patricia Fuk-Ying Tse, and Xiaojun Feng. 2019. "Labor Research under Coercive Authoritarianism: Comparative Reflections on Fieldwork Challenges in China." *Economic and Industrial Democracy* 40.1: 132–55.

Gåsymr, Hans Jørgen. 2017. "Navigation, Circumvention, and Brokerage: The Tricks of the Trade Developing NGOs in China." *China Quarterly* 222: 86–106.

Gold, Thomas, William Hurst, Jaeyoun Won, and Qiang Li, eds. 2009. *Laid-Off Workers in a Workers' State: Unemployment with Chinese Characteristics*. New York: Palgrave Macmillan.

Goldman, Merle, and Roderick MacFarquhar, eds. 1999. *The Paradox of China's Post-Mao Reforms*. Cambridge, MA: Harvard University Press.

Goodman, David S. G., and Minglu Chen, eds. 2013. *Middle Class China: Identity and Behavior*. Northhampton, MA: Edward Elgar.

Gries, Peter, and Stanley Rosen, eds. 2010. *Chinese Politics: State, Society and the Market.* New York: Routledge.

Habich, Sabrina. 2015. "Strategies of Soft Coercion in Chinese Dam Resettlement." *Issues and Studies* 51.1: 165–99.

———. 2016. *Dams, Migration and Authoritarianism in China: The Local State in Yunan.* Abingdon: Routledge.

Han, Jun. 2016. "The Emergence of Social Corporatism in China: Nonprofit Organizations, Private Foundations, and the State." *China Review* 16.2 (June): 27–53.

Harding, Harry. 1987. *China's Second Reform: Reform after Mao.* Washington, DC: Brookings Institution.

He, Baogang, and Stig Thøgerson. 2010. "Giving the People a Voice? Experiments with Consultative Authoritarian Institutions in China." *Journal of Contemporary China* 19: 675–92.

He, Baogang, and Mark E. Warren. 2011. "Authoritarian Deliberation: The Deliberative Turn in Chinese Political Development." *Perspectives on Politics* 9.2: 269–89.

Heilmann, Sebastian. 2018. *Red Swan: How Unorthodox Policy Making Facilitated China's Rise.* New York: Columbia University Press.

Heilmann, Sebastian, and Elizabeth Perry. 2011. "Embracing Uncertainty: Guerrilla Policy Style and Adaptive Governance in China." In *Mao's Invisible Hand: The Political Foundations of Adaptive Governance in China*, edited by Sebastian Heilmann and Elizabeth Perry, 1–29. Cambridge, MA: Harvard University Press.

Heurlin, Christopher. 2016. *Responsive Authoritarianism in China: Land, Protests, and Policy Making.* New York: Cambridge University Press.

Hsu, Carolyn L., and Yuzhou Zhang. 2015. "An Institutional Approach to Chinese NGOs: State Alliance versus State Avoidance Resource Strategies." *China Quarterly* 221: 100–122.

Hsueh, Roselyn. 2011. *China's Regulatory State: A New Strategy for Globalization.* Ithaca, NY: Cornell University Press.

Huang, Philip. 1993. "'Public Sphere'/'Civil Society' in China?: The Third Realm between State and Society." *Modern China* 19.2: 216–40.

Huntington, Samuel P. 1968. *Political Order in Changing Societies.* New Haven, CT: Yale University Press.

———. 1970. "Social and Institutional Dynamics of One-Party Systems." In *Authoritarian Politics in Modern Society*, edited by Samuel Huntington and Clement Henry Moore, 3–47. New York: Basic Books.

———. 1991. *The Third Wave: Democratization in the Late Twentieth Century.* Norman: University of Oklahoma Press.

Hurst, William. 2012. *The Chinese Worker after Socialism.* New York: Cambridge University Press.

Kelliher, Daniel R. 1992. *Peasant Power in China: The Era of Rural Reform, 1979–1989.* New Haven, CT: Yale University Press.

Kennedy, Scott. 2008. *The Business of Lobbying in China.* Cambridge, MA: Harvard University Press.

Landry, Pierre. 2008. *Decentralized Authoritarianism in China: The Communist Party's Control of Local Elites in the Post-Mao Era.* Cambridge: Cambridge University Press.

Lee, Ching Kwan. 2007. *Against the Law: Labor Protests in China's Rustbelt and Sunbelt.* Berkeley: University of California Press.

Lee, Ching Kwan, and Yonghong Zhang. 2013. "The Power of Instability: Unraveling the Foundations of Bargained Authoritarianism in China." *American Journal of Sociology* 118.6: 1475–1508.

Lee, Sangkuk. 2017. "An Institutional Analysis of Xi Jinping's Centralization of Power." *Journal of Contemporary China* 26.105: 325–36.

Lewis, Orion A., and Sven Steinmo. 2012. "How Institutions Evolve: Evolutionary Theory and Institutional Change." *Polity* 44.3: 314–39.

Lai, Hongyi. 2016. *China's Governance Model: Flexibility and Durability of Pragmatic Authoritarianism.* London: Routledge.

Li, Cheng, ed. 2010. *China's Emerging Middle Class: Beyond Economic Transformation.* Washington, DC: Brookings Institution.

Lieberthal, Kenneth G., and David M. Lampton. 1992. *Bureaucracy, Politics, and Decision Making in Post-Mao China.* Berkeley: University of California Press.

Lieberthal, Kenneth G., and Michel Oksenberg. 1988. *Policy Making in China: Leaders, Structures, and Processes.* Princeton, NJ: Princeton University Press.

Linz, Juan J. 1964. "An Authoritarian Regime: The Case of Spain." In *Mass Politics: Studies in Political Sociology*, edited by Erik Allard and Stein Rokkan, 251–83, 374–81. New York: Free Press.

———. 1975. "Totalitarian and Authoritarian Regimes." In *Handbook of Political Science*, edited by Fred I. Greenstein and Nelson J. Polsby, 174–411. Reading, MA: Addison-Wesley.

———. 2000. *Totalitarian and Authoritarian Regimes.* Boulder, CO: Lynne Rienner.

Lü, Xiaobo. 2000. "Booty Socialism, Bureau-preneurs, and the State in Transition: Organizational Corruption." *Comparative Politics* 32: 273–94.

Ma, Quisha. 2006. *Non-Governmental Organizations in Contemporary China: Paving the Way to Civil Society?* London: Routledge.

MacKinnon, Rebecca. 2011. "Networked Authoritarianism." *Journal of Democracy* 22.2: 32–46.

Mann, Michael. 1984. "The Autonomous Power of the State: Its Origins, Mechanisms and Results." *European Journal of Sociology* 25.2: 185–213.

Marquis, Christopher, and Yanhua Bird. 2018. "The Paradox of Responsive Authoritarianism: How Civic Activism Spurs Environmental Penalties in China." *Organization Science* 29.5: 948–68. doi:10.1287/orsc.2018.1212.

Mertha, Andrew. 2009. "'Fragmented Authoritarianism 2.0': Political Pluralization in the Chinese Policy Process." *China Quarterly* 200: 995–1012.

Michelson, Ethan. 2007. "Lawyers, Political Embeddedness, and Institutional Continuity in China's Transition from Socialism." *American Journal of Sociology* 113.2: 352–414.

Minzner, Carl F. 2006. "Xinfang: Alternative to Formal Chinese Legal Institutions." *Stanford Journal of International Law* 42.1: 103–80.

Nathan, Andrew. 2003. "China's Changing of the Guard: Authoritarian Resilience." *Journal of Democracy* 14: 6–17.

Newland, Sarah A. 2018. "Innovators and Implementers: The Multilevel Politics of Civil Society Governance in Rural China." *China Quarterly* 233: 22–42.

O'Brien, Kevin. 1994. "Chinese People's Congresses and Legislative Embeddedness: Understanding Early Organizational Development." *Comparative Political Studies* 27.4: 80–107.

Oi, Jean C. 1995. "The Role of the Local State in China's Transitional Economy." *China Quarterly* 144: 1132–49.

———. 1999. *Rural China Takes Off: Institutional Foundations of Economic Reform*. Berkeley: University of California Press.

Parris, Kristen. 1993. "Local Initiative and National Reform: The Wenzhou Model of Development." *China Quarterly* 134: 242–63.

Pearson, Margaret M. 2000. *China's New Business Elite: The Political Consequences of Economic Reform*. Berkeley: University of California Press.

Perry, Elizabeth J. 2007. "Studying Chinese Politics: Farewell to Revolution?" *China Journal* 57: 1–22.

Perry, Elizabeth J., and Mark Selden, eds. 2010. *Chinese Society: Change, Conflict and Resistance*. London: Routledge.

Read, Benjamin L. 2003. "Democratizing the Neighborhood? New Private Housing and Homeowner Self-Organization in Urban China." *China Journal* 49: 31–59.

Reilly, James. 2011. *Strong Society, Smart State: The Rise of Public Opinion in China's Japan Policy*. New York: Columbia University Press.

Remick, Elizabeth J. 2004. *Building Local States: China during the Republican and Post-Mao Eras*. Cambridge, MA: Harvard University Press.

Robins, Verity. 2018. "Negotiated Authoritarianism: Older People's Associations and Social Governance in Contemporary China." Ph.D. diss., University of Oxford.

Rowe, William T. 1993. "The Problem of 'Civil Society' in Late Imperial China." *Modern China* 19.2: 139–57.

Segal, Adam. 2003. *Digital Dragon: High-Technology Enterprises in China*. Ithaca, NY: Cornell University Press.

Shirk, Susan L. 1993. *The Political Logic of Economic Reform in China*. Berkeley: University of California Press.

Shue, Vivienne. 1988. *The Reach of the State: Sketches of the Chinese Body Politic*. Stanford, CA: Stanford University Press.

Shue, Vivienne, and Patricia M. Thornton, eds. 2017. *To Govern China: Evolving Practices of Power*. New York: Cambridge University Press.

Simon, Karla W. 2013. *Civil Society in China: The Legal Framework from Ancient Times to the "New Reform Era."* New York: Oxford University Press.

Solinger, Dorothy J. 1993. *China's Transition from Socialism: Statist Legacies and Market Reforms 1980–1990*. Armonk, NY: M. E. Sharpe.

———. 1999. *Contesting Citizenship in Urban China: Peasant Migrants, the State, and the Logic of the Market*. Berkeley: University of California Press.

Spires, Anthony J. 2011. "Contingent Symbiosis and Civil Society in an Authoritarian State: Understanding the Survival of China's Grassroots NGOs." *American Journal of Sociology* 117.1: 1–45.

Stockman, Danielle. 2012. *Media Commercialization and Authoritarian Rule in China*. New York: Cambridge University Press.

Taleb, Nassim Nicholas. 2007. *The Black Swan: The Impact of the Highly Improbable*. New York: Random House.

Tang, Wenfang. 2016. *Populist Authoritarianism: Chinese Political Culture and Regime Sustainability*. New York: Oxford University Press.

Teets, Jessica. 2014. *Civil Society under Authoritarianism: The China Model*. New York: Cambridge University Press.

Thun, Eric. 2006. *Changing Lanes in China: Foreign Direct Investment, Local Governments, and Auto Sector Development*. New York: Cambridge University Press.

Tong, Yanqi. 1994. "State, Society, and Political Change in China and Hungary." *Comparative Politics* 26.3: 333–53.

Tsai, Kellee S. 2002. *Back-Alley Banking: Private Entrepreneurs in China*. Ithaca, NY: Cornell University Press.

———. 2007. *Capitalism without Democracy: The Private Sector in Contemporary China*. Ithaca, NY: Cornell University Press.

Tsai, Lily. 2007. *Accountability without Democracy: Solidary Groups and Public Goods Provision in Rural China*. New York: Cambridge University Press.

Tsai, Wen-Hsuan. 2016. "How 'Networked Authoritarianism' Was Operationalized in China: Methods and Procedures of Public Opinion Control." *Journal of Contemporary China* 25.101: 731–44.

Tsang, Steve. 2009. "Consultative Leninism: China's New Political Framework." *Journal of Contemporary China* 18.62: 865–80.

———. 2015. "Contextualizing the China Dream: A Reinforced Consultative Leninist Approach to Government." In *China's Many Dreams: Comparative Perspectives on China's Search for National Rejuvenation*, edited by David Kerr, 10–34. Basingstoke: Palgrave Macmillan.

Unger, Jonathan. 1989. "State and Peasant in Post-Revolution China." *Journal of Peasant Studies* 17.1: 114–36.

———. 2002. *The Transformation of Rural China*. Armonk, NY: M. E. Sharpe.

Wakeman, Frederic. 1993. "The Civil Society and Public Sphere Debate: Western Reflections on Chinese Political Culture." *Modern China* 19.2: 108–38.

Walder, Andrew G. 1986. *Communist Neo-Traditionalism: Work and Authority in Chinese Industry*. Berkeley: University of California Press.

Watson, Andrew. 2008. "Civil Society in a Transitional State: The Rise of Associations in China." In *Associations and the Chinese State: Contested Spaces*, edited by Jonathan Unger, 14–47. London: M. E. Sharpe.

Weller, Robert P. 2008. "Responsive Authoritarianism." In *Political Change in China: Comparisons with Taiwan*, edited by Bruce Gilley and Larry Diamond, 117–35. Boulder, CO: Lynne Rienner.

White, Gordon, Jude Howell, and Xiaoyuan Shang. 1996. *In Search of Civil Society*. Oxford: Clarendon Press.

White, Lynn T. III. 1999. *Unstately Power: Local Causes of China's Intellectual, Legal and Governmental Reforms*. Armonk, NY: M. E. Sharpe.

Wu, Wen-Cheng. 2015. "A Critical Review on the Important Classificatory Concepts of Modern Political Regimes." *Dongwu zhengzhi xuebao* (Dongwu Political Studies) 33.4: 211–80.

Xi Jinping. 2014. *Xi Jinping tan zhiguo lizheng* (Xi Jinping: the governance of China). Beijing: Foreign Languages Press.

———. 2016. "Zai qingzhu Zhongguo gongchandang chengli 95 zhounian dahui shang de jianghua" (Speech on the Chinese Communist Party's gathering to celebrate its 95th anniversary). *Xinhua wang*. http://www.xinhuanet.com//politics/2016-07/01 /c_1119150660.htm.

Yan, Xiaojun. 2016. "Patrolling Harmony: Pre-emptive Authoritarianism and the Preservation of Stability in W County." *Journal of Contemporary China* 25.99: 406–21.

Yang, Dali. 2004. *Remaking the Chinese Leviathan: Market Transition and the Politics of Governance in China.* Stanford, CA: Stanford University Press.

Yu, Keping. 2012. "Chonggou shehui zhixu zouxiang guanmin gongzhi" (Reshaping social order and moving towards co-governance between cadres and citizens). *Guojia xingzheng xueyuan xuebao* (Journal of Chinese Academy of Governance) 4.2: 4–5, 127.

Yue, Lori Qingyuan, Jue Wang, and Botao Yang. 2019. "Contesting Commercialization: Political Influence, Responsive Authoritarianism, and Cultural Resistance." *Administrative Science Quarterly* 64.2: 435–65.

Zheng, Yongnian. 2011. "Qiangzhengfu qiangshehui dangshi zhongguo shehui guanli de fangxiang" (A strong government and strong society is the direction of China's societal management). *Zhongguo qiyejia wang* (China Entrepreneur). http://www.iceo .com.cn/shangye/114/2011/0524/218578_2.shtml.

Zhou, Kate Xiao. 1996. *How the Farmers Changed China: Power of the People.* Boulder, CO: Westview Press.

Zhu, Jiangnan, Qi Zhang, and Zhikuo Liu. 2017. "Eating, Drinking, and Power Signaling in Institutionalized Authoritarianism: China's Antiwaste Campaign since 2012." *Journal of Contemporary China* 26.105: 337–52.

Zweig, David. 1997. "Rural People, the Politicians, and Power." *China Journal* 38: 153–68.

CHAPTER 2

Measuring State–
Society Interactions in China's
Evolutionary Governance

Examining Extant Literature (2005–2015)

Szu-chien Hsu and Chun-chih Chang

This chapter presents an analytic framework for specifying the mechanisms underlying evolutionary governance in China and applies the framework to an original database of 125 state–society cases collected from research articles in leading social science China journals. Through multistaged narrative analysis, information about the issue domain, state strategies, societal strategies, and the political outcomes were numerically coded for each case of state–society interaction. The political outcomes were evaluated according to whether such interactions generated changes in political power, governance, or public policy. We find that societal actors are most likely to have an impact on public policy and governance rather than gaining political power through interactions with the state. Furthermore, when the state adopts a tough stance, societal actors engage in confrontational strategies. China's party-state thus faces a dilemma. On one hand, it prefers to demonstrate strength to maintain political power. On the other hand, engaging societal actors in more conciliatory manner improves governance. Striking a balance between these competing goals is an ongoing challenge for the regime.

> Civil society in China is clearly playing an increasingly independent and important role in both service delivery and policy advocacy.
>
> —Jessica Teets (2009)

In the great majority of associational arenas, a relatively vigilant Party state has exhibited a reluctance to cede any control over the associations that count.

—Jonathan Unger and Anita Chan (2008)

Social science scholars of contemporary China have yet to reach consensus on the mechanisms underlying regime durability and authoritarian governance. In the extant literature examining China's state–society relations and governance, studies of different types of cases have reached disparate conclusions about the power dynamics between state and society. Meanwhile, there has been limited dialogue among researchers focusing on particular social sectors or dimensions of governance. The resulting fragmentation of research may lead us to misrepresent the nature of state–society relations by, for example, focusing on party-state coercion in some cases, versus highlighting societal empowerment in others. Generalizing about state–society relations from discrete cases further runs the risk of missing out on governance mechanisms present in other contexts.

Is there a dominant strategy for the state and society in their mutual engagements over time? What are the range of consequences in state and society interactions? This chapter proposes a more integrated analytic framework for identifying the interactive mechanisms underlying evolutionary governance in authoritarian China, and it operationalizes core hypotheses by analyzing an original database of 125 state–society interaction cases published in leading English-language social science China journals between 2005 to 2015. Through multistaged narrative analysis, information about the issue domain, state strategies, societal strategies, and the political outcomes were numerically coded for each instance of state–society interaction. The political outcomes were evaluated according to whether such interactions generated changes in political power, governance, or public policy.

Overall, we found that societal actors are most likely to have an impact on public policy and governance rather than gaining political power by their interactions with the state. In particular, the state adopting a soft strategy toward society and society adopting a hard strategy yields the greatest change in various indicators of political power and public policy. When both state and society employ soft strategies, improvements in governance are most likely to occur. Furthermore, when the state uses a softer strategy, there is scope for societal actors to induce changes in governance or policy and, on occasion, even accrue marginal political power. When the state adopts a tough stance, however, societal actors often respond in a confrontational manner. China's party-state faces a dilemma. On one hand, it prefers to demonstrate strength to maintain political power. On the other hand, engaging societal actors in more conciliatory manner improves governance. Striking a balance between these competing goals is an ongoing challenge.

The chapter proceeds as follows. The first section reviews contemporary scholarship on authoritarianism to build the case for why analyzing state–society relations is important for identifying the mechanisms of governance and regime resilience. The literature review also summarizes the varying conclusions that China scholars have reached about state–society relations. The second part introduces the quantitative case survey (QCS) methodology that we used to derive insights more systematically from existing studies of state–society interactions. The results of this QCS analysis are detailed in the remaining sections, followed by discussion of the broader implications of our findings.

Literature Review

THE LIMITS OF COMPARATIVE AUTHORITARIANISM

Contrary to the general expectations of third-wave theory, authoritarian regimes persist and have demonstrated a degree of longevity unexpected by many observers. The study of comparative authoritarianism has thus emerged as a central concern in political science, with the aim of explaining the sources of authoritarian resilience in the 21st century.

The conventional perspective of comparative authoritarianism suggests that elections and legislatures are critical instruments for dictators to overcome their deficit of accurate information about the population and earn support from a coalition of elites. For example, in studies of political regimes, elections are the main standard for differentiating among regime types. Differing from totalitarian and democratic regimes, in hybrid regimes elections provide a channel of participation while enabling rulers to gauge social intentions. By manipulating the media and electoral procedures, rulers can discourage opposition, muffle social contention, and consolidate their legitimacy (Diamond 2002; Levitsky and Way 2002, 2010; Schedler 2006). Such tools have served to incorporate potential opposition members into the ruling alliance (Brownlee 2007; Bueno de Mesquita and Smith 2009; Bueno de Mesquita et al. 2003; Gandhi 2008; Gandhi and Przeworski 2007; Svolik 2012).

The foregoing contentions are based on the following assumptions about the nature of political competition. First, social forces are expected to have the capacity to organize themselves and articulate their interests. When society is organized, electoral competition and legislatures are assumed to exist. Second, it is assumed that political elites enjoy the support of certain societal sectors and that societal sectors are represented in elite circles. Third, a certain degree of electoral competition is presumed to exist, and the legislature performs more than a symbolic function. Thus, competing for seats in the legislature denotes sharing political power with the dictator. These assumptions may not be valid for understanding non-competitive authoritarian regimes.

Arguably, conventional frameworks in the study of comparative authoritarianism overemphasize the role of political elites and institutions. Although this perspective may be constructive for explaining the survival of electoral and competitive authoritarian regimes, a theoretical gap must be filled to explain authoritarian resilience in non-competitive authoritarian contexts. Moreover, because certain studies have indicated that single-party regimes are less likely to collapse or democratize compared with other types of authoritarian regimes (Geddes 1999; Hadenius and Teorell 2007), a theoretical explanation is more urgently required for the governance and resilience of one-party regimes compared with their competitive counterparts.

Moreover, mainstream research on comparative authoritarianism has neglected analysis of state–society interactions because of its focus on formal political institutions. We assume that state–society interactions differ widely and are more critical for explaining the authoritarian resilience of non-competitive regimes. In this type of regime, de facto competition does not exist, and pseudo-democratic institutions are not empowered for power sharing. Our focus is thus on state–society interactions using China as a non-trivial example of a non-competitive authoritarian regime. In the following section, we elaborate on three camps of China's state–society interactions from the existing literature.

THREE PERSPECTIVES OF STATE–SOCIETY RELATIONS IN CHINA

Within the study of state–society relations in contemporary China, one approach contends that the rise of civil society compromises state power. Saich (2000) coined the phrase "negotiating the state" to reflect the observation that new social organizations have devised strategies to accommodate the state's requests and evade penetration. Howell (2007) depicts civil society in China as "chipping away at the edges" of the state, and Ho (2008) describes the strategies adopted by environmental nongovernmental organizations (ENGOs) as "embedded activism." Other scholars underscore the coherence and autonomy embraced by various kinds of NGOs, such as AIDS-related NGOs (Gåsemyr 2017), business associations (Ji 2018), disaster relief NGOs (Peng and Wu 2018), and ENGOs (H. Han 2014). Underlying the rise of civil society and democratic pluralism, these studies exhibit an overly optimistic view of empowered societal actors and overlook potential reactions from the state. In other words, they provide only a partial explanation, overstating the influence of societal dynamics in China's authoritarian regime.

By contrast, the second perspective on state–society relations observes constant renewal of state domination over social sectors. Unger and Chan (2008) believe that China's party-state did not design the corporatist system as a transmission belt with society, but as a tool for separating societal associations from interactions and collaboration. Hsu and Hasmath (2014) highlight the tacit sanctioning of the local corporatist state and the complementary relations between the local government and NGOs. According to Thornton (2013), the Chinese Communist Party (CCP) strives to extend its reach into grassroots communities through party-organized NGOs. Newland (2018) argues that NGOs' autonomy depends on varieties of individual officials who face different career incentives. Contrary to the previous society-centric approach, these studies embrace an overly state-centered view, and societal actors are depicted as too feeble to generate social dynamism. Moreover, the word "corporatism" is not used accurately in studies on state corporatism because a system of interest representation does not exist. The "governance" phenomenon cannot be fully accounted for by state control of the political system as well.

The third approach to state–society relations in China emphasizes mutual dependence and collaboration in local governance. Spires (2011) proposed the concept of "contingent symbiosis" to explain the survival of illegal NGOs under a state-dominant system. J. Han (2016) interprets state–society relations in China as "social corporatism," whereby grassroots social organizations act as intermediators for facilitating interdependence and enhancing local welfare. Other studies have vividly demonstrated the collaborative relationship embedded in the local context, using terms such as "network governance" (Fulda, Li, and Song 2012), "soft coercion" (Habich 2015a), and "fragmented control" (Fu 2017). These studies may offer a more comprehensive perspective by underscoring mutually beneficial relations between state and society. However, their consideration of the political implications are limited and underspecified.

The foregoing critical summary points to significant gaps in the literature on state–society relations and local governance in China and amplifies the need for more systematic analysis to explain their political implications for regime durability under authoritarian governance. This chapter examines the varying political implications of different types of state–society interactions, with a view to identifying the mechanisms underlying evolutionary governance in contemporary China.

Research Design: Hypotheses, Method, Data, and Variables

HYPOTHESES

The premise of this analysis is that divergent interpretations of state–society relations may coexist under varying circumstances. Interactions between state and society may be expected to differ across local governance structures and types of social organizations.

We propose an evolutionary framework to categorize the dynamics of state–society relations across multiple cases in the social science literature on contemporary China. Similar concepts have been used in earlier studies. Tsai (2006, 122) contends that endogenous institutional change may derive from state–society interactions at the local level that generate adaptive informal institutions (see Hsu and Jiang 2015). Heilmann and Perry (2011, 8) have pointed out "'the capacity of actors in a system to further resilience' through their actions and interactions, intentionally or unintentionally." Lewis and Steinmo (2012) illustrate the logic of evolutionary theory such that agents' preferences, ideas, and strategies may foster institutional change over time. Borrowing the term from Charles Tilly, Shue and Thornton (2017, 18–19) refer to the various strategies and models of state–society interactions as "repertoires." Other scholars have delineated the process of mutual interaction and adaptation in their case studies (Ang 2016; Habich 2015a, 2015b; O'Brien and Li 2006). Of particular note, Ang (2016)'s book *How China Escaped the Poverty Trap* provides detailed methodological guidance on mapping coevolution, which mirrors the approach in this volume. Building on these insights, our overarching conceptual hypothesis is that the intermediate outcomes of policy change, public governance, and political power hinge on how state and society interact with each other. The government's attitude and treatment of societal actors may depend on the type of concern. Likewise, societal actors engaged in different issue domains may choose distinctive forms of interactive strategies in expressing their preferences to state entities. Hence, diverse configurations of state–society interactions are likely to have differential effects on the resulting political outcome.

In terms of the state's strategy toward society, the authoritarian state may exert forthright repression against society, which here is treated as the strongest action the state can take toward society. Conversely, the state may yield to society by engaging in advocacy and requesting a delay for future cooperation. When it comes to society's strategy toward the state, societal actors may adopt a confrontational approach against the state as the most assertive option. Conversely, society may simply comply with the will of the state, conform with its expectations, and work on its behalf. Given that state and society have alternative strategies on either end of the spectrum, we propose a heuristic 2 × 2 typology of state–society

Table 2.1
Typology of state–society relations in China

		Society's Strategy	
		Soft	Hard
State's strategy	Soft	III: More likely to change	IV: Most likely to change
	Hard	I: Least likely to change	II: Less likely to change

NOTE: Likelihood of change in governance or policy: IV>III>II>I.

relations. The first dimension is the "state's strategy toward society," ranging from hard to soft; the second is "society's strategy toward the state," also ranging from hard to soft.

Therefore, a heuristic 2×2 matrix is constructed to capture the spectrum of state–society interactions from a coevolutionary perspective. Table 2.1 lists the four resulting types of state–society interaction. In the table, Type I refers to when the state pursues a hard strategy, while society employs a soft strategy; Type II refers to when state and society both use hard strategies; Type III refers to when both employ soft strategies; and Type IV refers to the use of a soft strategy by the state and a hard strategy for society.

Among the four types of state–society interactions, we propose the following hypotheses. When the state adopts a hard strategy and society adopts a soft strategy (Type I), it is least likely that society could generate changes in public governance or public policy vis-à-vis the state. Conversely, when the state adopts a soft strategy and society adopts a hard one (Type IV), society is most likely to effect changes in public governance or public policy. These assumptions are intuitively relatively straightforward compared with the other two types. We hypothesize that the type when state and society both pursue hard strategies (Type II) tends to generate greater tension, and societal demands are thus less likely to succeed compared with the scenario where both parties exercise soft strategies (Type III). In brief, we hypothesize that the likelihood of societal impact on the state, going from most likely to least likely, is as follows: Type IV > Type III > Type II > Type I.

METHODOLOGY

We used the QCS methodology to process well-researched studies of state and society interactions in contemporary China. The process entailed six steps: (1) formulating the problem, (2) analyzing existing literature, (3) gathering information from studies, (4) analyzing and integrating their outcomes, (5) interpreting the evidence, and (6) presenting the results (Cooper 2010; see Major and Savin-Baden 2010).

In operationalizing these steps, we first flagged the issue of state–society interactions, which is overlooked in the comparative authoritarianism literature, followed by identifying the three main positions in studies of these interactions in China. The first stage enabled us to generate initial hypotheses. Next we collected articles that discussed concrete cases of state–society relations, governance, or public policies to construct a data set from the three most influential Social Science Citation Index journals in China studies: *China Quarterly*, *China Journal*, and *Journal of Contemporary China*. The QCS period covered 2005 to 2015, and all the surveyed cases occurred prior to Xi Jinping's leadership. Valid cases were selected by screening all of the articles from the three journals in this period that match the following seven criteria:

1. whether the case concerns state–society relations for a specific governance issue;
2. whether a qualitative study exists of the referred case(s);
3. whether the case occurred during the post-Mao reform era;
4. whether at least one specific state actor is involved;
5. whether at least one specific societal actor is involved;
6. whether an interaction between the state and society exists; and
7. whether a specific outcome of the state–society interaction exists in the governance issue discussed in the article.

In the first round of the case selection process, coders read each article to determine whether it met the first three criteria. Articles were excluded if they failed to meet any one of these initial three conditions. Coders then assessed the remaining articles on the other four criteria and further excluded articles from the sample if they did not fulfill any one of the conditions. This screening process yielded 89 articles that met all seven criteria for our analysis. Because some articles included more than one state–society case or addressed different governance issues or incidents, in total 125 cases were identified as eligible for analysis.

The third step entailed collecting information from the 125 cases according to the issue domain, state/society strategies, and political outcomes. The strategies adopted by state and societal actor(s) were coded according to the narratives provided in the context of the reviewed paper. For each case, we tracked up to four phases of state–society interactions. Next we assigned numerical values to the strategies of all the state and societal actors in each stage, calculated the mean of the strategy adopted by the state and society, and typologized the cases according to their average scores during the whole process of interaction.

Individual cases were coded quantitatively by at least two researchers to ensure data reliability. The first coder coded all the case information, and the second coder was tasked with double-checking. Discrepancies between coders were subject to systematic review and discussion by research teams led by the coauthors in Taiwan and Hong Kong. The team-based review process enabled us to develop intercoder reliability and translate case evidence into variables to populate a database for statistical analysis.

Issue Domains Table 2.2 lists the distribution of the cases across eight issue domains. The categories with the highest numbers of cases were equal

Table 2.2
Distribution of issue domains

Issue domain	Frequency	Percentage	Cumulative %
Land	10	8.0	8.0
Environment/public health	26	20.8	28.8
Labor	14	11.2	40.0
Economic management	12	9.6	49.6
Community	13	10.4	60.0
Equal rights	28	22.4	82.4
Culture/religion/ethnicity	12	9.6	92.0
Patriotism/nationalism	10	8.0	100.0
Total	125	100	

rights ($n=28$) and environment/public health ($n=26$). Four issue domains involved more than 10 cases: labor ($n=14$), community ($n=13$), economic management ($n=12$), and culture/religion/ethnicity ($n=12$). The topics of land and patriotism/nationalism involved 10 cases each. This distribution of cases mirrors the issues examined in the other chapters of this volume. Note, however, that we make no claims about the representativeness of these cases regarding their frequency of occurrence. The particular distribution of cases across issue domains only reflects their publication in the leading journals.

State and Societal Strategies State strategies were coded according to the following three criteria: the policy position of the state actor, the degree to which the outcome of the state's action is certain or irreversible, and the cost of the state's action. The underlying logic is that a tougher and more clearly specified policy position results in a more certain and irreversible outcome, and a lower cost leads the state to adopt a harder strategy. State strategies were classified into the following categories, ranging from cooperation (1) to repression (14) (see Appendix Table 2.1 at the end of the chapter for details):

1. Cooperation with society
2. Policy innovation
3. Mediation
4. Consultation
5. Compensation
6. Accepting the case
7. Exhausting
8. Competition
9. Propaganda
10. Purchasing services
11. Rewarding
12. Co-optation
13. Penalizing
14. Repression

Societal strategies were interpreted according to whether society's policy position was in opposition to the state and the relative assertiveness of measures taken. Ranging from softest to hardest (i.e., from cooperation (1) to resistance (7)), societal strategies were coded as follows (see Appendix Table 2. 2 for details):

1. Cooperation with the state
2. Allowing state co-optation
3. Contacting officials
4. Appealing to state organs
5. International cooperation
6. Appealing to public opinion
7. Resistance

In each research article, a concrete public governance issue or event was treated as a single case. Some articles included multiple cases, and some cases entailed up to four phases of state–society interactions over time. State strategies were considered to be hard/tough if the average score was greater than or equal to 7, whereas an average score below 7 was coded as a soft strategy. Societal strategies were defined as hard if the mean was greater than or equal to 3.5, and considered soft if the mean was less than 3.5.

Table 2.3 shows the distribution of the cases across the four types of state–society interactions. Interestingly, societal actors adopted hard strategies in 60.8 percent of the cases, and those were divided equally between cases in the Type II category where the state responded with a hard strategy ($n = 38$) and those in the Type IV category where the state responded with a soft strategy ($n = 38$). The plurality of cases—40 cases, accounting for 32 percent of the total—were in the Type III category, where both state and societal actors used soft strategies.

Table 2.3
Distribution of cases across the four categories
of state–society interactions

		Society's Strategy	
		Soft	Hard
State's strategy	Soft	III: 40 (32.0%)	IV: 38 (30.4%)
	Hard	I: 9 (7.2%)	II: 38 (30.4%)

Type I cases would be expected to be the most typical form of inter-action in an authoritarian regime, where the state exerts tough measures against submissive societal actors. Yet this mode of interaction was the least common in our QCS review, with only nine strong state/soft soci-ety cases, accounting for 7.2 percent of the total. This underrepresenta-tion of "normal" authoritarian state–society interactions in the sample may be attributed to selection bias on the part of researchers who do not find it worthwhile to describe expected outcomes. It may be more novel to highlight cases with deviant or unexpected outcomes. Out of the 125 cases, there were 78 instances (62.4 percent) in which the state adopted a soft strategy, and 76 cases (60.8 percent) in which society adopted a hard strategy.

Outcome Variables: Political Power, Governance, and Policy Change The outcomes were divided into three categories: political power, governance, and policy change. Political power represents a zero-sum power relation between the state and society, which we measured based on four indica-tors: political mobilization, political accountability, agenda setting, and representation. As Juan Linz (2000, 159) argued in his classic definition of authoritarianism, this type of regime typically suppresses political mobili-zation and holds limited political accountability. This is generally the case in China's authoritarian regime. Therefore, in the process of state–society interactions, if society is politically mobilized or any state actor is held ac-countable, the political power of society vis-à-vis the state has increased. The representation indicator is also relevant in authoritarian regimes. Lev-itsky and Way (2010) analyzed how "competitive authoritarianism" as a particular category of autocracy has its own institutional mechanism for maintaining rule, namely, that of society generating representatives via competitive election. But even in non-competitive authoritarian contexts such as China, representation can be an important indicator of societal power. The power of agenda setting was highlighted in Steven Lukes (1974, 16–20) as the second dimension of power. When a societal actor can set the agenda on governance or public policy in state–society interactions, society has gained political power vis-à-vis the state. Appendix Table 2.3 details the definition of these indicators of political power.

The outcome of governance also includes four dimensions: respon-siveness, transparency, input channels, and societal empowerment (see

Appendix Table 2.4 for definitions of these terms). According to governance theory in public administration and political science, governance entails a cooperative and mutually dependent network between society and the state in accomplishing tasks and having services delivered in public affairs. It is an approach to managing public affairs that differs from the traditional mode of sole management by the government (Rhodes 1996, 660; Stoker 1998, 17). Such an approach to managing public affairs underscores the continuous communication and information sharing between the public and private sectors (i.e., between the state and societal actors). Moreover, the goal of governance is to resolve public issues that concern society. Through such a process, a relatively autonomous network, particularly among societal actors, should emerge. For these reasons, we chose responsiveness, transparency, input channels, and societal empowerment as indicators for governance.[1] State and societal actors typically share common goals and interests in resolving public issues. Therefore, state–society relations are not zero-sum when it comes to governance and can even be positive-sum.

Finally, the policy outcome variable was measured dichotomously—there is either "policy change with a positive response to society" or "no change." Appendix Table 2.5 provides definitions of these outcome variables.

Testing Hypotheses: Cross-Tabulation of Outcome Variables and Types

We hypothesized that four types of state–society interactions would lead to different political outcomes, and we expected that the likelihood of reforms as intended by society would be ranked as follows: Type IV > Type III > Type II > Type I. Table 2.4 shows the cross-tabulation analysis of the four types of interactions and all nine outcome variables. Using the mean score of the internal indicators, Table 2.5 shows the cross-tabulation analysis of the four types of state–society interactions with political power, governance, and policy change. In policy change, the results conformed with the hypothesized sequence. However, the other two outcomes diverged from the original hypotheses. The sequence for political power was

Table 2.4

Cross-tabulation among interactions and outcome variables

Dimensions		Political Power				Governance				Policy Change
State–Society Relations		Political Mobilization	Political Accountability	Agenda Setting	Representation	Responsiveness	Transparency	Input Channels	Societal Empowerment	Policy Change
I. state hard, society soft	Cases	9	9	9	9	9	9	9	9	9
	Mean	0.22	0	0.22	0	0.44	0	0.22	0.56	0.11
	SD	0.44	0	0.44	0	0.53	0	0.44	0.53	0.33
II. state hard, society hard	Cases	38	38	38	38	38	38	38	38	38
	Mean	0.68	0.13	0.05	0.13	0.74	0	0.29	0.50	0.50
	SD	0.47	0.34	0.23	0.34	0.45	0	0.46	0.51	0.51
III. state soft, society soft	Cases	40	40	40	40	40	40	40	40	40
	Mean	0.25	0	0.45	0.20	0.90	0.32	0.65	0.55	0.80
	SD	0.44	0	0.50	0.41	0.30	0.48	0.48	0.50	0.41
IV. state soft, society hard	Cases	38	38	38	38	38	38	38	38	38
	Mean	0.66	0.24	0.29	0.16	0.97	0.13	0.50	0.58	0.92
	SD	0.48	0.43	0.46	0.37	0.16	0.34	0.51	0.50	0.27
Total	Cases	125	125	125	125	125	125	125	125	125
	Mean	0.50	0.11	0.26	0.15	0.84	0.14	0.46	0.54	0.70
	SD	0.50	0.32	0.44	0.36	0.37	0.35	0.50	0.50	0.46

ANOVA for Table 2.4

	F-value	Post-Hoc Tests (LSD)
Political mobilization	8.481***	II > I, IV > I, II > III, IV > III
Political accountability	4.395**	IV > I, IV > III
Agenda setting	5.949**	III > II, IV > II
Representation	0.810	No significant difference
Responsiveness	7.505***	II > I, III > I, IV > I, III > II, IV > II
Transparency	7.044***	III > I, III > II, III > IV
Input channels	4.494**	III > I, III > II
Societal empowerment	0.160	No significant difference
Policy change	14.225***	I > I, III > I, IV > I, III > II, IV > II

NOTE: ***$p < 0.001$; **$p < 0.01$; *$p < 0.05$.

Table 2.5

Cross-tabulation between interactions and aggregate outcome variables

Issue Domain	N		Political Power	Governance	Policy Change
I. state hard, society soft	9	Mean	0.44 (0.11)	1.22 (0.31)	0.11
		SD	0.53	0.97	0.33
II. state hard, society hard	38	Mean	1.00 (0.25)	1.53 (0.38)	0.50
		SD	0.70	0.92	0.51
III. state soft, society soft	40	Mean	0.90 (0.23)	2.43 (0.61)	0.80
		SD	0.84	1.01	0.41
IV. state soft, society hard	38	Mean	1.34 (0.34)	2.18 (0.55)	0.92
		SD	0.97	0.80	0.27
Total	125	Mean	1.03 (0.26)	1.99 (0.50)	0.70
		SD	0.85	1.00	0.46

NOTE: The 0–4 scores for political power and governance are converted into a 0–1 range (numbers in parentheses).

ANOVA

	F-value	Post-Hoc Tests (LSD)
Political power	3.671*	IV > I, IV > III
Governance	8.843***	III > I, IV > I, III > II, IV > II
Policy change	14.225***	II > I, III > I, IV > I, III > II, IV > II

NOTE: *** $p < 0.001$; ** $p < 0.01$; * $p < 0.05$.

Type IV > Type II> Type III > Type I, and contrary to our expectations, Type II (hard/hard) scored higher than Type III (soft/soft). For governance, the sequence was Type III > Type IV > Type II > Type I. Overall, Type IV (soft state/hard society) secured the highest score for two dimensions of political power and policy change and the second-highest for governance. In other words, when societal actors take a strong stance, they are more likely to succeed in changing power relations and policy if the state adopts a more receptive position. However, the highest score was generated in governance when state and societal actors both interacted in a cooperative manner.

Our findings reveal a trade-off in outcomes from a societal perspective: when the state adopts a soft strategy, societal actors may either use a soft strategy for higher performance in governance or pursue a more assertive strategy for higher scores in political power and policy change. Overall, when the state pursues a tough strategy, society generally benefits by also exercising a hard strategy. In sum, when the state adopts a soft strategy, society has different choices; when the state uses a hard strategy, society faces constraints in all three kinds of political outcomes. As detailed in the cross-tabulation calculations and empirical chapters of this volume, the conditions under which the state deploys stronger strategies is contextually contingent on the issue domain and nature of societal engagement. Indeed, the epistemological essence of evolutionary governance is the expectation that actors may recalibrate their strategies but not necessarily in a predictable way. As Orion Lewis and Sven Steinmo (2012, 330–31) explain, "The iterated interaction of agent preferences with institutional and environmental factors ultimately determines behavior." This means "one should expect significant variation even within the same local institutional system" (Lewis and Steinmo 2012, 331).

Having said that, the QCS analysis finds that irrespective of societal strategies, the overall score for political power for society is lower when the state is tough ($0.44 < 0.90$; $1.00 < 1.34$). This result is consistent with our expectations of how an authoritarian regime behaves. Furthermore, in governance, the score is always lower when the state adopts a hard strategy, irrespective of societal strategies ($1.22 < 2.43$; $1.53 < 2.18$). For policy change, it is difficult to discern whether more or less change serves state interests. The state thus faces a dilemma: pursuing a hard strategy maintains its political power over society, but taking a soft strategy enhances the quality of governance. The results show that governance always scores higher than political power in all of the indicators, which means there is always a greater change in governance compared with that in political power.

Whenever a certain quality of governance was enhanced and policy change occurred, the change in political power was generally minimal, except for the Type I interactions, which yielded the same scores in political power and policy change. Finally, we note that the overall score of 0.70 for policy change indicates that the state's original policy position can indeed occur following state–society interactions.

One such example is the case of peasant protests in Qizong, which involved two rounds of state–society interactions in 1993 and 1998. During the first round, Xie Weimin, the Parents' Association, and elected representatives from 18 villages staged a march to the township government. They pleaded for the retraction of a policy that would increase tuition fees at the village school. The local government had a cooperative and positive attitude and, following a three-day negotiation, agreed not to raise local school fees. The second round of interaction became violent, however. Local citizens established an informal "burden reduction council," which evolved out of the original Parents' Association, to express their vehement opposition to heavy taxation. They pointed to several official documents issued by higher-level governments as a means to discredit local authorities and mobilize villagers. Over the course of three years, Qizong activists repeatedly kidnapped local cadres, besieged the township government, and ransacked offices. The local government eventually repressed the protests in 1998. Surprisingly, even though both sides adopted extreme tactics in the second round of interaction, the villagers ultimately achieved their goals as taxes and fees were kept lower than average for many years (Zhang 2015). We infer from this outcome that the local government opted for stability over increased fiscal revenues. In our coding, this case eventually scored positively on political mobilization, representation, responsiveness, societal empowerment, and policy change. It also illustrates the value of adopting the lens of evolutionary governance rather than a static conclusion that societal actors triumphed over the state (or vice versa) during a preceding phase of interaction.

These findings are more sanguine than initially expected and offer insight into the mechanisms underlying authoritarian resilience in China. Although China is not a competitive authoritarian regime, our analysis indicates that the party-state can be responsive to societal demands. Policy reforms and improvements in governance have occurred despite the state's general monopoly of political power.

Examining the individual indicators of political power in Table 2.4 shows that political mobilization scored highest (0.50), followed by agenda setting (0.26). Representation and political accountability scored substantially lower, with 0.15 and 0.11, respectively, which is not surprising given that these processes occur in formal political institutions. By contrast, political mobilization and agenda setting can emerge beyond the parameters of existing political institutions. These findings reflect the rigidity of China's political institutions and the regime's unwillingness to share formal political power with society. This result reveals that when changes do occur in various dimensions of political power, these shifts are generated by societal efforts, rather than those of the state.

Among the four governance indicators, responsiveness scored the highest (0.84), followed by societal empowerment (0.54), and input channels (0.46). Transparency scored the lowest (0.14). The high score of responsiveness shows that despite its institutional rigidity, the CCP regime is in practice relatively agile in responding to societal needs, particularly when the state adopts softer approaches (0.90 and 0.97). A similar dynamic can be observed with input channels: when the state uses soft strategies, societal actors are more likely to reach a higher quality of governance. Although the societal empowerment score is greater than or equal to 0.5, there is no appreciable difference among the four types. Transparency is distinguished from the other governance variables, such that there is a score only when the state uses soft strategies.

In the area of political mobilization, the reviewed studies show a clear and cross-categorical tendency of societal actors to mobilize and seek empowerment. Social activism in public governance is notable in China. However, social activism faces restrictions in holding the state and its agencies accountable, having representatives recruited in the formal system of public decisionmaking, and rendering the relevant public governance more transparent.

Cross-Tabulation Analyses of Issue Domain and Outcome Variables

The distribution of outcome categories varies across different issue domains, as seen in the cross-tabulation results presented in tables 2.6 and 2.7.

In the area of political mobilization, the issues of patriotism/nationalism, culture/religion/ethnicity, and environment/public health all scored above the mean. Notably, patriotism/nationalism scored 1, meaning that all of the coded cases ($n = 10$) involved meaningful societal participation. In political accountability, the land, equal rights, and culture/religion/ethnicity cases received above average scores, though none scored higher than 0.5. In agenda setting, community, economic management, and equal rights issues scored higher than average. In representation, community issues scored the highest, signaling that leaders of residential communities have been recruited into official organizations. Except for political mobilization, none of the issues scored 0.5 or higher on the other three indicators of political power.

By contrast, among the four governance indicators, responsiveness and societal empowerment scored higher than 0.5. In particular, land issues scored highest (1) and environment/public health scored second-highest (0.92) in responsiveness. In terms of transparency, community cases scored highest (0.38), although this is lower than 0.5. Three issues scored 0 on transparency: including land, economic management, and culture/religion/ethnicity. For input channels, environment/public health (0.65) and community (0.62) scored higher than 0.50. In societal empowerment, community issues scored the highest (0.92), and patriotism/nationalism (0.80) and labor (0.64) also scored above average.

Overall, three issue domains emerged as having the most political traction for societal actors: community, environment/public health, and equal rights. Community interactions scored the highest among four outcome variables: agenda setting, representation, transparency, and societal empowerment. It also scored second-highest on the variables of input channels and policy change. Community scored low, however, in political mobilization and political accountability. Environment/public health scored the highest on the input channels indicator and scored second-highest on responsiveness and transparency. In addition to community

Table 2.6

Cross-tabulation between issue domains and outcome variables

Dimensions Outcomes Issue domains		Political Power				Governance				Policy Change
		Political Mobilization	Political Accountability	Agenda Setting	Representation	Responsiveness	Transparency	Input Channels	Societal Empowerment	Policy Change
Land	Cases	10	10	10	10	10	10	10	10	10
	Mean	0.40	0.30	0.10	0.10	1.00	0	0.40	0.50	0.90
	SD	0.52	0.48	0.32	0.32	0	0	0.52	0.53	0.32
Environment / public health	Cases	26	26	26	26	26	26	26	26	26
	Mean	0.62	0.08	0.23	0.04	0.92	0.27	0.65	0.46	0.77
	SD	0.50	0.27	0.43	0.20	0.27	0.45	0.49	0.51	0.43
Labor	Cases	14	14	14	14	14	14	14	14	14
	Mean	0.43	0	0.21	0.21	0.71	0.14	0.43	0.64	0.43
	SD	0.51	0	0.43	0.43	0.47	0.36	0.51	0.50	0.51
Economic management	Cases	12	12	12	12	12	12	12	12	12
	Mean	0.25	0.08	0.33	0.33	0.83	0	0.33	0.50	0.67
	SD	0.45	0.29	0.49	0.49	0.39	0	0.49	0.52	0.49
Community	Cases	13	13	13	13	13	13	13	13	13
	Mean	0.31	0.08	0.54	0.38	0.85	0.38	0.62	0.92	0.85
	SD	0.48	0.28	0.52	0.51	0.38	0.51	0.51	0.28	0.38
Equal rights	Cases	28	28	28	28	28	28	28	28	28
	Mean	0.43	0.18	0.29	0.18	0.89	0.11	0.46	0.43	0.79
	SD	0.50	0.39	0.46	0.39	0.32	0.32	0.51	0.50	0.42
Culture / religion / ethnicity	Cases	12	12	12	12	12	12	12	12	12
	Mean	0.67	0.17	0.25	0	0.58	0	0.50	0.33	0.25
	SD	0.49	0.39	0.45	0	0.52	0	0.52	0.49	0.45
Patriotism/ nationalism	Cases	10	10	10	10	10	10	10	10	10
	Mean	1.00	0	0.10	0	0.80	0.10	0	0.80	0.80
	SD	0	0	0.32	0	0.42	0.32	0	0.42	0.42
Total	Cases	125	125	125	125	125	125	125	125	125
	Mean	0.50	0.11	0.26	0.15	0.84	0.14	0.46	0.54	0.70
	SD	0.50	0.32	0.44	0.36	0.37	0.35	0.50	0.50	0.46

Table 2.7
Cross-tabulation between issue domains and aggregate outcome variables

Issue Domain	N		Political Power	Governance	Policy Change
Land	10	Mean	0.90 (0.23)	1.90 (0.48)	0.90
		SD	1.10	0.74	0.32
Environment/ public health	26	Mean	0.96 (0.24)	2.31 (0.58)	0.77
		SD	0.66	0.84	0.43
Labor	14	Mean	0.86 (0.21)	1.93 (0.48)	0.43
		SD	1.03	0.83	0.51
Economic management	12	Mean	1.00 (0.25)	1.67 (0.42)	0.67
		SD	1.04	0.98	0.49
Community	13	Mean	1.31 (0.33)	2.77 (0.69)	0.85
		SD	0.75	1.09	0.38
Equal rights	28	Mean	1.07 (0.27)	1.89 (0.47)	0.79
		SD	1.02	1.07	0.42
Culture/religion/ ethnicity	12	Mean	1.08 (0.27)	1.42 (0.35)	0.25
		SD	0.67	1.16	0.45
Patriotism/nationalism	10	Mean	1.10 (0.28)	1.70 (0.43)	0.80
		SD	0.32	0.82	0.42
Total	125	Mean	1.03 (0.26)	1.99 (0.50)	0.70
		SD	0.85	1.00	0.46

NOTE: Numbers in parentheses are the scores in a 0–1 range.

and environment/public health, equal rights received above average scores on most outcome variables except for political mobilization, transparency, and societal empowerment.

A typical example of a community case is Shining Stone Community Action (SSCA). Founded in 2002 by Song Qinghua, SSCA is an NGO that works with migrant communities in Beijing (Teets 2013). In particular, SSCA encourages residents to participate in community affairs and trains residential committees in delivering social services. The Qingyuan Street Office has served as a local government partner of SSCA by funding and implementing public service projects needed by its residents. Because societal concerns are mediated through participatory governance, we regard the local state and society as pursuing cooperative strategies. In terms of impact, the case received a full score of 1 in the areas of agenda setting, responsiveness, input channels, societal empowerment, and policy outcomes, but it did not make progress on political mobilization, political accountability, representation, and transparency.

In terms of aggregate findings across the three main outcome categories (summarized in Table 2.7), as mentioned earlier, none of the eight issue domains had meaningful effect on the political power indicators. In the governance category, community and environment/public health issues scored the highest, while the lowest score was in culture/religion/ethnicity, followed by economic management and patriotism/nationalism issues. For the outcome of policy change, six of eight issues scored higher than 0.5. State–society interactions concerning land attained the highest score (0.90), such that some forms of policy reform occurred in 70 percent of the cases. Only two issue areas scored below 0.5 in the policy change category—labor (0.43) and culture/religion/ethnicity (0.25).

Conclusion

The QCS approach and resulting set of variables for analyzing state–society interactions presented here serve as the organizing framework for the empirical chapters that follow. Specifically, we developed a typology of state–society strategies, generated hypotheses about political outcomes associated with different patterns of interactions, and used QCS to develop a more integrated and systematic evolutionary approach for understanding the political implications of state–society relations in contemporary China. Our findings may be summarized as follows.

First, the QCS analysis revealed that state–society interactions are much more likely to induce changes in public policy and governance than in shifting political power toward societal actors. The significant disjuncture between scores in governance and policy change on one hand, and political power on the other, provides insights into the mechanisms of authoritarian resilience. China's party-state is often pragmatic in responding to societal concerns, yet it rarely concedes to indicators of power sharing and thus continues to maintain a tight grip on political power.

Second, out of the three categories of political outcomes, change in public policy proved to be the most prevalent result. Our analysis revealed that the likelihood of policy change is maximized when the state adopts a soft strategy and society takes a more assertive strategy. Policy changes are also likely when both state and society pursue soft strategies. Conversely, when both sides take hard positions, policy change is less likely—and it is the least likely under regular authoritarian state–society conditions (hard state, soft society). These hypotheses were confirmed by the cross-tabulation analysis of coded data.

Third, it is evident that when facing a tough counterpart, the state confronts a more difficult choice than societal actors do in an apparently similar situation. When met with a hard state strategy, societal actors who stand firm are more likely to induce positive changes on all three of the outcomes—political power, governance, and policy change. As such, the dominant strategy for society in light of a firm state stance is relatively clear: pursue a hard strategy. The reverse does not hold for the state, however. The state faces more of a predicament when society adopts a strong strategy. If the state uses a hard strategy in return, it exerts and maintains political power but may not be able to achieve improvements in governance or policy change. If the state adopts a soft strategy in response, governance may improve, but it will cede a certain degree of political power to society. In other words, the state faces a trade-off between political power and good governance. There is not an obvious dominant strategy for the state in tactical terms. The decision depends on whether the state chooses to prioritize political power or governance as the source of its legitimacy.

Finally and relatedly, our results point to variation in state–society dynamics across sectors/topics, which suggests that the different perspectives may be more apt in some domains than others. For example, our QCS analysis found that societal actors had the most impact on community issues, which scored the highest in dimensions of political power and governance out of all the issue domains and second highest in public policy. Hence, for community concerns, both the "rising civil society" and "mutual collaboration" perspectives are borne out. When it comes to land and environment/public health, however, state domination of political power persists even when there is state–society collaboration in governance. By contrast, in the areas of equal rights, religion/ethnicity, and patriotism/nationalism, societal actors are able to gain political power vis-à-vis the state, usually through political mobilization, but collaboration with the state in governance is limited.

These findings have implications for understanding ongoing debates in the study of state–society relations in China. As indicated in the literature review, three main perspectives emphasize the rise of civil society, state dominance, or mutual dependence between state and society. Applying our evolutionary framework to this debate reveals that the three approaches are not actually examining the same dimensions of state–society relations. Some are focused on the balance of political power between state and society, whereas others are more concerned about governance. The three camps are not debating at the same level or about the same outcomes. Although the state may seek to strengthen its dominance over society in terms of political power, it may nonetheless have a more collaborative relationship with society on governance issues and public policies. By the same token, social organizations may exhibit growing capacity and participation in public governance, yet their efforts to compete with the state's political authority are likely to be thwarted.

Given that China has a strong central government, these findings may seem counterintuitive in the study of comparative authoritarianism. Nevertheless, they demonstrate how authoritarian governance, and in turn resilience, was initially enhanced following the Cultural Revolution. China's party-state faced a legitimacy crisis by the late 1970s. For regime survival, it not only turned to market-oriented sources of economic growth but collaborated with newly rising societal actors for developing good governance to rebuild its legitimacy. In the process, the party-state yielded incremental political power in some areas, while societal groups emerged that proved to be mutually beneficial and gained political power, which the state was reluctant to relinquish. During this evolutionary process, the state and society made interest-driven choices. A dilemma for the rule of Xi Jinping, particularly in his second term, is that adopting a hard strategy seems to be the preferred means for preserving his political power, and as a result, its governance relationship with society has deteriorated.

The outbreak of COVID-19 echoed our QCS findings on public health issues: the state refused to relinquish its domination of political power, and thus effective governance was absent in the critical initial weeks of the viral outbreak.

These general findings are illustrated with more contextual content in the forthcoming chapters through in-depth case studies structured around the same framework of state–society strategic interactions and particular types of public policy, governance, and political power outcomes. Although outright authoritarian repression remains a viable tool for the party-state when deemed necessary, it is ultimately suboptimal for enhancing legitimacy and managing complex policy issues. Evolutionary governance is interactive, multidimensional, dynamic, and a quotidian source of both authoritarian resilience and fragility.

Appendix Table 2.1
State strategy toward societal actors

Dimension	Score	Strategy	Definition
Soft	1	Cooperation with society	Regarding a public governance or policy issue, the state and its agencies adopt a compatible, harmonious, or even similar position to societal (including international) actors' appeals and demands, and express their coordinative—or at least not unfavorable—attitudes toward societal actors. In this manner, the state and society actors may correspond or coordinate with each other side by side on such an issue on official or nonofficial occasions.
	2	Policy innovation	Regarding a public governance or policy issue, the state and its agencies initiate a policy position, content, act, or thinking that is distinguished from conventional policy or has never been employed as a response to the issue instigating societal (including international) actors to take action and appeal.
	3	Mediation	Regarding a public governance or policy issue, the state and its agencies reach a consensus with the societal actors involved or devise a solution for resolving problems by mediating diverse opinions among the state and societal actors.
	4	Consultation	Regarding a public governance or policy issue, the state and its agencies offer societal actors an opportunity to express their opinion or preferences through an institutional or non-institutional channel.
	5	Compensation	The state and its agencies appropriate public finances or nonpublic funds to redeem the harm or losses incurred by societal actors.
	6	Accepting the case	Regarding a public governance or policy issue, the state and its agencies offer societal actors an opportunity or a channel to voice their requests and officially accept their appeals or demands.
	7	Exhausting	Regarding a public governance or policy issue, the state and its agencies adopt various measures (e.g., delays, perfunctoriness, deception, concealment, misleading, obstruction, procrastination, raising costs, and complications) to frustrate societal actors' intentions to continue or intensify similar actions.

Appendix Table 2.1 (continued)
State strategy toward societal actors

Dimension	Score	Strategy	Definition
	8	Competition	Regarding a public governance or policy issue, the state and its agencies would not take opposing, denying, or repressing attitudes directly toward societal actors who submit a request or take action. Instead, they perform speeches or take action that is favorable to the state's position to win public support on such an issue.
	9	Propaganda	Regarding a public governance or policy issue, the state and its agencies spread or promote a certain argument, message, or impression that is distinct from the view of societal actors and/or favorable to the state's inherent values, aiming to leverage the public position.
	10	Purchasing services	Regarding a public governance or policy issue, the state and its agencies use public finances to purchase services provided by societal actors.
	11	Rewarding	Regarding a public governance or policy issue, the state and its agencies assign political posts to societal actors who make appeals or take action as a reward or in exchange for a compromise or renouncement of their original position or goal.
	12	Cooptation	Regarding a public governance or policy issue, the state and its agencies allow societal actors to perform certain institutional or noninstitutional (albeit state-authorized) roles or functions to coordinate with or to work for the state to realize the agenda set forth by the state on such an issue.
	13	Penalizing	Regarding a public governance or policy issue, the state and its agencies enforce punitive measures with public effectiveness on societal actors who have made appeals or taken action but have violated legal regulations or administrative mandates in the process.
Hard	14	Repression	Regarding a public governance or policy issue, the state and its agencies exercise measures involving harassment, suppression, intimidation, prevention, forbiddance, arrests, or violent coercion on societal actors who make appeals or take action.

Appendix Table 2.2

Strategies adopted by societal actors toward state actors

Dimension	Score	Strategy	Definition
Soft	1	Cooperation with the state	Societal actors who appeal to the state or participate in a public governance or policy issue adopt actions of coordination, cooperation, or assistance to correspond with or support the state and its agencies, which hold compatible, corresponding, or even similar positions on the issue.
	2	Allowing state cooptation	Societal actors who appeal to the state or participate in a public governance or policy issue accept offers with the nature of the rewarding, cooptation, purchasing, compensation, or appointment of official posts or functions provided by the state or its agencies, the positions of which are incompatible with, do not correspond to, or even conflict with their own original position, so that these societal actors compromise their position on the issue.
	3	Contacting officials	Societal actors who appeal to the state or participate in a public governance or policy issue, through formal or informal channels, contact and exert influence on officials or representatives of government to make them realize, accept, or adopt values or preferences that favor the societal actors.
	4	Appealing to state organs	Societal actors who appeal to the state or participate in a public governance or policy issue use institutional opportunities or channels provided by the state to influence the state and its agencies to adopt positions or preferences on issues that are closer to the ones held by themselves.

Appendix Table 2.2 (continued)
Strategies adopted by societal actors toward state actors

Dimension	Score	Strategy	Definition
	5	International cooperation	Societal actors who appeal to the state or participate in a public governance or policy issue take harmonious, cooperative, or assisting action to work and correspond with or support those international actors who hold compatible, corresponding, or even similar positions on an issue.
	6	Appealing to public opinion	Societal actors who appeal to the state or participate in a public governance or policy issue, holding positions dissimilar, contrary, or opposite to that of the state and its agencies, spread arguments, messages, or impressions favorable to themselves through various channels and the media, aiming to leverage the public position.
Hard	7	Resistance	Societal actors who appeal to the state or participate in a public governance or policy issue, holding a position that is dissimilar, contrary, or opposite to that of the state and its agencies, adopt individual or collective measures to disturb public order, garner public attention, and exert pressure on the state.

Appendix Table 2.3
Political power

Political Power	Definition
Political mobilization	Societal actors who appeal to the state or participate in a public governance or policy issue make speeches or take action, which induces other societal actors to conduct more numerous, more intensive, more frequent, or higher levels of speech and action, aiming to pronounce their appeal or participation in related public issues.
Political accountability	The decisions, reactions, and measures adopted by the state and its agencies in response to the appeals made by societal actors regarding relevant public governance or policy issues are imbued with corresponding political responsibility for those who adopt them in the formal political system and process. These political responsibilities have the potential effect of generating a proportional deduction in the salary of officials or minimizes their chance of a promotion.
Agenda setting	Societal actors who appeal to the state or participate in a public governance or policy issue present a new policy position or goal dissimilar to the status quo position of the state. Accordingly, the new policy position or goal directly or indirectly affects the state and its agencies, forcing them to reframe or change their positions, and allows the public to discuss the new position or goal in the public sphere.
Representation	In a formal system of public decisionmaking, certain representatives recruited from an open, fair, universal, and competitive procedure of public choice could reflect the opinions, preferences, or interests of societal actors who appeal to the state or take action on a public governance or policy issue.

Appendix Table 2.4
Governance

Governance	Definition
Responsiveness	In public processes, the state and its agencies make a public decision or distribution on procedural or substantial issues as a response to appeals made by societal actors regarding the relevant public governance or policy issue.
Transparency	The state and its agencies disclose information on public governance or a policy issue, as requested by societal actors, regarding the relevant public governance or policy issues.
Input channels	Societal actors who appeal to the state or participate in a public governance or policy issue can articulate their opinions, preferences, or interests through channels that eventually lead to the government, thereby affecting the relevant public decision or the result of public distribution.
Societal empowerment	Societal actors who appeal to the state or participate in a public governance or policy issue can enhance their financing or participation capabilities to strengthen or expand their organization, or to consolidate or extend social links with other societal actors in the public process relevant to the public issues.

Appendix Table 2.5
Policy change

Policy Change	Definition
Positive change	The state and its agencies make changes and respond to public governance or policy issues in accordance or in parallel with the appeals made by societal actors.
No change or negative change	The state and its agencies do not make changes or respond to public governance or policy issues in accordance or in parallel with the appeals made by societal actors.

Note

1. Although these four terms may seem to overlap conceptually, Appendix Table 2.4 clarifies that they were coded in a way that distinguishes them. Furthermore, their definitional differentiation is reflected in both the cross-tabulation and analysis of variance (ANOVA) results.

References

Ang, Yuen Yuen. 2016. *How China Escaped the Poverty Trap*. Ithaca, NY: Cornell University Press.

Brownlee, Jason. 2007. *Authoritarianism in an Age of Democratization*. New York: Cambridge University Press.

Bueno de Mesquita, Bruce, and Alastair Smith. 2009. "Political Survival and Endogenous Institutional Change." *Comparative Political Studies* 42: 167–97.

Bueno de Mesquita, Bruce, Alastair Smith, Randolph M. Siverson, and James D. Morrow. 2003. *The Logic of Political Survival*. Cambridge, MA: MIT Press.

Cooper, Harris. 2010. *Research Synthesis and Meta-Analysis: A Step-by-Step Approach*. Los Angeles: SAGE Publications.

Diamond, Larry. 2002. "Thinking about Hybrid Regimes." *Journal of Democracy* 13: 21–35.

Fu, Diana. 2017. "Fragmented Control: Governing Contentious Labor Organizations in China." *Governance* 30: 445–62.

Fulda, Andreas, Yanyan Li, and Qinghua Song. 2012. "New Strategies of Civil Society in China: A Case Study of the Network Governance Approach." *Journal of Contemporary China* 21.76: 675–93.

Gandhi, Jennifer. 2008. *Political Institutions under Dictatorship*. New York: Cambridge University Press.

Gandhi, Jennifer, and Adam Przeworski. 2007. "Authoritarian Institutions and the Survival of Autocrats." *Comparative Political Studies* 40.11: 1279–301.

Gåsemyr, Hans Jørgen. 2017. "Navigation, Circumvention and Brokerage: The Tricks of the Trade of Developing NGOs in China." *China Quarterly* 229: 86–106.

Geddes, Barbara. 1999. "What Do We Know about Democratization after Twenty Years." *Annual Review of Political Science* 2: 115–44.

Habich, Sabrina. 2015a. "Strategies of Soft Coercion in Chinese Dam Resettlement." *Issues and Studies* 51.1: 165–99.

———. 2015b. *Dam, Migration, and Authoritarianism in China: The Local State in Yunnan*. London: Routledge.

Hadenius, Alex, and Jan Teorell. 2007. "Pathways from Authoritarianism." *Journal of Democracy* 18.1: 143–56.

Han, Heejin. 2014. "Policy Deliberation as a Goal: The Case of Chinese ENGO Activism." *Journal of Chinese Political Science* 19.2: 173–90.

Han, Jun. 2016. "The Emergence of Social Corporatism in China: Nonprofit Organizations, Private Foundations, and the State." *China Review* 16.2: 27–53.

Heilmann, Sebastian, and Elizabeth J. Perry. 2011. "Embracing Uncertainty: Guerrilla Policy Style and Adaptive Governance in China." In *Mao's Invisible Hand: The Political Foundations of Adaptive Governance in China*, edited by Sebastian Heilmann and Elizabeth J. Perry, 1–29. Cambridge, MA: Harvard University Asia Center.

Ho, Peter. 2008. "Introduction: Embedded Activism and Political Change in a Semi-Authoritarian Context." In *China's Embedded Activism: Opportunities and Constraints of a Social Movement*, edited by Peter Ho and Richard Louis Edmonds, 1–19. London: Routledge.

Howell, Jude. 2007. "Civil Society in China: Chipping Away at the Edges." *Development* 50.3: 17–23.

Hsu, Carolyn L., and Yuzhou Jiang. 2015. "An Institutional Approach to Chinese NGOs: State Alliance versus State Avoidance Resource Strategies." *China Quarterly* 221: 100–122.

Hsu, Jennifer Y. J., and Reza Hasmath. 2014. "The Local Corporatist State and NGO Relations in China." *Journal of Contemporary China* 23.87: 516–34.

Ji, Yingying. 2018. "Emerging State–Business Contention in China: Collective Action of a Business Association and China's Fragmented Governance Structure." *China Information* 32.3: 463–84.

Levitsky, Steven, and Lucan A. Way. 2002. "The Rise of Competitive Authoritarianism." *Journal of Democracy* 13: 51–65.

———. 2010. *Competitive Authoritarianism: Hybrid Regimes after the Cold War.* New York: Cambridge University Press.

Lewis, Orion A., and Sven Steinmo. 2012. "How Institutions Evolve: Evolutionary Theory and Institutional Change." *Polity* 44.3: 314–39.

Linz, Juan. 2000. *Totalitarian and Authoritarian Regimes.* Boulder, CO: Lynne Rienner.

Lukes, Steven. 1974. *Power: A Radical View.* London: Macmillan.

Major, Claire Howell, and Maggi Savin-Baden. 2010. *An Introduction to Qualitative Research Synthesis: Managing the Information Explosion in Social Science Research.* Abingdon: Routledge.

Newland, Sara A. 2018. "Multilevel Politics of Civil Society Governance in Rural China." *China Quarterly* 233: 22–42.

O'Brien, Kevin J., and Lianjiang Li. 2006. *Rightful Resistance in Rural China.* New York: Cambridge University Press.

Peng, Lin, and Fengshi Wu. 2018. "Building Up Alliances and Breaking Down the State Monopoly: The Rise of Non-Governmental Disaster Relief in China." *China Quarterly* 234: 463–85.

Rhodes, Roderick A. W. 1996. "The New Governance Governing without Government." *Political Studies* 44: 652–67.

Saich, Anthony. 2000. "Negotiating the State: The Development of Social Organization in China." *China Quarterly* 161: 124–41.

Schedler, Andreas. 2006. *Electoral Authoritarianism: The Dynamics of Unfree Competition*. Boulder, CO: Lynne Rienner.

Shue, Vivienne, and Patricia M. Thornton. 2017. "Introduction: Beyond Implicit Political Dichotomies and Linear Models of Change in China." In *To Govern China: Evolving Practices of Power*, edited by Vivienne Shue and Patricia M. Thornton, 1–26. New York: Cambridge University Press.

Spires, Anthony J. 2011. "Contingent Symbiosis and Civil Society in an Authoritarian State: Understanding the Survival of China's Grassroots NGOs." *American Journal of Sociology* 117.1: 1–45.

Stoker, Gerry. 1998. "Governance as Theory: Five Propositions." *International Social Science Journal* 50: 17–28.

Svolik, Milan W. 2012. *The Politics of Authoritarian Rule*. New York: Cambridge University Press.

Teets, Jessica C. 2009. "Post-Earthquake Relief and Reconstruction Efforts: The Emergence of Civil Society in China?" *China Quarterly* 198: 330–47.

———. 2013. "Let Many Civil Societies Bloom: The Rise of Consultative Authoritarianism in China." *China Quarterly* 213: 19–38.

Thornton, Patricia M. 2013. "The Advance of the Party: Transformation or Takeover of Urban Grassroots Society?" *China Quarterly* 213: 1–18.

Tsai, Kellee S. 2006. "Adaptive Informal Institutions and Endogenous Institutional Change in China." *World Politics* 59.1: 116–41.

Unger, Jonathan, and Anita Chan. 2008. "Association in a Bind: The Emergence of Political Corporatism." In *Associations and the Chinese State: Contested Spaces*, ed. Jonathan Unger, 48–68. Armonk, NY: M.E. Sharpe.

Zhang, Wu. 2015. "Protest Leadership and State Boundaries: Protest Diffusion in Contemporary China." *China Quarterly* 222: 360–79.

PART II

Community Governance

CHAPTER 3

Participation under Authoritarianism?

Legislative Impact of Homeowner Activism in Beijing

Yousun Chung

Since the 2000s, homeowners in Beijing have promoted representation of their collective interests through increasingly institutionalized channels. In particular, their dominant strategy of engagement with local and central government entities has evolved from contention to meaningful participation in the public policy process. Their achievements include enactment of local legislation on property management such as the Property Law (2007), Ordinance on Property Management in Beijing (2010), and the pending passage of revised legislation to protect homeowners. Increasing participation in community governance by private citizens demonstrates the authoritarian regime's adaptation to changing realities. Rather than repression, the state has allowed and even encouraged feedback from societal actors on local governance issues. However, terms of participation are under continuous negotiation within the parameters of authoritarian governance. Identifying the mechanisms through which important socioeconomic agendas are negotiated between state and societal actors requires empirical investigation over time.

The emergence of private property rights in China has created new forms of state–society interaction in the area of community governance. While all urban housing was managed and allocated by work units in the Mao era, the wholesale commodification of housing (*shangpin fang* 商品房) since 1998 has given rise to a new social group: middle-class homeowners. As well-informed urbanites, homeowners are conscious of their legal rights over purchased properties and have begun to mobilize and devise strategies to defend their interests. These tactics range from organizing contentious activities to claiming their rights to participate in relevant policy processes. Homeowners have even established countrywide virtual networks to share successful stories and legal strategies. As a group, they are politically attuned and engaged (e.g., Guan and Cai 2015).

This raises the empirical issue of how and to what extent urban homeowners have managed to develop a sense of political efficacy and influence public governance. While they have pushed for better representation of homeowner interests, there has also been a shift in the state's perceptions and treatment of homeowners, from initial suspicion of a new social group to greater inclusion of them in relevant policy processes. Although this is an ongoing interaction, the case of Beijing homeowners' legislative influence has implications for understanding how interactive governance takes place in an important socioeconomic domain.

Drawing on longitudinal fieldwork conducted in Beijing, this chapter traces the evolutionary process through which homeowners have influenced new local legislation on property management in Beijing over the course of 2010 to 2018. The author conducted in-depth interviews with local scholars, government officials, and homeowner activists involved in local legislation. Before proceeding, the next section reviews the framework used in this volume for discussing the evolution of state–society interactions in China. The bulk of the chapter focuses on the case study and analyzes three main phases of the state–society interaction: changes in the macro-legal environment, the policymaking process, and policy implementation and feedback. The chapter concludes with a brief summary and discussion of theoretical implications and offers suggestions for future research on this topic.

Analytical Framework

In contrast to competitive authoritarianism, electoral competition and legislatures do not play major roles in a regime like China's. A nuanced understanding of state–society interactions is necessary for comprehending the alternative methods through which the Chinese state gains legitimacy. Coercion (or repression) remains a valid tool in authoritarian governance

(D. Yang 2017); however, coercive measures are accompanied by costs the regime would prefer to avoid (e.g., loss of legitimacy). Finding a balance between repression and concession through "political arrangements" is a preferable approach (Cai 2008).[1] As such, it is worth examining how the Chinese state has attempted to use non-coercive methods to govern and how these strategies contribute to regime durability.

State–society relations in contemporary China can be depicted as a strategic interaction between the two sides. The party-state authorities have begun to pay attention to the demands of society; accordingly, there are also opportunities for citizens to influence public policy. Arguably, state–society interactions have become a process of negotiation such that interest representation is selectively granted in exchange for regime legitimacy. Although it does not rely on competing parties and representative bodies, the state must show its capacity to deal with growing interest articulated by its constituencies (Chung 2015). Relatedly, the state has even taken intentional steps to buy stability and proactively monitor protests to gather information about citizen complaints (Heurlin 2016). Given that the state acts on this gathered information, we can see that China's authoritarian state exhibits adaptation to a rapidly changing reality. In this vein, social actors' participation in public governance is an advanced form of communication between state and society. Yet the mechanisms through which this participation promotes regime durability warrant further study. In particular, what are the channels for participation and to what extent can societal actors actually influence public governance in China?

Given that state–society interaction can take many forms and the way social actors can influence public policy differs by issue domain, generalizing about state–society interactions in a uniform and succinct manner can be challenging. Table 3.1 presents a 2 × 2 table similar to that discussed in chapter 2. Put simply, a state strategy can adopt a strong or soft form, and the same can be said for societal strategies. However, the typological boundaries in table 3.1 do not necessarily mean that the division between strong and soft strategies is dichotomous; rather, it implies a range of possible options that can be used by the state and social actors. More specifically, strategies adopted by the state lie on a spectrum from total repression at one end to cooperation with society at the other. Similarly, societal strategies range from determined resistance to cooperation with the state.

Table 3.1
Typology of state–society relations in China

		Society's Strategy	
		Soft	Hard
State's strategy	Soft	III	IV
	Hard	I	II

NOTE: Possibility of change in governance or policy: IV > III > II > I.

The particular community governance issue discussed in this chapter belongs to Category III, a soft–soft interaction. This does not exclude the use of contentious strategies by some homeowners because they do not act homogeneously; homeowners demonstrate diversified patterns of interest representation (Chung 2015; Xie and Xie 2019). Compared with other issue domains in which state–society interaction is more tense (such as labor and religion), the state–society interaction in private property rights/community governance can be categorized as a soft–soft interaction. The likelihood of policy change is expected to be relatively high in this category. To be sure, analyzing only one category of state–society interaction limits broader generalizations, but we can at least develop a deeper understanding of a soft–soft interaction in authoritarian contexts. Relatedly, although a soft–soft interaction may not introduce dramatic changes to governance, it is expected to engender positive change in the quality of governance. Hence, even if social actors consider their achievements to be limited, piecemeal changes contribute to the regime's broader goal of keeping the Chinese Communist Party in power (Stockmann and Gallagher 2011), a point revisited at the end of this chapter.

Case Study of a New Mode of Property Management in Beijing

Urban homeowners (*yezhu* 业主) are characterized by acquisition of purchased properties. However, the issue of private property rights is more than a materialist concern. Equipped with a strong awareness of rights and resources to actively defend their rights over major assets, urban homeowners differ from their counterparts at the periphery, such as farmers and migrant workers. As relative winners of reform,[2] these social actors belong to China's new middle class and have explored their relationship with the state in more nuanced ways. Earlier research revealed that the interests of homeowners often collide with those of the state, particularly the local state. Generally speaking, the state has not been active in processing requests from homeowners to clarify the nature of their property rights. Indeed, the state has often delayed or otherwise interfered with the process. Attempts to establish a homeowners committee have encountered obstacles. Local state agencies at the grassroots level, such as street offices (*jiedaoban* 街道办) and residents' committees (*juweihui* 居委会), have been reluctant to grant permission to establish such committees (Cai 2005; Read 2003; Shi and Cai 2006; Tomba 2005).

Nonetheless, some meaningful changes have occurred in the relationship between homeowners and the state. Although disgruntled homeowners have not directly challenged state authority, activism has become effective in requesting more responsibility from the state to clearly define and guarantee the protection of private property rights. A prime example is homeowner activists' participation in local legislation in Beijing. Through the Beijing Housing Construction Committee (*Beijing zhujianwei* 北京住建委, the main state actor in property management), the local state in Beijing has openly expressed its position to allow more room for homeowner interest representation. The Ordinance on Property Management in Beijing (*Beijingshi wuye guanli banfa* 北京市物业管理办法), announced in May 2010, mandated such changes.[3]

Several key features in the ordinance are worth highlighting: (1) homeowners are the main actors in property management (*yezhu zixing guanli* 业主自行管理); (2) more specific steps regarding the establishment of homeowner organizations (i.e., homeowner committees [*yezhu weiyuanhui* 业主委员会] and homeowner assemblies [*yezhu dahui* 业主大会]) have been suggested, including establishing a preparation team (*choubeizu* 筹备组), a preregistration process (*beian* 备案), a fixed-term appointment system with partial reelection (*renqizhi* 任期制), and a board of supervisors (*jianshehui* 監事会); and (3) ideas about how to enable homeowner organizations to become substantial entities (*shitihua* 实体化) have been proposed, including securing full-time staff equipped with professional knowledge of property management.

In terms of formalizing homeowner organizations, the idea of turning homeowners assemblies into legal entities (*faren* 法人) is noteworthy. Given that the official status of homeowner organizations has not been recognized, the concept was regarded as revolutionary. According to the ordinance, it is possible for a homeowners assembly, which represents all homeowners in a particular neighborhood, to be registered as a legal entity. Upon acquiring legal status, a homeowners assembly can serve as the main actor in litigation, fund management, and interaction with the state. In addition, the deputy director of the Beijing Housing Construction Committee, who played a key role in preparing the ordinance, confirmed the shifting stance of the local state by publicizing documents he had authored.[4]

Instead of full-scale application of the newly proposed agenda to transform homeowners assemblies into legal entities (*yezhu dahui farenhua* 业主大会发言稿), Beijing introduced an experimental application in a specific district and then stopped. Full-scale incorporation of homeowners assemblies in Beijing requires more time. This experimental incorporation plan garnered mixed reviews when first launched by the Beijing municipal government. Some welcomed it as a meaningful breakthrough in the history of Beijing homeowner activism, whereas others responded with skepticism and derided it as a hollow experiment. Despite these mixed reactions, allowing the experimentation to occur is meaningful for local governance in China. This new mode of property management in Beijing provides an instructive case study of how the opportunity for social input has translated into relevant policy outputs.

Despite some limitations, the attempt at local legislation in Beijing in 2010 did not necessarily fail. Because of the fierce contest between the two camps representing vested interests and new interests (i.e., citizens' interests), experimental application in one district could not be expanded across the city, and a leadership change in the Beijing Housing Construction Committee followed. However, governance is essentially about solving problems through institutionalized methods, and such attempts are under way in Beijing. After this experimental attempt ended in incompletion, problems surrounding property management remained, and citizens' requests for responsibility in governance have persisted. Thus, another round of social participation in property management has begun. The city of Beijing is preparing a new version of local legislation on property management, involving new actors, such as the Association of Lawyers in Beijing (*Beijingshi lüshi xiehui* 北京市律师协会) and the Beijing People's Congress (*Beijingshi renda* 北京市人大).

Beijing was selected as the core case in this chapter for several reasons. First, it is a pioneer in homeowner activism in China, as well as social movements in other issue domains. In terms of state–society interaction, the attitude of the Beijing local state is regarded as one of the most progressive instances that the local state has accepted and responded to voices from society.[5] Although Beijing's situation is not necessarily representative of changes occurring throughout China, it satisfies some conditions to be considered a critically groundbreaking case. In addition, the Beijing case holds future applicability. Once institutionalized, its mode of homeowner governance may spread to other areas.[6]

Changing Dynamics

PHASE I: CHANGES IN THE MACRO-LEGAL ENVIRONMENT

Up until the 2000s, the macro-legal environment grounding the protection of private property rights was precarious. Two higher laws with potential for nationwide application were in play: the Property Law (*wuquanfa* 物权法) of 2007 and the Ordinance on Property Management (*wuye guanli tiaoli* 物业管理条例) of 2003 and then 2007. The Property Law defined ownership broadly, whereas the Ordinance on Property Management recommended necessary conditions for establishing and managing homeowner organizations. However, many details regarding actual property rights practice were missing. The initial version of the Ordinance on Property Management (2003) was released much earlier than the Property Law (2007), creating a paradoxical regulatory situation such that many clauses regarding homeowner organizations in the ordinance were not backed by the highest law of the country. Some ambiguous clauses in the Property Law that left room for interpretation were harshly denounced.[7] Actual implementation of property rights thus fell under the discretion of local governments.

Prior to the new version in 2010, the earlier version of the local Ordinance on Property Management in Beijing, called the Ordinance on Community Management in Beijing (*Beijingshi zhuzhai xiaoqu guanli banfa* 北京市住宅小区管理办法), was issued in 1995. The long period between these ordinances created uncertainty, and a few observations regarding this gap can be drawn. First, the lack of a clearly defined legal environment for property rights unexpectedly left room for social power to grow. One homeowner activist commented, "In a sense, after the issuance of a very specific local ordinance with legal standing, I am afraid that social space will shrink. When everything was murky, we had more freedom."[8] This remark reveals that the absence of a clearly defined institutional environment can be perceived as a window of opportunity for social actors. Second, neither the local state nor society initially had sufficient information about the true intentions of the other party; frequent encounters facilitated mutual understanding. Many homeowner activists testified that the hostile attitude of the state toward citizen actors diminished gradually, which was a testament to the state's changed perception toward social actors.[9]

Throughout the transition period, homeowners emerged and grew in terms of social power. They responded to perceived opportunities by mobilizing and transforming into actors who could effectively represent the collective interests of homeowners. With the development of commodified housing, homeowners started to form homeowner committees in each neighborhood as representative organizations with their interests at heart. Homeowners can now purchase housing in a given neighborhood, elect representatives, and turn to their leaders and organizations to convey complaints about housing maintenance, living conditions, and general quality of life to housing business actors (e.g., real estate developers and property management companies) and relevant government units (Cai 2005; Read 2003; Shi and Cai 2006; Tomba 2005).

In the early stages of housing commodification, many conflicts around property management occurred between housing business actors and homeowners because of disparate expectations. Some initial conflicts emanated from developers who built poor-quality housing, and others stemmed from a lack of clearly specified property ownership (*suoyouquan*

所有权). More conflicts surrounded the issue of how purchased properties were managed, including maintaining communal public facilities such as elevators, green spaces, and parking lots, and providing security and cleaning services in residential complexes. Homeowner committees have played a central role in conveying residents' complaints about such issues to other relevant actors. For instance, based on the approval of a majority of homeowners, homeowner committees have attempted to dismiss unsatisfactory management companies and recruit new ones. They have also resorted to collecting petitions, initiating litigation, and pursuing collective action to articulate and defend homeowners' interests.

Horizontal linkages connecting homeowner committees across multiple neighborhoods have emerged over time, and homeowners have begun to mobilize beyond state-set boundaries of individual neighborhoods (Chung 2015; Yip and Jiang 2011). As their social force expands, horizontal homeowner linkages across Beijing have facilitated representation of their collective interests. These horizontal linkages now represent the main actors representing society in this specific issue domain. Changes in the macro-legal environment (such as the Property Law in 2007) have offered opportunities for social groups to come forward and raise their voices. Open forums, press conferences, and signature-collecting campaigns have followed. The main goal of social group activities has evolved beyond fighting unethical housing entrepreneurs. Homeowners now seek to change rules and regulations binding their rights over purchased properties.[10]

There are two representative horizontal linkages of homeowners in Beijing: the Governance and Community Institute (*hexie shequ fazhan zhongxin* 和谐社区发展中心) and the Beijing Association of Homeowners' Committees' Bidding Committee (*Beijingshi yezhu weiyuanhui xiehui shenban weiyuanhui* 北京市业主委员会协会申办委员会). The Governance and Community Institute purports to be a research-oriented organization that interacts with homeowners and other actors through forums, seminars, and conferences. As a formally registered social organization, the institute has developed with relative stability while avoiding direct confrontation with the state. In the Beijing Association of Homeowners' Committees' Bidding Committee, members are heads of homeowner committees from multiple neighborhoods. The committee claims to be more independent and directly representative of homeowner interests while being open to using aggressive strategies in interactions with the state. It has been engaged in many neighborhood disputes and has provided help to contending homeowners.

These two organizations assume somewhat different stances toward interaction with the state. Compared with the Governance and Community Institute, the Bidding Committee adopts more aggressive behavioral strategies. The state has responded differently to each body—granting formal legal status to the former but not the latter. However, these organizations have been steadily seeking engagement with the state. Social organizations in China have learned that their survival is better assured when they engage with the state than by seeking absolute autonomy (Lu 2009). Meanwhile, the state has realized that interactions with these organizations—regardless of their differences—contribute to governance because the state can gather information about issues of growing importance in local society. The following sections demonstrate how these horizontal homeowner linkages have been actively involved in the relevant policy process.

PHASE 2: HOMEOWNER PARTICIPATION IN LOCAL LEGISLATION AROUND 2010

At this stage, meaningful changes occurred in the concept and practice of property management (*wuye guanli* 物业管理). Homeowners came to care about the quality, comfort, and value of the properties they purchased and became disgruntled upon feeling that they were not receiving due service in proportion to management service fees. Moreover, they felt helpless when they were unable to dismiss an unsatisfactory management company at will. There were three underlying problems, involving identifying the main actor controlling property management, how conflicts of interest were discussed, and whether homeowners' interests were duly addressed in this process. As tensions in commodified residential complexes continued to rise, the state began to notice the seriousness of this issue.

The changed perception of the state with respect to property management was reflected through substantial evidence. At the 17th National Congress of the Chinese Communist Party, the central state mentioned that "grassroots self-governance is an important definition of self-governance pushed by the PRC" (*jiceng zizhishi zhonggong zizhi zhiyi* 基层自治是中共自治之一).[11] This statement implies that top leaders have come to regard self-governance among urban residents as equally crucial as that of ethnic minorities and that promoting self-governance among urban residents is included in the macro-level policy directions of the central state. The stance of the Beijing local state seemed to follow similar lines. In preparing a new version of the local ordinance around 2010, the municipal government appeared willing to allow more room for home-owners' rights in deciding matters relevant to their everyday lives in residential complexes. Despite some limitations, more feasible action plans to absorb citizen requests were suggested by promulgating the new ordinance in 2010.

Incessant complaints and requests from society have played a role in inducing a change in the mind-set of the state. The primary target of complaints by homeowners has been housing business actors. The local state, whether in general or specific state agencies related to property management, has also become a target of homeowner complaints. The Beijing Housing and Construction Committee previously received approximately 6,000 cases of complaints or disputes annually, which posed a considerable administrative burden (interview, August 2012).[12] An official in the Housing Construction Committee acknowledged that committee members had been paying close attention to increasing rights awareness, advancement, and sophistication in homeowner rights protection strategies. The same official added that his own agency and many others had come to realize the importance of facilitating the growth of homeowner organizations because doing so should ease their burdens.[13]

Similarly, the change in objective conditions of property management has affected the perspective of relevant bureaucrats. In contrast to previous years, property management is no longer likely to remain lucrative. Because of continuing inflation and the opposition to increases in service fees, many management companies now worry about operating at a deficit or maintaining the status quo. Supposing that such a situation becomes exacerbated, if the state continues to support management companies that fall short of providing quality service, the responsibility falls on the shoulders of the local state. The state would have to continue to provide direct material subsidies to malfunctioning management companies. An interviewee working as an adviser to the Beijing city government

stated, "It would be like going back to the mode of property management prior to housing commodification, and the burden shouldered by
the state would be insurmountable," thereby projecting a dim future for
property management.[14]

Faced with the aforementioned scenario, a rational choice for the state
would be to acknowledge homeowners as the primary actors in property
management. The state has come to expect that such action would alle-
viate growing disputes in the commodified housing sector and enhance
the long-term sustainability of property management.[15] The ordinance of
2010 established a policy agenda that has since drawn considerable attention with respect to transforming homeowner assemblies into legal entities. The phrase "de facto legal entities" (*shizhi faren* 实质法人) refers to
this agenda due to unresolved issues. To be a de facto legal entity, a homeowner assembly must be registered with the county or township government and street office. Final ratification is completed by obtaining a stamp
from the local Housing Land and Resource Bureau (*fangdiju* 房地局).
Once considered a legal entity, a homeowner assembly can open independent bank accounts and control funds such as management fees and
public funding earmarked for repairs (*gonggong weixiu jijin* 公共维修基金).
Because controlling funds is at the center of disputes in many residential
complexes, the goal of pushing this policy agenda is to mitigate disputes
and dissatisfaction with property management among homeowners.
An official at the Beijing Housing Construction Committee predicted,
"By granting officially recognized legal status to homeowner organizations, we encourage homeowners to resolve issues through legitimate
channels. It may help to either decrease or prevent disputes related to property management."[16]

The aforementioned change in the policy position of the state seeks
to actively recognize homeowner organizations and consider them partners in governance. In other words, the state regards homeowners and
their organizations as the main agents for outsourcing governance in a
particular issue domain where the state's continuous assumption of responsibility is inefficient and potentially high risk. Under the previous
workplace system (*danweizhi* 单位制), the state managed long-term public housing rentals through the Housing Authority (*fangguanju* 房管局
or *fangguansuo* 房管所); however, the state has since recognized that an
administrative approach where the state takes responsibility in this man-

ner is unsuitable for commodified housing. Intensifying the responsibility of business actors has also proven inefficient. An alternative solution is for the state to offer homeowners greater leeway to express their thoughts and incorporate feedback into property management in residential complexes. The primary policy agency of the state in dealing with such issues is the Beijing Housing Construction Committee. Most major local regulations concerning property management are prepared by this committee, even though such regulations are publicized by the Beijing city government. Given the necessity of cooperation, state agencies in charge of taxes, public security, quality control, and civil affairs are also involved in property management. For example, when promoting the agenda to turn homeowner assemblies into legal entities, securing the agreement of related functional agencies was crucial. The procedure to confirm the legal status of homeowner assemblies hinged on the consent of these agencies. The Beijing Housing Construction Committee took the initiative in persuading these agencies individually, but the agencies did not welcome the idea initially.[17]

Because different levels or lines (*xitong* 系统) of state agencies have different interests, tension is unavoidable. The Beijing Housing Construction Committee and lower-level government organizations have disparate interests. Grassroots government organizations, which have traditionally exerted territorial control in local society, still do not regard homeowner organizations as equal counterparts. Economic incentives also matter because district governments and street offices often have symbiotic interests with business actors in the commodified housing sector.[18] However, higher-level governments or agencies (i.e., the Beijing city government and Housing Construction Committee) are more interested in maintaining general stability, minimizing conflicts in residential complexes, and increasing efficiency in community management. Divergent local state interests and goals reflect fragmented state authority, and societal actors can leverage such chasms to advance their goals (Spires 2011). Interviewed homeowners were well aware of potential points of access.[19]

The policymaking process of the 2010 ordinance contained certain levels of inclusiveness, responsiveness, and deliberation, such that state agencies' decisionmaking processes elicited opinions from social actors. While preparing drafts of the new ordinance, the Beijing Housing Construction Committee held many public hearings (*tingzhenghui* 听证会)

to seek opinions from legal professionals, officials in related government agencies, business actors, and social activists.[20] Well-known homeowner activists in Beijing shared the experience of being invited to attend such meetings, hosted by relevant state agencies,[21] with some being individually consulted. The aforementioned horizontal linkages of homeowners across Beijing have participated actively in these processes. The case of the Bidding Committee is especially noteworthy. Although the committee does not have formal legal status and tends to express critical opinions toward government policies, it has been frequently contacted and consulted.[22] Field interviews with activists revealed that the idea of transforming homeowner assemblies into legal entities was proposed by homeowners rather than by state agencies.[23]

Communications technology has facilitated discussion among stakeholders. In addition to traditional media (television and newspapers), the influence of new media is crucial for engaging in political discourse in contemporary society. Regardless of the state's intention, new media has contributed to increased transparency in policymaking. Drafts of groundbreaking policies are disclosed to the public through formal legal documents and made available online almost instantaneously. For instance, through microblogging (*weibo* 微博), homeowner activists, relevant state agencies, and even ordinary homeowners can engage in debates. One informant shared, "I used to argue with those who are working in the Housing Construction Committee about the new version of local legislation. I gushed out critical opinions without reservation. After a few intense debates, they disappeared from the web space. Maybe they were offended by my criticism."[24] Despite the possibility of censorship, online discussion has provided a channel through which the local state and social actors can interact and exchange opinions.[25]

Pluralization of the policymaking process enables multiple interest groups to be collectively involved; thus, state agencies involved in policymaking may encounter challenges or face repercussions when attempting to compromise between multiple interests. On many occasions before and after the promulgation of the new ordinance, then-deputy director of the Beijing Housing Construction Committee Zhang Nongke openly acknowledged the shortcomings of earlier property management practices.[26] Zhang had a clear sense about the direction of upcoming local legislation. This was somewhat surprising given that it is not easy for a leader of a government agency overseeing the property management of a city to openly acknowledge problems within his own agency. Most of my interviewees underscored the importance of individual leadership in facilitating progress in the Housing Construction Committee.[27]

At this stage, social actors' participation in public governance (i.e., agenda setting and decisionmaking) became readily apparent since the local state altered its perception of homeowners and property management. A reform-minded leader in the core agency relevant to property management was proactive in meeting with social actors. My interviews with activists substantiated that such efforts were not superficial, but genuine attempts to improve communication on the part of the Beijing Housing Construction Committee.[28] The new local legislation eventually contained many clauses allowing more room for homeowner interest representation through methods such as transforming homeowner assemblies.

PHASE 3: HOMEOWNER PARTICIPATION IN IMPLEMENTATION AND FEEDBACK

During the third phase of interaction, a two-pronged approach was adopted for implementation of the new ordinance: (1) direct implementation by the state, and (2) implementation through state-sponsored social organizations. Direct implementation by the state refers to state-directed experimental implementation of incorporated homeowner assemblies, which entailed narrow-scope experimentation in a specific district in Beijing. Implementation through state-sponsored social organizations refers to these organizations' assistance in establishing homeowner groups across the city. Homeowner committees and homeowner assemblies have been established in every community of the experimental district. However, state-directed implementation has faced criticism; some have likened it to "planned economy-style implementation" (*jihua jingji fangshi* 计画经济方式) and "forced democracy" (*beiminzhu* 被民主), thereby expressing disappointment over how the agenda has been implemented.[29]

In terms of facilitating the establishment of homeowner organizations across the city, the local state supported the opening of two "guidance centers" (*fudao zhongxin* 辅导中心) in late 2011, directed by two well-known homeowner activists.[30] The stated goals of these centers include aiding the establishment of homeowner organizations, educating and producing human resources with professional knowledge in property management, and building platforms conducive to knowledge exchange among homeowners. These intermediary organizations emerged as a result of overlapping interests between state agencies and social actors. Because the state requires social stability, if disputes can be minimized by establishing more homeowner organizations, then the "work outcomes" (*zhengji* 政绩) of local state units will benefit. The state's provision of financial subsidies to social organizations can be understood as purchases of social services.[31] Social actors directing these new organizations indicated that they intended to capitalize on the opportunity to conduct activities for the benefit of society. They know that the state relies on their services and that state sponsorship can stabilize social organizations.

The two-track approach was implemented for about a year before being halted. In September 2012, after an experimental application at a district in Beijing had been completed, incorporation expansion stopped. Meanwhile, opinions of social actors were sought to evaluate the implementation of the plan. The Housing Construction Committee has since invited the Governance and Community Institute—a well-known horizontal linkage of homeowners who played an active role in the legislation process—to conduct an across-the-board evaluation of the new local ordinance. Thus, social actors have played a role in providing feedback or evaluating the policy. According to Fulda, Li, and Song (2012), social actors' transference of expert knowledge into policy evaluation is a crucial aspect of state–society collaboration.

Despite attempted innovations, whether the idea suggested in the new ordinance can be further implemented remains unclear,[32] primarily because the deputy director of the Housing Construction Committee has been assigned elsewhere. As noted, Zhang was open to considering requests from social actors. Under his leadership, the committee requested opinions from homeowner activists and devised many clauses in the local ordinance that were highly progressive at that time; it likely would have been impossible to issue the new ordinance in 2010 without him. While homeowner activists welcomed him (Bei 2011), backlash from the other side forced Zhang to leave his post. Pressured by housing business actors (developers and management companies) who believed that their vested interests were being encroached on by recent changes initiated by the Beijing Housing Construction Committee, Zhang was reassigned to a position that did not deal directly with property management or related legislation.[33]

Property management is a sector where the conflicting interests between stakeholders are fierce. Those with vested interests in close relations between the state and housing-related industry do not want to see the pendulum swing in favor of social actors, and thus oppose radical change in dynamics between property management stakeholders. Nevertheless, the voice of social actors has continued to increase. Homeowners continually endeavor to share their opinions regarding unresolved problems in property management with policymakers. A major change related to the Housing Construction Committee did not quell citizens' interest in this issue; rather, awareness of the public's legal rights has been raised.

Today, the local state is situated between old and new actors and seeks to find a solution that balances multiple parties. An eventual answer to this issue domain will presumably be determined through multiactor involvement because coordinating clashing interests appears to be the macro-direction of policy in this domain. After Zhang's departure, the Beijing city government realized that one specific government agency could not manage such a heavy burden, and thus the Beijing People's Congress, which was assumed to be better positioned to oversee local legislation and gather opinions from multiple actors, took control. Since 2012, key figures in the Beijing People's Congress have expressed that they are well aware of this task. In addition, the Association of Lawyers in Beijing has assumed an important role in preparing for another round of local legislation.[34] Ongoing attempts by multiple actors yielded a new draft of the Ordinance on Property Management in Beijing, which had gone through several rounds of public hearings by late 2019.[35]

Discussion and Conclusion

When it comes to clarification and protection of private property rights, recent state–society dynamics indicate that the policymaking process in China has become more pluralized than in previous years. The changing shape of property management in Beijing suggests that requests from society, corresponding acknowledgment from the state, and communication between these parties contributed to the innovative outcome of local legislation in 2010. Despite meaningful breakthroughs, residual limitations in the system warrant attention, and implementation of some innovative ideas remains incomplete. The 2010 revolution enjoyed limited success. However, a local attempt to prepare a new version of local legislation through multiactor involvement is under way, and social actors continue to add their voices to policymaking while positioning themselves as virtual "policy entrepreneurs" (Mertha 2009).

To summarize, social actors in this issue domain have succeeded in political mobilization to some extent. Homeowners have become actors who express their opinions about relevant policies. The resultant social empowerment can be considered an achievement by social actors. Reactions from the state reflect a certain degree of responsiveness because they provide social actors with a feedback channel. Regarding policy outcomes, no drastic change has occurred; narrow experimentation in a specific district in Beijing has not expanded. Although not dramatic in terms of amendment, a change in the quality of governance is notable. In contrast to its former stance, the local state now seems willing to interact with society and listen to homeowners by inviting them to participate in the local legislation process. As of this writing, a new version of property management–related local legislation is in development, and homeowner activists in Beijing are making sustained efforts to add their voices to a new legal document.

Because mutual needs have facilitated nonadversarial state–society interaction, this case is categorized as a soft–soft interaction in table 3.1; both state and society are motivated to engage with one another while avoiding direct confrontation.[36] The state tends to invite social actors to solve problems and enhance the quality of governance, and society attempts to use this opportunity to promote their cause. In this form of complementary state–society interaction, experimental applications are likely even if dramatic changes in institutions or policies remain elusive. At the same time, when both parties benefit from mutual engagement, the state–society relationship is likely to be collaborative.[37] Although this scenario does not represent a complete picture of the state–society relationship in contemporary China,[38] other issue domains exhibit similar trends (e.g., environmental issues and the anti-incineration campaign discussed in chapter 7), especially those involving urban middle-class actors with legal knowledge, material resources, and networking abilities.[39]

The case presented in this chapter offers implications about governance capacity and societal perceptions of state legitimacy. The state is aware it can enhance legitimacy by including urban middle-class citizens in relevant policy processes and enabling them to experience political efficacy. Unless these actors cross an ultimate red line, such exposure is less costly and more efficient than repression. Rather than leaving citizens disgruntled with the system and isolated, offering them opportunities to add their voices to policymaking can bolster their faith in the system.[40] Thus, China's modernized authoritarian state demonstrates adaptability by striking a balance between repression and concession. To be sure, citizens with enhanced political awareness may test the boundaries of state tolerance (Cai 2008; Yang 2005). It is preferable for the state to retain them as supporters of the regime while granting them selected opportunities to test political efficacy. Furthermore, incremental systemic changes gained through such state–society interaction help avoid abrupt shifts that may result in subversive outcomes. In this sense, policy- and issue-based contention could also reinforce the regime's legitimacy. Allowing expression of societal grievances in a specific scope can contribute to regime durability (Liu 2017).

The main focus of this chapter was private property rights and homeowners in urban China. Despite encouraging findings about evolving state–society relations, the current status of urban homeowners is not necessarily transferable to other segments of the Chinese population. Different state strategies (e.g., the "divide and rule" strategy) could be applied to other issue domains and other population groups. Other chapters in this volume explore state–society interactions across other issue domains, which provide further insight on the sustenance or erosion of regime legitimacy in contemporary China.

Notes

1. According to Cai (2008, 411), authoritarian resilience is explained by "political arrangements (that) grant conditional autonomy (to local governments)." This idea may be extended to the relations between state and society.

2. It could also be said that homeowners have benefited from the state project of creating a housing market and consumers. Negotiated sales of work unit housing to employees and many other subsidization policies followed to boost the nascent housing market in the 1990s (Tomba 2014).

3. The ordinance went into effect in October 2010. For the full text, see *Zhongguowang* (2010).

4. A representative one is "Zhongguo tese wuye guanli moshide zaizao 中国特色物业管理模式的再造" (Rebuilding property management with Chinese characteristics), which has been publicized online.

5. Interview with activist, August 2012.

Fulda, Li, and Song (2012) have shown how social actors in Beijing, despite their relative inferiority in power relations, can access the state proactively and induce changes.

6. Comparative case studies, if available and possible, will enhance generalizability.

7. For instance, unclearly defined divisional ownership (*qufen suoyouquan* 区分所有权) has brought about much controversy.

8. Interview with activist, August 2012.

9. Interviews with activists, August 2012 and August 2014. Regarding the process of how "mutual suspicion" can change into "mutual benefit," see Spires (2011).

10. Given this development, homeowners committees in specific neighborhoods are not the focus of this chapter.

11. For the full text of what was discussed at the 17th National Congress of the Chinese Communist Party, see *Zhongguowang* (2007).

12. However, the complaints directed to this committee decreased rapidly after the promulgation of the new local ordinance in 2010 (interview, September 2012).

13. Interview with official, September 2012.

14. Interview with activist, September 2012.

15. Interview with activist, September 2012.

16. Interview with official, September 2012.

17. Interviews with activists, August and September 2012.

18. This kind of business (i.e., land and/or housing sales) adds to local government budgets to a great extent. For instance, see Dong and Wang (2017).

19. Interviews with activists, August and September 2012.

20. According to He and Warren (2011), these are "deliberate" mechanisms that undergird Chinese authoritarianism.

21. One homeowner activist testified that the number of meetings (*huiyi* 会议) he has participated in is more than 20. He also added that he has contributed to making at least four clauses of the 2010 ordinance (interview, September 2014).

22. Regarding similar cases of environmental NGOs, Yang (2005) points out that this shows the state's tolerance of spontaneous social groups in the given issue domain.

23. Interviews with activists, August and September 2012.

24. Interview with activist, September 2012.

25. Online forum of homeowners also facilitates interaction among them within neighborhoods (Li and Li 2013).

26. Zhang was recruited from outside the organization. Because he is not a lifelong bureaucrat, he did not have entrenched interests with relevant stakeholders and was able to take bold steps to intensify homeowners' voices vis-à-vis those of business actors.

27. Interviews with activists, September 2012 and September 2014.

28. Interviews with activists, August and September 2012.

29. Interviews with activists, September 2012.

30. The leaders of these guidance centers are from the horizontal linkages of homeowners, respectively.

31. In addition to the basic subsidy to run organizations, a performance-based subsidy (in the amount of RMB10,000 for every additional homeowners committee established) has been offered (interviews with activists, August and September 2012).

32. Interviews with activists, August and September 2012, August 2014.

33. Interview with activist, September 2014. Zhang's story implies that the individual leader factor still holds in the Chinese system. In regard to the importance of "first-in-command" (*yibashou* 一把手), see Fulda, Li, and Song (2012). Others point out this factor as the shortcoming of the current system, which cannot guarantee continuity of reform policies, adding uncertainty to the future direction.

34. Interviews with activists, August and September 2014.

35. The October 22, 2019, draft of the Beijing Property Management Regulations is available at http://zjw.beijing.gov.cn/bjjs/xxgk/yjzj/53603652/index.shtml.

36. Early works focused on emerging homeowner organizations within neighborhoods and their confrontational potential. Homeowner activism has now entered a more mature phase. The focus of this chapter is on the latest phase, which is more toward participatory.

37. Making the relationship "mutually beneficial" guarantees sustainable development of a given social group (Spires 2011).

38. For instance, the landscape of state–society relations would be quite different in the issue domains of labor, religion, and ethnicity, which are regarded as politically sensitive.

39. On how citizens have turned themselves into participants in waste-sorting projects, see Johnson (2013).

40. On how inclusion of social actors may forestall their dissent, see Hsu and Hasmath (2014).

References

Bei, Ye. 2011. "Yige zhenzheng dong wuye guanlide lingdao, zan shijianwei lingdao zhang nongke tongzhi" (A leader who truly understood property management: praising the City Housing Construction Committee leader Zhang Nongke). Forum for League of Homeowners (yeweihui lianmeng luntan), September 22. http://house.focus.cn /msgview/2429/219863611.html.

Cai, Yongshun. 2005. "China's Moderate Middle Class: The Case of Homeowners' Resistance." *Asian Survey* 45.5: 777–99.

———. 2008. "Power Structure and Regime Resilience: Contentious Politics in China." *British Journal of Political Science* 38.3: 411–32.

Chung, Yousun. 2015. "Pushing the Envelope for Representation and Participation: The Case of Homeowner Activism in Beijing." *Journal of Contemporary China* 24.91: 1–20.

Dong, G. Nathan, and Zigan Wang. 2017. "House Price, Land Sales and Local Government Finance in Developing Economies: Evidence from China." Working Paper. https://pdfs.semanticscholar.org/b0f5/a85cad272d387e4b3b2c5e9201f3bd936dce.pdf

Fulda, Andreas, Yanyan Li, and Qinghua Song. 2012. "New Strategies of Civil Society in China: A Case Study of the Network Governance Approach." *Journal of Contemporary China* 21.76: 675–93.

Guan, Bing, and Yongshun Cai. 2015. "Interests and Political Participation in Urban China: The Case of Residents' Committee Elections." *China Review* 15.1: 95–116.

He, Baogang, and Mark E. Warren. 2011. "Authoritarian Deliberation: The Deliberative Turn in Chinese Political Development." *Perspectives on Politics* 9.2: 269–89.

Heurlin, Christopher. 2016. *Responsive Authoritarianism in China*. New York: Cambridge University Press.

Hsu, Jennifer Y. J., and Reza Hasmath. 2014. "The Local Corporatist State and NGO Relations in China." *Journal of Contemporary China* 23.87: 516–34.

Johnson, Thomas. 2013. "The Health Factor in Anti-Waste Incinerator Campaigns in Beijing and Guangzhou." *China Quarterly* 214: 356–75.

Li, Limei, and Li Si-Ming. 2013. "Becoming Homeowners: The Emergence and Use of Online Neighborhood Forums in Transitional Urban China." *Habitat International* 38: 232–39.

Liu, Chunrong. 2017. "Beyond Coercion: The New Politics of Conflict Processing in China." *Chinese Political Science Review* 2.2: 221–36.

Lu, Yiyi. 2009. *Non-Governmental Organizations in China: The Rise of Dependent Autonomy*. London: Routledge.

Mertha, Andrew. 2009. "'Fragmented Authoritarianism 2.0': Political Pluralization in the Chinese Policy Process." *China Quarterly* 200: 995–1012.

Read, Benjamin L. 2003. "Democratizing the Neighbourhood? New Private Housing and Home-Owner Self-Organization in Urban China." *China Journal* 49: 31–59.

Shi, Fayong, and Yongshun Cai. 2006. "Disaggregating the State: Networks and Collective Resistance in Shanghai." *China Quarterly* 186: 314–32.

Spires, Anthony J. 2011. "Contingent Symbiosis and Civil Society in an Authoritarian State: Understanding the Survival of China's Grassroots NGOs." *American Journal of Sociology* 117.1: 1–45.

Stockmann, Daniela, and Mary E. Gallagher. 2011. "Remote Control: How the Media Sustain Authoritarian Rule in China." *Comparative Political Studies* 44.4: 1–32.

Tomba, Luigi. 2005. "Residential Space and Collective Interest Formation in Beijing's Housing Disputes." *China Quarterly* 184: 934–51.

———. 2014. *The Government Next Door: Neighborhood Politics in Urban China*. Ithaca, NY: Cornell University Press.

Xie, Yue, and Sirui Xie. 2019. "Contentious versus Compliant: Diversified Patterns of Shanghai Homeowners' Collective Mobilizations." *Journal of Contemporary China* 28.115: 81–98.

Yang, Dali. 2017. "China's Troubled Quest for Order: Leadership, Organization and the Contradictions of the Stability Maintenance Regime." *Journal of Contemporary China* 26.103: 35–53.

Yang, Guobin. 2005. "Environmental NGOs and Institutional Dynamics in China." *China Quarterly* 181: 46–66.

Yip, Ngai-Ming, and Yihong Jiang. 2011. "Homeowners United: The Attempt to Create Lateral Networks of Homeowners Associations in Urban China." *Journal of Contemporary China* 20.72: 735–50.

Zhongguowang. 2007. "Hu Jintao zai zhongguo gongchandang di shiqi ci quanguo daibiao dahui shangde baogao" (Hu Jintao makes a report on the 17th National Congress of Communist Party of China). *Zhongguowang*, October 24. http://www.china.com .cn/17da/2007-10/24/content_9119449_6.htm.

———. 2010. "Beijingshi wuye guanli banfa" (The Ordinance on Property Management in Beijing). *Zhongguowang*, May 27. http://www.china.com.cn/policy/txt/2010 -05/27/content_20129188.htm.

CHAPTER 4

Cellularized Civil Society

Public Participation in Community Governance

Szu-chien Hsu and Muyi Chou

L ocal governments in China have increasingly co-opted social forces by building apparently cooperative or complementary partnerships. In evolutionary response, civil society organizations (CSOs) have helped local governments establish bottom-up mechanisms of governance. This chapter focuses on CSOs at the community level and how they participate in community governance. Two cases demonstrate that local governments can retain considerable political power, even when societal actors self-organize and participate in local governance with greater autonomy. Although the activism and autonomy of local societal actors appear to provide space for the emergence of "local civil society," this expression of autonomous social dynamism is only allowed to occur within limited administrative spatial or issue boundaries and under the auspices of local governments or party organs. This type of state–society cooperation in local governance under Chinese authoritarianism is best described as a "cellularized civil society." In such a society, the possibility for cross-boundary or cross-issue coalitions to arise among registered CSOs is limited because the local party-state continues to monopolize agenda setting and the authority to renew or withdraw CSOs' registered certificates. It is a structural arrangement within which bottom-up social autonomy and public participation are conditionally encouraged by local party-state agencies. In turn, this reinforces authoritarian survival rather than planting seeds for the growth of democratization.

During the Mao era, local governments in China delivered social services through work units or top-down administrative bureaucracies. As Chinese society has become increasingly diversified, sophisticated, and mobile, perfunctory supply of public services has generated increasing dissatisfaction. This is not surprising given that authoritarian regimes typically struggle to maintain an organic connection between state and society in the absence of meaningful elections for political leaders. In contemporary China, urban residents lack appropriate channels through which to express their needs and concerns about community affairs. Meanwhile, governments at the grassroots level have neither the incentive nor the platform to communicate effectively with local communities. The expenditure of public funds without solving problems often creates more discord in local state–society relations. The resulting accumulation of unsolved problems undermines trust between local citizens and the implementing branches of the local state. Communication becomes more fraught, the local government becomes increasingly anxious, and local communities become frustrated. As this happens, an authoritarian regime that was originally intended to be benevolent runs the risk of becoming increasingly alienated from society.

To forestall such a downward spiral in state–society relations, social organizations (SOs, *shehui zuzhi* 社会组织) dedicated to engaging local residents in local governance have emerged. This chapter presents in-depth case studies of how two SOs, Cultivation and Local Tube,[1] have assisted subdistrict governments in Beijing by communicating and cooperating with local citizens with the explicit objective of enhancing the quality of community-level public governance. Both organizations specialize in mediating disputes using participatory methods and have succeeded in achieving their stated objectives. Through horizontal communication, the gap between local government and residents has been effectively narrowed, and residents have become empowered with the capacity to communicate and self-organize. However, this development could become a double-edged sword for the local government. Although residents' capacity for self-organization can be conducive and instrumental to improvements in community governance, it can become problematic if harnessed for collective mobilization against local authorities. Indeed, some scholars regard grassroots SOs as the types of nonstate actors that portend the development of civil society in China. We contend that such an assessment would not be appropriate because of structural limits on their capacity to challenge party-state authority beyond their immediate communities.

This chapter proceeds as follows. The first section discusses relevant literature on state–society relations and presents contextual background on China's reforms in "social management." Some contributions harbor an optimistic view regarding the political implications of an expanding civil society, referencing the increasing number and capacity of grassroots SOs like Cultivation and Local Tube. By contrast, we argue that although these organizations can implement government projects and inspire local community residents to participate in local governance, their political role is limited. To the extent that such SOs empower residents to become participatory at the grassroots level, the "civil society" they create is at best "cellularized" because it is bounded spatially within a specific administrative area. Both SOs have demonstrated that they can change how the local government implements policies, but they have yet to change the fundamental asymmetry in power relations between the local government and society. There are limits to evolutionary governance as the party-state continues to dominate agenda setting and decisionmaking. We propose the concept of a cellularized civil society to capture this dynamic.

The empirical sections of this chapter review the relevant policies on the management of SOs, followed by case studies of Cultivation and Local Tube to illustrate the characteristics of a cellularized civil society and how SOs mediate between the local government and residents to improve community governance. Subsequently, the advantages and limitations of these two models of state–society cooperation are analyzed. In the final section, we argue that the development of this type of SO may not necessarily facilitate a pluralist civil society and democratization; at most it will generate a cellularized civil society, which will likely contribute to authoritarian resilience in China. In our two case studies, state–society interactions are cooperative rather than confrontational. Thus, the state–society strategy here is shown as soft state and soft society. The party-state still wields power in shaping civil society. Public participation has influenced the mode of governance rather than the distribution of power between local state and society.

Literature Review: Cellularized Civil Society

A BRIEF REVIEW OF RELEVANT LITERATURE

Debate persists over whether civil society has emerged in China. Three major approaches are typically used to explain SOs in Chinese society (Wang, Fei, and Song 2015): the civil society, corporatism, and contingent approaches. However, none are adequate for explaining empirical developments, which is why researchers have instead applied a meso-level framework that links theoretical discourse to the actual practices of SOs in contemporary Chinese society (Wang, Fei, and Song 2015, 421). We advance this research agenda by discussing the relationship between the government and SOs and reflecting on the political implications arising from their interactions. Earlier debates tended to be black-and-white in nature, focusing on the tension between a dominant state and a thriving civil society. A more nuanced position articulated by more recent scholarship is that SOs (or nongovernmental organizations, NGOs) not only coexist or collaborate with the state but also expand, grow, or become more autonomous without compromising the authoritarian nature of the regime. This line of argument has multiple versions, ranging from weak to strong. In a weak version, Shieh (2009, 38) argued that "the majority of NGOs in China see their future as being not in opposition to, but in collaboration with, the state," and that "civil society is too dependent on the goodwill and resources of the state to challenge it openly." Similarly, Woodman (2016, 342) highlighted the existence of "socialized governance" through "face-to-face" politics, which "blurs the boundaries between political compliance and social conformity" through the institutionalization of participation, welfare entitlement, and citizenship. Thus, civil society is depicted as extremely passive.

Fulda, Li, and Song (2012) presented a stronger version of the argument by depicting the state and SOs as engaging in cross-sector collaboration with local state agencies, which represents a shift from "government control" toward "network governance." Similarly, Shen and Yu (2017) applied a performance-based framework to explain the win-win situation between local governments and SOs. They argued that this collaboration is conducive to the local economy and social services, thereby empowering

SOs. Moreover, Hsu and Hasmath (2014) argued that contributions to SOs in local governance may feed back into their own organizational development. In these versions, civil society plays a supplementary role, contributing positively to public governance. This view of civil society is less passive than in Shieh's version.

An even stronger version of the argument claims that when collaborating with the state, civil society does not remain in a static condition. Instead, it grows and may even become autonomous. For example, Spires (2011) views the state–society relationship as a form of "contingent symbiosis." Similarly, Tang (2015, 106–7) argues that public deliberation in urban communities, particularly those with healthy socioeconomic conditions, is conducive to conflict resolution and the development of democratic values and abilities among citizens. Going beyond the previous arguments, Spires and Tang both claim that state and society need each other, making them relatively equal. The boldest version of the argument is that of Teets (2013), who argues that a relatively autonomous civil society may expand under authoritarianism without threatening the regime's political dominance. Even in this version, a more assertive civil society is still regarded as nonconfrontational and unlikely to challenge party-state authority.

This chapter echoes the observations made by these scholars, but proposes that state–society relations in China should not be examined from just one level of analysis. It is important to specify the level at which we are making our argument and in which dimension society is achieving gains. For example, this chapter shows that at the micro-level, SOs may be able to expand their network, develop their capabilities and strengths, or gain autonomy from the state. But at the macro-level, society merely serves the purpose of state expansion or growth. The stronger, more autonomous, and connected SOs become at the micro- or implementation levels, the more resilient the authoritarian regime becomes at the macro-level. If the administration firmly controls agenda setting and the power to allocate public resources, then SOs have only two alternatives: to work with the government in exchange for opportunities for development, or not work with the government and become marginalized and eventually repressed.

CELLULARIZED CIVIL SOCIETY

This chapter proposes the concept of a cellularized civil society to characterize the phenomenon described above. Such a society contains the following elements.

First, it is a phenomenon observed in state–society relations in a noncompetitive authoritarian country, such as China. Because of its growing plurality and complexity of public affairs, such a society tends to develop multiple SOs. However, the regime cannot absorb them through electoral patronage, unlike competitive authoritarian regimes.

Second, the state has material resources and is willing to distribute them to society to attain greater legitimacy. Again, unlike competitive authoritarianism, in full authoritarianism, the state lacks an organic linkage with a pluralizing, complex, and mobile society. Nonetheless, although SOs typically lack access to public resources, they may have the patience and skills to communicate with people and transform their needs and problems into a workable project. When successful, SOs earn high levels of trust and build strong ties with local communities and ordinary people. This means that SOs own something that the authoritarian state needs, and the state also has something that SOs lack.

Third, SOs may wish to empower citizens to become more politically active and participatory. Instead of repressing SOs, local state agencies might allow or even encourage SOs to transform the local community into one that is more self-organized, has a greater interest and concern in community public affairs, and exhibits a greater degree of participatory activism.

Fourth, once SOs are recruited by the state to help improve local governance, they are confined to a particular role. Their activism is limited within a certain administrative level and space, and the civic activism of local residents therefore remains within their community.

Fifth, SOs are restricted by certain functions and disciplines delimited by the party-state. Cross-boundary or cross-issue agendas are limited according to related regulations and laws.[2] However, in practice, it depends on the type of issue. For example, charity and service-oriented activities may have more flexibility to operate.[3] By contrast, rights and advocacy-oriented organizations are restricted, and any issue that concerns rights or political demands is not tolerated by the party-state.

These five dimensions constitute our definition of a cellularized civil society. Participatory activism may exist for public governance in the community, but such a circumscribed society does not challenge an authoritarian regime. Although facilitating SOs may enjoy trust or even authority within an empowered community, building cross-community leadership remains difficult. Without public authority or resources, the extent to which SOs can build an organic linkage with various communities is largely dictated by local state agencies. Therefore, the concept of a cellularized civil society helps explain why "contingent symbiosis" exists and why this type of society cannot undermine the existing authoritarian political order.

Background of the Problem and Methodology

POLICY REFORM ON THE MANAGEMENT OF SOs

Confronted with increasingly diverse social interests of society, maintaining social stability has become key to the governance of the Chinese Communist Party (CCP). In its report to the 17th National People's Congress in 2007, the CCP emphasized the importance of strengthening social development. To support this aim, the party proposed "a social management system characterized by Party committee leadership, government execution, nongovernmental support, and public participation" (*dangwei lingdao, zhengfu fuze, shehui xietong, gongzhong canyu* 党委领导、政府负责、社会协同、公众参与) (Xinhua Net, November 17, 2012). Moreover, it shifted its attitude toward SOs away from heavy control toward greater tolerance. Accordingly, the CCP government has promulgated several relevant documents relating to the innovative management of SOs in 2011.[4] For example, since 2008, the Beijing municipal government has disseminated several official documents pertaining to social construction (i.e., a series of 1 + 4 documents).[5]

Three crucial aspects must be addressed regarding this innovative management and development of SOs. First, relaxing restrictions on registration provides SOs with more social space, and a considerable number of them now have legal status. Second, government procurement of the services provided by SOs has created additional resources and funding for their development. Third, the government has created a state-corporatist hub system based on united front people's organizations, such as the Communist Youth League, All-China Federation of Trade Unions, Women's Federation, and several government-organized NGOs. These hubs function as a bridge between the party-state and grassroots SOs by maintaining close ties to the party-state and serving as "professional supervising units" for SOs. They are responsible for incubating and guiding grassroots SOs and facilitating state–SO collaboration to include controllable SOs. In practice, the hub system does not play a crucial role in Beijing because the bureaucratic characteristics of people's organizations are not easily changed, and they do not have the extra budget required to manage grassroots SOs. Thus, for most SOs in Beijing, people's organizations are still viewed as being part of the party-state.

Furthermore, the political mandate of "fulfilling a social management system characterized by Party committee leadership, government execution, non-governmental support, and public participation" was reinforced in the 18th National People's Congress Report in 2012 (Xinhua Net, November 17, 2012). Thus, facilitating community self-governance is encouraged by the policy of innovation in community governance and viewed as a foundation of local democracy (Xinhua Net, November 17, 2012). The abovementioned official statements and policy reforms provide a framework of policy openness within which SOs such as Cultivation and Local Tube have emerged and participated meaningfully in local governance.

METHODOLOGY

This study used qualitative methodology through in-depth field interviews with SO founders and staff members to develop a grounded narrative explanation. Interviews explored how participants implement projects authorized by the local government; how they communicate with officials and local residents; and how they interact with other SOs and relevant stakeholders. In addition, we interviewed local officials who frequently interact with these SOs to gain an understanding of policies on social management at the community level. Using case study analysis, we explored the factors encouraging or discouraging state–society interactions and how SOs influence state–society relations in practice. Our focus was on subdistrict- and community-level governance. In the following section, we briefly explain the challenges faced by the local government, the background to collaborative SOs, the relationship between the SOs and local government, and how the SOs work with the local government.

The Case of Cultivation: Participatory Planning for Activity Room Renovation in Golden Community

CULTIVATION IN THE YOUJING DISTRICT OF BEIJING

In response to rapid development and urbanization, Beijing and other large cities have become increasingly diversified, creating numerous new challenges in public governance, such as environmental pollution, social welfare provision, access to social services, and social conflict. In response, the local government has tried innovative methods to ease social tensions and maintain effective governance. However, with the collapse of the work unit (*danwei*) system, it must determine new methods for detecting poten- tial problems in an increasingly pluralized and mobile society to imple- ment policies effectively and deliver services efficiently. The current bu- reaucratic nature of the administration cannot address residents' needs and solve urgent problems. A considerable gap often exists between what the government provides and what residents want (Saich 2007).

Meanwhile, the party-state increasingly recognizes the challenges faced by local governance. For instance, the director of the Construction Division of the Beijing Social Affairs Committee (*shehui gongzuo weiyuan- hui* 社会工作委员会) acknowledges that "there are four main problems regarding community governance, including narrowly identified issues, the bureaucratized mechanism, low levels of participation, and incompetent self-governance" (Sun 2012). Thus, the purpose of reforming community governance is to identify diverse needs, promote public participation, and establish sustainable institutions. The government cannot implement such reforms on its own. It needs to cooperate with societal forces, which provide SOs with space to enhance local governance at the community level.

Cultivation is an SO that specializes in mediating disputes using participatory methods. It was originally registered as a company under the Bureau of Industry and Commerce and received grants from international foundations. Subsequently, it was registered as an SO under the Bureau of Civil Affairs (BOCA) and developed close working relations with the subdistrict government in Beijing. This evolution in its status occurred in three stages.

During the first stage, Cultivation conducted independent projects and received grants from international foundations. It persuaded the local government to allow them to design a project designed to solve community-based problems. Cultivation provided human resources and grants for the execution of these activities. Local officials and residents were satisfied with the results. This successful experience established trust between the local government and Cultivation and led to more opportunities for the SO to work with communities.

In the second stage, the subdistrict government became increasingly dependent on Cultivation to solve community disputes, even though the project grants and human resources still came from Cultivation. These interactions promoted Cultivation's reputation, and subsequently the group was invited to present and explain its performance to local officials, during which several officials from Youjing District noticed its participatory methods.[6] After the meeting, they approached Cultivation's founder and sought cooperation. Cultivation was then offered an opportunity to conduct an experiment in a subdistrict government in Youjing District. The subdistrict government provided project grants and invited Cultivation to implement the project.

This development steered the relationship into a third stage, during which Cultivation and the subdistrict government became partners. However, to receive government grants and execute government-authorized projects, Cultivation had to be a legal SO registered with BOCA. The leader of Youjing District invited Cultivation to register under its BOCA. Registration proceeded smoothly. Its newly acquired legal status consolidated Cultivation's working relationship with subdistricts in Youjing District. However, it retained its company registration with the Bureau of

Industry and Commerce, which it used in projects elsewhere. By keeping this double registration, Cultivation retained its autonomy and flexibility in implementation. The BOCA strove not to interfere with Cultivation's performance elsewhere, provided it continued to perform well in Youjing District.

ENGAGEMENT IN THE SPRING SUBDISTRICT PROJECT

In 2008, the Beijing Municipal Commission of Urban Planning (BMCUP, *Beijingshi guihua weiyuanhui* 北京市规划委员会) devised a pilot project titled "Urban Planning in the Community." It chose three districts for the pilot, including Youjing. The Youjing Branch of the BMCUP invited Cultivation's director to design a participatory method to encourage public participation in community development planning. The head of the Youjing branch of the BMCUP approved this method and invited residents and officials to discuss and plan the community project. The Youjing branch of the BMCUP later hosted a meeting to promote public participation in community development planning and invited an urban planning apparatus, Spring Subdistrict,[7] Cultivation, community residential committees, and residents to participate. To reach consensus and pave the way for planning and future implementation, introducing a participatory method was regarded as vital. The head of the Spring Subdistrict was interested in this method and thought it could be applied to community governance in his administrative area to help overcome distrust between local cadres and residents.

The Spring Subdistrict comprises seven communities. The composition of residents is so diverse that the traditional model cannot satisfy their varying needs. Therefore, the Youjing District government provided a public welfare fund that was devolved to subdistrict offices (*jiedao banshichu* 街道办事处) to handle community affairs. The community residential committee can apply to this fund for financial support. Most applications were for celebratory activities or giving souvenirs. These activities were generally mobilized from the top down and involved onetime consumption. Community residential committees (*jumin weiyuanhui* 居民委员会) were responsible for organizing and mobilizing residents to participate in these activities. However, such activities did not meet residents' actual needs. In response, the Spring Subdistrict office collaborated with Cultivation to develop an innovative model to fill this gap and improve community governance (interview, Golden Community Residential Committee, February 26, 2013). According to Cultivation's director, participatory governance should facilitate collaboration between the government, community, and SOs (interview, Cultivation's director, October 31, 2012). Under participatory governance, each member has a role to play in contributing to public affairs. Community residents are encouraged to participate in the process of decisionmaking and in the management, implementation, supervision, and interest-sharing involved in community development. In using this model of collaboration between the state and society, local governance was able to deliver demand-oriented community services (interview, Cultivation's director, October 31, 2012).

At the end of 2008, Cultivation was invited by the Spring Subdistrict street office (*jiedao* 街道) to work on a participatory project for designing an activity room. Cultivation helped the Spring Subdistrict organize an open space meeting for residents to discuss what type of activity room they wanted for their community. Approximately 100 people participated in the discussion session, including subdistrict officials, community social workers, community residential committees, Cultivation, and nearly 60 residents. After this meeting, Spring Subdistrict officials chose Golden Community as the place to implement this participatory planning project.[8] An old public activity room already existed in Golden Community, but it was dilapidated and required renovation. In fact, it had already been renovated once. However, residents were not satisfied, and thus the activity room was left idle and broken. Subdistrict officials did not want to make the same mistake, which is why they invited Cultivation to help execute the new planning project.

CULTIVATION IN ACTION: BRIDGING RESIDENTS AND CADRES

Cultivation first summoned relevant local cadres and active residents and provided them with basic training in participatory methods. Then Cultivation and local cadres held several open meetings to canvas residents' opinions. Based on these, Cultivation ascertained the current resources and capacity of Golden Community. Participants in open space meetings included cadres of the Spring Subdistrict and Golden Community residential committees, community residents, and Cultivation staff, which included approximately 60 people. During the meeting, residents expressed and exchanged opinions regarding the activity room. Participants then divided themselves into several groups to discuss problems. Subsequently, each group summarized and presented its conclusions to all participants in a plenary session. After the presentation, each participant had three votes to be cast for his or her favored proposals. The five most popular proposals were selected. Participants were then divided into five groups, with each discussing how to implement one of these proposals, followed by group presentations to all participants.

After the first open meeting, Spring Subdistrict officials, other relevant local officials, several experts, and Cultivation convened to discuss the feasibility of the residents' demands. The Spring Subdistrict government invited a company to submit a renovation tender based on residents' demands with an estimation of the price (approximately RMB600,000). All participants assembled to discuss and revise the renovation tender. As a result, the revised renovation plan was priced at approximately RMB200,000, which was much lower than the one designed by the company.

During the renovation, conflicts arose between local cadres and residents regarding the noise and mess created by the construction. Cultivation and the local cadres cohosted a meeting and invited residents to solve the problems together. Through discussion, residents came to an understanding of the reasons for the disruption and even volunteered to supervise the construction process. The activity room was eventually renovated according to residents' demands and at a reasonable cost. Residents decorated the activity room themselves and made new rules for its use. As their ideas were adopted and their demands met, they became more willing to use the activity room and ensure its tidiness. Whereas previously residents felt the activity room had nothing to do with them, they now felt that the activity room was "theirs" (interview with Cultivation's project manager, November 9, 2012).

This pilot project was generally successful and took 1.5 years to complete. To sustain it, Cultivation learned that the aim of the model should be to transform residents' needs into a concrete program. Cultivation guided and trained local cadres in how to design a program based on residents' demands. Compared with previous attempts at holding a festival or providing entertainment activities, these programs were more sustainable and responsive to residents' needs. Once the residents' demands were met, local cadres found that implementing numerous policies and delivering services proceeded much more smoothly. Through this pilot project, the level of trust between the local government, residents, and Cultivation was strengthened, which made further cooperation for community governance more likely.

The Case of Local Tube: A Party–Government–People Mutual Consultation and Co-Governance Model in Summer Subdistrict

LOCAL TUBE IN THE ZUOJING DISTRICT OF BEIJING

Facing similar challenges, another district in Beijing adopted a different strategy. In 2012, Zuojing District conducted a project titled "Solving Problems for the People" (*weimin jieyou* 为民解忧), which involved canvassing people's demands and responding to them.[9] These projects were mainly concerned with improving people's well-being on concerns such as improving living conditions and public facilities. In 2013, this project was initiated by inviting a media company, Local Tube, to work with the district administration. Local Tube is registered under the Propaganda Department of Zuojing District, and its role is to publish a community-based newspaper. Its business model aims to integrate business opportunities, community services (corporate social responsibility), and government propaganda (community newspapers), as well as to run community media in print and online. It has been successful in reaching the district's residential population.

A community service SO was subsequently established under Local Tube. This SO has several service centers in the communities where Local Tube provides social services to teenagers, elderly people, and disadvantaged groups. It is registered with the BOCA of Zuojing District and is mainly financed by government procurement projects. This SO later became the major platform for Local Tube's involvement in community governance.

Initially, Local Tube conducted a pilot project on participatory budgeting in the subdistrict, which was widely applauded by the academic community. However, its "independence" meant that local officials were afraid that the proposed projects from residents would be difficult to control. Consequently, this model was not adopted.

Following this experience, Local Tube modified the model by allowing local party cadres and local government to take a more active role in the procedure and develop initiatives. To further public participation in Zuojing District, Local Tube was invited to design a procedure to encourage residents' participation in community affairs. The Solving Problems for the People project encouraged some residents to participate and deliver their demands. Local Tube's experience in participatory budgeting not only mobilized residents but also provided channels for them to participate in the process of local governance and jointly realize projects. The mixture of experiences from the Solving Problems for the People and Participatory Budgeting projects became the model for "Party–Government–People Mutual Consultation and Co-governance" (*dangzhengqun gonshang gongzhi* 党政群共商共治; hereafter referred to as Co-governance) in Zuojing District. This co-governance model won the Prize for Ten Innovative Results of Community Governance in China (*Zhongguo shequ zhili shida chuangxin chengguo* 中国社区治理十大创新成果).

Based on this model, several subdistricts in Zuojing introduced specific procedures. For example, the Summer Subdistrict established a Three-level Residents' Assembly (*sanji yishihui* 三级议事会)—consisting of the subdistrict, community, and apartments (*louyuan* 楼院)—to improve local governance.[10] The assembly was designed according to four pillars of co-governance: "demand, solution, consultation, and evaluation" (*wenxu, wenji, wenzheng, wenxiao* 问需、问计、问政、问效) (interview, Local Tube staff, September 4, 2014). The characteristics of co-governance are "the CCP's leadership, the government's guidance, pluralistic participation, reciprocal negotiation, resource integration, social mobilization, and community self-governance" (interview, Local Tube staff, September 4, 2014).

HOW THE CO-GOVERNANCE MODEL WORKS

The whole process of co-governance comprises four main phases: (1) collecting needs and suggesting proposals, (2) discussing and sequencing the proposals, (3) implementation, and (4) evaluation. In practice, the procedure is as follows. First, local cadres deliver questionnaires to every household in the community through the apartment assembly. This questionnaire includes basic information, "demands with reasons," and "suggestions." Thus, residents can express their opinions by completing the questionnaires. The apartment assembly was a meeting held by local cadres with residents. In this meeting, cadres collected information from residents, talked with them, and excluded issues that could be dealt with by residents themselves. Some of them were also known as the "self-management group" (*ziguanhui* 自管会).

Second, a community assembly was held, which included resident representatives, SOs, deputies to the District People's Congress (DPC deputies), members of the district committee of the Chinese People's Political Consultative Conference (district CPPCC members), and estate management companies. Overall, 25 to 35 representatives participated in the community assembly. The assembly discussed the proposals collected from apartment assemblies and classified them into two categories. If the demands could be dealt with by the CCP community committee (*shequ dangwei* 社区党委) and community residential committee (*juweihui* 居委会), then community cadres would solve these issues by themselves. If the proposals were related to large-scale public needs or infrastructure, they were referred to the subdistrict office.

Third, a subdistrict assembly was held, which comprised community representatives (each community has six representatives), DPC deputies, district CPPCC members, SOs, and administrative representatives of the subdistrict government. In total, the subdistrict assembly had 100 representatives and is also known as the hundred-person deliberation assembly (*bairen yishituan* 百人议事团). It discussed and sequenced community proposals based on the degree of public urgency, finally selecting approximately 10 proposals for implementation. Fourth, the co-governance office of the subdistrict government managed these proposals and distributed them to relevant offices for implementation. Fifth, implementation will be evaluated the following year by subdistrict assembly representatives. Thus, when the subdistrict assembly is held, representatives decide which projects to implement in the coming year and evaluate the projects implemented in the previous year.

This co-governance model has narrowed the gap between local government implementation and residents' needs and improved relations between local cadres and residents. More important, it has facilitated and advanced residents' participation in community governance. The residents transformed from passively receiving public services to exercising agency in improving them.

Moreover, regarding the degree of public urgency for which the projects were scrutinized during the competition, the hundred-person assembly typically excludes proposals from wealthier communities that pertain to entertainment, learning, or cultural activities. To care for the needs of prosperous communities, the subdistrict government created another project category called integrated projects (*ronghe xiangmu* 融合项目) since 2015. This project encourages cooperation and mutual learning among neighborhood communities. Cultural, educational, or entertainment-based activities belong to this category. Unlike other projects, its implementation is mainly conducted by the local government, such that integrated projects are selected through competition among communities. The winner receives a budget from the subdistrict government and is responsible for implementing the project. Other communities in the subdistrict participate in the activities and each can learn from the other. Cross-community activities are led by local party organs, run by one host community, and financed by the subdistrict government. The purpose of this is to strengthen the solidarity and stability of communities under the leadership of the subdistrict party office and government. The implementation of integrated projects is then evaluated by representatives at the end of the year. In 2015, four projects were implemented in this category, including a table tennis match, a karaoke event, a flea market, and a knitting class.

THE ROLE OF LOCAL TUBE

Local Tube was both the designer and key implementer of this co-governance model. It was probably the only entity that could play such a role, given its deep penetration into the grassroots community, access to government officials, strong grasp of public opinion, and the trust engendered to community leaders.

Local Tube developed its own smartphone and online app that links local stores, restaurants, and hospitals, as well as administrative and social services. This platform provided not only commercial information but also news about public affairs in the community, and later provided a virtual public sphere within which residents could exchange information and discuss community issues.

Local Tube was highly strategic in striking a balance between the "party/government's control" and "social participation." In the three processes, both cadres and residents or their representatives were involved. The most critical of these was the hundred-person deliberation assembly that wielded agenda-setting power. The 100 members included subdistrict governmental officials, but these did not form the majority. The DPC and CCPCC deputies' function is half official and half social. They are typically elected with the agreement of the local party office, but they also have a certain representative role within society. If representatives of the residents and the SOs are considered social elements, then the social component has a stronger voice in the hundred-person assembly than does the official component.

Nevertheless, the subdistrict party/government officials are not worried about losing control over Local Tube. First, Local Tube is registered with the subdistrict Propaganda Department. Second, Local Tube is politically savvy and has used official discourse to frame how civic participation should be incorporated into local governance. Party leadership is always guaranteed. With the trust of local government, Local Tube has been able to duplicate the format of participatory governance and civic involvement throughout Zuojing District. Third, Local Tube was wise enough not to monopolize credit for such a reform. Instead, it gave credit to the local party and government. The reform originally began as one of participatory budgeting, but Local Tube changed the title to

"Party–Government–People Mutual Consultation and Co-governance," with the party at the helm. This is also the title that won the award for the Top Ten Innovative Results of Community Governance in China. Thus, the winner of the award was not Local Tube but the DPC.

This reform has indeed empowered numerous residents as well as Local Tube. However, Local Tube remains deeply embedded within the party and state apparatus. Civic participatory activism at the community level is robust and active, and Local Tube has succeeded in implementing reforms on a cross-community scale. But this occurs only within the framework stipulated by the subdistrict government under its supervision. Such a reform can only contribute to improving local governance under the party's leadership.

Analysis and Discussion

WHAT HAS CHANGED?

With participatory methods, the local government has improved its governance using professional techniques and by building trust with residents of the SOs. SOs serve as a bridge between local government and community residents, which has helped ease tension, solve conflicts, and narrow gaps. Introducing participatory methods into community governance provides an alternative way of delivering social services. Furthermore, local officials and residents have increased mutual understanding by engaging in public meetings. These meetings provided residents with a channel for dealing with conflicts through rational discussion, gradually learning how to express their opinions about public affairs and listen to others' ideas. More important, the local government initially had doubts about residents' competence for participating in solving community problems. These doubts were dispelled after officials witnessed firsthand the changes in the residents. Through participatory discussions, disadvantaged groups or individuals became active contributors to community development (interview, Cultivation's director, October 31, 2012). They came to realize that they themselves were able to contribute toward improving community governance. With this realization, the behavior of the residents changed from being disgruntled, passive recipients of government services to active citizens of the community. The local government also changed its attitude toward SOs and community activists from viewing them as a threat to viewing them as a partner in community development (interview, Golden Community Residential Committee, February 26, 2013).

For example, in Golden Community, Spring Subdistrict, the Golden Community residential committee, Cultivation, and residents all have incentives to work together in public governance. For the Spring Subdistrict and Golden Community residential committee, the incentive was the ability to achieve tasks and use budgets more efficiently. Cultivation's incentive was realizing its goal of empowering the community, establishing positive relationships with local officials and residents, and building its reputation. The residents' incentive was the fact that by participating in the process of community governance, their demands were articulated and then met by the local government.

In the second case, the Summer Subdistrict government, local party cadres, community residential committees, Local Tube, and residents all benefited from co-governance. For the Summer Subdistrict government, this meant that the budget could be used efficiently to meet residents' needs. Community residential committee functions were enhanced, and they were able to communicate more confidently with residents. For local party cadres, the distance between residents and the party was narrowed to some extent. The function of the party machine was also enhanced by this new co-governance model because it gave the party a constructive role in bringing everyone together and a useful mechanism for motivating rank-and-file party members. Furthermore, the party was able to recruit community activists through this process. The mass line strategy was revived by the co-governance model, and the relationship between local cadres and residents was improved. Residents' needs were now satisfied, and the process of distributing the budget became more transparent.

Local Tube played a crucial role in designing mechanisms that facilitated co-governance. It used government procurement to expand its projects and influence, thereby developing positive relationships with the local government. Local Tube not only designed mechanisms that bridged the gap between the local party-state and residents, it also provided a virtual public sphere for residents and other stakeholders to communicate and share information. Thus, living conditions and the community environment were improved, which in turn motivated residents to participate in the co-governance process. Improvements in quality of local governance bolstered the legitimacy of the local government.

Local Tube achieved slightly more than Cultivation in terms of the scale of local governance. It constructed a more comprehensive mechanism that integrated information sharing, communication, and service provision. Moreover, the co-governance model reached a higher level of institutionalization with the establishment of a three-level assembly. Co-governance was easy to adopt and modify according to various contexts and the varying composition of communities. Its underlying logic was to use good services to replace control, thereby achieving the goal of social stability and simultaneously satisfying residents' needs, the SOs, and the party/government.

LIMITATIONS: THE CELLULARIZATION OF ACTIVISM

Ultimately, SO development is a double-edged sword for local government. Residents' capacity for self-organization can be beneficial for improving governance. However, SOs can also be a problem for local government if they become a collective force opposed to its rule.

In the first case study, Cultivation's involvement in empowering community participation in public governance seems to encourage the development of civil society. Residents are motivated not only to participate but also to organize themselves. Cultivation was able to directly mobilize residents and simultaneously earn the trust of the local government. At the community level, this seems to be win-win for the local state and society. At the macro-level, the political domination of the authoritarian regime remains intact. Over time, Cultivation became known more for introducing participatory methods; thus, their work gradually shifted from implementing projects to training projects. Cultivation now provides training courses for local officials and SOs, and most of these projects are financed by government procurement. This means Cultivation is now less likely to spend time with residents and its role as a mediator between local government and residents seems to be less powerful. The organization's potential is therefore credited but also restricted by its profession and skill. In the long run, empowering the community and facilitating its ability to self-organize by working and practicing with residents can be beneficial. However, when Cultivation focuses on training, spreading the use of participatory methods may be limited to a onetime activity, rather than laying the foundation for long-term empowerment.[11]

In the second case study, Local Tube formed a partnership with the local government and relied on government procurement to run the business. It provided techniques and participatory methods that enabled the local government to govern. Its goal was to deliver happiness and promote civilization. It believed that "drawing closer to people generates power" (*tiejin jiushi liliang* 贴近就是力量) (interview, Local Tube staff, September 4, 2014). This belief is akin to the mass line strategy of the CCP. Thus, a specialized niche emerged within which Local Tube works with the local government and party organs. Using Local Tube's techniques and skills, the local party-state can preempt social forces and channel their energies into improving the quality of local governance. The mission delegated to Local Tube is tied to the task of maintaining social stability. Thus, for Local Tube to diverge from this principle and drift toward democratic reform would be difficult.

Several limitations exist that are shared by these cases. First, participatory discussion is time-consuming and depends on the local government's willingness to apply it. Thus, it is not suitable beyond the community level because it is difficult to hold constant meetings and engage in deliberative discussions with a larger population. Furthermore, social trust is difficult to form beyond the scope of a neighborhood community. When participatory discussion is applied, it must deal with difficult issues.

Second, in both cases, neither SOs nor the community residents initiated the participatory process; this was led by the subdistrict government. As mentioned, participatory discussion is typically focused on solving difficult problems. However, in everyday practice, it is not implemented routinely. Thus, societal actors do not have the power to set an agenda for reform.

Third, the government is indispensable as a facilitator. If SOs took the initiative to approach more communities to promote participatory discussion, would it be able to do this? If the SO has its own resources, could it not use them to solve problems in the community? The SO can certainly take the initiative to approach more communities or use its own resources to resolve local concerns. However, this cannot be conducted on a large scale because when community residents do not see any sub-district- or district-level government agencies present, they do not take the project seriously. Issues or problems at the community level typically require more than the commitment of government finance. They require public authority from multiple government agencies, which in turn requires coordination and commitment from a government leading official. This is something the SOs can never replace or provide.

Fourth, in the rare cases where an SO can solve problems using its own resources or its public reputation, it remains under the control of the government. An SO is only allowed to operate in the administrative area in which it is registered. Cross-boundary mobilization is difficult. Furthermore, any SO must face annual inspections, even when formally registered.

In addition to these institutional constraints, other uncertainties remain. For example, if the leader with whom the SO has a connection is transferred to another location or position, the cooperation that has been granted can be terminated at any time. A successor is usually unwilling to continue the original plan, and thus everything must start fresh (interview, Cultivation's project manager X, November 9, 2012). Moreover, while the policy of increasing government procurement for the services of SOs seems conducive to their development, the reality is more complicated. Typically, local officials may approach SOs such as Cultivation and Local Tube, and the organization would formulate a plan based on the government's needs before submitting an application. Once the application is approved, the SO can implement the project without significant interference from officials (interview, Cultivation's project manager H, November 9, 2012). However, sometimes officials approach SOs to seek innovative reforms that benefit their own political promotion and consequently may have a short-sighted perspective.

Another type of mentality officials may display is known as "dumping the load" (*shuai baofu* 甩包袱). According to a Cultivation staff member, once an SO had accepted a government's procurement, "it seemed that we were hired by the local government to do a job that is supposed to be done by the local government itself." To ensure the quality of the project, government officials tend to intervene with the implementation of the project or ask a third-party auditing organization to do so. Government procurement renders the relationship between the local government and SO more like that of an employer and employee rather than a partnership. For Cultivation's staff, the experience of government procurement has done more harm than good. They became exhausted writing proposals and reports and had little time for their professional work (interview, Cultivation's project manager X, November 9, 2012).

The empowered residents also face serious constraints. At the beginning, residents requested and welcomed intervention from the SOs. However, once the SO played a successful mediation role, the residents and the organization were constrained by a model in which the government distributes public resources to the community. If the empowered residents or the SO extend their activism beyond the boundaries of the local community, they face potential penalties from the local government, such as the suspension of public funding or subsidies.

Therefore, although numerous dynamic interactions exist between the local party-state and society in the evolution of local community governance, there has not been redistribution of political power between the local party-state and society. In both cases, the local government and party organs remain dominant when it comes to agenda setting and decisionmaking.

Conclusion: Comparative Discussion and Implications

In Hsu and Chang's quantitative case analysis (chapter 2), the category community governance scored first in representation, transparency, and social empowerment. It scored second in agenda setting, the aggregate governance index, and policy change. The community and environment/public health are two categories that generally earn the highest scores. The cases in this chapter do not align fully with those aggregate findings. In our two cases, transparency of public information indeed improved and residents were empowered. However, no genuine representation was generated, either through the local People's Congress or CPPCC. Instead, representatives from these institutions were summoned to screen the proposals. By contrast, the power of agenda setting is mainly in the hands of the party-state. For Cultivation, it was the subdistrict government that decided which issues would be delegated to SOs for the local residents to discuss. For Local Tube, although affiliated SOs helped the local government design the procedure for the co-governance model and several democratic or participatory mechanisms were embedded to ensure the party/government could not easily decide which items should be implemented, the subdistrict party office or government still had the overall power to make decisions about the reforms, irrespective of their speed, scale, or depth.

Based on our findings, SOs clearly serve as a bridge between the local government and residents, and they can change the modalities of public governance. But the basic power relationships between the local government and residents has not changed. SOs help moderate the tension that exists between local government and society. Yet the trust between SOs and the local government is contingent rather than unconditional, and their collaboration is ad hoc rather than institutionalized. The sustainability of the interaction between SOs and the subdistrict governments, as well as the bonds between SOs and local residents, remain uncertain. Although public participation improves the quality of local governance, it does not necessarily increase residents' political rights. Residents may be empowered to become more active in community public affairs. Yet this does not necessarily translate into political participation at a higher level. Relatedly, SOs may facilitate social solidarity within a community, but they do not facilitate social solidarity on a larger scale.

SOs help the local government communicate with residents and teach them how to solve disputes or conflicts through deliberative discussion. This type of approach is time-consuming and labor-intensive, which may not be scalable. The projects conducted using the participatory method were mainly concerned with improving residents' living conditions and community harmony rather than addressing citizens' rights. This form of participatory governance is unlikely to be sustainable if it is not supported by the local leader. The local government still dominates agenda setting. The collaboration between SOs, the local community, and the subdistrict government has unquestionably helped soften the tension between the local government and residents. Nonetheless, such a model does not resolve the origins of such problems, particularly those that are structural or institutional. Moreover, it cannot effectively transform representation into higher level decisionmaking (articulation) or hold the local government accountable.

Unlike state–society relations in democracies that exist in a competitive form, those in China are organized in a complementary and cooperative manner that benefits the survival of an authoritarian regime. This chapter presented two case studies that elucidate how local governments in China provide incentives to absorb social forces by building seemingly complementary partnerships. In response, SOs help local governments create a bottom-up mechanism for local governance. In both cases, although societal actors can self-organize and participate in local governance with greater autonomy, this does not weaken the political power of local governments. Instead, societal participation enhances local state capacity in functional terms and strengthens their penetration into the local community. The activism and autonomy of local social actors appear to create the room for a "local civil society." However, in reality, such autonomous social dynamism is only allowed to exist and grow in limited administrative spatial or issue boundaries and under the auspices of local governments or party organs. We characterize such state–society cooperation in local governance under Chinese authoritarianism as a cellularized civil society. In such a society, cross-boundary or cross-issue coalitions are limited because local governments or party organs control agenda setting and have the authority to renew or withdraw CSOs' registered certificates. Thus, the evolutionary emergence of bottom-up social autonomy and public participation in local governance benefits authoritarian survival rather than sowing the seeds for democratization.

Under Xi Jinping's rule, some regulations and laws related to CSOs have been revised or promulgated. In 2016, the Charity Law was introduced, which encourages charitable organizations to develop by providing institutional, tax and financial incentives. The Provisional Regulation on the Registration and Management of Civil Non-Enterprise Units (Revised Draft for Public Consultation) was released by the Ministry of Civil Affairs of the People's Republic of China in 2016. It has since been renamed Regulations on the Registration and Management of Social Service Organizations. To be consistent with the Charity Law, the phrase "civil nonenterprise units" was changed to "social service organizations."

These two documents show the CCP's intention in shaping the development of SOs for social services and charities. Furthermore, the enactment of the Law of the People's Republic of China on the Administration of Activities of Overseas Non-Governmental Organizations within the Territory of China (Foreign NGO Law, 2016) reinforced this trend and implies that the development of SOs has become even more dependent on government procurement. This is because foreign NGOs are required to register under "the public security department of the State Council and the public security organs of provincial people's governments," which restricts the administrative functions of foreign NGOs.[12] The CCP uses these policies to shape the development of SOs and defines SOs as helpers. In so doing, the CCP intends to prevent SOs from becoming forces that oppose its rule. To ensure that the seeds of civil society are "cellularized" at community level is a useful strategy from this perspective.

In the long run, whether a cellularized civil society in the community can reach out and connect with others remains to be seen. If the whole society or a wider range of local communities in a region face a common crisis or shock, empowered cellularized civil societies may be more willing to take action than are communities that have never been empowered. Before the occurrence of such an extreme scenario, cellularized civil society operates within the parameters of authoritarian rule. Furthermore, the space for social forces to engage in public governance relies heavily on how much information the state is willing to share with society. Take the outbreak of the novel coronavirus in late 2019, for example. The local government decided to control the information from the outset and punished the doctor who posted one of the warnings (Zhou, Zhu, and Yang 2020). The government subsequently manipulated relevant information, and party organs led and implemented related containment work at the community level (Tian 2020). With the asymmetry of information between the state and society at the local and community levels, it is difficult for societal forces to address this issue unless the local government allows them to do so. In some cases, local governments permitted societal actors to be involved in activities such as designing posters to educate the public about home quarantining (Liu and Zhu 2020). In line with our findings, agenda setting and transparency of information are controlled by the local government. Voluntary assistance coordination, governance collaboration, or information exchange across the community are strictly forbidden. Public participation at the community level remains cellularized by the state.

Notes

1. Cultivation and Local Tube are pseudonyms for two SOs that are deeply engaged in community governance in Beijing.

2. See Articles 13 and 25 in "Minban feiqiye danwei dengji guanli zhanxing tiaoli" (1998). In practice, there is some flexibility for SOs to operate depending on the attitude of the local government. In 2016, the Provisional Regulation on the Registration and Management of Civil Non-Enterprise Units (Revised Draft for Public Consultation) was released by the Ministry of Civil Affairs of the People's Republic of China. It was renamed Regulations on the Registration and Management of Social Service Organizations. The name of Civil Non-Enterprise Units is modified as Social Service Organizations (SSOs), consistent with the Charity Law. Nevertheless, according to Article 56 in the draft of Regulations on the Registration and Management of Social Service Organizations, the registered SSOs are still required to obey that their activities shall not go beyond the principles and area of work as defined in the charter. Central Government of the PRC (2016).

3. For example, see chapter 9, "Promotional Measures" in the Charity Law (2016). The charitable organizations are encouraged by providing friendly institutional conditions and tax preferences. An English translation of the Charity Law is available at http://www.chinadevelopmentbrief.cn/wp-content/uploads/2016/04/Charity-Law-CDB-Translation.pdf.

4. According to the 12th Five-Year Plan (2011), the CCP government proposed that the registration regulation of SOs would change from dual registration to single registration. Literally, this is viewed as a reform that lowers the threshold for registration and may be conducive to the development of SOs.

5. The series of 1 + 4 documents are as follows: Outlines of Enhancing Beijing Municipal Social Construction Implementation (*Beijing shi jiaqiang shehui jianshe shishi gangyao* 北京市加强社会建设实施纲要), The Trial Measures for Beijing Municipal Community Management (*Beijing shi shequ guanli banfa (shixing)* 北京市社区管理办法（试行）), The Trial Measures for Beijing Municipal Community Social Workers (*Beijing shi shequ gongzuozhe guanli banfa (shixing)* 北京市社区工作者管理办法（试行）), Opinions on Enhancing the Facilitation of the Reform and Development of Social Organizations (*Guanyu jiakuai tuijin shehui zuzhi gaige yu fazhan de yijian* 关于加快推进社会组织改革与发展的意见), Opinions on Further Enhancement and Improvement of the Construction of Party-branches in Social Sector (*Guanyu jinyibu jiaqiang he gaijin shehui lingyu dangjian gongzuo de yijian* 关于进一步加强和改进社会领域党建工作的意见). Central Government of the PRC (2008).

6. Youjing District is a pseudonym for the involved district in this case.

7. Spring Subdistrict is a pseudonym for the involved subdistrict in this case.

8. Golden Community is a pseudonym for the community in which Cultivation implemented the project.

9. Zuojing District is a pseudonym for the involved district in this case.

10. Summer Subdistrict is a pseudonym for the involved subdistrict in this case.

11. According to Cultivation's staff, it is difficult to follow up with the trainees after training courses because the organization does not have enough staff to do so, and the trainees (like local officials) are less likely to keep in touch once they are transferred. Interview, Cultivation staff, March 1, 2013.

12. According to Foreign NGO Law, Article 6, the public security department of the State Council and the public security organs of provincial people's governments are the registration administrative authorities for foreign NGOs conducting activities within the territory of China. Also see List of Fields of Activity (2016).

References

Central Government of the PRC (*Zhongguo zhengfu wang*, 中国政府网). 2008. Beijing Government Spreads the Series of 1+4 Documents of Strengthening Social Building (*Beijing shiwei shizhengfu yinfa jiaqiang shehui jianshe 1+4 wenjian*, 北京市委市政府印发加强社会建设1+4 文件). http://www.gov.cn/gzdt/2008-09/27/content_1107627.htm.

———. 2016. The Draft of Regulations on the Registration and Management of Social Service Organizations (Call for Feedback to This Revised Draft) (*Minban fei qiye danwei dengji guanli zhanxing tiaoli (xiuding caoan zhengqiu yijian gao)*, 民办非企业单位登记管理暂行条例（修订草案征求意见稿）). http://www.gov.cn/xinwen/2016-05/26/content_5077073.htm.

Charity Law. 2016. *China Development Brief* (*Zhongguo fazhan jianbao*, 中国发展简报). http://www.chinadevelopmentbrief.cn/wp-content/uploads/2016/04/Charity-Law-CDB-Translation.pdf.

Fulda, Andreas, Yanyan Li, and Qinghua Song. 2012. "New Strategies of Civil Society in China: A Case Study of the Network Governance Approach." *Journal of Contemporary China* 21.76: 675–93.

Hsu, Jennifer Y. J., and Reza Hasmath. 2014. "The Local Corporatist State and NGO Relations in China." *Journal of Contemporary China* 2.87: 516–54.

Law of the People's Republic of China on the Administration of Activities of Overseas Non-Governmental Organizations within the Territory of China (Foreign NGO Law). 2016. (*Zhonghua renmin gongheguo jingwai fei zhengfu zuzhi jingnei huodong guanlifa*, 中华人民共和国境外非政府组织境内活动管理法). PKU LAW (*Fabao beida*, 法宝北大). http://en.pkulaw.cn/display.aspx?cgid=269422&lib=law.

List of Fields of Activity, Categories of Projects and Professional Supervisory Units for Overseas NGOs Carrying Out Activities in Mainland China. 2016. *China Development Brief* (*Zhongguo fazhan jianbao*, 中国发展简报). http://www.chinadevelopmentbrief.cn

/articles/the-list-of-fields-of-activity-categories-of-projects-and-professional-supervisory
-units-for-overseas-ngos-carrying-out-activities-in-mainland-china/.

Liu, Xiaoyang, and Lichen Zhu. 2020. "Young People of Cultural and Creative Industries Design the Propaganda Illustration of Coronavirus Containment to Serve Residents" (*Wenchuang qingnian hui fangyi xuanchuan chahua fuwu jumin* 文创青年绘防疫宣传插画服务居民). *Zhongguo wenming wang* (中国文明网). http://www.wenming.cn/dfcz/bj/202002/t20200211_5415713.shtml.

"Minban feiqiye danwei dengji guanli zanxing tiaoli" (The Provisional Regulations for the Registration and Management of Civil Non-Enterprise Work Units). 1998. *China Development Brief* (*Zhongguo fazhan jianbao*, 中国发展简报). http://www.chinadevelopmentbrief.cn/wp-content/uploads/2014/08/PROVISIONAL-REGULATIONS-FOR-THE-REGISTRATION-AND-MANAGEMENT-OF-CIVIL-NON-ENTERPRISE-WORK-UNITS1.pdf.

Saich, Anthony. 2007. "Citizens' Perception on Governance in Rural and Urban China." *Journal of Chinese Political Science* 12.1:1–28.

Shen Yongdong and Yu Jianxing. 2017. "Local Government and NGOs in China: Performance-Based Collaboration." *China: An International Journal* 15.2: 177–91.

Shieh, Shawn. 2009. "Beyond Corporatism and Civil Society: Three Modes of State-NGO Interaction in China." In *State and Society Responses to Social Welfare Needs in China*, edited by Jonathan Schwartz and Shawn Shieh, 22–43. London: Routledge.

Spires, Anthony J. 2011. "Contingent Symbiosis and Civil Society in an Authoritarian State: Understanding the Survival of China's Grassroots NGOs." *American Journal of Sociology* 117.1: 1–45.

Sun, Zhixiang. 2012. "Shequ zhili xin shijian: Beijing shi shequ guifanhua jianshe" (The new practice of community governance: The construction of Beijing municipal community normalization). Participation Center (*Hui zhi canyu zhongxin* 汇智参与中心). http://www.participation.cn/a/zhutiwenzhang/2012/0714/1465.html (accessed May 28, 2013).

Tang, Beibei. 2015. "Deliberating Governance in Chinese Urban Communities." *China Journal* 73: 84–107.

Teets, Jessica C. 2013. "Let Many Civil Societies Bloom: The Rise of Consultative Authoritarianism in China." *China Quarterly* 213: 19–38.

Tian, Chao. 2020. "11.7 Thousand Party Members in Dongcheng Take Responsibility of Coronavirus Containment Work in Communities" (*Dongcheng 1.17 Wan zaizhi dangyuan chongfeng shequ fangyi yixian* 东城 1.17 万在职党员冲锋社区防疫一线). *Beijing News* (京报网). http://www.bjd.com.cn/tx.

Twelfth Five-Year Plan for National Economic and Social Development of the People's Republic of China (*Guomin jingji he shehui fazhan di shi'erge wunian guihua gangyao* 国民经济和社会发展第十二个五年规划纲要). 2011. Central Government of the PRC (*Zhongguo zhengfu wang*, 中国政府网). http://www.gov.cn/2011lh/content_1825838_10.htm.

Wang, Shizong, Di Fei, and Chengcheng Song. 2015. "Characteristics of China's Non-governmental Organizations: A Critical Review." *Journal of Chinese Political Science* 20: 409–23.

Woodman, Sophia. 2016. "Local Politics, Local Citizenship? Socialized Governance in Contemporary China." *China Quarterly* 226: 342–62.

Xinhua Net (Xinhua wang, 新华网). November 17, 2012. Hu Jintao's Report at the 18th National Congress of the Communist Party of China (*Hu Jintao zai Zhongguo gongchandang di shiba ci quanguo daibiao dahui shang de baogao* 胡锦涛在中国共产党第十八次全国代表大会上的报告). http://www.xinhuanet.com//18cpcnc/2012-11/17/c_113711665_8.htm.

———. November 17, 2012. Hu Jintao's Report at the 18th National Congress of the Communist Party of China (*Hu Jintao zai Zhongguo gongchandang di shiba ci quanguo daibiao dahui shang de baogao* 胡锦涛在中国共产党第十八次全国代表大会上的报告). http://www.xinhuanet.com//18cpcnc/2012-11/17/c_113711665_6.htm.

Zhou, Huiying, Jianling Zhu, and Shengru Yang. 2020. "Wuhan Coronavirus Whistleblower Li Wenliang Confirmed Dead: Freedom of Speech Is Rising" (*Wuhan feiyan chuishaoren Li Wenliang bingshi, Zhongguo xian qi yanlun ziyou hushen* 武漢肺炎吹哨人李文亮病逝 中國掀言論自由呼聲). Central News Agency, February 7. https://www.cna.com.tw/news/firstnews/202002070150.aspx.

CHAPTER 5

Contention and Inclusion of a Grassroots Community

Conflict over Rural Land Requisition in Nanhai, Guangdong

Yi-chun Tao

This chapter traces the evolution of land management and legal awakening in a rural village to illustrate the possibilities and limits of societal contention under authoritarian governance in China. Reform of the farmland shareholding system in rural Guangdong in the 1990s aroused broad grassroots conflict that initially erupted in 2000. After the local government ordered the clearance of agricultural land for construction, villagers in Sanshan mounted a rights defense campaign in 2005, pitting themselves against the municipality of Nanhai. Local residents brought their grievances to the highest level petitioning office in Beijing and sought support from lawyers, NGOs, intellectuals, and journalists. Tension between Sanshan villagers and local authorities escalated, plunging grassroots society in Sanshan into a governance crisis. In response, the Nanhai municipal government enforced "regulatory inclusion" through existing laws and arbitrary coercion. Conflict between Sanshan residents and authorities began to subside in 2012, and the rights defense movement diverged as its nonlocal supporters shifted their focus to land rights disputes in other regions. This nearly decade-long grassroots resistance was suppressed by another municipal crackdown in 2014. Since then, Nanhai has continued to flourish economically and won awards from the central and provincial governments for governance performance. In the absence of an evolutionary approach to state–society relations, the preceding conflict would be buried under the veneer of these awards.

Well located in a fertile region of Guangdong province, Nanhai district in Foshan has developed vibrant markets and outperformed other rural counterparts in the Pearl River Delta since the earliest years of China's "reform and opening." Because of its progressive stance toward economic development, Nanhai was designated as a pilot site for several reform experiments and is currently lauded by various official awards for its success in governance performance. Adopting the evolutionary framework in this volume reveals multiple stages of protracted state–society conflict over the past three decades. In the 1990s, the introduction of the rural land shareholding cooperative system (*nongcun tudi gufen hezuozhi* 农村土地股份合作制) aroused broad grassroots opposition that erupted in 2000, particularly in Nanhai's islet of Sanshan. This escalated into a rights defense (*weiquan* 维权) movement in 2005. Pitting themselves against the municipality of Nanhai, villagers brought their grievances to the highest-level petitioning office in Beijing and sought support from lawyers, nongovernmental organizations (NGOs), intellectuals, and journalists. Tension between Sanshan villagers and local authorities worsened, plunging the grassroots society in Sanshan into a governance crisis.

In response, the municipality of Nanhai enforced "regulatory inclusion" with existing laws and arbitrary coercion. The conflict between the Sanshan locals and authorities over land rights began to subside in 2012, and the rights defense movement diverged, with its outside supporters shifting their focus to land rights disputes in other regions. After being suppressed by another municipal crackdown in 2014, this nearly decade-long grassroots resistance came to an end. Since then, Nanhai has continued to flourish economically and won a national award that labeled it as an innovative local government and a flagship city in Guangdong for "successfully" reforming its collective economic organization, which involved addressing corrupt practices that plagued the rural land shareholding cooperative system. Furthermore, in 2013, Nanhai implemented a new system of social control called "grid management" (*wanggehua guanli* 网格化管理) and stabilized its political economy.[1] A concurrent wave of urbanization transformed Nanhai from a rural to an urban community that boasts a self-sufficient economy, less use of government resources, and a social structure characterized by limited official penetration into the general public. Nanhai has been hailed as the archetype of social governance by researchers from the social policy think tank of the central government. However, as detailed in this chapter, earning this national reputation was accompanied by social conflict over the loss of farmland and grassroots legal awakening—a process that is revealed through an evolutionary approach to state–society relations.[2]

Economic and Social Structure of Nanhai

Situated in the Pearl River Delta, Nanhai has geographic advantages for economic development (Vogel 1990). Its economic scale and fixed asset investment have been among the top ranked in the nation for many years, and it has ranked several times among the 10 most economically competitive counties or county-level cities in China. With a robust market economy and continued foreign investment, Nanhai has a relatively small state sector, and its residents rely little on government resources.

Nanhai has undergone rapid economic growth. Its market contracts have developed on a long-term basis and created demand for legislation. A nationwide campaign to popularize legal education was launched in the 1980s to facilitate China's economic reforms. The National People's Congress (NPC) passed a law in 1985 regarding the implementation of a popular five-year compulsory legal education program spanning 1985 to 1990. During this period, basic legal knowledge was disseminated to as many as 700 million people across China. Guangdong province was among the most active participants in this program (State Council Information Office 2008). The faculty of Southwest University of Political Science and Law, one of China's most reputable educational institutions in this field, were invited to travel from Chongqing to teach in Guangdong. Many locals worked as citizen agents and rights protectors for approximately 10 years after receiving training in the program.

With mandatory legal education taking root across China and the expanding markets, some regions in the Pearl River Delta have been home to growing rights consciousness at the grassroots level. The general public in these regions is inclined to pursue legal means to settle disputes, as demonstrated by the statistics of keyword searches related to rights defense on the Baidu Index, a big data tool for identifying keyword trends

Table 5.1

Top 10 Chinese provinces with the highest volume of online searches
for keywords related to rights defense

keywords rank	*weiquan* (rights defense)	*xinfang* (petitioning)	*weiwen* (maintenance of social stability)
1	Guangdong	Guangdong	Guangdong
2	Jiangsu	Beijing	Beijing
3	Beijing	Henan	Jiangsu
4	Zhejiang	Shandong	Zhejiang
5	Shandong	Hebei	Xinjiang
6	Shanghai	Zhejiang	Shandong
7	Hunan	Jiangsu	Sichuan
8	Henan	Shanghai	Hubei
9	Hubei	Hubei	Henan
10	Hebei	Sichuan	Shanghai

SOURCE: Baidu Index (data period: July 2013 to December 2014).

in the Chinese internet. Between the earliest available search date, July 2013, and December 2014, the keywords rights defense, petitioning (*xinfang* 信访), and maintenance of social stability (*weiwen* 维稳) were most widely searched in Guangdong and Beijing (where China's highest-level petitioning authority is located) (table 5.1). Guangdong is the first province in China where comprehensive governance and policies for maintaining social stability have been implemented at the county, township, and district levels. In 2009, the offices of comprehensive governance, petitioning, and social stability maintenance were established across Guangdong, and a news website on local legal matters was launched. This site, which encompasses the resources of Nanfang Baoye Media Group Corporation, the publicity and legal affairs departments of the Guangdong Provincial Committee, the Standing Committee of the People's Congress of Guangdong, the Higher People's Court of Guangdong, the People's Procuratorate of Guangdong, the Public Security Department of Guangdong, the Department of Justice of Guangdong, and the Legal Affairs Office of Guangdong, is intended to facilitate the establishment of a comprehensive mechanism of social governance that is best described as "regulatory inclusion."

Abstract social governance mechanisms based on legal norms create a social structure that facilitates autonomy. Such a social structure pro-

Table 5.2
The development of a rights defense movement

		Altruistic rights defenders	
		Negotiation	Resistance
Self-centered rights defenders	Negotiation	Stability at the grassroots level ←	Divergence in community actions ↑
	Resistance	Weak contention →	Strong contention

vides a context through which a municipality can implement strategies and policies regarding social governance and yields community actions and various forms of social power that the municipality must manage. Participants in community actions can be divided into "self-centered rights defenders" involved in rights-related conflicts, and "altruistic rights defenders" who are not involved in such conflicts. "Negotiation" and "resistance" characterize the decisionmaking of both types of rights defenders. Negotiation, in a broad sense, comprises noncontentious acts, such as engaging institutional processes, agreeing to concessions, bandwagoning, and onlooking.

When self-centered rights defenders operate independently, they can only demonstrate weak resistance; but they can offer strong resistance if they actively seek support from altruistic rights defenders (table 5.2). In response, the municipality exerts governance mechanisms and uses the coercive power of laws to derail community actions involving strong resistance. If the municipality successfully eliminates most of the outside support for community actions, this collective action relapses into weak resistance. In this case, self-centered rights defenders either concede or continue to seek support. In the context of strong resistance, if self-centered rights defenders are assimilated into a municipality's governance mechanism, their actions may diverge from those of their outside supporters, providing favorable conditions for the municipality to exert further legal authority and institutional decisionmaking. Moreover, if the self-centered and altruistic rights defenders are both assimilated into the municipality's negotiation mechanism, then grassroots society stabilizes, which constitutes what is known in China as successful performance of local governance.

Accordingly, one of the primary aims of grassroots governance is to exert governance mechanisms and legal authority to coerce community actions to shift from resistance to negotiation and eventually concessions. Such governance mechanisms in Nanhai, which feature an abstract, autonomous social structure, enable the institutional inclusion of dissenters and are regarded as a politically effective method of grassroots governance. Therefore, it can be assumed that when community actions and social forces in this social structure are eliminated by authorities, then those in other regions and social contexts might be unable to grow, let alone thrive. Thus, governance cases within abstract, autonomous social structures are necessary to determine how effectively a macro-political power regime establishes stability at the grassroots level on the basis of its governance performance. This requires contextual conditions: if the leadership of the Chinese government stabilizes along with its abstract, autonomous social structures, then most grassroots societies across China will achieve stability, and unrest at the grassroots level will be briefly smothered to avoid disunity and conflict in the upper echelons of the government.

The social structure of Nanhai can be characterized by abstract independence. Its grassroots community makes little use of institutional political and economic resources. Local talent and resources do not flow to political organizations, and grassroots society exhibits relatively high autonomy and agency. In addition, the organizational structure and action patterns of this community, which are based on contractual rules and rights awareness, are abstract in nature. This indicates that community actions, as well as their associated groups and social movements, can be connected through close bonding between certain clans and grassroots members (as is typical of Wukan village in Guangdong) and laws and decrees. Specifically, a community action can be more effective when it is led by legal professionals than by clan elders or grassroots officials. These characteristics constitute different social structures, complicating the already challenging governance of grassroots society.

Notably, the social structures of Guangdong and the Pearl River Delta are not always characterized by abstract independence. Such social structures typically exist in a region with an expansive market, consistently strong economy, high social autonomy, free flows of labor and capital, and a close connection between abstract contractual rules and community organizations. Economically robust coastal regions (particularly in Guangdong) are a case in point. Thus, the occurrence of major governance crises in these regions and how they are handled merit attention. In short, if a social structure is only defined as involving abstract independence, then that of Sanshan and other Pearl River Delta regions can be defined identically. However, in areas where clans, factionalism, and interpersonal networking prevail (such as the village of Wukan), distinct social structures, social governance mechanisms, and social relationship styles are present. Noninstitutional community actions and social governance crises in regions where social structures are characterized by autonomy and abstraction, such as Zhejiang (which ranked among provinces with the most frequent online keyword searches on rights defense–related words), are almost as equally complicated as those in Nanhai. More critically, conflicts and governance tactics regarding farmland in Sanshan are so distinctive and sophisticated that they warrant further investigation from an evolutionary perspective.

Marketization and Reform of the Rural Land Shareholding Cooperative System

China's rapid economic development and growing industrialization in the 1980s resulted in two challenges over land use in Nanhai and the Pearl River Delta region. The first challenge was that many farmers requested changing the use of their fields because of the increasing earning capacity of nonagricultural land. The second challenge was related to disorderly town infrastructure caused by a lack of rigorous regulations governing land use.[3] In the early 1990s, the rural land shareholding cooperative system was first implemented in a few villages in Nanhai; by 1993, it had taken root in much of the area through advocacy by the municipal government. The framework of this system composed two components: (1) designating farm preservation areas, economic development areas, and commercial and residential areas, and (2) incorporating farmers' collective assets and land contract rights into stakeholding at a discount and establishing guidelines on the arrangement and management of equities and the distribution of bonus shares, which are collectively known as a "village constitution" (Jiang and Liu 2005, 56).

As stated by Jiang and Liu:

> After the implementation of the rural land shareholding cooperative system, the land contract rights of family units have been replaced by the collective land operation rights of villagers' committees and groups. That is, the shift in the use of rural land from individual management to collective ownership and operation, which unified ownership and operation rights, has once again placed the land under the control of collective economic organizations. (2005, 56)

Moreover, the characteristic enclosure of the exertion of authority by rural municipalities in China, which helps concentrate rural land rights in the hands of collective economic organizations, provides money-making and rent-seeking incentives to village officials. In their capacity as the "agents" of executive orders, cadres are often understandably tempted to sell land or rent it cheaper in response to changes in the rural land shareholding cooperative system. This has been the chief cause of numerous rural land disputes. Various municipal officials involved in such disputes have been foiled, thus compromising grassroots governance (Shu, Yin, and Li 2014). Rural land reforms based on the "Nanhai model" have triggered unrest in Nanhai itself (Ma 2008, 16–17). Many farmers have faced reprisals from local agents (Y. Liu 2008, 75–81), and the rural land shareholding cooperative system has degenerated, increasing the nationalization of rural land and dooming the rural land reform model (X. Liu 2010, 69–132). This may pose a challenge for policymaking economists who intend to confirm land rights through such a system. This method entails a localized political mechanism that allows for procedural, public, deliberative, and representative decisionmaking, but in the absence of a governance framework that corresponds to social structures at the grassroots.

With an abstract, autonomous social structure, the municipality of Nanhai has experienced highly resistant community actions characterized by high coherence, agency, and capacity for escalation in reaction to a grassroots crisis associated with the reform of the rural land shareholding cooperative system. Because the municipality's policies and human resources outstrip that of grassroots resources, including specific core members of community actions into the municipality prevents marginal costs from rising. Moreover, because the leadership of a community action based on abstract rules typically comprises members with legal knowledge, rights awareness, and agency (rather than clan elders or grassroots officials designated through personal connections), information exchange and negotiation processes among personally connected grassroots members should be integrated with judicial regulations and processes to transform this inclusion mechanism into a social governance mechanism that enables institutional inclusion. The typical mechanisms of regulatory inclusion include litigation agents and the representative power of grassroots people's congresses on behalf of the general public. However, a highly resistant community action may encounter bitter internal dissension and harsh suppression if its core members detach themselves from institutional inclusion mechanisms to engage in rights defense and seek broader action by raising awareness of political and social aspirations, such as trans-locality and universality. As such, the governance mechanisms of regulatory inclusion work in a coherent manner. Together, the implementation of the rural land shareholding cooperative system in Sanshan, with its attendant rights defense movements, social governance tactics, and ubiquitous coercive suppression, defines the conflict over the district's rulings on rural land.

Conflict over Rural Land in Sanshan

OVERVIEW OF SANSHAN

Sanshan is located in the Guicheng subdistrict of Nanhai and spans 12.42 km². The northern area includes boat households working on the Pearl River; no fixed system of collective ownership of rural land is implemented here. The eastern and central areas each have one administrative village that comprises four natural villages; the combined eight natural villages total approximately 2,000 households and 7,100 residents (table 5.3). The largest clans in Sanshan bear the surnames of Chen, Shao, Wang, and Cui and maintain ancestral shrines. However, because these clans are

Table 5.3
Villages in Sanshan, Nanhai

Region	Administrative Village	Village Group/Natural Village
Sanshan (the members of the local People's Congress are all elected officials)	Eastern	Heyang, Zhengjie, Yixi, and Yidong
	Central	Xintiandi, Nan, Xijiang, and Chongyuan
	Northern (no administrative village has been formally established)	Boat households

made up of recent immigrants and are small in size—and because Sanshan has a robust economy, convenient transportation infrastructure, and high population mobility—a clear relationship between the clans and traditional society does not exist. In fact, before the People's Republic of China (PRC) was established in 1949, the role of the clan chief was already extinct, and nearly all local ancestral shrines had been demolished without subsequent reconstruction. Guo Huojia (郭伙佳), the leader of a local rights defense movement, was born in 1951 in Sanshan and studied at a local elementary school that had been built on a piece of land previously occupied by an ancestral shrine. He once lamented that "no clan chiefs had been around before emancipation. If they were around, then land expropriation would be a less difficult matter to deal with."

CONSEQUENCES OF THE RURAL LAND SHAREHOLDING COOPERATIVE SYSTEM AND WEAK RESISTANCE

In 2005, the residents of villages in Sanshan received notices from the municipality stating that land in their villages would be requisitioned by the government of Nanhai and should be vacated for fill construction. The villagers requested expropriation documents from the officials of their villages and the government but received none. Having failed in various attempts to obtain these documents, the villagers resorted to asking someone to secretly view them and were shocked to know that when the rural land shareholding cooperative system was launched thirteen years earlier, the local land and resources department had signed a land prerequisition agreement with former village officials allowing the ownership of land in the villages to be transferred to the government.

Villagers in Sanshan fought this decision, arguing that this land prerequisition agreement was completely illegitimate on the following grounds: "First, the agreement does not come with any letters of authorization issued by the government of Nanhai County.[4] Second, there is no legal signature on the agreement. Third, no effective date is noted on the agreement. Above all, no meetings were hosted for villagers, and no details regarding this agreement were provided to all Sanshan villagers" (fieldnotes, Sanshan, November 2012).

The villagers united against the official order. In March 2005, their representatives sent petitions to the provincial government, people's congress, prosecutor's office, and public security department, as well as the city government and land administration department of Foshan and the land and resources department of Nanhai. Only Guangdong's public security department issued a response, but this did not improve the situation.

Whenever the municipal officials of Nanhai arrived at Sanshan to start construction, villagers surrounded their land in defense. However, at midnight on May 31, 2005, the local police, demolition workers, and unidentified thugs (some of whom were reportedly from other provinces and numbered in the thousands) raided the villages in Nanhai by blockading surrounding roads and seizing and razing great expanses of orchards. Numerous villagers resisted while half-awake. Some were caught in the violent conflict while chanting a slogan of resistance, and many were injured during the confrontation. Feeling indignant yet helpless (fieldnotes, Sanshan, November 2012), the residents of Sanshan began to seek support from various sources to fortify their resistance.

EXTERNAL SUPPORT AND REINFORCEMENT

Following the conflict, Sanshan villagers staged a rights defense movement, clashed with municipal officials, sent petitions to the petitioning office in Beijing, and sought support from rights defense lawyers, journalists, NGOs, intellectuals, and social activists. Word of the incident in Sanshan soon spread, intensifying the movement. All individuals who offered outside support were harassed. According to local villagers, a US scholar who claimed to have been unfamiliar with the conflict while briefly filming in Sanshan was detained for three hours on July 2, 2005.[5] On July 23, Hou Wenzhuo, the founder of the Empowerment and Rights Institute, an NGO dedicated to promoting human rights across China, was detained and interrogated by the Foshan police after investigating land confiscations in Sanshan, speaking with local farmers, and joining their rights defense movement. The organization subsequently faced reprisals from the Chinese government, and Hou ended up leaving for the United States. Two days later, Guo Feixiong, a renowned rights defense lawyer, was listed as wanted for his involvement in the rights defense movement in Sanshan. The villagers involved in self-centered rights defense were detained, arrested, and sentenced for various crimes, including blackmail and extortion, disturbing public security, and vandalism.

Even when this community action transformed into strong resistance and began to spread, it continued to be inhibited by the municipality. By 2007, outside support for the movement had subsided, and Sanshan villagers sought legal means to defend their land rights. Chen Qitang (陈启棠), a Foshan native popularly known by his online handle Tian Li (heavenly principles 天理), played a vital role in helping the villagers in that regard.

INSTITUTIONAL MECHANISM: REPRESENTATIVE LITIGATION

Numerous rights defense lawyers and citizen agents rallied behind the villagers, facilitating their resistance and litigation against the municipality. Moreover, when the villagers' resistance was suppressed, the rights defenders turned to legal means.

In ancient China's grassroots culture, litigation masters (law practitioners who prepared documents for lawsuits) were hired to litigate on behalf of citizens or help with their litigation processes. Many of them did so for financial gain, and because the ancient Chinese generally regarded involvement in legal matters as an act of intimidation, the job carried the same social stigma as pettifoggers from time to time (Fei 2012, 107). Therefore, the system of agency litigation exhibited little (if any) improvement for centuries. Although the role of lawyers was formally established following the implementation of the contemporary legal system, laws regarding the practice of litigation agents remained unclear. Thus, the Ministry of Justice issued a notice on the revocation of unethical lawyers and litigation pettifoggers in 1950, pledging to reform the practices of litigation agents. In 1954, the PRC Law on the Organization of the People's Courts took effect, stipulating: "The accused have the right to legal defense. In addition to defending himself, the accused has the right to delegate a lawyer to defend him. He may also be defended by a near relative or guardian or by a citizen either recommended by a people's organization or approved by the people's court."[6]

This law has obvious ambiguities, particularly in terms of "a citizen approved by the people's court." Currently, its implications continue to manifest in three major litigation statutes in China: (1) Article 32 of the PRC Criminal Procedure Law, (2) Article 58 of the PRC Civil Procedure Law, and (3) Article 29 of the PRC Administrative Procedure Law.

Article 32 of the PRC Criminal Procedure Law, which was passed in July 1979 and amended in March 1996, states:

> In addition to exercising the right to defend himself, a criminal suspect or a defendant may entrust one or two persons as his defenders. The following persons may be entrusted as defenders: (1) lawyers, (2) persons recommended by a public organization or the unit to which the criminal suspect or the defendant belongs, and (3) guardians or relatives and friends of the criminal suspect or the defendant. Persons who are under criminal punishment or whose personal freedom is deprived or restricted according to law shall not serve as defenders.[7]

Article 58 of the PRC Civil Procedure Law, which was passed and promulgated in April 1991, states: "Each party or legal representative may appoint one or two persons to act as his litigation agent(s). Lawyers, a party's near relatives, persons recommended by relevant public organizations or the units to which a party belongs, or any other citizens approved by a people's court may be entrusted as the party's litigation agents."[8]

Article 29 of the PRC Administrative Procedure Law, passed and enacted in April 1989, states: "Each party or legal representative may entrust one or two persons to represent him or her in proceedings. A lawyer, a social group, near relatives of a citizen who has initiated an action, or a person recommended by the unit to which the citizen belongs or any other citizen approved by the people's court may be entrusted as an agent."[9]

In these litigation statutes, "relatives" (as opposed to "near relatives") and "any other citizen approved by the people's court" are vaguely defined. However, this definitional ambiguity has allowed for broader interpretation of ordinary citizens as "citizen agents," although qualifications for serving as a litigation agent were subsequently clearly defined. Article 58 of the amended PRC Civil Procedure Law, which took effect on January 1, 2013, stipulates: "Each party or legal representative may entrust one or two persons as his defenders. The following persons may be entrusted as defenders: (1) lawyers or grassroots legal workers; (2) a near relative or employee (if the party is a juristic person or unincorporated organization) of the party; or (3) citizens recommended by the community, unit, or social group to which the party belongs." The Chinese government reserves the right to interpret the role of a litigation agent in a more concrete manner.[10]

When the rights defense movement against land requisition began in Sanshan, Chen Qitang, a rights defense activist, joined as a citizen agent. Born in Foshan in 1959, Chen said that he had acquired basic legal knowledge at a law-popularizing program hosted in the 1980s by the Southwest University of Political Science and Law. He later carved out a business career, eventually rising to the position of CEO, while remaining informed of political issues. In 1998, when the internet was becoming increasingly ubiquitous, Chen served as a moderator, editor, and administrator for multiple online forums; published numerous commentaries on current social and political events under his online handle, Tian Li; and soon became popular among online rights defense communities. By 2000, he was engaged in grassroots rights defense; in 2007, he cofounded Chinese Human Rights Defenders (CHRD), a human rights NGO.[11]

When Sanshan villagers began their rights defense movement and sought outside support, they visited the newly established CHRD in 2007. Headquartered in Beijing, the organization has offices and volunteers in various regions; most of its activity is concentrated in the provinces of Fujian and Guangdong. Across China, 300 to 400 CHRD-affiliated lawyers and citizen agents provide legal assistance to people involved in rights defense. Volunteers offer free assistance to rights defense movements in regions to which the volunteers are assigned. They charge only travel fees if they are asked to assist in other regions. Sanshan villagers, who predominantly speak Cantonese and have limited fluency in Mandarin, requested help from CHRD, which then asked Chen, who also lived in Guangdong, to provide help. After having gained a full picture of the incident of disputed land requisition in Sanshan, he began to throw himself into the case. As the incident escalated, his involvement increased. On April 26, 2007, Chen started to help the villagers prepare legal documents, instructed them to negotiate with the municipality, and filed petitions to the court as their citizen agent. He visited a municipal intermediate people's court to address the cases of seven villagers who were involved in the movement and indicted by the Nanhai government for blackmail and extortion; he wrote to the mayor of Nanhai, the court's judges, and former Premier Wen Jiabao regarding these cases. Chen then enlisted the support of citizen agents and rights lawyers from other regions.

Chen's efforts seemed to have enabled the villagers to successfully negotiate with the local government, persuading it to relax its attitudes. Gu Jiajin, a judge from Foshan, assured Chen in 2007 that "we have submitted all documents about the Sanshan case to the Higher People's Court of Guangdong. Please unwind in the midst of the 17th National Congress. As soon as the Congress is over, you will receive a satisfactory reply. Don't worry; things will look up for Sanshan after the Congress" (fieldnotes, Sanshan, November 2012). In fact, official replies were not as favorable as the villagers had expected. The grassroots community exhausted considerable human and material resources in the litigation process, thus draining its resources. As a veteran rights defender, Chen had anticipated this and continued to stage protests to galvanize the municipality. In October 2007, he accompanied 14 Sanshan villagers to the Department of Land Inspection in Guangzhou and obtained a RMB100,000 subsidy for a villager on medical parole who had become seriously ill after being indicted. Nonetheless, Chen was arrested on October 25, imprisoned for "having impersonated a police officer to carry out deceptive acts," and was released 28 months later in February 2010.

Under the local government's policies and coercive tactics, rights defense in Sanshan was divided into two patterns: (1) exploring opportunities for rights defense through other institutional means and (2) upgrading, elevating, and expanding a movement by enabling all rights defense activists involved to work in an organized fashion and connecting it with movements that operate in other regions and focus on different cases or issues. Chen helped the residents of Sanshan undertake the first pattern of rights defense and encouraged them to attempt the second, although the villagers became increasingly reliant on the first. Both patterns were staged differently, yielded different consequences, and entailed different challenges. However, the rights defense movement against land requisition in Sanshan was gradually undermined by a further occurrence of regulatory inclusion.

INSTITUTIONAL MECHANISM: LOCAL PEOPLE'S CONGRESS

Most Sanshan villagers sought to strengthen their rights defense through institutional means. Local people's congresses are arguably the key institutional vehicle through which the public at large exercises their rights. Article 2 of the PRC constitution (2004) stipulates that "all power belongs to the people. The NPC and the local people's congresses at various levels are the organizations through which the people can exercise state power."[12] Article 3 states, "The NPC and local people's congresses at various levels are established through democratic elections, and they are accountable to the general public and subject to their supervision." Article 34 states: "Any citizen of the People's Republic of China who has reached the age of 18 has the right to vote and stand for election, regardless of ethnicity, race, sex, occupation, family background, religion, education, financial situation, and length of residence, except for those who are deprived of political rights in accordance with the law."

Article 97 of the Constitution states:

> Deputies to the people's congresses of provinces, municipalities under the central government, and cities divided into districts are elected by the people's congresses at the next lower level; deputies to the people's congresses of counties, cities not divided into districts, municipal districts, townships, nationality townships, and towns are elected directly by their

constituencies. The number of deputies to local people's congresses at different levels and the manner of their election are prescribed by law.

The election regulations of local people's congresses are detailed in the PRC Election Law for the National People's Congress and Local People's Congresses at All Levels (passed in 1979, amended in 1982, 1986, and 1995), the Provisions of the Standing Committee of the National People's Congress for the Direct Election of Deputies to People's Congresses at or Below the County Level (passed in 1983), and the PRC Organic Law of the Local People's Congress and Local People's Governments (passed in 1979, amended in 1982, 1986, and 1995). Furthermore, Article 34 of the PRC Election Law for the National People's Congress and Local People's Congresses at All Levels (2010) stipulates, "The elections of the NPC and local people's congresses at various levels shall be conducted in strict compliance with legal procedures and supervised. Any organization or person shall not, in any way, impede voters or deputies exercising their rights to vote." On the basis of the PRC's constitution, "people's congresses at various levels" are a crucial institutional vehicle that allows the public to exercise their political rights, and the rights of the deputies of people's congresses to vote and stand for election are legally protected. Elections for local people's congresses take place in a specific period; for example, the elections of deputies to people's congresses in the majority of regions at the county, township, and city levels were held between July 1, 2011, and December 31, 2012.

However, the suffrage and electoral eligibility of candidates running for local people's congresses at various levels are persistently impeded by the government. Many independent candidates have vied for seats, but only a few have been successful. This indicates that candidates who run for people's congress and are elected are exceptions to the institutional decisionmaking mechanisms of Chinese municipalities. Such mechanisms are characterized by enforcing chronically neglected statutes specified in the constitution and laws, rather than initiating interference or suppression, to facilitate grassroots social governance.

In 2007, some Sanshan villagers began to seek institutional means to defend their land rights. They perused legal documents, searched for favorable evidence, and received constant legal assistance from Chen

Qitang and other rights defenders equipped with solid legal knowledge. Following his release in 2010, Chen continued to fight alongside Sanshan villagers, primarily through institutional means. The villagers demanded that the land and resources department of Guangdong disclose all documents on land requisition after Guo Huojia pointed out that the Regulation of the People's Republic of China on the Disclosure of Government Information had come into force in 2008. In March 2010, the provincial land and resources department published 19 approved documents on land requisition. An investigation led by Guo showed that because of these documents, the application of the requisition of rural land in Sanshan was approved hastily at the end of December 1997—an action that exceeded the limits of authority. Accordingly, Guo and Chen led the villagers to file lawsuits at the court against the land and resources departments of Guangdong and Sanshan.

Despite having been approved, their lawsuits encountered obstacles. Once again, the pursuit of institutional means weakened their resistance against the government. However, these experiences collectively strengthened Guo's audacity and legal knowledge and bolstered his reputation. He was soon promoted to lead two administrative villages in Sanshan. As a fruit retailer known locally as Uncle Jia (*jiashu* 佳叔) who earned less than RMB600 a month and came from a small clan in Sanshan, Guo earned considerable trust for his reliable legal knowledge related to rights defense.

In 2011, Guo was nominated by many of his fellow villagers to be elected deputy to the People's Congress of Sanshan. Chen worked with volunteers in and outside of Sanshan to help Guo formulate election campaign strategies and prepare a manifesto. "In the first place, I began rights defense work for myself, not for everyone," Guo recalled plainly, "but they saw me as capable of speaking out for them, so I decided to run for the election" (fieldnotes, Sanshan, October 2014). After the nomination round, which lasted August 9–13, 2011, he began his candidacy for deputy.

Guo ran his election campaign with so much support that the district office announced the withdrawal of two female candidates one week after announcing their candidacy on September 13. On September 21, the municipality of Nanhai nominated another candidate, Chen Guanqiu. Several days of intense campaigning in which the candidates delivered blistering assaults gave rise to a rumor that "the municipality was cheating." On election day, September 28, 2011, Guo and his relatives monitored the voting process. Many Sanshan villagers feared for the local government and watched the vote counting gingerly without even "eating anything or using restrooms" (fieldnotes, Sanshan, October 2014) to ensure the municipality had no opportunity to manipulate the voting results. According to the announcement of the final results, of 8,136 eligible voters in the electorate of Sanshan, 8,021 cast ballots, of which 7,718 were valid. Guo won by a landslide with 4,827 ballots (62.54 percent), compared with 2,837 for Chen Guanqiu. This election victory caused a huge sensation in and beyond Sanshan. Guo and Chen Qitang remarked that Yao Lifa (姚立法) was also an independent candidate who had been elected to the position of deputy to a local people's congress but that he "had a political background" (fieldnotes, Sanshan, November 2012). As such, Guo is arguably the first rights activist elected as a people's congress deputy and the first "real" democratically elected people's congress deputy in China.

Interestingly, Nanhai permitted only Guo to take the office. In fact, some of the Sanshan villagers involved in rights defense had run in previous village elections, but the municipality manipulated the elections in favor of its chosen candidates. However, as stipulated by terms and conditions that have not been promulgated to date,[13] as well as procedures published on March 2012 by the Ministry of Civil Affairs: "The chairman, vice-chairman, and members of a villagers' committee shall be elected directly by villagers, and no organization or individual shall appoint or replace any member of the committee." As such, the chair of the committee shall be democratically elected by villagers. This system fails in many grassroots communities where government officials exploit legal loopholes and deliberately flout the law. The chair of the villagers' committee in Sanshan is appointed either by the votes of local villagers or by a representative elected by the villagers. Normally, the latter manner of appointing the chair requires that a village meeting be called. However, the municipality of Nanhai bypasses the meeting and requires the villagers' representative to appoint the chair. "That's the reason we fail every time," a Sanshan villager said. "This whittles down the candidates for the position and ensures elections turn out the way the government expects" (fieldnotes, Sanshan, October 2014). The municipality influences the appointment of not only the villagers' committee chair but also the party chief of Sanshan, implying that it has exploited the local people's congress to enhance its inclusion of Sanshan and undermined the system of villager self-governance.

Once elected, Guo felt "honored but stressed." His fellow villagers were triumphant about his victory, which shocked the municipality. However, Guo soon realized that his power was limited in practice and placed no further pressure on the municipality to yield to the demands of the rights defense movement against land requisition in Sanshan. At the People's Congress in Nanhai, whose membership was made up of approximately 380 deputies of local people's congresses, a motion required more than 10 signatures to be approved, whereas that proposed by only one member would be deemed a suggestion. Because of this, Guo noted that "when these deputies are preparing to propose motions, they have no interest in talking with me because they were all selected by their governments" (fieldnotes, Sanshan, October 2014). Guo was included in the People's Congress of Sanshan and shouldered the expectations of the other villagers, and he found himself gradually restricted by the rules of the Nanhai People's Congress. Moreover, he and some of the other local leaders of the *weiquan* movement were constantly watched in their neighborhoods by thugs hired by the municipality. "They watch me day and night. This damages my image as a people's congress deputy, and no villager dares to come to me to offer suggestions," Guo complained (fieldnotes, Sanshan, October 2014).

Villagers' fears of talking to Guo were perhaps an intended objective of the municipality's monitoring. In the end, Sanshan villagers became increasingly disappointed, and Guo could not continue. Each year, they submitted three to four suggestions, which ended up rejected or heavily altered to force them to acquiesce. At the beginning of 2012, the retirement pension of RMB75 a month to which all Nanhai farmers aged 60 years or older were entitled, was distributed by the village. Guo demanded an increase, and Nanhai raised the retirement pension to RMB300 in August of that year and stipulated that half of it would be distributed by the village and the other half by the municipality. However, only when Sanshan villagers accepted the land requisition plans would they receive the half from the municipality. Guo had no choice but to comply with this provision. Although he was democratically elected, he was unable to fulfill the expectations of his constituents or bolster the grassroots resistance against land requisition.

DIVERGENCE AND DISPERSION OF THE RIGHTS DEFENSE MOVEMENT

Meanwhile, Chen Qitang and Su Changlan (苏昌兰), a Sanshan villager, had foreseen how the municipality's institutional inclusion would affect the rights defense movement in Sanshan. They used representative litigation and Guo's authority and intensified the rights defense movement. The law-savvy core members of the movement avoided institutional inclusion and advanced to the stage of strong resistance. Inevitably, they faced continued repression. For example, Chen was constantly monitored and harassed, and although he experienced no systematic suppression, he was eventually arrested in October of that year. As the movement began to weaken in Sanshan, CHRD and Sanshan villagers began to diverge in their tactics. Few villagers were as visionary as Su Changlan. In her opinion, Chen needed to seek more legal assistance to enhance his representative litigation, and Guo was too "conservative" and would end up in the hands of the municipality.

Chen and Su (fig. 5.1) went above and beyond rights defense and framed the defense of human rights in abstract terms. CHRD founded an online forum in 2006 and issued its founding declaration (drafted by Chen and revised by more than 10 CHRD members) in March 2007 "to fight for the human rights of the Chinese people." CHRD began its operations with a membership of approximately 100 people and soon recruited many rights defense lawyers, citizen agents, and legal specialists. CHRD currently boasts 300 to 400 active members and sends volunteers to offer free assistance in grassroots rights defense cases in regions for which they are responsible and other regions as required. In terms of municipal reprisal, local volunteers face harassment, and nonlocal volunteers are often forced to leave. However, CHRD typically assigns its volunteers to specific regions "to safeguard human rights at the local level." Chen knew that it was never easy to win a lawsuit against the municipality. He stressed that "we want to let more people know that [CHRD] has greater aims than winning lawsuits," adding that "we only help people involved in rights defense and keep our mouths shut about other matters,

FIGURE 5.1 Rights activist Su Changlan in Sanshan Village
Source: By author, Yi-chun Tao.

such as the use of excessive force by the Urban Administrative and Law Enforcement Bureau (*chengguan* 城管) in Gulangyu Island at Fujian province" (fieldnotes, Sanshan, November 2012). He even revealed his political aspirations: "If democracy is realized, then CHRD will need votes."

Chen Qitang was imprisoned in October 2007 as retaliation by the municipal government for CHRD's frequent activity. Upon his release in 2010, he continued to support the rights defense movement in Sanshan and help Guo in his litigation and local election campaign. Meanwhile, Chen engaged in CHRD activity across China and expanded its nationwide presence, particularly after Guo was elected. On February 27, 2013, Zhang Anni, the 10-year-old daughter of Zhang Lin (张林), a civil rights dissident from Anhui province, was seized from her elementary school in Hefei by four national security officials and detained with her father in Bengbu. Three days later, Chen started a group discussion on Skype in which he and others discussed how to rescue the Zhangs. In early April, lawyers and netizens arrived in Hefei from across the country to demand their release. On April 10, lawyers staged a relay hunger strike at Zhang's school, and netizens held a candlelight vigil and delivered speeches at an office of the Department of Public Security. After they were dispersed on April 16, they continued to voice their support through other forms of protest. In September, Zhang Anni and her elder sister, accompanied by officials from the US consulate in Shanghai, flew from Shanghai to San Francisco, where she started a new life under the guardianship of a women's rights activist. These events demonstrate the extent of government harassment faced by the families of rights defenders in China.

In March 2014, Chen was jailed on charges of "gathering crowds to disturb public order," owing to his support for Zhang Anni's return to school and his organization of a group of lawyers for regional petitioners. In November 2014, Chen was placed under "criminal investigation custody" for the violation of instigation and subversion of the political power of the state by publishing articles on the internet. He was officially arrested and sentenced to about 4.5 years of imprisonment. Chen was released in May 2019. Meanwhile, in October 2014 Su Changlan was under criminal investigation custody for the violation of instigation and subversion of the political power of the state from forwarding photographs of the Occupy Central movement in Hong Kong through the WeChat social media app. In March 2017, she was sentenced to about three years in prison by the Guangdong Foshan Intermediate People's Court and was released in October 2017. Both Chen and Su have remained under close surveillance since their release. The radical fringe of the rights defense movement in Sanshan, led by Chen and Su, was virtually disbanded under the double blow of the municipality's inclusion mechanism and its coercive authority.

DEVELOPMENT OF THE RIGHTS DEFENSE
MOVEMENT AGAINST RURAL LAND
REQUISITION IN SANSHAN

Overall, the evolution of grassroots opposition to land requisition in San-shan comprised five stages. During the first stage, when the rural land shareholding cooperative system was implemented in Nanhai in 1992, Sanshan villagers did not recognize the threat it could pose to their in-terests or the need to defend their land rights. It was not until the second stage, when the prerequisition land agreement was revealed in March 2005, that they started to fight for their land rights. This weak rights defense movement against the local government was thoroughly crushed on May 31, 2005, which the villagers described as "the darkest day in San-shan" (fieldnotes, Sanshan, November 2012).

Furious and anxious, the villagers sought external support, entering the third stage of the conflict. They received various forms of support to take stronger action against the municipality, which in turn became more vigilant and was quicker to suppress them. The municipality used tactics such as involving the villagers in negotiations through administrative liti-gation and the system of the local people's congress; these events charac-terized the fourth and fifth stages of the conflict. However, as is often the case when dealing with government officials in China, such negotiation did not affect the municipality's initial decisions, and the opportunity to voice opinions weakened rather than strengthened local resistance.

When self-centered rights defenders felt increasingly helpless and when altruistic rights defenders avoided these negotiations out of their firm convictions, the rights defense movement began to diverge, making it difficult for acquiescent villagers, radical villagers, and their outside sup-porters to work coherently toward a common goal. The municipal govern-ment took advantage of this development to further splinter and suppress active villagers and their supporters, increasingly isolating the weak resis-tance faction of the movement. Following its resistance and divergence, the grassroots community in Sanshan restabilized, but the achievement of unity within and outside of the community may never materialize. Table 5.4, which adheres to the same general structure of rights defense movements as depicted in table 5.2, outlines the municipality's use of inclusion and coercion as governance mechanisms.

Table 5.4
Evolution of the rights defense movement against rural land requisition in Sanshan

| | | Altruistic rights defenders | |
		Negotiation	Resistance
Self-centered rights defenders	Negotiation	**Grassroots stability** **1st stage:** Before the prerequisition land agreement was revealed **5th stage:** In 2007, Chen Qitang started to litigate for Sanshan villagers in opposition to land requisition. Outside supporters of Sanshan villagers were suppressed; the villagers gave in.	**Divergence in Actions** **4th stage:** Sanshan villagers resorted to institutional means and were urged by their supporters to strengthen resistance.
	Resistance	**Weak Contention** **2nd stage:** The prerequisition land agreement was revealed in March 2005, and the rights defense movement was crushed at the end of May 2005.	**Strong Contention** **3rd stage:** After having been crushed by the government, Sanshan villagers sought external support to bolster their movement. In April 2007, Chen served as a citizen agent for the villagers.

Conclusion

Tracing the evolution of land conflict and legal rights awareness in Sanshan reveals various relevant contextual factors. First, without the abstract, autonomous social configuration of Sanshan, local villagers might not have been permitted to elect their rights defense leader, and Guo might not have been able to lead them or be elected as a deputy to the People's

Congress of Nanhai. Second, where social structure at the grassroots level is characterized by the strict enforcement of rules and regulations, weak patrilineal awareness, high social autonomy, and solid self-organizing capacity (due to local economic development), the local government focuses its institutional governance mechanism on coopting the activists of grassroots movements when such organizations emerge. Moreover, an institutional governance mechanism functions largely through the judicious enforcement of existing laws.

Around 2007, the rights defense movement in Sanshan escalated to the stage of strong resistance, with tension between local officials and villagers showing no signs of subsiding. However, the movement was gradually weakened and fragmented by their involvement in representative litigation. In the years leading up to 2011, when Chen and other outside supporters were trying to negotiate with the municipality, the Nanhai government allowed Sanshan villagers to participate in the local People's Congress and suppressed rights defense actions devoted to trans-local and crosscutting political issues.

After Guo was elected to the People's Congress of Nanhai, he shouldered the tension between his fellow villagers and the municipality. The divergence of the rights defense movement prompted its citizen agents, outside supporters, and radical villagers to cooperatively support rights defense cases in other regions, which inevitably radicalized the movement and narrowed its base. Hit by several waves of suppression, this 10-year movement eventually came to an end. Nanhai's economy continued to grow, and the city was recognized as an innovative local government for "successfully" reforming its collective economic organization after being tasked with addressing corrupt practices in the rural land shareholding cooperative system. In addition, following the 18th Party Congress in 2013, Nanhai implemented the grid management system of social surveillance and control and stabilized its political economy.

These governance outcomes were attributed to a complex of regular inclusion mechanisms, as well as institutional suppression of rights defense actions concerning trans-local problems. Despite its high agency and abundant political possibilities, Sanshan remains on the margins of the domestic political arena. This style of social governance can prompt a municipality to tighten its grip on political and social resources, thereby improving its governance performance and cementing its relationship with the grassroots. As a result, we have seen the municipality's governance mechanism and social structure coevolve dynamically. Possible widespread dispersion associated with the effective social governance of atomic interpersonal relationships makes the close relationship between the boundaries of micro-governance and the development of macro-regimes a topic worthy of further study. In China's contemporary authoritarian context, however, the space for national diffusion of local governance practices is at the highly restricted end of the spectrum.

Notes

1. Initiated by Shanghai municipality in 2013, "grid management" refers to a mode of urban management that divides a city's jurisdiction into various grids. Each district (or county) delegates a grid supervisor (*wangge jianduyuan* 网格监督员) to monitor (infrastructure and illegal) activities in the grid and report any issue directly to relevant government departments through a digitalized urban information system. Grid supervisors then follow up and rate the relevant departments on how they deal with the reported issues.

2. Case data used in this study were obtained from field notes (dated November 2012, October 2014, and April 2015) that the researcher prepared on Sanshan.

3. See Jiang and Liu (2005, 54–55) for more information on how the rural land shareholding cooperative system has been implemented in Nanhai.

4. Nanhai County was upgraded to a county-level city in 1992 and incorporated as a district of the city of Foshan in 2002.

5. This scholar, whom the villagers identified by the transliterated name "German," was from Yale University. Many news articles cited this name accordingly; however, the scholar's real name could not be found online.

6. Translation mine. The law was abolished in 1979.

7. The translation of law references to Chinalawinfo Co., Peking University Center for Legal Information (北京大学法制信息中心), https://www.pkulaw.com/en_law/2eca790ee72fb2c8bdfb.html.

8. Peking University Center for Legal Information, https://www.pkulaw.com/en_law/83de2d9699832a9ebdfb.html.

9. Peking University Center for Legal Information, https://www.pkulaw.com/en_law/7cfb5b6f6ed411f3bdfb.html.

10. Peking University Center for Legal Information, https://www.pkulaw.com/en_law/68957aaf4c3a793dbdfb.html.

11. CHRD differs from the Open Constitution Initiative (OCI), which was cofounded by civil rights activist Xu Zhiyong. CHRD comprises different core members from those in the OCI. However, both groups frequently work together and support each other. See CHRD's website, https://www.nchrd.org/ (accessed March 5, 2020).

12. The translations of the Constitution of the People's Republic of China are from the Peking University Center for Legal Information, https://www.pkulaw.com/en_law /b62e1b65233709b3bdfb.html.

13. A legislative proposal for the draft version of the Organic Law of the Villagers' Committees of the People's Republic of China has been circulated on the internet but remains unofficial.

References

Fei, Xiaotong. 2012. *From the Soil: The Foundations of Chinese Society.* Beijing: Foreign Language Teaching and Research Press.

Jiang, Xingsan, and Shouying Liu. 2005. "The Nature of the Rural Land Shareholding Cooperative System in Nanhai." In *Land Capitalization and Rural Industrialization: Nanhai Model and Institutional Innovation*, edited by Xingsan Jiang and Jun Han, 54–70. Shanxi Economic Publishing House.

Liu, Xianfa. 2010. "The Formation, Transformation and Outcomes of the Nanhai Model." In *Case Studies in China's Institutional Change*, edited by Shuguang Zhang, 69–132. Beijing: China Financial and Economic Publishing House.

Liu, Yuan. 2008. "What Are Farmers Getting from the Rural Land Shareholding System? The Nanhai Rural Shareholding Economy." *Management World* 1: 75–81.

Ma, Jian. 2008. "Nanhai Model: Innovations and Predicaments—The Survey of Rural Land Shareholding Cooperative System in Nanhai." *Newsletter about Work in Rural Areas* 17: 16–17.

Shu, Taifeng, Jikun Yin, and Cheng Li. 2014. *The Change in Rural Governance: Nanhai Enlightenment for Local Governance in China.* Peking: Peking University Press.

State Council Information Office of the People's Republic of China. 2008. "China's Efforts and Achievements in Promoting the Rule of Law." *People's Daily Online*, February 28. http://politics.people.com.cn/GB/1026/6937141.html.

Vogel, Ezra F. 1990. *One Step Ahead in China: Guangdong under Reform.* Cambridge, MA: Harvard University Press.

PART III

Environmental and Public Health Governance

CHAPTER 6

AIDS Governance in China

Transitional Tripartite Interaction among State, Societal, and International Actors

CHANHSI WANG

A lthough the Chinese government launched public health sector reform after SARS, the outbreak of COVID-19 in late 2019 and early 2020 reminded us of the Chinese government's weakness in controlling infectious diseases. The trajectory of AIDS governance in China offers insights for understanding the reform process and outcomes in public health since about 2000. This chapter tracks the tripartite interactions among the state, civil society, and the international community through three different phases of AIDS governance in the past 20 years and shows how the interactive dynamics varied across different phases. The evolution of HIV/AIDS governance in China reveals the potential influence of external actors on state–society relations, as well as the instability and limits of authoritarian rule. When external actors from international society increased their engagement in the policy process and threatened the party-state's monopoly of political power, the state adopted repressive strategies to keep its status. However, this reaction has compromised the regime's performance in governing public health.

Following the disruptive outbreak of SARS in 2003, the Chinese government began to reform its public health sector to build a modern system for controlling infectious diseases (L. Wang et al. 2019; Ming and Li 2015). Xi Jinping called for implementing a national strategy of "healthy China" in his report to the Chinese Communist Party (CCP)'s 19th National Congress in 2017. However, the outbreak of COVID-19 in late 2019 and early 2020 reminded us of the authoritarian regime's vulnerabilities in detecting emerging infectious diseases. The evolution of AIDS governance in China offers insights for understanding the reform process and outcomes in public health over the past two decades.

In the mid-1990s, the Chinese government considered HIV/AIDS to be mainly confined to drug users in the southwest, sex workers in the southeast, and gay men in urban areas. The government was confident in its ability to manage the problem. But the alarming spread of HIV/AIDS in central rural China in 1995 transformed the landscape of state–society interactions in this issue. As the epidemic continued over the next two decades, AIDS governance evolved in unexpected directions. These shifts were driven by more than the Chinese government's top-down response to a growing health crisis; in fact, a complicated tripartite interaction among state, societal, and international actors fueled various adaptations in framing and managing HIV/AIDS.

In the early 2000s, the Chinese government regarded AIDS as a politically sensitive issue to be managed in an authoritarian manner. The state controlled information related to the epidemic, did nothing in terms of prevention or treatment, and excluded nonstate actors from the issue. In late 2002, a major shift occurred: China's new state leaders responded positively to the increasing advocacy efforts by the international community. In subsequent years, international actors involved in AIDS governance in China built a co-governance relationship with the Chinese government. Furthermore, grassroots AIDS nongovernmental organizations (NGOs), as self-organizing societal forces, grew rapidly with international support and gained formal status to participate in policy processes at the national level. In 2011, the governance structure shifted again as international actors' interest waned and the state reclaimed its dominant position in the policy process and state–society relations. According to the evolutionary framework and the typology of state–society relations in China delineated in chapters 1 and 2 of this volume, four forms of state–society interaction were generated that depended on state and societal actors' strategies. The interactive dynamics in AIDS governance clearly shifted between different types: from Type I (strong state/weak society) to Type IV (weak state/strong society), and back to Type I in recent years.

In the field of China studies, the dynamics of state–society relations in AIDS governance has attracted attention from diverse theoretical perspectives. Some studies emphasize how social forces seek opportunities in the state's institutional framework and develop survival strategies through service provision (Cai and Zhang 2016; Gåsemyr 2017). Others focus on how the organizational processes of social forces are controlled by the state (Gåsemyr 2016). By contrast, other studies trace the emergence of cooperation between the state and NGOs (Hildebrandt 2015) and explore the response of social forces to international actors (Gåsemyr 2015; Long 2018). In addition, some studies use resource dependence and organizational ecology perspectives in organization theory to illustrate the dynamic development of local AIDS NGOs (Q. Wang and Yao 2016; Yu 2016). A final approach examines the impact of the disease's threat on state–society relations (Lo 2018). These studies have not focused on longitudinal processes and have not captured the interaction among different sectors in this field.

Applying the evolutionary framework of this volume, this chapter examines the continuous interaction among the state, civil society, and the international community through three different phases of AIDS governance in the past 20 years (since about 2000). In so doing, we address the following questions. How did these sectors interact and what was the outcome at different times? Why was the state willing to improve governance by sharing power with external actors during a particular period but then revive authoritarian tactics later on? What are the implications of such shifts for the regime?

Phase 1: An Authoritarian Approach to AIDS Governance (1995–2002)

HIV/AIDS was first diagnosed in central rural China in 1995. Even as it developed into a serious health crisis, the local government concealed information regarding the epidemic to avoid political responsibility. Social activists were powerless to influence the authoritarian state to respond appropriately. In late 2002, the AIDS governance situation changed because of the involvement of the international community and the rotation of state leaders. Only then did China recognize AIDS as a public concern.

AIDS EPIDEMIC COVERED UP IN
RURAL HENAN

In the early 1990s, a "plasma economy" emerged in rural central China, particularly in Henan province. Local governments established plasma-pheresis stations to purchase blood plasma from farmers, which would be then resold to pharmaceutical companies to manufacture plasma products. Lured by substantial economic rewards and government mobilization, millions of people participated in the program. However, low health and safety standards in the collection process led hundreds of thousands of farmers to contract HIV.

In 1995, Wang Shuping, an officer from the China Center for Disease Control and Prevention (CDC) in Zhoukou, Henan, discovered a 100 percent HIV infection rate in 111 rural plasma donors. This was the first time HIV/AIDS was discovered in rural China. Wang issued an urgent report to the Henan government but was forbidden from making his discovery public. He defied the local government's orders and brought the blood samples to the Ministry of Health (MOH) in Beijing. After confirming the samples, MOH directed Henan to immediately suspend its plasma collection program. However, governments in Henan continued to operate the plasmapheresis stations for another two to three years. Moreover, the province took no disease prevention or control actions, such as informing people who may be HIV-positive or reporting the results of epidemic monitoring to the MOH. Over the following years, the AIDS epidemic spread in rural China without any prevention or medical care until the infection rate in rural villages reached 35.9 to 73.9 percent (Zhu et al. 2008). In 1999, numerous farmers began dying from the disease, unaware of the cause. Although the MOH knew that HIV/AIDS was spreading, it could not persuade Henan to address the epidemic.

In the late 1990s, activists Gao Yaojie, Wan Yanhai, and Zhang Ji-chen began working to expose the AIDS problem in rural areas. As a doctor, Gao had detected HIV/AIDS in her patients and then discovered the large-scale spread of the virus and the disease through her field surveys of rural villages. She contacted the Henan government, which warned her to abandon the issue. Gao decided to publish her findings by herself. At the same time, Wan, the director of a health education institution, received an unpublished Henan government document and posted it on the internet. This document revealed that the Henan government already knew about the AIDS epidemic in 1995 but continued to conceal it from the public. Several months later, Zhang, a reporter at *Dahe Daily*, produced two special reports about the AIDS problem in Henan. Zhang's work attracted the attention of domestic and international groups. The Henan government suppressed these activists and continued to deny the widespread existence of AIDS.

ADVOCACY EFFORTS FROM THE INTERNATIONAL COMMUNITY

By the late 1990s, the fight against HIV/AIDS had become global and reached the agenda of the United Nations. The UN placed this health crisis in its Millennium Development Goals, and a framework of global AIDS governance was developed for coordinating the resources and actions of different countries. This framework included a set of principles and ideas and was improved by the major organizations, Joint United Nations Programme on HIV and AIDS (UNAIDS) and the Global Fund.

In this context, the efforts of domestic activists in China attracted international attention. The international community worried that the Chinese government had neither the will nor the capacity to win the fight against HIV/AIDS and considered their feeble response to its AIDS crisis to be irresponsible. China's AIDS problem was also seen as a new risk factor in the context of the "China threat" thesis and the "collapse of China." Western countries feared the AIDS epidemic could hinder China's development and eventually pose a health threat to neighboring countries. They also worried about human rights violations that could accompany the spread of AIDS in China.

During 2000–2003, the international community adopted a series of actions. First came critiques from Western media and international advocacy organizations. The *New York Times*, Human Rights Watch, and Reporters Without Borders criticized the Chinese government's irresponsibility in AIDS governance and related human rights issues. Next were warnings and advocacy efforts from international organizations. In 2002, UNAIDS declared China unable to control the epidemic at the local level and warned that HIV/AIDS had become a major public health threat (UNAIDS 2002). In 2003, the UN Development Programme warned that its efforts to address the AIDS crisis in China were the slowest part of implementing the Millennium Development Goals. The Global Fund, which controls global financial resources in AIDS governance, twice refused applications from the Chinese government to protest China's inaction regarding its rural AIDS problem. In addition to attracting the attention of state leaders and citizens, UNAIDS substantially contributed to soft advocacy efforts in China, such as organizing the 15th International HIV/AIDS Conference 2002 in Beijing. Finally, global leaders started to lobby around the world. UN Secretary-General Kofi Annan and former US President Bill Clinton visited China in 2002 and 2003, respectively. They warned that the AIDS epidemic could quickly destroy China's achievements in economic reform and encouraged the Chinese government to redouble its efforts on this issue.

CHINA'S NEW LEADERS BRING A NEW ATTITUDE

Before mid-2002, China did little to deal with the AIDS crisis and rejected criticism from the international community. A turning point was when new state leaders took over. In late 2002, Hu Jintao and Wen Jiabao delivered a critical speech about China's approach to AIDS governance. In October 2002, the evening before he assumed leadership of the CCP, Hu (2003) announced, "HIV/AIDS prevention and control is a major issue pertinent to the quality and prosperity of the nation." This was the first time China's top leader had publicly addressed the HIV/AIDS issue. In December 2002, Wen spoke as new premier of the state council, acknowledging the local government's responsibility and emphasizing the urgent need for AIDS governance. He said, "The real situation of HIV/AIDS is probably more serious than we think, local governments in some high-diffusion areas have not adopted and implemented the prevention work . . . dealing with HIV/AIDS as an urgent and major issue, which is related to the fundamental interests of the whole Chinese nation" (Wen 2004). China's leaders also addressed the international community.

In September 2003, at the UN General Assembly Special Session on HIV/AIDS, Vice Health Minister Gao Qiang, entrusted by Hu, proclaimed, "The Chinese government has attached great importance to HIV/AIDS prevention and treatment and has treated it as a strategic issue for social stability, economic development, national prosperity and security, making it a first priority of the government work" (Gao 2003).

In 2004, Vice Premier and Minister of Health Wu Yi acknowledged the role of the international community in these changes: "HIV/AIDS prevention and control is demanded and expected by the Chinese people and is also a great concern for international society. In such a phase with both inner drive and outer pull, we are required to face the epidemic of HIV/AIDS. . . . with a more open and practical attitude, we ought to strengthen international communication and cooperation" (Wu 2004).

Changes at the highest level of government elevated AIDS to the top of the Chinese political agenda. What caused the new leaders to adopt a positive response? Susan Shirk (2007) argued that the Hu-Wen regime paid greater attention to domestic social problems than the international community expected. In this vein, it is possible that central leaders decided to enhance HIV/AIDS prevention and control to avoid a serious public health crisis. This was not the only reason for the changed attitude.

Several factors indicate that the international community played a crucial role in this shift. First, China's disease monitoring system was too weak to evaluate the HIV/AIDS situation accurately. Official data from the Chinese government showed that the number of HIV infections increased from 8,219 in 2001 to 9,732 in 2002, implying a slower rate of increase than during 2000–2001 (Sun et al. 2007; Wu et al. 2007). These numbers do not suggest an emergent crisis, so state leaders must have been considering international opinion to judge the severity of HIV/AIDS in China. Second, although public health issues such as smoking and hepatitis also needed to be addressed, the government chose to prioritize HIV/AIDS (Hesketh 2007). Third, although Wu Yi's speech mentioned the Chinese people's expectations and international concerns, local actors lacked the power or channels to influence the government's attitude, particularly because Gao and Wan were suppressed in 2002. Moreover, many believed that the SARS experience would change the government's attitude toward public health threats (Xue 2005). However, when state leaders began to prioritize AIDS governance in late 2002, SARS had not yet become a major problem.

The new leaders' attitudes were reflected in their macro-strategies. During the final years of the Jiang Zemin government, China faced various international pressures, such as the threat of military conflict with the United States and criticism for oppressing the Falun Gong. Under the Hu regime, China aimed to stabilize international relations to improve the domestic economy. Hu emphasized China's "peaceful rise" and constructed the image of "responsible power" to mitigate doubt in the international community. Given this context, the AIDS issue was an easy compromise that allowed China to demonstrate to the world its goodwill.

RESULTS

As new leaders brought a new attitude, the Chinese government began adopting numerous policies to address the AIDS problem in rural areas, such as improving monitoring systems and conducting a general survey of former plasma donors in Henan. It also improved the lives of HIV-positive people in rural areas with two crucial policies: "four free and one care" and "five-one construction." The first policy promised to provide HIV-positive people with free medical treatment, antivirus drugs, education for children, and subsidies; the second policy pledged to improve the infrastructure of villages with high levels of infection. In addition, the budget for AIDS governance was tripled in 2003 and then doubled in 2004 (see fig. 6.1).

At the same time, the Chinese government strengthened international cooperation and communication to gain trust from the international

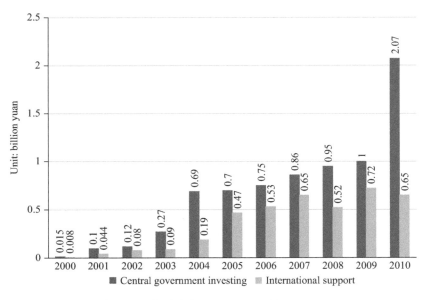

FIGURE 6.1 Financial support for AIDS governance in China, 2000–2010
Source: Wu et al. (2007); MOH (2009, 2010).

community. In 2003, a government report about the AIDS epidemic in China was copublished by the MOH, UNAIDS, and World Health Organization (WHO). This was the first time China released a report to the public on its AIDS epidemic and related policy plan. The report was based on a joint effort by the Chinese government and international organizations. In addition, the Global Fund awarded 800 million yuan in financial aid to the Chinese government to focus on rural areas with high infection rates.

Phase 2: Co-Governance with the International Community and the Growth of AIDS NGOs (2003–2010)

With the support of new state leaders, in 2003 AIDS governance in China underwent considerable changes in participants and structure. International actors became very involved in China's AIDS governance by helping the government plan, implementing AIDS-prevention projects, and providing considerable financial support. Thus, a co-governance relationship developed between the Chinese government and international actors. An unintended consequence for the state was the rapid growth of AIDS NGOs with the support of international actors.

CO-GOVERNANCE BETWEEN THE CHINESE GOVERNMENT AND THE INTERNATIONAL COMMUNITY

After 2003, numerous international actors emerged in the AIDS governance field. International organizations in the UN system, such as UNAIDS, United Nations Children's Fund, United Nations Educational, Scientific, and Cultural Organization, and the International Labour Organization, began cooperating with related government departments in China to promote various AIDS prevention projects. The United States, Canada, Sweden, and other countries established bilateral cooperation projects. In addition, numerous international NGOs became involved. These emerging international actors brought abundant resources and advanced technology that yielded strong influence on policy planning and practices in China's AIDS governance.

The international actors had the most direct influence through their substantial grants. From 2003 to 2009, the Chinese central government set aside a total of 5.22 billion yuan for AIDS prevention, and international organizations contributed another 3.17 billion yuan—more than one-third of China's AIDS prevention budget (see fig. 6.1). The Global Fund was the largest source of international grants, donating more than 1.8 billion yuan from 2003 to 2010. Notably, the Global Fund also gave the Chinese government funding to control malaria and tuberculosis, with total funds of 6.4 billion yuan as of 2012.

The effects of international grants surpassed expectations. Due to budgetary constraints in China's public health system, most of the government's budget was spent on salaries and daily operating expenses. By contrast, international grants met the real needs of the MOH and increased the ministry's administrative influence. In a 2011 interview, an international NGO director in China stated, "For MOH, money from government budget is dead money, but international grants are flexible. It can be the tool to enhance MOH's power" (personal interview, December 8, 2010).

Moreover, international grants improved the capacity of the public health system. In a 2007 interview, one midlevel official stressed the importance of international grants to the public health system:

> It is hard to obtain funding in the disease control sector. Funding means a lot. AIDS prevention is all about money and it can definitely promote the whole public health system in China. . . . External funding can improve the condition of epidemic prevention stations or offer various training. If the personnel in county level receive consistent professional training, everything will be different. (personal interview, August 2, 2007)

In fact, international aid helped almost all aspects of AIDS governance. For example, in 2010 the MOH published *Managing Project Programs for Preventing HIV/AIDS*. This document asserted that the financial base of AIDS governance in every area was to "integrate central and provincial government budgets with the projects of the Global Fund and other international organizations." The document also asked the local government to "complete the tasks required by international cooperation projects."

International actors were also directly involved in the policymaking process. After 2003, the Chinese government continued to set their aims and work agenda according to the advice of international organizations. This was reflected in official documents such as China 2005 Declaration of Commitment on HIV/AIDS Progress Report and China's Action Plan for Reducing and Preventing the Spread of HIV/AIDS (2006–2010). The international community responded positively by enhancing technical and administrative support. In 2007, the UN system in China formulated the UN Joint Programme on AIDS in China (2007–2010) (UNDP 2007) and declared close cooperation with the Chinese government. It was developed with a coherent vision and strategy for achieving the objectives of the UN Development Assistance Framework in China and in support of China's Action Plan for Reducing and Preventing the spread of HIV/AIDS (2006–2010).

The Chinese government entered partnerships with international NGOs such as the Clinton Initiative and the Bill and Melinda Gates Foundation. In a 2007 interview, senior staff in the Clinton initiative explained,

> Our current chief used to be chief consultant in the Clinton government who guided and planned AIDS prevention policy for the United States. Now he also helps the Chinese government to create their guidelines . . . Our institution works with the whole health system. Our experts from the US will draw up the policy revision recommendation and provide specific technical support to MOH after their discussion with WHO. For MOH, this is a stakeholder's opinion, and they will respect it. (personal interview, July 30, 2007)

The involvement of international actors meant a lot to the Chinese government in this period because the government sought to move past the negative image that resulted from concealing the epidemic and the international community's involvement boosted the government's response to international expectations. In addition, the resources and technical support from the international community improved the Chinese government's ability in AIDS governance substantially and enhanced the public health system. Thus, the MOH attached great importance to the opinions and perceptions of the international community.

An appropriate example of this is the "HIV/AIDS Epidemic Annual Report" in 2005, which estimated that 650,000 people in China had contracted HIV. This number was almost 200,000 fewer people than reported in the previous year, causing the public to question whether the Chinese government was underestimating the size of the epidemic. However, a government officer from the State Council's Office of AIDS Prevention who participated in the investigation and drafting of the report explained in a 2006 interview, "The evaluation model in 2005 was based on the suggestion of WHO. Theoretically, it should be even more reliable compared to the report last year. In fact, we also worried that international communities wouldn't believe us. Therefore, we corrected the number upward to 650,000. The actual statistics were lower than this number" (personal interview, July 8, 2006).

Another example of China's openness to international influence was its swift reform of domestic regulations. In 2009, UNAIDS began appealing to countries to ease travel restrictions on people with HIV/AIDS. The Global Fund announced that it would reduce its cooperation with countries denying entrance to people with HIV/AIDS. The Chinese government responded in 2010 when it rescinded its related border control policies from 1985. China was the second country to respond to this appeal after the United States. This shows that the Chinese government was highly sensitive to international expectations during this phase.

INTERNATIONAL COMMUNITY'S SUPPORT
FOR CIVIL SOCIETY

The international community's goal was not just to assist the Chinese government in its fight against HIV/AIDS but also to actively promote the engagement of domestic civil society. In the 1990s, when global AIDS governance was developing, the involvement of civil society and HIV carriers was identified as crucial to the success of the HIV/AIDS prevention program. Specific principles of action and objectives were created, called the "greater involvement of people living with HIV/AIDS" (GIPA; see UNAIDS 1999). In brief, GIPA aimed to involve relevant social groups in the AIDS governance policy process, eventually including them in decisionmaking bodies (fig. 6.2).

This pyramid models the increasing levels of involvement advocated by GIPA, with the highest level representing complete application of the GIPA principle. Ideally, GIPA is applied at all levels of organization.

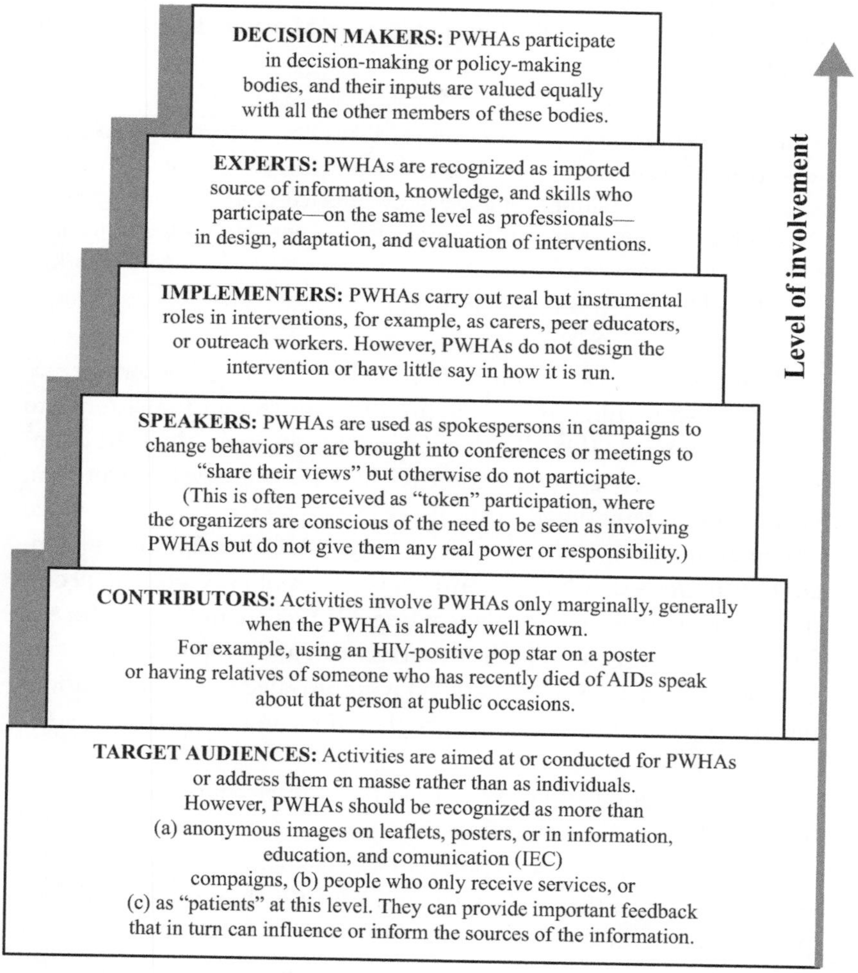

DECISION MAKERS: PWHAs participate in decision-making or policy-making bodies, and their inputs are valued equally with all the other members of these bodies.

EXPERTS: PWHAs are recognized as imported source of information, knowledge, and skills who participate—on the same level as professionals— in design, adaptation, and evaluation of interventions.

IMPLEMENTERS: PWHAs carry out real but instrumental roles in interventions, for example, as carers, peer educators, or outreach workers. However, PWHAs do not design the intervention or have little say in how it is run.

SPEAKERS: PWHAs are used as spokespersons in campaigns to change behaviors or are brought into conferences or meetings to "share their views" but otherwise do not participate. (This is often perceived as "token" participation, where the organizers are conscious of the need to be seen as involving PWHAs but do not give them any real power or responsibility.)

CONTRIBUTORS: Activities involve PWHAs only marginally, generally when the PWHA is already well known. For example, using an HIV-positive pop star on a poster or having relatives of someone who has recently died of AIDs speak about that person at public occasions.

TARGET AUDIENCES: Activities are aimed at or conducted for PWHAs or address them en masse rather than as individuals. However, PWHAs should be recognized as more than (a) anonymous images on leaflets, posters, or in information, education, and comunication (IEC) compaigns, (b) people who only receive services, or (c) as "patients" at this level. They can provide important feedback that in turn can influence or inform the sources of the information.

Level of involvement

FIGURE 6.2 Different stages of the GIPA (PWHAs are people with HIV/AIDS)
Source: Reproduced from UNAIDS (1999, 3).

International actors in China also took improving the practice of GIPA as a key goal and followed this guideline to build the capacity of social forces to participate in AIDS governance. In a 2007 interview, a senior officer of a UNAIDS office in China spoke on the crucial role of NGOs:

> One of the most important principles of UNAIDS is the GIPA and the way to practice GIPA is to introduce and to promote the idea of GIPA and to assist the organizations established by infected groups. . . . Assisting NGOs is a very important part in social participation. NGOs is one major weakness in China's social participation; therefore, all the focus of the work transferred to NGOs. (personal interview, August 26, 2007)

With this objective established, UNAIDS mobilized other international NGOs in China to provide funding and technical assistance to support developing AIDS NGOs in China. For example, the Ford Foundation, which paid close attention to civil society development, and Marie Stopes International, dedicated to reproductive health, provided substantial support to AIDS NGOs under UNAIDS' mobilization. Concurrently, many AIDS NGOs formed by groups of HIV-positive people began appearing around 2003, including AIDS Care in China, the Ark of AIDS, and Red Forest. With encouragement and support from the international community, these early NGOs cultivated more organizations from local groups of HIV-positive people and focused on grassroots community work.

The Global Fund also played a crucial role in promoting civil society. To ensure the opportunity and ability for civil participation, the Global Fund stipulated that at least 15 percent of the applied prevention grants must be allotted to the NGO sector, and NGOs should have sufficient representation in the decisionmaking process of the fund's projects. These regulations were general and applied to every recipient country. In China, the Global Fund allowed unregistered grassroots NGOs to propose work so they could contribute to the project directly. The Global Fund also initiated the "NGO Capability Building" project to strengthen operating skills at AIDS NGOs. In addition to the Global Fund, some international NGOs focused on civil society, including the United Fund (created by 10 international NGOs to provide funding support directly to grassroots AIDS NGOs in China) and the Bill and Melinda Gates Foundation,

FIGURE 6.3 Capacity-building seminar for grassroots NGOs
Source: Photo by author, Shenyang, Liaoning province, 2007.

which established a five-year 0.4 billion yuan project in 2007 to sponsor AIDS NGOs through government channels.

Western groups also actively sponsored AIDS NGOs with the goal of policy advocacy and human rights protection. For instance, Wan Yanhai was arrested for disclosing information about the AIDS epidemic in 2002. During a visit to the United States after his release, he received grants from the National Endowment for Democracy and the Open Society Institute. He returned to China to establish an NGO named Aizhixing (爱知行) to promote legal advocacy and human rights protection. Aizhixing also actively sponsored local HIV-positive groups to establish NGOs and supported them in protesting for the group interests and rights protection (fig. 6.3).

DEVELOPMENT OF AIDS NGOS AND THEIR INTERACTION WITH THE STATE

The Chinese government was ready to address AIDS-related issues and comply with most international norms but had not anticipated and could not accept the rapid growth of AIDS NGOs. In response to international requests to improve social engagement, government-organized NGOs (GONGOs) were mobilized at different levels to handle AIDS prevention work, but grassroots NGOs were given no assistance. Similar to grassroots NGOs in other fields in China, almost none of the grassroots AIDS NGOs could be registered legally. UNAIDS tried to persuade the MOH and the Ministry of Civil Affairs to accept societal participation and allow AIDS NGOs to register. The government refused. In response to the Global Fund's requests to provide financial support to NGOs, in 2005 Beijing established the National HIV Prevention Social Mobilization Project. But it only funded registered NGOs, thereby excluding most grassroots AIDS NGOs.

With sponsorship and support from the international community, China's local grassroots AIDS NGOs developed rapidly and obtained access to abundant resources. Before 2003, there were fewer than 10 AIDS NGOs in China, and half of these were GONGOs. In 2006, AIDS NGOs totaled more than 100, most of which were organized by HIV-positive people. By 2010, the Global Fund's list included nearly 1,000 AIDS NGO recipients, most of which were grassroots organizations unable to register legally. As they grew in number, the AIDS NGOs developed strong connections with each other. My investigation of an AIDS NGO network in 2007 revealed close communications and a tight collaborative network of 85 nonstate actors, including grassroots NGOs, international NGOs, and other international groups in this field (C. Wang, 2015; fig. 6.4).

In fig. 6.4, each node is an independent organizational actor, and each line means there is a specific interaction between these two organizations. In the communication network (left), interaction is defined as a stable information exchange relationship. As for the collaboration network (right), interaction is defined as resource exchange for a particular project or task. On average, each actor in the AIDS field shared their information with 32 actors and established cooperation with more than 10 actors. In addition, the size and location of each node reflects its importance in the whole network. UNAIDS was named too in fig. 6.4, and it obtained a larger interactive scope than others and was able to maintain the operation of the network. Advanced analysis also shows that international actors' role in this network were like "peak organization" (C. Wang 2015).

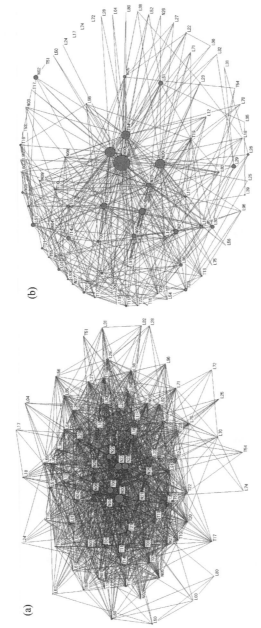

FIGURE 6.4 AIDS NGO communication and collaboration networks in China

Note: (a) represents the communication network; (b) represents the collaboration network.

Source: C. Wang (2015).

Table 6.1
Three AIDS NGO coalitions

Name	Established	Initiator	Number of Members
China HIV/AIDS CBO Network	2006/5	Aizhixing	55
China Alliance of People Living with HIV/AIDS	2006/11	The Ark of AIDS	24
China Network of Activists Advocating for HIV Treatment Access	2006/12	AIDS Care in China Red Forest	Unknown

Based on close connections, AIDS NGOs established three organizational coalitions in 2006, establishing horizontal connections and organizational mobilization between groups (table 6.1).

The main work of AIDS NGOs was to support various assistance and prevention projects, protect people's rights during protests, and engage in policy advocacy. Because AIDS NGOs still faced substantial oppression in their daily operations, they developed strategies to expand their living space in front of the state, with three major types of working area and related strategies: AIDS relief and prevention, policy advocacy and rights protection amid protests, and horizontal connections among NGOs.

AIDS Relief and Prevention For the local government, obtaining grants from international actors was crucial for initiating prevention projects at the community level. In addition to a few professional GONGOs, such as the Chinese Association of STD and AIDS Prevention and Control, most GONGOs, such as the All-China Women's Federation and the All-China Federation of Industry and Commerce, could not execute complex behavioral intervention and prevention projects with HIV-positive groups, which made up most grassroots NGOs. This gave grassroots NGOs an advantage during prevention work at the community level. Although most local governments were not pleased with the activities of grassroots NGOs for fears they might expose poor AIDS governance at the local level, the achievements of these organizations could be used to gain recognition for the local government.

This type of government recognition typically originated from a limited collaboration based on resource exchange. For example, with the support of an international group, a grassroots NGO in Xincai County, Henan, took in dozens of AIDS orphans. Using a central government compensation program, the local health bureau established an orphanage. However, the local government did not provide care for the orphans, and instead leased the orphanage's building for commercial use. But the local government used the orphan list from the grassroots NGO to apply for funding grants and "borrowed" these orphans during visits by superiors or international organizations to demonstrate their care for orphans. This allowed grassroots NGOs to gain acceptance from local governments.

Policy Advocacy and Rights Protection amid Protests A crucial aim of advocacy efforts was to investigate the government's responsibility in blood safety issues. When local governments could not implement the assistance policies of the central government, HIV-positive groups generally came out to protest. The Chinese government has no tolerance for activists. Active policy advocators such as Wan Yanhai, Hu Jia, and Li Dan were all under long-term surveillance by the security department. One night in August 2007, I met Wan and Li in Beijing. Li was set to host a policy initiative event in Guangzhou three days later. After dinner, however, Li was arrested by a security officer and put in custody to prevent him from traveling to Guangzhou.

Protests in China can result in the arrest of key advocates. The international community often steps in to support AIDS NGOs in these events. For example, Li Xige, the leader of a rural NGO in Henan, appealed to the MOH in Beijing and was arrested because she chained the doors of the MOH office. Long-term supporters of Li and Aizhixing publicized the news of her arrest through international media. Under pressure from the international community, the Chinese government released her three days later.

Horizontal Connections among NGOs The Chinese government does not allow transregional mobilization or horizontal connections between social forces to develop. However, a crucial characteristic in the development of China's AIDS NGOs was the dense organizational network. The horizontal connections among AIDS NGOs comprised frequent meetings, training programs, and collaborations. These events were usually part of international projects and were cosponsored by international groups, international NGOs, and local governments. The close collaborative relationship between the Chinese government and the international community meant that security departments were unable to stop these events for being illegal gatherings. Thus, the support of the international community helped legitimate the connections among AIDS NGOs in China.

NGOS PROMOTED IN PARTICIPATION
AND RESOURCE DISTRIBUTION

With increasing involvement by the international community, the Chinese government gradually became dependent on international resources, creating new opportunities for civil society to participate in the policy process. Two crucial events in this phase were the reform of the country coordinating mechanism in China and the Global Fund's suspension of its grants. The former event endowed AIDS NGOs and local HIV-positive populations formal power to join the policy process related to Global Fund projects, whereas the latter eliminated obstruction by the Chinese government in the process of grants flowing to NGOs.

Reform of China's Country Coordinating Mechanism with the Global Fund
The Global Fund's operational framework states that each country accepting grants must establish a country coordinating mechanism (CCM) as a top administrative and supervisory institution. The CCM is responsible for planning national projects to apply for grants and controlling the distribution, management, and supervision of funds. The Global Fund stipulates that the CCM must include representatives from the government, international organizations, and civil society and that the civil society representatives must hold more than 40 percent of the seats in the CCM. In China's CCM, the government assigned civil society representatives to GONGOs for safeguarding affairs under the state's control. Without representatives in the CCM, civil society was excluded from the operational process of the fund projects and resource distribution—and therefore could not fulfill the Global Fund's needs.

Since its establishment in 2003, the China CCM has been criticized for its size, nontransparency, and limited civil society participation. Most international actors did not recognize GONGOs as real NGOs and thought the China CCM was not following the Global Fund rules. In 2004, international NGO representatives in the China CCM—the Clinton Global Initiative, the Salvation Army, and Save the Children, UK—jointly asked the Global Fund's secretariat in Geneva to reform the China CCM. After investigation, the fund's secretariat presented the China CCM with a reform plan, calling on it to simplify its structure, elect representatives from different sectors, and add a representative seat for community-based NGOs and a seat for organizations of HIV-positive people.

In March 2006, the China CCM restructured and elected new representatives. However, AIDS NGOs were not satisfied with the outcome. Aizhixing and 27 other grassroots NGOs sent a signed protest letter to the Global Fund questioning the election results and complaining that the China CCM constitution still limited the participation of civil society by asking the representatives of the two new sectors to register. The Global Fund's secretariat asked the China CCM to elect new representatives of these two new sectors before 2007 and asked that the outcome fully represent the relative groups' opinions and interests. The Global Fund also warned that the outcome of the election would influence future grants.

Following this request, the China CCM formed a special work group to organize a new election. The MOH, the government representative in the China CCM, declared, "Although the MOH is voluntary as member of the special work group, the MOH did not join in the evaluation and practices" (Jia 2009). Rather than risking the loss of grants from the Global Fund, the Chinese government opted not to interfere in this election.

The new election was organized by UNAIDS and with complex processes to ensure transparency and fair representation. First, a conference was held in Wuhan in November 2006 to decide election procedures. The conference allowed 108 grassroots AIDS NGOs to discuss related issues, including the qualifications of the voters and candidates, the method of dividing electoral districts, and the method of ensuring that representatives reflect voter interests. AIDS NGOs voted on electoral procedures. Then, conferences were held in Xian, Beijing, and Kunming to ensure local NGOs in different areas understood the election method and encourage them to join the election. More than 170 grassroots NGOs joined these conferences. Third, two national rounds of voting were held in March 2007. The majority of the two sectors voted on a working committee, and then these two working committees voted two formal representatives and two attending observers to join the China CCM. In communist China, this marked the first time that nonparty organizations elected national representatives through open and direct election and that civil society actors participated in a public policy process with equal status to the government.

The Global Fund Suspends Its Grants Although civil society gained more power to participate than ever before, decisionmaking power remained with the Chinese government and resource distribution was heavily skewed to official sectors. This went against the Global Fund's stipulation that NGOs should receive at least 20 percent of the grants in a sponsored country. In May 2010, Meng Lin, a representative of HIV-positive populations in CCM and an NGO leader, sent a letter to the Global Fund secretariat complaining that the Chinese government was not fulfilling its funding requirement about supporting NGOs. This letter attracted the fund's attention.

In July 2010, the Global Fund attempted to negotiate with the Chinese government to improve the situation, but the government gave a lukewarm response. The fund started independent investigations to assess the performance and operational process of its projects in China. Reports from two independent investigators confirmed that grassroots AIDS NGOs were not receiving enough financial and managerial support. They found other problems, such as misuse of funds and a lack of coordination on project operations. In response to these reports, in October 2010 the fund secretariat suspended its grants for AIDS projects in China. Six months later, the fund suspended all of its grants to China to protest the government's lack of action to remedy the problems.

Although Beijing had doubled its budget for the AIDS epidemic in 2010, it was affected by the Global Fund's decision. The Chinese government conceded. To demonstrate goodwill about improving the situation for NGOs, MOH minister Chen Zhu convened a special work group to investigate related issues and met with NGO representatives to gather their opinions. The government then made an agreement with the Global

Fund promising to give NGOs sufficient financial support and resolve problems on the use of funds. In May 2011, the Global Fund resumed grantmaking to China. In this process, the fund exercised financial leverage to secure the government's compliance.

RESULTS

The representative seats of AIDS NGOs in the China CCM provide civil society and HIV-positive groups equal status with the Chinese government. Such power did not originate from the Chinese government or in the formal policy process but was embedded in the institutional framework the Global Fund erected in China. Given the crucial role of the Global Fund in China's AIDS governance, its power was sufficient to involve civil society in related policymaking and resource distribution and increase their bargaining power with the government.

By using such power, AIDS NGOs could improve the policy process to protect their rights. For example, in March 2008, HIV-positive people in Henan could not obtain the free antiviral drugs on time because the local government did not have enough in reserve. People asked the local government to solve this urgent medical need, but the response was unfriendly. They contacted Duan Jun, a Henan-based NGO leader and attending observer in the China CCM. Duan instantly requested the CDC to solve this problem. The next day, the CDC sent 3,500 units of an antiviral drug to Henan by air transport and asked other provinces to offer another 8,000 units. The drug shortage crisis was solved in just a few days. Clearly, without the power of a seat in the China CCM, it would have been impossible for HIV-positive people in villages to express their needs to the CDC at the central level and receive a direct response.

With continued development of cooperation between China and the international community, the influence of the latter peaked in 2010. In addition to pressuring China to comply with international norms, the Global Fund successfully changed the government's attitude toward supporting NGOs by withholding its grants. It could have been a new opportunity for NGOs to grow and for state–society relations to improve. However, before this could happen, the international community began leaving China, sending the evolution of AIDS governance in a different direction over the next five years.

Phase 3: The State Regains Control (2011–2015)

After 2011, important changes appeared on the international and domestic stages. At the beginning, the international community changed its attitude toward China as the Global Fund withdrew from the country. Xi Jinping took over and began tightening social controls, working to weaken or sever connections between domestic social actors and their international sponsors. These changes led the AIDS governance structure to return to a state-dominant model.

CHANGES IN THE INTERNATIONAL COMMUNITY

The Global Fund's Withdrawal In the previous phase, the Global Fund played a crucial role in AIDS governance in China, particularly in promoting NGO participation. In 2011 the fund stopped funding projects and exited China for two reasons.

First, most of the Global Fund donors were advanced Western countries. The global financial crisis in 2007–2008 had affected these countries' economies and reduced their willingness and capacity to support the Global Fund and other international programs (WHO 2009). By contrast, China maintained high economic growth and had become an upper middle-income economy by 2010. Thus, the international community began to question why China was still being given enormous international grants for AIDS prevention and other health issues. Jack Chow, one of the Global Fund's establishers, indicated that China being the fund's fourth largest recipient did not match its economic strength, its contributions to the international community, and its real health needs. Moreover, China was competing for limited funds with the poorest countries in sub-Saharan Africa. Chow (2010) warned that this was eroding the financial base of the Global Fund. Meanwhile, the international community expected China to begin shouldering more international responsibility, as Russia did when it shifted from being an international aid recipient to donor status in 2006. Under pressure from major donors and public opinion, the Global Fund gradually changed its funding decisions.

Second, the Global Fund was disappointed with the Chinese government's inefficient work and misused funds. At the central level, a 2009

McKinsey Global Institute Report noted that fund projects in China were being managed independently without central coordination and that different bureaucratic areas were not cooperating with each other. Local governments considered the fund's grants as extra budget and used the money without following the fund's standards (Huang and Jia 2014). In addition, the Chinese government at the central and local levels had no interest in improving NGO involvement in financing and implementing projects. Taken together, these problems hindered the effectiveness and performance of Global Fund projects in China, leading the fund to lose confidence and will to invest there.

The Global Fund resumed disbursing grants to China in May 2011, but at barely half of the previous level. Six months later, the Global Fund decided to exclude China and other G20 high-income countries from its aid list, and it ended existing projects over the next three years. The Global Fund offered to help China ensure its institutional framework continued to work, but China refused. Thus, the Global Fund's influence in China rapidly declined as it withdrew.

CHANGING ATTITUDE OF OTHER INTERNATIONAL NGOS TOWARD CHINA

The Global Fund's retreat marked a turning point in the evolution of AIDS governance, as many international NGOs similarly reduced their support for domestic NGOs. Wan Yanhai, a famous AIDS activist, complained in a 2012 interview: "In recent years, international NGOs no longer insist the value of democracy, human rights and social participation, and decreased their support to domestic AIDS NGOs. Instead, they turned to follow the state's will to ensure their space for survival in China" (interview, June 15, 2012).

International NGOs changed their attitudes for three reasons. First, some international groups were dissatisfied with the performance of AIDS NGOs. AIDS NGOs grew quickly, outpacing organizations in other domains, but the quality of their operations never reached the level expected by international NGOs. For example, the Bill and Melinda Gates Foundation sponsored domestic AIDS NGOs to administer HIV tests on high-risk populations and created financial incentives for NGOs and potential HIV carriers by paying people to take the blood tests. However, this project was criticized because some NGOs and people being tested saw the service as an easy way to earn money and took the test several times a day. In 2009, the *New York Times* reported on this story, critiquing domestic NGOs and the foundation (Jacobs 2009). Such media accounts tarnished the image of AIDS NGOs and their international sponsors. After the foundation's project to improve NGO participation ended in 2012, its objectives in China turned to developing medical instruments and away from supporting civil society.

Second, other international NGOs' capacity to support domestic civil society was affected by the Global Fund's withdrawal. Many international groups worked in specific sectors. For example, the Salvation Army focused on rural poverty alleviation, whereas Marie Stopes International focused on improving reproductive health. They became involved in supporting domestic NGOs under the institutional framework the Global Fund built in China, or they relied on the fund's grants to get additional resources to conduct their work for domestic NGOs. Although they remained willing to support domestic AIDS NGOs, they lost the necessary institutional environment and external resources after the Global Fund withdrew.

Third, international NGOs were under increased pressure from the Chinese government, particularly after the CCM reform in 2007. A director of an international NGO said in a 2007 interview: "Security offices more frequently asked international NGOs to report their work plans and interactions with domestic NGOs. Although it did not threaten our survival, we still felt increasing pressure" (interview, August 20, 2007).

Like other international NGOs in China, those dealing with AIDS governance face an ambiguous regulatory environment and must manage relations with the government. As government pressure increased, some of them gradually reduced their support for civil society.

Changes in the international community considerably reduced the resources and institutional space available to domestic AIDS NGOs. After 2011, the number of AIDS NGOs decreased rapidly. Some NGO leaders changed to careers in business, whereas others moved abroad.

CHANGES AT THE STATE LEVEL

China's Response to the Global Fund Withdrawal Around 2010, China was facing pressure from the international community and the uncertainty of international aid, particularly because the Global Fund suspended its grants for AIDS projects. Despite these changes, China kept its promise to win the fight against HIV/AIDS, and the international community reacted positively. In September 2010, Wen Jiabao promised to increase China's contributions to the Global Fund to US$14 million over the next three years. The government also increased its investment in AIDS governance.

Another important factor at the time was medical reform. In 2009, China began deep reform of its medical and health care system, increasing government health care investment from 481.6 billion yuan in 2009 to 1,253.3 billion yuan in 2015 (Meng et al. 2015). Although AIDS governance was not a focal point of the medical reform, it benefited from the larger total health care budget.

In 2010, central government investment in AIDS governance reached 2.2 billion yuan—twice that of the previous year. In 2014, central government investment reached 4.66 billion yuan; meanwhile, international grants declined to 0.054 billion yuan (just 1.1 percent of total funds for AIDS governance; fig. 6.5). As financing rapidly became dominated by the state, the influence of the international community in AIDS governance declined quickly.

State Governance Strategy during the Xi Jinping Era The governance structure of AIDS prevention changed in the later years of the Hu era, and Xi Jinping's rule accelerated this transition starting in 2012. In contrast to Hu, Xi took a stricter stance toward NGOs, particularly those receiving foreign aid. In 2015 and 2016, the government arrested numerous lawyers nationwide and several women's rights activists in Beijing and labor NGO leaders in Guangdong. The government accused them of collaborating with foreign forces to affect social stability. Xi increased direct control over international NGOs by enacting the Foreign NGOs Law in 2016. This law required international NGOs to obtain governmental approval for almost every action, preventing them from cooperating or supporting domestic NGOs without government approval. Obviously, the Chinese government wants to prevent international actors from strengthening social forces through resource subsidies and action support, as in AIDS governance and other similar policy domains.

Although AIDS NGOs rapidly declined before 2012, Xi's repressive actions raised pressure on the remaining social service groups. A few international organizations still funded domestic social welfare groups after

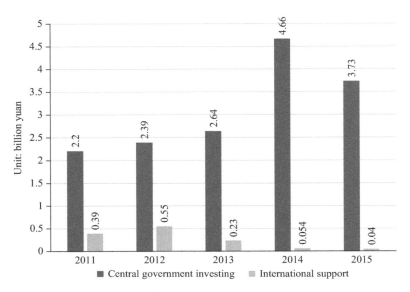

FIGURE 6.5 Financial support for AIDS governance in China, 2011–2015
Source: National Health and Family Planning Commission (2015); Ma et al. (2016).

2012, but such connections became illegal after 2017. The Chinese government increased its monitoring of AIDS activists to prevent protests. A Chinese writer and AIDS activist in Henan complained, "Although I have almost retreated from the AIDS issue, police or agents from security sector still visit me almost every week, ask me whom I contact, where I plan to travel, and what I do. If I leave to other city for a few days, they come to visit me on the second day I come back" (interview, July 20, 2017).

The Chinese government still allowed NGOs to participate in AIDS governance but only under the government's system. In 2015, the government built a new official fund called the China AIDS Fund for Non-Governmental Organizations to tighten state control over resource collection and distribution for AIDS NGOs. It integrated different international aid sources under an official funding mechanism and created a unified single channel to distribute resources to AIDS NGOs. In 2016, the first round of this new fund provided money to nearly 1,000 NGOs. Half of these were newly established hospital-based NGOs organized by nurses and patients to support HIV/AIDS patients; the other half were local GONGOs established by the local health sector or community-based NGOs from the population of homosexual men. Each contributed meaningfully to AIDS prevention and treatment. However, they worked under the government's plan and were no longer interested in rights protection, legal advocacy, or participating in AIDS policy.

RESULT

In recent years, there have been no influential international actors or domestic advocacy NGOs in China's AIDS governance. After the dramatic funding changes in 2010–2012 and amid increased government control under Xi, the state reclaimed its dominant position and rebuilt state–society relations under a state purchase service model. With the state's control over external resources, domestic AIDS NGOs face a situation similar to other health philanthropy groups that are widely subject to the space and restrictions granted by the state (Huang 2019). Following the withdrawal of independent social forces and external actors, the government once again covers up problems, such as misused funds, correctly addressing the needs of virus carriers, and new ways of infection. Civil society participation remains limited in practice and excluded from the policy process.

Analysis and Conclusion

Since the early 2000s, AIDS governance in China has evolved in a circular manner. During the first phase, the Chinese government adopted a traditional authoritarian approach: doing nothing to control the epidemic, hiding information, and ignoring the appeals of domestic and international actors. In the second phase, the AIDS governance model opened to stakeholders. The state allowed the international community to influence policy and began to rely on international assistance to handle HIV/AIDS and other health problems. International support also helped AIDS NGOs grow rapidly. Under pressure from the international community, the Chinese government was eventually pressured to allow civil society to participate in policymaking. However, when international actors withdrew, AIDS governance returned to a state-dominant model as state capacity increased.

The changes in AIDS governance in China were so extreme that methodologically, it could be viewed as a crucial case study to understand the dynamics of state–society relations and the flexibility and limitations of resilience in China.

MULTILEVEL AND ONGOING
INTERACTIVE PROCESS

In the multiphased evolutionary process, tripartite relations among the state, civil society, and international community led to numerous changes over time. This reflects the unstable nature of these relations: the situation could develop quickly in one direction and then rapidly turn the other way. Explaining such fluidity or evaluating the state or society as strong or weak is difficult under a single static model. Reviewing the state–society interactions diachronically is useful for understanding the intentions, capacity, and opportunities of each actor, and how their strategic interaction shaped the intermediate outcomes at different phases.

The dynamics of the transition process entailed interactions at multiple levels. At the top level was the interaction between China and the international community. This refers to the international community's expectations of and influence on China, and China's willingness to comply. The middle level was the interaction between international actors in China (such as the Global Fund) and particular government departments, including the MOH. This reflected the capacity and intentions of these two sides. At the bottom level were AIDS NGOs and their surrounding political environment, including the MOH and local governments. Interactions at the top level drove changes in AIDS governance that carried over from one phase to the next. At the lower levels, actors' intentions, capacity, and opportunities were constrained by the environment that was constantly being shaped by interactions at the higher level. Transitions at the bottom and middle levels were not completely determined by the top level but were crystallized by the outcome of actors' interactions. At these levels, actors pursuing change used opportunities and mobilized resources in the environment to affect other actors' attitudes and behavior in the iterative engagements. It was a continuously dynamic process: the outcome of each step affected the conditions of the next interaction.

INTERNATIONAL COMMUNITY'S INFLUENCE

During the first decade of 21st century, international actors generally supported particular domestic NGOs and social actors made use of international norms as tools to persuade the government. In this case, international actors changed China's attitude toward a domestic social problem, expanded their influence at the national and systematic level, and helped domestic NGOs gain the status required to participate in policy. This unusual situation showed the context in which the international community could influence the Chinese government and state–society relations.

The international community had considerable normative, institutional, and financial resources, and the state desired international recognition. The specific outcomes of different phases were shaped by international actors' strategic actions and their interaction with the state. By the end of the first phase, international advocacy efforts had made the international community's hopes clear to China and attracted new central leaders' attention and a positive response. Interactions at the top level led AIDS governance to the second phase, when interaction occurred at the middle level. State agencies, such as the MOH, were responsible for AIDS governance but had little administrative power or financial resources and had to depend on international resources to improve their capacity. Under these circumstances, international actors, such as the Global Fund, gained considerable bargaining power with the MOH. The Global Fund used this power to push the ministry to provide participation rights to civil society along with sufficient financial support. These changes were achieved through the fund's strategic actions, such as investigations, protests, and suspending grants.

However, this case illustrates the limits and instability of the international community's gains. Even during the second phase, the international community hoped to bring external norms and institutions into China but was blocked by political conditions. In addition to the MOH, other departments and the local governments were unwilling to change their behavior, resisting international influence and delaying changes the international community had hoped for. The decline in international influence after 2011 was a reminder of the uncertain role of international actors in China. When further changes occurred at the top level, international actors abandoned their efforts in China, leaving domestic societal actors to deal with the state on their own.

STRENGTH OF SOCIAL ACTORS' STRATEGIC ACTIONS

The growth of AIDS NGOs was an unintended consequence for the Chinese government. Without international support, the social sector could not have developed as described in the second phase. However, the role of civil society actors should not be ignored. Facing state suppression, social actors mobilized international resources to push for state change, reflecting the fortitude of an otherwise weak social sector.

During the first phase, activists Gao and Wen successfully attracted international attention to the HIV/AIDS problem in China. In the second phase, international actors became involved in AIDS governance, and AIDS NGOs grew with international support, though they still had to deal with the government without goodwill and expand their operational space vis-á-vis the state by offering AIDS prevention services to the local government or using international protection to improve self-organizing and protest. AIDS NGOs strived for formal status to participate in policy and access to resources. Civil society actors proactively launched a reform agenda and mobilized international support to change their relations with the state. In other words, state–society relations were not unilaterally decided by the state but were embedded in the interactive process between the two sides. Yet these achievements did not ensure the status of AIDS NGOs after international actors withdrew their support.

In the third phase, social actors rapidly declined as international actors left. The remaining AIDS NGOs had no choice but to submit to the state and rely on government resources. Civil society was not strong enough to develop itself without international support.

AUTHORITARIAN RESILIENCE AND ADAPTATION

Since about 2000, the role of nonstate actors in the AIDS governance policy process has expanded and contracted. For instance, the Chinese government shared its power in the policy process with stakeholders in a particular situation, but this change proved to be unstable. The flexibility and limits of the state to change are attributable to several aspects of the regime.

First, the attitudes of state leaders were a necessary condition in this case. Without Hu and Wen's support, the MOH could not move to strengthen cooperation with the international community by itself. State leaders' attitudes reflected their characters and strategic objectives in a particular time. Hu and Wen pursued international recognition by resolving domestic social problems, which created the political space for closer interaction between the MOH and the international community. Xi then reshaped the political space according to his own strategic objectives, such as excluding international actors from intervening in domestic affairs. Even if the Global Fund had not left on its own, it was clear that Xi would not have allowed such an influential external actor to continue operating in the same mode in China. In other words, the resilience of authoritarianism depends on the state leader.

Second, the preferences of the main state agents also mattered. In this case, the MOH lacked the administrative power and financial resources to deal with a health crisis. The political environment was subsequently restructured at the top level, giving the MOH the chance to boost its governing capacity and administrative power through the international community. Thus, the MOH allowed external actors to join the policy process and exert their influence. This resource dependency even changed the attitudes of the MOH toward civil society. In other domains, where the main state agent was replaced by more powerful entities, such as the Ministry of Public Security, the outcome would be different.

Third, flexibility was constrained by political inertia. Even with central leaders' support and main agents' concession, the flexibility to adapt was still limited by other bureaucratic sectors. During the second phase, although the MOH gradually accepted the more influential role of civil society, the Ministry of Civil Affairs did not accept it, and their space was threatened by the security department and local government. International actors' efforts to change the government's behavior were also impeded by resistance in the government. It is difficult for a single state agent in a particular domain or an individual state leader to overcome systemic obstacles, such as misused funds, lack of coordination between sectors, and reluctance to share power with civil society. Perhaps the most stable factor limiting the regime's ability to adapt was not the leader's will or the preferences of a particular agent but the ideas and customs embedded in the authoritarian bureaucracy.

Fourth, accountability was limited. Since 2010, some local officers have been punished for corruption in AIDS governance, but the cover-up of the HIV/AIDS epidemic in the late 1990s still has not been investigated. Li Changchun and Li Keqiang were party secretaries of Henan province at the time and should have been held responsible. Yet both were later appointed as members of the Standing Committee of the CCP. In effect, lower-level officers are held accountable for crimes, but officers at higher levels are free of political responsibility. Political stability and the interests of the ruling group take priority.

Finally, the regime's mode of social management was inefficient. The rapid growth of AIDS NGOs and their appeals to participate under international support taught a valuable lesson to China's rulers. The state learned to preempt such situations from arising. After Xi took power, social actors' international links were seen as a serious threat to the regime's stability, and the Foreign NGOs Law forbade direct international support to domestic NGOs. In addition to these firm tactics, the state tightened control over resources to the social sector. As the role of international actors changed and the state strengthened its control, pressure from nonstate actors declined, as did the state's will to respond to social needs and share government power. Although the state was willing to provide social actors limited access to the policy process, it would not allow advanced political change to occur with social participation.

Overall, this case reminds us that state–society relations in China are neither homogeneous nor stable. They depend on the context of particular issues and ongoing interactions among different actors. Even in a specific domain, in addition to the state's preference, state–society interactions play a role. Furthermore, interactions in each phase brought unintended consequences. Ultimately, the analytic framework of evolutionary governance provides insight into the transitional mechanisms of state–society relationships by capturing different actors' interests and strategies in a dynamic manner.

AUTHORITARIAN GOVERNANCE OF DISEASES

When international and societal actors have attempted to participate in AIDS governance, their basic aims are to improve the transparency, efficiency, fairness, and accountability of the Chinese government's disease control and prevention work. However, during the Xi era, the party-state has reinvigorated its monopoly on political power in almost every policy field and repressed external actors' survival and space for engagement. Although the official disease control system has improved in the past two decades, the outbreak of COVID-19 in late 2019 and early 2020 posed a sharp reminder of the authoritarian regime's limits in managing infectious diseases.

When independent external actors are only peripherally permitted to monitor and participate in the surveillance of an epidemic, the speed and accuracy of public health information released by the Chinese government may be affected by high-level politics, thereby compromising the trust of domestic society and the international community. Meanwhile, without the assistance of social forces, efforts to curtail the spread of the disease means that the Chinese government relies on coercive means. The public lacks channels to influence public policy in the face of improper regulation or inadequate medical treatment. Moreover, during the party-state's top-down resource mobilization process, NGOs are unable to perform aid functions as they did following the Sichuan earthquake in 2008.

Ultimately, in the absence of societal support and trust, the threat of (another) public health crisis looms. COVID-19 not only caused more severe economic, social, and health shocks than SARS, it also eroded the CCP's legitimacy under Xi. Whether the party-state exerts repressive strategies to maintain its political power or engages society for enhancing the quality of governance remains the core dilemma of evolutionary governance under authoritarianism.

References

Cai, Yongshun, and Jing Zhang. 2016. "Niche, Connections and NGO Operation in China." *Journal of Chinese Governance* 1.2: 269–83.

Chow, Jack. 2010. "China's Billion-Dollar Aid Appetite." *Foreign Policy*, July 19. http://www.foreignpolicy.com/articles/2010/07/19/chinas_billion_dollar_aid_appetite.

Gao Qiang. 2003. "Speech by Executive Vice Minister of Health, Mr. Gao Qiang, at the HIV/AIDS High-level Meeting of the UN General Assembly." http://www.china-un.ch/eng/tsjg/jgthsm/t85551.htm.

Gåsemyr, Hans Jørgen. 2015. "Twenty Years of Mobilising around AIDS in China: The Main Actors and Influences behind Organisational Growth." *Asian Studies Review* 39.4: 609–27.

———. 2016. "Networks and Campaigns but Not Movements: Collective Action in the Disciplining Chinese State." *Journal of Civil Society* 12.4: 394–410.

———. 2017. "Navigation, Circumvention and Brokerage: The Tricks of the Trade of Developing NGOs in China." *China Quarterly* 229: 86–106.

Hesketh, Therese. 2007. "HIV/AIDS in China: The Numbers Problem." *Lancet* 369.9562: 621–23.

Hildebreadt, Timothy. 2015. "From NGO to Enterprise: The Political Economy of Activist Adaptation in China." In *NGO Governance and Management in China*, edited by R. Hasmath and J. Y. J. Hsu, 121–35. London: Routledge.

Hu, Jintao. 2003. "President of the State Hu Jintao's Appointment of HIV/AIDS Prevention." *Information of HIV/AIDS Prevention and Control* 38: 1.

Huang, Yanzhong. 2019. "At the Mercy of the State: Health Philanthropy in China." *VOLUNTAS: International Journal of Voluntary and Nonprofit Organizations* 30: 634–46.

Huang Yanzhong and Jia Ping. 2014. "The Global Fund's China Legacy." International Institutions and Global Governance Working Paper, Council on Foreign Relations.

Jacobs, Andrew. 2009. "H.I.V. Tests Turn Blood into Cash in China." *New York Times*, December 2. http://www.nytimes.com/2009/12/03/health/policy/03china.html.

Jia, Ping. 2009. *Democracy in Bud: Report on 2006/07 China CBO/NGO Representative Elector.* Beijing: China Global Fund Watch Initiative.

Lo, Catherine Yuk-ping. 2018. "Securitizing HIV/AIDS: A Game Changer in State-Societal Relations in China?" *Globalization and Health* 14.1: 50.

Long, Yan. 2018. "The Contradictory Impact of Transnational AIDS Institutions on State Repression in China, 1989–2013." *American Journal of Sociology* 124.2: 309–66.

Ma, Yingpeng, Dongyi Yu, Rong Gu, and Ke Lü. 2016. "Analysis of Fund Inputs for HIV/AIDS Prevention and Control from 2010 to 2015 in China." *Chinese Journal of AIDS & STD* 22.12: 991–93.

Meng Qingyue, Yang Hongwei, Chen Wen, Sun Qiang, and Liu Xiaoyun. 2015. "People's Republic of China Health System Review." *Health Systems in Transition* 5.7.

Ming Xu and Shi-xue Li. 2015. "Analysis of Good Practice of Public Health Emergency Operations Centers." *Asian Pacific Journal of Tropical Medicine* 8.8: 677–82.

Ministry of Health. 2009. "Minister Chen Zhu Attended 5th Conference of International Cooperation Projects in China's HIV/AIDS Prevention." *Sina*, November 24. http://news.sina.com.cn/o/2009-11-24/103616659429s.shtml.

———. 2010. "Project Management Program in HIV/AIDS Prevention." Ministry of Health. http://www.nhc.gov.cn/wjw/ghjh/201009/49049.shtml.

National Health and Family Planning Commission. 2015. "2015 China AIDS Response Progress Report." http://www.unaids.org.cn/cn/index/Document_view.asp?id=875.

Shirk, Susan. 2007. *China: Fragile Superpower.* Oxford: Oxford University Press.

Sun, Xinhua, Ning Wang, Dongmin Li, Xiwen Zheng, Shuquan Qu, Lan Wang, Fan Lu, Katharine Poundstone, and Lu Wang. 2007. "The Development of HIV/AIDS Surveillance in China." *AIDS* 21: S33–S38.

UNAIDS. 1999. "From Principle to Practice: Greater Involvement of People Living with or Affected by HIV/AIDS (GIPA)." UNAIDS. http://data.unaids.org/Publications /IRC-pub01/JC252-GIPA-i_en.pdf.

UNDP. 2007. "United Nations Development Programme at Work in China: Annual Report 2007/2008." UNDP. http://www.undp.org/content/dam/china/docs/Publica tions/UNDP-CH-AR-Publications-Annual-Report-20072008.pdf.

Wang, Chanhsi. 2015. "Social Network Analysis and China Studies: Measurement and Analysis of Relational Network." *Mainland China Studies* 58.2: 23–59.

Wang, Li, Zhihao Wang, Qinglian Ma, Guixia Fang, and Jinxia Yang. 2019. "The Development and Reform of Public Health in China from 1949 to 2019." *Global Health* 15.1: 45.

Wang, Qun, and Yanran Yao. 2016. "Resource Dependence and Government-NGO Relationship in China." *China Nonprofit Review* 8.1: 27–51.

Wen, Jiabao. 2004. "Joint Efforts for Effective Prevention and Control of HIV/AIDS." In *Collection of Policies and Documents on HIV/AIDS Control and Prevention in China*, edited by China Center for AIDS/STD Control and Prevention, 1–9. Beijing: State Council AIDS Working Committee Office.

WHO. 2009. "The Financial Crisis and Global Health." WHO Information Note 2009/1. http://www.who.int/mediacentre/events/meetings/2009_financial_crisis_report _en_.pdf.

Wu, Yi. 2004. "Seizing the Opportunity to Search Further, Accelerating the Work of HIV/AIDS Prevention and Control in an All-Around Way." In *Collection of Policies and Documents on HIV/AIDS Control and Prevention in China*, edited by China Center for AIDS/STD Control and Prevention, 10–30. Beijing: State Council AIDS Working Committee Office.

Wu Zunyou, Sheena G. Sullivan, Wang Yu, Mary Jane Rotheram-Borus, and Roger Detels. 2007. "Evolution of China's Response to HIV/AIDS." *Lancet* 369.9562: 679–90.

Xue, Bin. 2007. "HIV/AIDS Policy and Policy Evolution in China." *International Journal of STD and AIDS* 16: 459–64.

Yu, Zhiyuan. 2016. "The Effects of Resources, Political Opportunities and Organisational Ecology on the Growth Trajectories of AIDS NGOs in China." *VOLUNTAS: International Journal of Voluntary and Nonprofit Organizations* 27.5: 2252–73.

Zhu, Xinyi, Zhao-lin Cui, Zuojun Huang, Bojian Zhu, and Ning Wang. 2008. "Study on AIDS Incidence and Death in Previous Paid Blood-Donated Population, Central China." *Chinese Journal of Preventive Medicine* 42.12: 906–10.

CHAPTER 7

Not a Zero-Sum Game

State–Society Interaction and Anti-Incinerator Campaigns in China

Szu-chien Hsu and Chin-chih Wang

Since 2009, there have been numerous campaigns to prevent the construction of waste incinerator plants in residential neighborhoods. These not-in-my-backyard protests have inspired debates on whether everyday citizens can have an effect on or even reverse policy decisions under authoritarian rule. Studies on anti-incinerator activism in China are often misleading, as they tend to focus on first-round interactions between protesters and local authorities, thereby overemphasizing the conflictual element of state–society interactions. Based on two anti-incinerator campaigns, in Asuwei, Beijing, and Panyu, Guangzhou, this chapter makes the following observations. First, an evolutionary analysis reveals that state–society interactions in anti-incinerator campaigns are not necessarily zero-sum in nature. Second, the strategies pursued by state and societal actors affect the outcome of their interactions. Third, policy discourse can be used as a tool to accommodate rather than overwhelm the other side. In summary, when initially contentious episodes are followed by appropriate interactions, state and societal actors in China may cooperate effectively in managing public governance issues.

According to a World Bank (2005) report, China replaced the United States in 2004 as the country creating the largest volume of municipal solid waste in the world. The report also estimated that the volume of municipal waste in China in 2030 will grow by 150 percent, compared with the volume in 2004. The explosive growth of municipal waste has resulted in a phenomenon that the Chinese media has called "cities besieged by waste." How to appropriately process waste created by rapid industrialization and urbanization has become a serious concern for many local governments in China. In 2007, the People's Republic of China (PRC) State Council published the "11th Five-Year National Guideline for the Construction of Innocuous Processing Facilities for Municipal Waste." The guidelines noted that because of the shortage of land in eastern China, landfills can no longer be used as the primary method for processing municipal waste. Therefore, incineration should be considered as an alternative. With such an explicit policy direction from the central government, many local governments began to build incinerators. This wave of construction was described by the Chinese media as the "Great Leap Forward of waste incineration" (*Caixin Online* 2012).

Given China's authoritarian context, there is little opportunity for democratic participation in which citizens can express their views on public governance issues, such as municipal waste management. Few local governments in China consulted with residents on construction plans for incinerators, and they did not inform residents of the potential risks once the incinerators came into operation. This set the background for waves of opposition against the incinerators across the country. Since 2006, when local residents organized a campaign opposing the construction of a waste incinerator in Beijing's Liulitun neighborhood, there have been 16 cases of anti-incinerator campaigns in China. Some of these campaigns successfully halted incinerator construction. Scholars of Chinese politics studying these cases have argued that it is possible for Chinese society to influence public policy. For example, Xiaoyun Chen noted that the anti-incinerator campaign in City G developed the strategy of "being organized without organization" by using the internet instead of homeowner associations as the platform for mobilization. The campaign was thus able to evade suppression by the authoritarian state apparatus (X. Chen 2012). Thomas Johnson compared the cases of Liulitun and Asuwei in Beijing and Panyu in Guangzhou. He argued that these three campaigns successfully stopped the construction of incinerators because the contenders raised an "alternative narrative" in "issue framing" and an alternative policy agenda to challenge government policies. Furthermore, the contenders elevated the discontent from local campaigns to policy advocacy oriented toward broader public interest and environmental protection. By doing so, they successfully avoided being labeled selfish. The contenders occupied the moral high ground and ownership of agenda-setting power and were thus able to force the government to yield (Johnson 2013). Graeme Lang and Ying Xu (2013) also compared the case of Liulitun in Beijing and Panyu in Guangzhou. Their explanation of the success of these campaigns stressed two factors: the connections of the contenders and the "political opportunity structure." Residents in Liulitun mobilized support from experts or environmental protection officials through personal connections, whereas those in Panyu attracted media attention because many journalists in the neighborhood were affected by the incinerator. Moreover, these incidents occurred against the background of two international events. The Beijing case occurred before the 2008 Olympic Games, and the Guangzhou case happened before the 2010 Asian Games. Pressure to maintain public order for governments in these cities was a key reason they were willing to yield (Lang and Xu 2013).

In terms of the policy process, Andrew Mertha (2009) observes that the nature of "fragmented authoritarianism" in China has changed. The original top-down and state-centered policy process is no longer the only sphere. Multiple bottom-up policy initiatives and influences at various levels and in the policy implementation process have effectively changed the contours of public policymaking in China. Malte Benjamins (2014) makes a similar argument in his study of Nangong's anti-incinerator campaign. He contends that although China maintains an authoritarian regime in terms of decisionmaking and actors outside the political system may not have substantial political power, they can influence policy implementation through building policy coalitions. In the case of Nangong, the campaigning nongovernmental organization (NGO) exerted pressure by lobbying a German bank to reconsider its investment in the incinerator construction project. Although these efforts did not succeed, the case demonstrates that except for framing and mobilizing the masses, social actors without political power can still influence the outcome of public policies by developing coalitions with those who have bargaining or veto power.

Previous studies have provided explanations from various theoretical perspectives, but some limitations remain. First, such studies have put considerable emphasis on the strategies and behavior of societal actors while treating the state as passive or responsive. Second, most analyses have presented a snapshot of events, lacking an evolutionary perspective on how and why different actors may adjust their strategies in the process of interaction. Third, studies have generally limited the dependent variable to a narrow scope, mostly regarding whether society was able to change the state's policy position. They tend to treat the relationship between the state and society as zero-sum at the beginning and end of their case. By contrast, we observe that when society can influence the state's policy position, the change may be more likely to result from cooperative interaction than sheer confrontation.

This chapter divides the evolutionary analysis into different stages, emphasizes the strategies adopted by each actor, and explains how the strategy of one party affected the strategy of the other. This interactive approach also highlights the strategies that led the other side to adopt a more cooperative position, which eventually affected the result of each case. The second and third sections analyze the cases of Beijing and Guangzhou, respectively. We conclude with a comparative discussion of the cases and their implications for understanding evolutionary governance in China's authoritarian regime.

The Case of Beijing

PHASE I: CONFLICTING CONTENTION

The Asuwei Municipal Waste General Processing Center is located one kilometer from Asuwei Village, Xiaotangshan town, Changping submunicipal district, Beijing municipality. It is a landfill center that processes the daily municipal waste from Beijing's Dongcheng and Xicheng districts and part of the daily municipal waste from Changping and Chaoyang districts. The quantity of municipal waste the center can process has increased from the original figure of 1,500 tons to nearly 7,000 tons currently. It is the largest waste processing center in Beijing, serving nearly 3.5 million people. Because the available space for landfill was almost exhausted by Beijing's fast-increasing municipal waste, the municipal government planned to build incinerators. However, the locations of planned incinerators were not fully disclosed to the public.

At the end of July 2009, a homeowner in the neighborhood of Asuwei found a public document titled "Public Disclosure of the Results of

Environmental Appraisal of the Beijing Asuwei Municipal Waste Incinerator and Power Plant Construction Project" pasted to the announcement wall of the Xiaotangshan town government headquarters. The homeowner soon spread the information online and through his personal social network. Once the information began to disseminate, many homeowners in communities near the construction spot mobilized to oppose the construction. First, they tried to contact the Xiaotangshan town government and inquired why residents in adjacent neighborhoods had not been informed and consulted before a decision was made on such a controversial and risky project. The town government did not respond to their inquiry. They then appealed to the Beijing Municipal Bureau of Environmental Protection. Bureau officials hinted to the residents that it would be of limited assistance given its absence of veto power over projects like the incinerator. After failing in their appeals to the government through institutional channels, the homeowners and residents decided to pursue "noninstitutional channels" (interview, January 2013). On August 1, 2009, homeowners around Xiaotangshan organized a demonstration with 58 cars. On each car, a banner carried the slogan, "Resolutely opposing the threat of dioxin." The cars drove around the area that could be potentially affected by future emissions. That evening, demonstrating homeowners received a call from the Xiaotangshan town magistrate expressing willingness to communicate and asking them to send 20 people to the town government to discuss the matter.

On August 2, officials from the Beijing Municipal Commission of City Administration and Environment (MCOCAE), the deputy magistrate of Changping district, leading township government cadres, and environmental appraisal experts from Tsinghua University all arrived to speak with the homeowner delegation. The homeowners raised questions and complained about the smell from the incinerator and lack of transparency in the environmental appraisal of the project. The government delegation responded to questions and promised to address the homeowners' concerns. After the meeting, the MCOCAE adopted measures to eliminate the smell, and the environmental appraisal report was published in the *Beijing Daily*. From the government's perspective, the officials had responded to the residents' demands. From the homeowners' perspective, the government merely addressed minor issues and did not address the question of whether the incinerator should be built.

When these homeowners realized that the government was not sincere in resolving their main concerns and the institutional channels of appeal were ineffective, they decided to organize another protest by taking advantage of the political opportunity provided by the 2009 Beijing Environment and Sanitation Exhibition. They planned to hold a public protest during the event, aiming to attract attention from higher-level government officials and the public. The homeowners were aware of the political risks in doing so. They followed the formal legal process by issuing a public petition to the police station according to the Law on Assemblies, Processions and Demonstrations passed in 1989. They clearly stated the purpose, time frame, location, marching route, and number of participants in their application. However, the police station was unwilling to formally receive their application or issue a document to explain why (interview, December 2011). Consequently, the homeowners once again used noninstitutional means to express their opinions. On September 4, more than 100 participants mobilized at the exposition, raising slogans such as "Opposing the construction of the Asuwei incinerator; protecting Beijing." The homeowners originally decided not to yell slogans to avoid disrupting the event, and by doing so, they expected that the government would not react negatively. However, they did not account for the political timing. Their protest took place around the 60th anniversary of the founding of the People's Republic on October 1. Because the timing was far more sensitive than the homeowners had expected, their action was immediately and ruthlessly shut down. More than a dozen demonstrators were arrested and detained, with others later subpoenaed.

PHASE 2: ENGAGING TRANSFORMATION

What became known as the September 4th incident represented the first turning point for the anti-incinerator campaign in Asuwei. Many participant homeowners withdrew from the campaign because of the political risks. For those who persisted, the incident led them to reflect on whether direct confrontation was an effective strategy. Frustrated by the futility of both institutional and noninstitutional methods, the homeowners began to consider a third way: reframing the issue. Reflecting on the campaign, they realized that simply opposing the incinerator construction was not a responsible position because it did not propose a solution to the problem of processing ever-increasing municipal waste. Realizing this, the homeowners altered their strategy from simply opposing the construction to finding policy alternatives.

Several homeowners organized a North Olympic Park Volunteer Team,[1] which began to collect information and materials regarding waste processing and policies within and beyond China. Based on the materials they collected and studies conducted on China's conditions, they authored a report on future waste policy titled "A Choice of Life and Death for the Environment of China's Cities: Waste Incineration Policy and Public Opinions" ("Life and Death" hereafter). The report argued that making incineration the only policy choice for processing municipal waste would inevitably lead to an ecological disaster because most of the incinerated waste in China is unsorted and incineration emits heavy pollutants, such as dioxin. The report suggested that waste processing should adopt a model of "mechanical biological treatment" plus "refuse-derived fuel" (RDF), in which a machine first sorts recyclable waste and then uses the remaining waste with a high calorific value for generating energy. The waste not suitable for burning could be transferred into organic fertilizers and used for replanting efforts in areas suffering from desertification near Beijing. The homeowners sent this report to relevant government ministries, departments, National People's Congress deputies, Chinese People's Political Consultative Conference representatives, and experts. They also tried to deliver the report to "high-level leaders" in government through personal connections (interview, January 2013). Although the report was not written by scientific experts, it proposed a credible alternative policy, and many specialists applauded its content. Nevertheless, the report did not affect the policy. In fact, the homeowners did not receive any response or feedback from government departments related to waste management policy.

Although the Beijing municipal government expended considerable effort in persuading the homeowners and the public, there was no sign of any yielding or change in the policy position. The Beijing municipal government established a provisionary reception office at Asuwei, with the deputy director of the MCOCAE Solid Waste Office in charge and responsible for answering residents' questions and receiving their opinions. In the eyes of the homeowners, such actions were merely designed to placate them, as their requests for serious dialogue with those proposing incineration and allowing a public tour of the incinerator power plant failed to receive any response. It seemed that the officials were only interested in delivering propaganda about the incinerator's construction with empty guarantees on its safety and no desire to have a meaningful dialogue (interview, January 2013). As one official put it, "For such propaganda and assurances to be effective, they must be conducted before any decision is made. If it is conducted after the residents go to the streets, then it is no more than empty words, because the trust is no longer there" (*China News Weekly* 2010).

At this point, the Beijing municipal government and the homeowners sought to persuade the other side to their position to allow a resolution to be negotiated. Despite the self-assumed responsible position of the government or the righteous position of the homeowners, lack of mutual trust prevented the sides from establishing an efficient communication channel.

PHASE 3: POLICY ENTREPRENEURS AND BUILDING MUTUAL TRUST

The deadlock was eventually broken because of a connection between two key figures: a leader of the homeowners, Huang Xiaoshan, and an expert in the MCOCAE Solid Waste Office, Wang Weiping. They were invited to a TV program to discuss waste incineration. Huang was invited as a representative of the anti-incineration camp and Wang as a representative of the local government (pro-incineration camp). Huang realized that the program presented an opportunity to build a bridge between the homeowners and the government. He exchanged contact information with Wang and invited him to an informal exchange of opinions with the residents of Asuwei. Wang accepted his invitation. Later, Wang visited Asuwei five or six times and handed the "Life and Death" report to the leading officials of the Beijing municipal government. Through this relationship, Huang acquired the opportunity to express the homeowners' opinion directly to MCOCAE officials (interview, December 2011). This interaction presented both sides with trustworthy "messengers" to finally overcome the lack of communication.

These interactions led to mutual trust, and both sides were ready for new thinking. In 2010, the MCOCAE organized a team to visit Japan and learn about municipal waste management. Following efforts by

Huang and Wang, the Beijing municipal government decided to invite Huang as a citizen representative to join the team. The government maintained that the homeowners opposed incineration because they lacked understanding of the technology underlying the process. Therefore, the government believed the best way to overcome such a misunderstanding was to allow the homeowners to personally visit an incinerator with advanced technology (interview, February 2013). After more than half a year of campaigning, the homeowners, including Huang, came to realize that they were not powerful enough to change the government's position with head-on confrontation. They needed opportunities for communication and compromise more than the government did. According to Huang, "As a resident of Asuwei, we have been bewildered, indignant, resistant, under demonstration and protest, and also made formal appeals to the government. But none of these turned out to be effective. On the issue of waste processing, we have come to realize that we have no choice but to develop a communicative channel with the government" (*Jinhua Daily* 2010a).

Huang was already thinking ahead. After the trip to Japan, he believed it would be quite unlikely for the government to press ahead with constructing the incinerators, disregarding the homeowners' opinions, because his cooption into the group had been well publicized and the government had been depicted by media reports as "open minded" and "willing to accommodate society's opinions" (interview, December 2011).

The group left on February 20, 2010, and spent 10 days visiting incinerators and relevant facilities in Japan and Macau. In planning the trip, the government and Huang focused on the opportunity to learn technical skills; however, they approached it from different viewpoints. The government argued that incineration technology was now mature and widespread among other countries; thus, as long as it operated according to the regulations, there would be no risk of contamination or other inconvenience for residents. The government hoped the trip would be educational and cause the residents and wider public to correct their misconceptions and prejudice toward the project (interview, February 2013). By contrast, Huang emphasized that visiting more advanced countries provided an opportunity to examine how they had adopted alternative methods for processing waste. The Asuwei homeowners in the "Life and Death" report advocated the use of alternative techniques, such as RDF, and firmly opposed the incineration of unsorted waste. As Huang admitted, the main purpose of the trip in his mind was to observe how advanced alternative techniques, such as RDF, were applied in other countries (*Beijing News* 2010a).

In hindsight, despite the remaining differences, we can see that the positions of the homeowners and government had already moved closer before the trip, and both were focused on the technical aspects of waste processing rather than irreconcilable positions for or against incineration. This change can be seen as a compromise that the sides reached on the basis of the trust they developed through mutual interaction inspired by Huang and Wang as policy entrepreneurs.

PHASE 4: STATE–SOCIETY COOPERATION

During the trip, Huang was deeply impressed by the efficiency and strictness of waste sorting in Japan, which led him to reflect on whether the original strategy of emphasizing the end stage of waste processing was appropriate. He began to believe that the earlier stage, sorting, is what required emphasis. In his own words,

> I firmly opposed incineration before the trip. But after the trip, I came to the understanding that technologies such as landfill, incineration, vaporization, anaerobic fermentation, or even RDF are really not the key. What is most important is completely sorting the waste before it goes to the later stage. (*Beijing News* 2010c)

> If waste sorting is well implemented in the early stages, even if incineration is later adopted, it would not be such a worry for us. If we can process the waste and build the incinerator like the one in Japan, I am willing to live next to the incinerator plant. (*China News Weekly* 2010)

> We should focus on—and the government should turn its financial weight behind—the early and middle stages of waste processing. (*Beijing News* 2010b)

Huang came to the following conclusion from his trip: "no waste sorting, no waste incineration." He turned from an "opponent of incineration" to a "conditional advocate for waste incineration" (interview, December 2011). The trip thus marked the second turning point of the

Asuwei anti-incineration campaign. Huang had changed his view. The government also changed its perspective. When he put forth his new principle of "no waste sorting, no waste incineration," the government was unable to raise an objection. They were unable to refute the argument that minimizing the quantity of waste at the early and middle stages was much more important than the final stage. Huang's new line of discourse seized the moral high ground. Furthermore, as he had repeatedly praised the government in the press as "open minded" and "willing to listen to the people's voice," giving the government a positive public image (*Beijing News* 2010d; *Jinhua Daily* 2010c), the government found itself in a position where openly objecting to reasonable positions was untenable. This strategy is described by the Chinese saying "wearing a tall hat" (*daigaomao* 戴高帽), which means to use kind words and flattery to ingratiate oneself with others.

Huang not only put a high hat on the government's head, he also took concrete action to make the hat more robust. He was determined that his proposal for sorting waste would not just be an abstract idea; it required concrete actions. Huang and other homeowners in Asuwei organized the Asuwei Waste Sorting Committee, which experimented with various waste-sorting methods in the community to test their feasibility (fig. 7.1). They did not limit their activity to social advocacy. Huang invited Wang and other MCOCAE officials, including the deputy director of the Solid Waste Office. These officials expressed willingness to assist the waste-sorting experiment with beneficial policy, financial, and technical support. Huang also invited the press to cover the government officials' visit, and he prepared a question-and-answer session for the officials (interview, January 2013). Thus, the image of the Beijing municipal government as open-minded and willing to listen to the people was amplified once again in the press. At the event, when asked by media members, Deng Jun, the deputy director of the Solid Waste Office, commented that if the quantity of waste could be effectively minimized by sorting at the community level, then the necessity of building more incinerators could be reconsidered (*Jinhua Daily* 2010b).

Through such interactions, the Asuwei homeowners were able to obtain access to the landfill plant near them and other waste-processing facilities, such as the Gaoantun Incineration Power Plant and Nangong

FIGURE 7.1 Huang Xiaoshan started a waste-sorting station called "The Green House" at Napa Valley community and put up a sign thanking the Beijing government for its help
Source: Photo by author.

Waste Processing Plant. Although these exchanges did not imply that the government had changed its policy position, they were definitely a significant change from the previous confrontation to cooperation. In the process of these interactions, the government gradually came to accept that the homeowners were not simply a group of recalcitrant residents but a group of citizens defending their rights on justified grounds. Their proposals were constructive and helpful. Likewise, the homeowners, through interaction and communication with governmental officials, came to gradually understand that the government was under tremendous pressure to solve the problem presented by waste processing and that these officials were not intending to wreak havoc on citizens' lives.

The Case of Guangzhou

The anti-incinerator campaign in Panyu, Guangzhou, was a tug of war that began with media reports. September 23, 2009, as with every 23rd day of the month, was the official day on which the Guangzhou municipal government received citizens' petitions. Officials, including the mayor, district magistrate, and bureau chief, all gathered to publicly receive the visiting public and answer journalists' questions. The Environment Protection and Sanitation Bureau chief and the Garden and Forestry Bureau chief were asked by journalists whether an incinerator was going to be built in Huijiang village of Dashi subdistrict, Panyu district. One chief replied that although the project was still under environmental appraisal, part of the land had already been allocated, and they hoped for construction to start on October 1. The other chief replied that worries regarding dioxin emissions were baseless and unnecessary. However, the chiefs had not realized that the press had already prepared a report before interviewing them, and their remarks were the finishing touches (interview, August 2011). The next day, their comments led the headlines on the front page of the newspaper. The report inspired other news organizations around the country to follow the story and led to a series of mass campaigns for opposing the incinerator construction.

Before the press reported the story, the message that the incinerator was about to be built had already spread among the homeowners in neighboring communities, but relatively little attention was paid to it. One reason the press focused on the story was that many journalists lived in communities adjacent to the construction location. This personal interest later played a critical role and became an important distinction that differentiated the anti-incinerator campaign in Panyu from the case in Asuwei.

PHASE I: STATE–SOCIETY INTERACTION THROUGH THE MEDIA

When this story was made public by the media, homeowners in Panyu near the planned incinerator location began a series of campaigns opposing construction. The homeowners created anti-incineration fliers and distributed them in the densely populated areas of Panyu district. At the same time, they took the opportunity to explain to the public the potential risks and hazards to the environment and public health that could be caused by the incinerator. In some communities, the homeowners collected residents' signatures opposing the construction before sending them to the relevant government bureau. The homeowners organized a team to investigate and study the Likeng Incinerator in Guangzhou's Baiyun district, which had earned the title of "Guangdong Provincial Outstanding Model Project." Ironically, they found that the residents near the Likeng Incinerator were deeply troubled by the smell emanating from this "model project." According to local residents, a growing number of villagers were diagnosed with cancer following the commencement of the incinerator's operations. These findings were published by a community blogger on the internet and stimulated heated discussion among Panyu homeowners. They came up with an anti-incineration slogan: "The Likeng of yesterday shall become the Panyu of tomorrow." The Panyu homeowners, much like their Beijing counterparts, expressed their opinions to the government through regular official channels by visiting the petitions office or calling the government's complaint numbers.

What made the case in Guangzhou different from that in Beijing was not the government reaction but the positive media coverage by almost all the major newspapers in Guangzhou. Compared with anti-incineration campaigns elsewhere, the media coverage and attention in Guangzhou was exceptional. One reason for this was that many journalists and media workers lived in communities near the planned location for the incinerator at Panyu. Another important factor was the fiercely competitive media market in Guangzhou. Any event that related to local residents' interests and caused conflict between the public and government was made into a big story to increase newspaper sales, website traffic, and television viewing rates, thereby bringing in more advertisement income (H. Chen 2000). In Guangzhou, three newspapers were listed among the top 100 in the world in terms or circulation volume (*People's Daily Online* 2010), of which the *Nanfang Dushibao* (南方都市报) and *Xinkuai Bao* (新快报) are the two largest and compete intensely with one another. Even the local state newspaper, *Guangzhou Daily* (广州日报), is much livelier than other state newspapers in terms of its relatively liberal and open style.

At the start of the Panyu campaign, the homeowners wished to raise three major questions with the government. First, according to the Law on Environmental Impacts Appraisal, passed in 2002, a construction project cannot be started before an appraisal report is approved. The homeowners wanted to know why the government embarked on construction before an environmental appraisal was completed. Second, they requested the criteria on which the government chose the location for the incinerator. The government chose to build the incinerator at the original location of the landfill to save on land requisition, but the government did not consider "environmental capacity," particularly when the location was in a densely populated area. Third, they sought clarification on whether incineration was the optimal method for processing municipal waste. Given public suspicion of the risks of incineration and the lack of efficient supervision, homeowners believed that the government should have implemented waste sorting and recycling before pushing ahead with incineration.

Facing these questions, the Guangzhou municipal government did not respond until a month later at a press conference on October 30. Government officials provided the following responses. First, the government changed its position by promising that the construction of the incinerator would not start before the environmental appraisal was completed, and they promised that the government would not initiate a project that caused pollution. Second, regarding the location, they stated that because of the shortage of land appropriate for such a project, the existing location was the only one that could satisfy various conditions. Third, in terms of potential risks, the government invited four experts on incineration to endorse the plan, who said the technology was mature and could control dioxin emission. One expert even noted that dioxins emitted by barbecues are 1,000 times higher than those emitted by waste incineration and that the public should not act irrationally.

This press conference failed to assuage public suspicion of the project. First, the government did not invite any homeowners or journalists as representatives of the local community to participate. Access for other members of the press was strictly controlled. Thus, the government's explanation at the conference already seemed to lack fairness and transparency. Second, the press conference only conveyed one-way messages. Everything said was to endorse the official position and defend the security of the project. The lack of trust between the local communities and government rendered the event useless as a propaganda effort. The public perceived that it was not a genuine attempt to explain the project's safety, but an attempt to avoid challenges to the government's decision (*New Express Daily* 2009a).

The Beijing municipal government established a working station in the Asuwei community to receive residents' complaints and communicate with homeowners. By contrast, the Panyu district government believed such efforts were unnecessary because a public consultation was held in the process of the environment appraisal. This decision to avoid communication and contact with residents later proved to be a mistake.

The homeowners discovered that the South China Institute of Environmental Sciences, which was responsible for the environmental appraisal, had conducted appraisals for numerous incinerators in Guangdong province but each appraisal led to the same result: approval (*New Express Daily* 2009b). Thus, the public consultation process in the environmental appraisal seemed to be worthless. One article in the local press reported,

> The Guangzhou municipal government never seriously considered the "legitimacy crisis" that the incinerator project is facing. Instead, all the efforts the government has made are merely superficial responses to public suspicion. . . . The government was very clear in telling the public that the problem shall be resolved by the environmental appraisal, which the public does not trust. The rational moves of Panyu residents to defend their

rights turned out to have no chance of a resolution within the established institutions. (*New Express Daily* 2009c)

The mistrust that already existed between society and the government was amplified, and grievances grew following the ill-conceived press conference. Further aggravation soon followed. The Provincial Information Survey Research Center of Guangdong province published a report, the "Public Opinion Research Report on the Panyu Incinerator Project" ("Public Opinion Research Report" hereafter) on December 5, 2009. This report revealed the following. First, out of a valid sample of 1,550 respondents, 96.2 percent of interviewees were aware of the project. Second, 97.3 percent were not satisfied with the government's disclosure of relevant public information in handling the case. Third, 98.3 percent did not trust the government's guarantee that the incinerator would emit a minimal volume of dioxins and would not affect the life and health of nearby residents. Fourth, 83.9 percent of interviewees believed the environmental appraisal should not be approved. If passed, only 1.5 percent would trust the result. Last, 97.1 percent of interviewees objected to the construction of the incinerator (*Express Daily* 2009). However, on the same day, the official newspaper of the Panyu Communist Party Committee, *Panyu Daily* (2009), published an article titled "Construction of the Incinerator Power Plant Is a Project to Win the Heart of the Masses." The article said more than 70 representatives of the Panyu People's Congress expressed that the local consensus was that Panyu's waste should be processed within Panyu, and that they ardently supported the government speeding up construction.

PHASE 2: DISCONTENT DUE TO INADEQUATE STATE–SOCIETY COMMUNICATION

Because its original position of a "harmless project" was unconvincing, the government changed its position to emphasizing that Panyu had an obligation to process its own waste, and hinting that those who opposed incineration were irresponsible and held a not-in-my-backyard mentality, whereas the government was maintaining a responsible position (*Yangcheng Evening News* 2009). On this basis, the government argued that building the incinerator was not up for debate, although the location could be discussed.

On December 22, 2009, the Guangzhou municipal government held a second press conference on the incinerator issue. Lu Zhiyi, the deputy secretary general of the municipal government, claimed that the incinerator would adopt high technological standards that would not harm the environment or residents' health. He maintained that residents had panicked and objected irrationally because they did not have comprehensive information and had been misled by the media. Regarding waste sorting and recycling, Lu said the idea could reduce the volume of waste but it could not solve the processing problem; thus, incineration was inevitable. Replacing incineration with sorting and recycling was a "utopian" proposal. When a reporter asked him about the 97.1 percent of residents who objected to the construction according to the "Public Opinion Research Report," Lu responded that he had not read the report, but the environmental appraisal had its own process of public consultation that was more comprehensive than a survey. The conference concluded with officials affirming that because of the shortage of land and in support of central policy, the Guangzhou municipal government would firmly push ahead with incinerator construction, not only in Panyu but also in Conghua, Zengcheng, and Huadu.

The press conference not only failed to engage in dialogue with the opposing camp, it ignored objective public opinion and accused those opposed to the project of being underinformed and irrational. This seemingly arrogant and bureaucratic attitude infuriated opponents, who were mostly of the urban middle class. The day after the press conference, November 23, was once again the day petitions were accepted by the Guangzhou Municipal Commission of City Administration (GMCCA). Frustrated Panyu residents mobilized each other through phone calls, text messages, and online, resulting in more than 1,000 Panyu residents arriving before 9:00 a.m. in front of the GMCCA that day. Because the process of receiving the petitioners was slow, many Panyu residents collectively moved from the GMCCA building toward the municipal government building. In the process, the residents raised banners reading, "Oppose the incinerator, protect green Guangzhou," "Respect public opinion," "Officials should come and talk to the masses," and "Request for dialogue." The Panyu residents were restrained in their actions and had no confrontations with law enforcement. When they arrived at the municipality government building, the officials asked for five representatives of the residents to come inside for dialogue; however, this request was rejected. At that moment, the gathered residents shouted a line that came to represent their whole campaign: "We don't want to be represented!" The masses gathered in front of the government building until around 2:30 p.m. before gradually dissipating. The incident ended peacefully. It was reported that not even one piece of waste was left at the protest site.

News of the November 23 incident aroused national curiosity. Many national media and press publications from other provinces sent journalists to Guangzhou to follow the event and report on its background. The Panyu residents who made their way to the municipal government before peacefully dissipating were characterized as "rational citizens." The media interest soon meant the incident drew the attention of the central government. This created tremendous pressure on the Guangzhou municipal government (interview, September 2011).[2]

Two press reports further aggravated their already awkward position. The first was a report in the *Xikuaibao* (2009), stating that on December 2, 2009, a relative of Lu Zhiyi was working at the Guangri Corporation. Two days later, a second piece published in the *Nanfang Dushibao* (2009b) disclosed that the Guangri Corporation, which specialized in manufacturing elevators, had acquired the franchise from the government to process the municipal waste of Guangzhou without public bidding. More shocking still, the car that the GMCCA leader drove was provided by the Guangri Corporation (*Nanfang Dushibao* 2009a). All these reports alluded to a corrupt relationship between the Guangzhou municipal government and Guangri Corporation. This suspicion had a serious negative effect on the already shaky trust the public had in the local government.

Under pressure, the Panyu district government announced that the construction and location selection for the incinerator were to be deferred until after the Asian Games in November 2010, and public consultations on waste processing locations commenced. This public announcement did not provide the Panyu homeowners with much relief. A leader of the Panyu homeowners, Luo Jianming (known as Basuo Fengyun online, Basuo hereafter), invited the Panyu District Party Secretary Tan Yinghua for a face-to-face conversation with other homeowners in the Riverside Garden Community. After the press reported on the invitation, Tan accepted and met the homeowners. During the meeting, Tan publicly declared that the construction of the incinerator had been "formally suspended." The anti-incinerator campaign had "won" the first stage.

PHASE 3: DEEPENED ESTRANGEMENT

This victory was followed by a long period of cooling relations between residents and the local government. Although residents had opportunities for face-to-face meetings with officials, a lack of sincere dialogue remained. Learning from the Beijing case, the Guangzhou municipal government invited two leaders of the anti-incinerator camp on an overseas study trip together with government officials, but genuine mutual trust was not developed between officials and Panyu homeowners.[3]

One reason for this was that the Guangzhou municipal government continued to exclude homeowners from the decisionmaking process. In a public online event held by the government in January 2010 titled, "Asking the People for Strategies to Manage Municipal Waste in Guangzhou," the Panyu homeowners, despite being major stakeholders, were treated like ordinary netizens; thus, their opinions were diluted. Furthermore, the expert consultation meeting held by the government in February was not open to the public. The Panyu homeowners only learned about the consultation from the media after its conclusion, which is also when they learned about its final decision: incineration was to be the primary method of waste processing in Guangzhou, and the secondary method would be landfill.

Responding to this detached government attitude, the Panyu homeowners often reacted provocatively. One example is Basuo, who, to remind the government of the urgency of the matter, went to the GMCCA to personally present an official with a gift: a clock.[4] Such moves may have earned campaigners column inches and airtime, but they were not helpful when it came to building trust with government officials (interview, August 2011).[5] When the GMCCA chose the Riverside Garden Community (fig. 7.2) as the testing point for municipal waste sorting and recycling, the homeowners were not informed by the government. Although the homeowners had already been conducting waste sorting in the community for more than a year before the GMCCA announcement, this event indicated how strained the relationship between the local government and homeowners had become (interview, August 2011).

FIGURE 7.2 Basuo and other Panyu homeowners conducted a waste-sorting project at Riverside Garden Community
Source: Photo by author.

The only substantial interactions between the Panyu homeowners and government were on the 23rd of each month, when the government accepted petitions. Following the November 23rd incident, the government never took the initiative to contact or consult with the Panyu homeowners on anything related to the incinerator project. When the Guangzhou municipal government decided to restart the incinerator construction and announced that the government would choose from among the five possible locations on April 4, 2011, the Panyu homeowners once again only heard the news through media reports. The government publicized various channels for citizens to express their opinions and suggestions on the location, including a phone number, website, email address, and mailing address, but these channels were unidirectional. No mechanism existed for direct two-way communication between societal actors and the state. The government seemed unwilling to engage in direct dialogue with its opponents.

Guangzhou has often been praised as one of the most open cities in China, and its government's attitude toward different voices in the society is also seen as among the most accommodating and tolerant. However, in handling the anti-incinerator campaign, the government appeared to be exceptionally inflexible and bureaucratic. The reasons for this can be found in the pattern of interaction between state and society. In the process of interaction, Panyu homeowners formed a tacit coalition with the media. Homeowners relied on the media to provide a platform for their opinions to earn public sympathy and support, usually by revealing the stubbornness and self-assuming attitude of the Guangzhou government. The media, in turn, wanted the Panyu homeowners to be confrontational and challenging, which meant their reports could be more sensational and attractive in the fiercely competitive Guangzhou market. Such a coalition is naturally likely to alienate the government, because it relies on depicting the government as arrogant and careless. Consequently, the government intentionally maintained its distance from society.

PHASE 4: POLICY ENTREPRENEUR
BREAKS THE DEADLOCK

Deadlock persisted between the government and the homeowners until a new mayor of Guangzhou, Chen Jianhua, was appointed in 2012. Chen had no personal history with either the existing bureaucracy or the homeowners.

This allowed him much wider space for negotiation. In May 2012, he held a symposium on the waste processing work. Experts were invited to provide officials with lessons on waste sorting and recycling. The symposium concluded that the basic principle of incineration as the primary method and landfill as the second remained unchanged, but it would be supplemented with a new working guideline of "sorting, recycling, and decreasing waste volume first; then innocuous incineration, landfill, or biochemical processing." Several days later, Chen held another symposium, titled "Inquiring about the Needs of the People, Their Suggestions on Policy, and Their Ideas on Strategy." Thirteen citizen representatives were invited, including three major leaders of the homeowners' campaign. With Chen offering an olive branch, the symposium finally marked the beginning of a sincere dialogue between the state and society on the incinerator project. Chen transformed the previously passive position of the government by taking the initiative to invite the media for interviews (*Guangzhou Daily* 2012). The *Nanfang Dushibao* and the *Guangzhou Daily* both opened new columns titled "A Message to the Mayor" and "Inviting New Strategies for Managing Waste," respectively. Under Chen, the media had become an instrument for government propaganda.

Chen changed not only the relationship with the media but also the content of the government's policy discourse. Previously, the government tended to demand that Panyu citizens "give up individual interests for the sake of public interests." He turned this position, with its strong hierarchical tone, into a more magnanimous one. The new discourse stressed that although processing municipal waste was the obligation of the government, they nevertheless wanted the cooperation and assistance of society and its citizens. The mayor created a new slogan: "Sell what can be sold; separate the noxious; and divide the dry from the wet." The new discourse freed both sides from the zero-sum game and created a cooperative space for both. With this change, the government was ready to work more constructively with Panyu's homeowners.

On July 10, 2012, the Guangzhou municipal government held a high-profile public event called "Mobilization and Task-Deployment Rally for Managing Municipal Waste" (hereafter, the "mobilization rally"). The government urged citizens to join "people's warfare" on municipal waste management and vowed "to resolutely conduct the policy of waste sorting and recycling to make Guangzhou a model city of waste processing." During the mobilization rally, Chen deployed "responsibility command" to five districts (Panyu, Huadu, Conghua, Zengcheng, and Nansha), demanding that they solve the matter of waste processing together by using methods that were most appropriate for their situation. For old districts with a shortage of space for processing facilities, such as Yuexiu and Haizhu, the main task was waste sorting and recycling. For Luogang and Baiyun, which had more space available, the task was constructing waste-processing facilities to help other districts (*Nanfang Daily* 2012a). On the same day, Chen announced that four incinerator power plants in Panyu, Huadu, Zengcheng, and Conghua would commence construction within a year (*Nanfang Daily* 2012b). In short, Chen adopted a double-handed strategy. Although he vowed to adopt waste sorting and recycling, he was also unequivocal about moving ahead with the construction of the incinerator.

Although opposition to the incinerator construction was ultimately not accepted by the government, the anti-incinerator campaign cannot be described as a failure. The location of the incinerator in Panyu was eventually moved in a much more remote area, and with Chen's leadership as a policy entrepreneur, in 2012 Guangzhou started conducting municipality-wide waste sorting and recycling. Guangzhou represents the first local government in China to formally make waste sorting and recycling a governmental policy.

Despite the fact that Chen pushed ahead with the incinerator construction, there was little opposition from society. By accepting the waste sorting and recycling agenda originally proposed by the Panyu homeowners, he deprived them of the moral base for further contention. Chen even went further to incorporate previous opposition. He established a Supervision and Advisory Committee on the Management of Municipal Solid Waste and invited several of the original Panyu homeowner leaders (among them Basuo), journalists, and experts to sit on it. The committee serves as a formal platform for both criticism and constructive suggestions to be articulated and heard by the government. Furthermore, the government allowed Basuo to register a social organization and subcontracted the new organization for a project studying the progress and impediments to waste sorting and recycling in Guangzhou.

Conclusion: Comparative Discussion

Since 2012, the two cases described in this chapter have undergone notable changes because the policy entrepreneurs involved are from markedly different backgrounds. Chen Jianhua retired from his role as the mayor of Guangzhou in 2016, but his policies regarding waste processing have not been drastically altered by his successor. However, Chen's double-handed strategy of promoting waste sorting and recycling alongside incinerator construction can only be considered a partial success: the incinerators have been built, but the waste sorting and recycling targets are behind schedule.

In contrast to Chen, Asuwei's Huang Xiaoshan had no official position; thus, his ability to influence policymaking came from framing issues and getting media attention. Once other news events drew the public's attention, Huang lost his leverage against the Beijing municipal government. Consequently, construction of the Asuwei incineration plant resumed in 2015. The only difference lay in the project's name: they removed the word "incineration" from the project's title, which is now the Asuwei Circular Economy Park. As Mertha (2008) has observed, social actors in China need media coverage for leverage to alter policy decisions. Once media loses interest in particular cases, the government is likely to withdraw earlier compromises.

Comparing these two cases from an evolutionary governance perspective sheds light on the interaction between state and society in anti-incinerator campaigns in China. Unlike previous studies, this analysis did not use a zero-sum perspective to examine state–society relations. Instead, it found that after initial confrontation between state and society, without a state or societal actor able to break the deadlock, neither side could be victorious, producing a lose-lose result.

However, because there is no institutional basis for building trust between state and society, extra effort is required to form relationships between the sides. For state and society to develop a cooperative relationship, there needs to be mutual trust. Two factors are highlighted in the examined cases that allow for such a development: gradual informal interactions and the role of policy entrepreneurs. Regarding the interactive process, the case in Beijing was more successful than the one in Guangzhou. Through TV appearances and participation in a government-sponsored overseas study visit, Huang Xiaoshan was able to gradually develop trust with the Beijing municipal government official, Wang Weiping. Through this personal connection, the two sides were able to establish a cooperative relationship. By comparison, in Guangzhou several opportunities for interaction between state and societal actors were organized, but the two sides were unable to develop trust. The Panyu homeowners' use of the media to criticize the government meant that the relationship was difficult to repair. In Beijing, the policy entrepreneur was a societal actor, homeowner leader Huang Xiaoshan, whereas in Guangzhou, it was a government actor, Mayor Chen Jianhua.

This chapter differs from previous literature in another way: emphasis on interaction. This analysis emphasized how the strategies and behaviors of state and society result from interaction. For example, in the Beijing case, because Huang used the media to put a "high hat" on the government—that is, deliberately casting the government in a positive light—it was lured into a more cooperative position. By contrast, when homeowner leaders and the media in Guangdong cast the government in a negative light, it became reluctant to interact with the local community. Similarly, when Chen incorporated waste sorting and recycling into his policy agenda, the original opposing Panyu homeowners not only lessened their opposition to the mayor's policy of building incinerators in remote locations but became willing to cooperate with the government by conducting subcontracted research tasks.

This chapter also emphasizes the importance of policy discourse. This is similar to the framing argument, but the difference is that it is not about discontent or campaigns per se, but about how each side interacts with the other party. In these cases, successful discourse had the following characteristics. First, it not only appealed to the public interest, it also created a constructive position or a positive image for the other side. Second, it neither negated nor rejected the position of the other side, but tried to incorporate it. Third, the actor, be it state or society, usually presented the new discourse to the media and allowed the media to amplify it to the public; through this, they claimed the moral high ground and an advantageous position over the other side. However, the actor must first develop informal interactions with the opposition to develop a cooperative and non-zero-sum relationship prior to media interaction.

Under an authoritarian system, such as that in China, trust between the state and society is vulnerable by default. Much of the comparative politics literature posits that discontent in society against the state can send signals to the regime to execute a crackdown. Even so, this study shows that discontent, if followed by appropriate interaction, can also facilitate dialogue that alleviates mutual suspicion between state and society, creating opportunities for both sides to cooperate on public governance issues.

According to the volume's four dimensions of governance (responsiveness, transparency, input channels, and societal empowerment), the behavioral patterns of state actors in these two cases are very similar. Local authorities in Beijing and Guangzhou eventually responded to demands from local residents and tried to make the decisionmaking process more transparent to society, but they also showed no interest in empowering the social actors as partners of co-governance. There is one important difference between the cases, which is the policy entrepreneur in Guangzhou. Mayor Chen Jianhua established the Supervision and Advisory Committee on the Management of Municipal Solid Waste as a temporary input channel. This did not occur in Beijing because Huang Xiaoshan lacked official power to initiate such a platform.

However, the positive state–society interactions observed in both cases have not diffused in China since Xi Jinping assumed leadership in 2012. On June 28, 2019, another anti–incinerating plant demonstration began in Wuhan, Hubei, causing serious and violent confrontations between thousands of protesting citizens and riot police for several days. In the Wuhan case, we have not observed multiple phases of interaction as in Asuwei and Panyu. Instead, the state relied on surveillance technology and coercion to end the protest. Apparently, the regime under Xi's leadership would rather take unilateral state actions than consult with societal stakeholders to solve the problems. Meanwhile, most of the channels facilitating communication between officials and citizens, such as media and NGOs, have faced much tighter control or suffered from suppression since 2012. Compared with Hu Jintao's era, China has shifted away from interactive governance to the exercise of the party-state's despotic power.

Unfortunately, when the novel coronavirus (COVID-19) disease erupted in Wuhan at the end of 2019, the rigid responses of Chinese central and local authorities revealed serious governance problems as a result of such a shift away from interactive governance.

Notes

1. Asuwei is located at the north of some Beijing Olympics facilities, like the Bird's Nest and Water Cube, and this area is also called "Aobei," which in Chinese means "north of the Olympics."

2. According to the interview, the central government had received the internal reference reports about 11:23 on the day, but they didn't intervene or press when the Guangzhou government tried to fix the problem. Interview, Guangzhou, September 5, 2011.

3. Protesters defined this campaign as "everyone only represents themselves" and "without organization but with disincline," so they agreed this was a campaign without a leader. However, there were some "star homeowners" on media, like Basuo, Yingtaobai (樱桃白), and Ajiaxi (阿加西).

4. "Presenting people a clock as a gift" in Chinese is homophonous with "bidding someone farewell in a funeral."

5. Some homeowners thought "presenting a clock" (*song zhong* 送钟), as a kind of performance art, was not helpful for building a reliable relationship with the government, because it made the official look bad. Interview, Guangzhou, August 25, 2011.

References

Beijing News. 2010a. "Xiangkan riben shimin zenme dao lese" (Want to see how Japanese citizens dump their garbage). *Beijing News*, February 21. http://epaper.bjnews.com .cn/html/2010-02/21/content_67728.htm?div=-1.

———. 2010b. "Kaocha riji: lesechuli zhongzai qianduan" (Investigation diary: front-end process is the key of waste disposal). *Beijing News*, February 28. http://epaper .bjnews.com.cn/html/2010-02/28/content_70079.htm?div=-1.

———. 2010c. "Kaochatuan 'chizhong' guilai guanyuan chuyan jinshen" (Officials spoke cautiously after the investigation). *Beijing News*, March 4. http://epaper.bjnews .com.cn/html/2010-03/04/content_71731.htm?div=-1.

———. 2010d. "Asuwei jumin yanjing de zhengfu zhuanbian" (Changes of the government in the eyes of Asuwei residents). *Beijing News*, March 10. http://epaper.bjnews .com.cn/html/2010-03/10/content_74008.htm?div=-1.

Benjamins, Malte P. 2014. "International Actors in NIMBY Controversies: Obstacle or Opportunity for Environmental Campaigns?" *China Information* 28.3: 338–61.

Caixin Online. 2012. "Lese fenshao dayuejin" (The Great Leap Forward of incineration). *Caixin Online*, June 6.

Chen, Huai-lin. 2000. "Shixi zhonguo meiti zhidu de jianjin gaige: yi baoye wei anli" (An analysis of gradual progress of media institution reform in China: Using the newspaper industry as an example). *Xinwensxue Yanjiu* (*Mass Communication Research*) 62: 97–118.

Chen, Xiaoyun. 2012. "Quzuzhihua: Yezhu jiti xingdong de celüe: Yi Guangzhoushi fandui lese fenshaochang jianshe shijian weili" (Disorganize: the strategy of homeowners' collective activism: a survey of the anti-incinerator action in Guangzhou). *Gonggong Guanli Xuebao* (*Journal of Public Management*) 9.2: 67–75.

China News Weekly. 2010. "Asuwei de lese canzhengzhe" (Political participants of waste in Asuwei). *China News Weekly*, March 19. http://big5.chinanews.com:89/gn/news /2010/03-19/2180324.shtml.

Express Daily. 2009. "Shengqing diaoyan zhongxin fabu lese fenshaochang diaocha baogao" (Provincial Situation Survey Research Center publicized the research report of the incineration plant). *Express Daily*, November 5. http://news.xkb.com.cn /guangzhou/2009/1105/22491.html. =

Guangzhou Daily. 2012. "Lese chuli quancheng douke yangguang yunxing" (Making waste disposal known to the public). *Guangzhou Daily*, May 23. http://gzdaily.dayoo .com/html/2012-05/23/content_1711772.htm.

Jinghua Daily. 2010a. "Asuwei jumin qu Riben kaocha lesechuli" (The Asuwei resident visit Japan to investigate waste disposal). *Jinghua Daily*, February 22. http://epaper .jinghua.cn/html/2010-02/22/content_519767.htm. Accessed April 6, 2015.

———. 2010b. "'Lushihdan' bei jumin zhiyi yuezudaipao" ("Lushihdan" was called in question by Asuwei residents). *Jinghua Daily*, March 22. http://epaper.jinghua.cn/html /2010-03/22/content_529791.htm.

———. 2010c. "Lese weicheng xia de fenshao tuwei" (Incineration making breakthrough in front of the city besieged by waste). *Jinghua Daily*, June 27. http://big5 .xinhuanet.com/gate/big5/news.xinhuanet.com/politics/2010-06/27/c_12267639 .htm.

Johnson, Thomas. 2013. "The Health Factor in Anti-Waste Incinerator Campaigns in Beijing and Guangzhou." *China Quarterly* 214 (June): 356–75.

Lang, Graeme, and Ying Xu. 2013. "Anti-Incinerator Campaigns and the Evolution of Protest Politics in China." *Environmental Politics* 22.5: 832–48.

Mertha, Andrew. 2008. *China's Water Warriors: Citizen Action and Policy Change*. Ithaca, NY: Cornell University Press.

———. 2009. "Fragmented Authoritarianism 2.0: Political Pluralization in the Chinese Policy Process." *China Quarterly* 200: 995–1012.

Nanfang Daily. 2012a. "Quancheng zhanlese gequ lingrenwu" (All districts have their tasks on the battle to garbage). *Nanfang Daily*, July 11. http://epaper.southcn.com /nfdaily/html/2012-07/11/content_7103017.htm.

———. 2012b. "Panyu Huadu Zengcheng Conghua sizuo fenshaochang niandi qiandong gong" (Panyu, Huadu, Zengcheng and Conghua, four districts will build their own incinerator in the end of the year). *Nanfang Daily*, July 11. http://epaper.southcn .com/nfdaily/html/2012-07/11/content_7103016.htm.

Nanfang Dushibao. 2009a. "Yuan huanweiju fujuzhang zuojia jie Guangri jituan de" (Ex-chief of the Environmental Sanitation Bureau borrowed a car from Guangri).

Nanfang Dushibao, December 4. http://www.360doc.com/content/09/1204/11/142
_10335778.shtml.

———. 2009b. "Zuodianti de Guangri jituan ruhe jinjun lese chuli chanye de?" (How
Guangri, an elevator manufacture company, can march to the waste disposal industry?). *Nanfang Dushibao*, December 4. http://nf.nfdaily.cn/nfdsb/content/2009-12/04
/content_6824089.htm.

———. 2009c. "Guangri jituan youshi ruhe qude lese texu jingyingquan" (How
Guangri acquired the franchise of waste disposal). *Nanfang Dushibao*, December 4.
http://www.360doc.com/content/09/1204/10/142_10333844.shtml.

New Express Daily. 2009a. "Lesechang 'xinwen tongbaohui' yi kaishi jiu wushi gong-
zheng" (The press conference of the incineration plant isn't impartial at the beginning). *New Express Daily*, October 31. http://www.ycwb.com/ePaper/xkb/html/2009
-10/31/content_640074.htm.

———. 2009b. "Panyu shuo buhui zuzhi yezhu zuotan" (Panyu district government
said they won't organize a homeowner forum). *New Express Daily*, November 4. http://
epaper.xkb.com.cn/view/451134.

———. 2009c. "Bu zuzhi Panyu jumin zuotanhui zaici shixinyu min" (Government
said they won't organize a resident forum, which broke their own promise again). *New
Express Daily*, November 5. http://www.ycwb.com/epaper/xkb/html/2009-11/04
/content_644504.htm.

Panyu Daily. 2009. "Jian lese fenshao fadianchang shi minxin gongcheng" (Construction of the Incinerator Power Plant Is a Project to Win the Heart of the Masses). *Panyu
Daily*, November 5. http://pyrb.dayoo.com/html/2009-11/05/content_755062.htm.

People's Daily Online. 2010. "2010 shijie fufei ribao faxing liangqian baiming" (The one
hundred big daily newspapers in the world in 2010). *People's Daily*, November 16.
http://media.people.com.cn/BIG5/40606/13225351.html.

World Bank. 2005. "Waste Management in China: Issues and Recommendations." Ur-
ban Development Working Paper no. 9, East Asia Infrastructure Department, World
Bank. http://www-wds.worldbank.org/external/default/WDSContentServer/WDSP
/IB/2006/03/23/000160016_20060323131109/Rendered/PDF/332100CHA0Waste1
Management01PUBLC1.pdf.

Xinkuaibao. 2009. "Zhengfu ying lizheng lese fenshao xiangmu wu liyi goulian" (Government should prove there is no illegitimate connection in the incineration project).
Xinkuaibao, December 3. http://epaper.xkb.com.cn/view/459896.

Yangcheng Evening News. 2009. "Su Zequn: Panyu lese zhineng jiudi chuli" (Su Zequn:
Panyu has to dispose of their own garbage). *Yangcheng Evening News*, November 10.
http://www.ycwb.com/epaper/ycwb/html/2009-11/10/content_652832.htm.

PART IV

Economic and Labor Governance

CHAPTER 8

Decentralized and Differential Labor Policy Governance

The Implementation of China's Labor Contract Law in the Pearl River Delta

CHIH-PENG CHENG

Using an evolutionary ontology, this chapter traces interactions between two policy coalitions in the Pearl River Delta regarding implementation of China's Labor Contract Law. The first is the alliance between Taiwanese investors and local governments; the second is the alliance between rural migrant workers and the central government. The long-standing partnership between Taiwanese factory owners and local governments directly led to the underregulation of the Labor Contract Law between 2008 and 2014, particularly in the area of social insurance coverage. However, this arrangement was disrupted in 2014, when workers staged a strike at the world's largest shoe manufacturer: the Yue Yuen shoe factory in Dongguan, Guangdong. Initially, the central government appeared to defend the interests of workers by requiring Taiwanese factories to improve their social insurance coverage. However, the central state used the strike to increase its legitimacy in the eyes of workers while seizing the opportunity to move foreign investors inland. Following the strike, China's labor regime developed into a dual-track system, whereby Yue Yuen and other foreign-owned factories were required to enforce the Labor Contract Law more comprehensively, whereas domestic producers were not subject to similar expectations. The analysis in this chapter reveals the decentralized and differentiated nature of labor policy governance in China. After the strike, the original alliance between Taiwanese investors and local governments became increasingly unstable. Rather than moving production facilities inland, Taishang increasingly relocated their factories to Southeast Asia. From the perspective of the central party-state, the flight of foreign capital is an unintended by-product of the increased oversight of workers' benefits.

This chapter examines the implementation of China's Labor Contract Law in the Pearl River Delta following the 2008 global financial crisis. This law has had a substantial influence on foreign direct investment (FDI) in China. Foreign investors, including Taiwanese investors (*Taishang* 台商),[1] have begun to reevaluate China's role as the world factory and reconsidered the possibilities of westbound or offshore migration because of increasing costs and major acts of protest, including the Foxconn suicides in 2010 and the large-scale strike at the Taiwanese-run Yue Yuen Group in 2014 (C. Cheng and Lin 2017). Meanwhile, local private factories are increasingly being incorporated into the supply chains controlled by investors from Taiwan (C. Cheng 2016). Implementing the Labor Contract Law may generate a new mode of interaction among the state, capital, and labor. This chapter analyzes the transformation of Chinese state–society relations by examining how the Labor Contract Law has been applied in manufacturing factories, particularly in those that are foreign.

Why is it appropriate to use the Labor Contract Law to explore Chinese state–society relations? The answer is provided in a document titled "China's Social Security and its Policies" (*Zhongguo de shehui baozhang zhuangkuang zhengce* 中国的社会保障状况和政策), issued by the State Council in 2004. The central government clearly expresses its attitude toward social policies in this document:

> Social security is one of the most important social-economic systems for a country in modern times. . . . In light of China's actual situation and adhering to the principle of "putting people first," the Chinese government attaches great importance and devotes every effort to establishing and improving its social security system. The Constitution of the People's Republic of China stipulates that the state shall establish and improve a social security system corresponding to the level of economic development. The Chinese government regards economic development as the basic prerequisite for improving people's livelihood and affecting social security. . . . China's social security system includes social insurance, social welfare, the

specialized care and placement system, social relief, and housing services. As the core of the social security system, social insurance includes old-age insurance, unemployment insurance, medical insurance, work-related injury insurance, and maternity insurance.

The foreword to this document has two crucial implications. First, it implies that the state not only prioritizes national economic development but also views social policies as a means of solving the problems caused by economic development. Consequently, the establishment of a social security system is part of a national development strategy. It is also intended to build legitimacy for the state. The second implication is that social insurance is an essential part of the social security system. As such, this chapter examines state–society relations through the case of social insurance coverage as one of the central issues in the Labor Contract Law.

This study addresses three questions spanning the decade of 2008 to 2018: (1) Why did the central government enact the Labor Contract Law in 2008? (2) Why was the Labor Contract Law underregulated in Taishang factories, particularly in terms of social insurance coverage? (3) What effect did the 2014 strike at the Yue Yuen shoe factory have on the Labor Contract Law and state–society relations? To answer these questions, I conducted fieldwork in the Pearl River Delta, with a focus on the export-oriented footwear manufacturing industry controlled by Taishang. The rationale for choosing the shoe industry is that China was the largest shoe exporter in the world in 2017, with nearly 58 percent of shoes being made in China (APICCAPS 2018). Moreover, this industry employs a high proportion of rural migrant workers. Therefore, examining the shoe industry can provide insight into implementation of the Labor Contract Law and state–society relations in China.

Perspectives on the Development of Chinese Social Policies

Several perspectives have been employed to explain the development of Chinese social policies in the post-Mao reform period. First, the functionalist approach claims that the central government enacted social policies in response to social problems caused by economic transition (Duckett 1997; Guan 2005; Saunders and Shang 2001). For example, due to soft budget constraints and the iron rice bowl policy, the Chinese Communist Party (CCP) reformed state-owned enterprises to improve efficiency. However, this economic restructuring led to large-scale unemployment in state-owned enterprises and collapse of the state-sponsored social welfare system. A new relationship emerged between the owners of production and labor as capitalist–worker conflict has become a leading category of social protests in China (Chen 2017). Therefore, as a national social policy, the Labor Contract Law is regarded as an attempt by the central government to regulate interactions and solve conflict between capitalists and workers. The State Council document, "China's Social Security and Its Policies," reflects a functionalist perspective. However, this approach cannot explain how the policy is implemented and why it is underregulated in practice.

The second perspective may be called the local state approach. This approach focuses on what different local governments have done in terms of social policies. For example, coastal local governments with substantial financial resources have played an innovative role in creating the social welfare system, particularly with regard to pension insurance. The subnationalization of social protection not only influenced social policy-making at the national level but also transformed the spatial politics of Chinese social welfare (Shi 2009). This perspective originates from local state corporatism, highlighting the role of local governments in contributing to the growth of rural industry (Oi 1999; Y. Peng 2001; Walder 1995). This role is not always as positive as this approach assumes. Numerous local governments in coastal areas provide favorable policies for foreign investors, such as tax breaks, cheap land, and lax environmental monitoring. Some corrupt local officers even sacrificed workers' social welfare in exchange for their rent-seeking activities, particularly those of rural migrant workers (C. Cheng 2008). My research found that local governments may choose not to follow the Labor Contract Law because it jeopardizes local capital accumulation and the personal interests of local officials. This phenomenon is indicative of a Chinese-style social welfare system such that local governments play a more critical role than the central government. Local officials are ultimately the actors charged with implementation of state-driven social policies.

Differential citizenship is the third perspective and is more effective in explaining the development of social policies compared with the other two perspectives. Differential citizenship focuses on the discriminatory treatment of rural migrant workers, particularly in social welfare, due to the household registration (*hukou* 户口) system (Solinger 1999; Wu 2011). Migrant-receiving cities use rural–urban dualism from the household registration system to exclude rural migrant workers from enjoying urban public goods and create a repressive labor regime that favors capital accumulation. Several studies focusing on foreign factories in China have presented empirical evidence showing how labor conditions in these factories violate human rights (Chan 2001; C. Lee 1998; Lin, Lin, and Tseng 2016; Pun 2005). Although the Chinese factory regime is still classified as despotic because of coercive practices,[2] the central government enacted the 2008 Labor Contract Law and 2011 Social Insurance Law to protect workers. In other words, the differential citizenship approach cannot explain why the Labor Contract Law emerged in 2008, or why it was implemented completely by local states in the Pearl River Delta only after 2014.

In sum, the three perspectives are inadequate because they are overly state-centered, and societal actors are depicted as too weak to generate any form of social dynamism. These perspectives cannot explain the underlying reasons for the underregulation of the Labor Contract Law in Taishang factories and the occurrence of the Yue Yuen strike, resulting in differential treatment between foreign and local factories by the central and local governments. As shown in most studies on Asian social policies, the state, which is developmental and authoritarian, has been regarded as the major agent affecting the formation and transformation of social policies (Holliday 2000; Y. Lee and Gu 2003).

However, the state is not footloose and always embedded in society, as studies on the comparative welfare regime have often suggested in relation to state–society interactions (Esping-Anderson 1990; Haggard and Kaufman 2008; Skocpol 1992). Some studies focusing on Chinese state–society relations have even argued that an emerging civil society has compromised state power (Howell 2007; Mertha 2009; Saich 2000) or claimed that the relationship between them is mutually dependent in respect of local governance (Spires 2011). By contrast, other scholars have observed the continuing domination of state over society (Thorton 2013;

Unger and Chan 2008). However, neither state- nor society-centered perspectives pay adequate attention to the significant role of local governments in the process of implementing Chinese policy governance.

How policies are enforced by local governments has been a critical issue for the CCP since the establishment of socialist China (C. Lee 2007; C. Lee and Zhang 2013; Lieberthal and Lampton 1992; Liu 2017; Oi 1989). The discrepancy between the central and local governments has continued to deteriorate because of financial decentralization in the early 1980s (Oi 1992) and the reform of the tax-sharing system in 1994 (Liu 2010). These two fiscal policies also provide institutional incentives for local officials to develop their own financial resources and accumulate capital. Four ideal modes of local state economic involvement—entrepreneurial, clientelist, developmental, and predatory—are created through various responses of the local governments to the advent of marketization and the downward transfer of fiscal and administrative authority (Baum and Shevchenko 1999). For example, the entrepreneurial model refers to the direct involvement of local governments in profit-making activities by setting up their own enterprises or becoming joint venture partners with other enterprises. The concept of local state corporatism belongs to the entrepreneurial model, which was often found in the countryside of the Yangtze River Delta before the 2000s. The clientelist model is another pattern of local state involvement in the economy and refers to the symbiotic clientelism that exists between local governments and private or foreign enterprises. Local governments offer entrepreneurs licenses, tax benefits, access to resources, and protection from predators in exchange for kickbacks, favors, and access to profits. This model, which emphasizes personal ties (*guanxi* 关系), is often found in the southern coastal provinces of China (C. Cheng 2008; Wank 1999; Wu 2019), including the Pearl River Delta. Notably, "symbiotic clientelism" tends to operate at the expense of effective policy governance, ultimately undermining the institutional authority of the state (Baum and Shevchenko 1999). Nevertheless, the informal relationship between local governments and entrepreneurs becomes unstable when the institutional environment in which they are embedded is changed by external factors, such as the intervention of the central state (Wu 1997) and worker protests (Chen 2015). Consequently, a more dynamic approach toward state–society interactions, including the role of local states, is needed when examining the implementation of social policies in China. The following discussion thus uses an evolutionary framework to analyze three stages involved in the development of the labor law.

Stage I: Why Was the Labor Contract Law Enacted in 2008?

Prior to the enactment of the Labor Contract Law by the central government in 2008, workers in China were subject to a Labor Law introduced in 1995.[3] This was the first time China had enacted a law to regulate labor relations, and it set the standard for other labor and social policies. However, the implementation of the 1995 Labor Law was ineffective. The central government then enacted the Labor Contract Law to resolve the increasing number of labor disputes caused by inadequate content of the Labor Law. For example, although the Labor Law stipulated that employers must sign a contract with their employees, the regulation was intentionally ignored because the cost of punishment was low. This led to an increase in labor disputes. Between 1995 and 2007, labor disputes rose, on average, by approximately 25 percent each year (Gallagher et al. 2015, 215). The Labor Contract Law stipulates that employees are entitled to monthly double pay if employers do not sign a contract with them after they have worked in the factory for one month. Employees who have worked for more than one year are entitled to an unlimited contract if employers still have not signed a contract. The Labor Contract Law is intended to increase labor contract coverage by raising the cost of punishment. Its primary goal is to formalize labor disputes. However, the Labor Contract Law also led to a substantial increase in the number of labor disputes. For example, the number of labor disputes rose from about 900,000 in 2009 to nearly 1.6 million in 2012 (Gallagher et al. 2015, 215–16). Chapter 10 in this volume makes a similar observation. In addition to different interpretations from local officials regarding the provisions of the law, labor disputes increased dramatically after 2008 in response to the global financial crisis. Numerous labor disputes arose in relation to issues such as severance payments and unpaid wages, which particularly affected rural migrant workers. The enactment of the Labor Contract Law provided both parties with a more formalized channel for negotiation.

Increasing labor disputes began to raise doubts regarding national development strategies. Since the economic transition of 1978, China had already embraced capitalism for more than 30 years. During this time, the country became deeply embedded in a world economic system through foreign trade and investment. An abundance of cheap land and lax social and environmental policies enabled China to become a world factory. Since the 2000s, social instability caused by income inequality, an inadequate social welfare system, and environmental problems have forced the central government to reconsider the costs of being a world factory. The 11th Five-Year Plan, which began in 2006, was a turning point for the economic policies of the central state.

In this plan, the central government redefined the content of development and aimed to transform economic growth in several key ways. First, it would change from being driven by industry and quantitative expansion to being driven by structural optimization and upgrading. Second, it would shift from being driven by substantial resource consumption to greater efficiency in resource use. Third, it would change from relying on the input of capital and substance factors to relying on the advancement of science and technology and human resources. Consequently, industries with high resource consumption and low output became unfavorable targets. Thus, in Guangdong province, the policy of "cleaning the cage to make way for new birds" (*tenglong huanniao* 腾龙换鸟)—to replace traditional manufacturing industries with high-tech and low-pollution industries—could be perceived as a response to the 11th Five-Year Plan. Furthermore, the plan emphasized the need for balanced economic and social development, which implied that economic growth should not be at the expense of citizens' social welfare. The Labor Contract Law was thus the product of a policy desire for balanced economic and social development. In addition, the 2008 tax reform enshrined one of the goals of the 11th Five-Year Plan, which was to increase the income tax paid by foreign enterprises from 17 to 25 percent and reduce the income tax paid by local enterprises from 33 to 25 percent. This equivalent rate of income tax increased the competitiveness of local enterprises and affected the implementation of the Labor Contract Law. For foreign investors, China's favorable policies regarding FDI were ending.

Overall, the central government's decision to enact the Labor Contract Law was motivated by two reasons. One was the need to regulate capitalist–worker interactions and formalize labor disputes, and the other was to accelerate inland economic development by moving capitalists, particularly foreign investors, from coastal to inland areas. The latter motive is a part of a hidden agenda by the central government, although its purpose in managing capital can be clearly observed in the *tenglong huan-niao* policy (C. Cheng 2008). Thus, the Labor Contract Law more clearly specifies the provisions of the labor contract, which were somewhat vague in the preexisting Labor Law. Table 8.1 highlights the differences in labor contracts between the 1995 Labor Law and the 2008 Labor Contract Law. Although the first, second, fifth, seventh, and ninth provisions were contained in the Labor Law, they were not included in the labor contract. The Social Insurance Law, enforced in 2011, further strengthened the efficiency of the Labor Contract Law in promoting the provision of social insurance. Consequently, bureaus and departments in charge of social security can now charge enterprises as much as three times the amount of insurance fees if they do not take responsibility for workers' social insurance.

Table 8.1
Comparison of labor contracts in the Labor Law and
the Labor Contract Law

Labor Contract Law (2008)	Labor Law (1995)
1. Name and location of the enterprise, and the name of the employer	N/A
2. Name, address, and ID of the employee	N/A
3. Period of the labor contract	Period of the labor contract
4. Work content and location	Work content
5. Work time	N/A
6. Work pay	Work pay
7. Social insurance	N/A
8. Labor condition and labor protection	Labor condition and labor protection
9. Other labor items included in the contract	N/A

According to *Taiwan Business Weekly* (Hsiao 2007), President Terry Guo of Foxconn, the world's largest manufacturer in terms of employment, flew to Xiamen to see Wu Yi, vice premier of the State Council, to discuss the forthcoming Labor Contract Law. The central government officially replied that it was impossible for them to delay the enforcement of the law.

Stage II: Evaluating Implementation of the Labor Contract Law, 2008–2014

By the 2010s, Taishang, the main foreign investors in the Pearl River Delta, started reevaluating the attractiveness of China as a world factory and considering the possibilities of westbound or offshore migration. It was not just the Labor Contract Law but also the global financial crisis that led to the "big escape of Taishang" (*taishang da taowang* 台商大逃亡, Lu and Yu 2008). One of the interviewees in this study, a shoemaker in Dongguan, estimated that almost 40 percent of Taiwanese shoe factories did not survive the 2008 crisis. Therefore, it appears that the global financial crisis and the transformation of the Chinese regulatory regime, particularly enactment of the Labor Contract Law, affected the attractiveness of China to Taishang and other foreign investors. Even so, the enactment of the Labor Contract Law does not mean it has been implemented. A substantial number of Taishang factories remaining in the Pearl River Delta do not comply fully with the Labor Contract Law.

On October 1, 2010, when the general manager of a large Taiwanese shoe company located in Dongguan was asked how his company reacted to the Labor Contract Law, his reply was intriguing: "Of course, we signed the labor contract with each of our employees. But no one regulated us to buy social insurance for everyone." According to him, the core issue for Taishang and other foreign enterprises was social insurance coverage, rather than the labor contract coverage enshrined within the Labor Contract Law. This is because social insurance coverage is directly related to production costs. When the manager was asked how it was possible for his company to avoid purchasing social insurance for each employee, he responded as follows:

Over 90 percent of local officials in Dongguan are bribed by Taishang . . . no company can afford social insurance for all of its workers. To be honest, the social insurance coverage in my company was only 10 percent. Of course, local states in some areas, such as the Yangtze River Delta, regulated that the social insurance coverage should be 40–60 percent at least, higher than 30–40 percent in the Pearl River Delta. But I doubted the credibility of what Taishang said over there. . . . The most important of all was that the department in charge of labor contracts (human resource department, *renli ziyuanju* 人力资源局) differed from the department in charge of social insurance (social security department, *shehui baozhangju* 社会保障局). So these two departments were in conflict with one another. (interview, October 1, 2010)

On the basis of his description, the local governments concealed the illegal behavior of Taishang. The coalition between Taishang and local officials had been an "open secret" in the Pearl River Delta since the early 1990s (C. Cheng 2008; L. Cheng 1999; Hsing 1996; Wu 1997). Local governments played a crucial role in helping Taishang resolve market uncertainties and establish a repressive labor regime. Consequently, local governments did not require comprehensive social insurance coverage. Local officials always had "one eye open with another one closed" (*zhengyizhiyan biyizhiyan* 睁一只眼闭一只眼) regarding the implementation of the Labor Contract Law in Taishang factories. This meant they could receive a "management fee" or "service fee" from Taishang, although the amount depended on the nature of their social relations.

The issue of social insurance coverage requires further clarification. Five types of social insurance are present in the Chinese social security system: old-age insurance (pension insurance), unemployment insurance, medical insurance, work-related injury insurance, and maternity insurance. The coverage varies for these five types of insurance. Coverage of medical and work-related injury insurance is typically 100 percent, particularly in foreign-owned factories, because these two types of insurance are crucial for labor reproduction and the fees are low. Pension insurance coverage is the lowest because its fee is the highest among the five types of insurance—nearly 90 percent of the amount both employers and employees pay for social insurance. The manager's statement regarding 10 percent social insurance coverage in his company mostly refers to pension insurance. This also applies to other Chinese coastal areas, including the Pearl River Delta and Yangtze River Delta.

Using the Dongguan social insurance system in September 2010 as an example, the city government charged RMB287.2 for each worker hired by factories. Employers needed to pay RMB185.2 and employees needed to pay RMB102. The ratio was 6.5:3.5. If we assume that the Taiwanese shoe company had 10,000 workers, then according to the Labor Contract Law, it needed to pay RMB1,852,000 a month. It only paid RMB185,200 because of the 10 percent social insurance coverage. Even taking into consideration the higher coverage provided by the other four kinds of insurance, the coalition with local officials saved this shoe company a substantial amount of money. This indicates why implementation of the state-driven Labor Contract Law was underregulated at the local level.

The Dongguan city government's social insurance system was characterized by stratification, particularly in relation to medical insurance. The city government divided medical insurance into two categories: golden card and silver card. Employees with a golden card could receive better medical treatment. For example, they could go to higher-ranked hospitals and get a greater level of reimbursement for hospitalization. Only employees working in state- and city-owned enterprises qualified for a golden card. Employees working in foreign, private, and township-owned enterprises belonged to the silver card category. For the Dongguan city government, the stratified medical insurance system that began in 2000 helped attract FDI because the golden card payment for enterprises was substantially higher than that for the silver card. The difference in payment for each worker was RMB156.38 in 2013.[4] This further illustrates the coalition that existed between foreign investors and local governments. Consequently, Taishang companies could have higher medical insurance coverage in their factories.

Figure 8.1 illustrates the underregulation of the Labor Contract Law at the national level. In 2009, the coverage of old-age, medical, unemployment, work-related injury, and maternity insurance in industrial and service sectors was 38 percent, 47 percent, 27 percent, 32 percent, and 23 percent, respectively. In 2007, the coverage of these five social insurances was 34 percent, 40 percent, 26 percent, 27 percent, and 17 percent. This shows that they did not increase substantially with the enforcement of the Labor Contract Law. Although the coverage of each social insur-

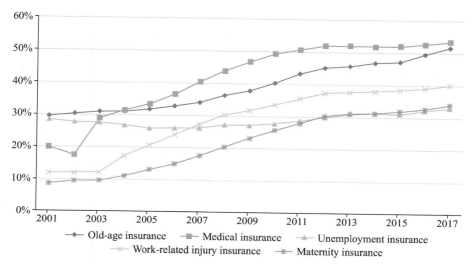

FIGURE 8.1 Coverage of the five types of social insurance in industrial and service sectors in China, 2001–2017
Source: Lin (2013); National Bureau of Statistics of China (2018).

ance has increased from 2008 to 2017, about half of the working population in China is still not covered by social insurance in 2017. The coverage of work-related injury, unemployment, and maternity insurance is even less than 40 percent.

For Taishang, another factor resulting in the underregulation of the Labor Contract Law was the extension of the global commodity chain. In response to the global financial crisis and the transformation of the Chinese regulatory regime, Taishang, involved in an original equipment manufacturer (OEM) and an original design manufacturer embedded in the international division of labor began to place orders in local private factories so that they could survive in the Pearl River Delta (C. Cheng 2014).

This was crucial for Taishang because of the high-risk investment environment created by socialist economic transition and the rampant rent-seeking activities of local officials. Some of the FDI pioneers in China, the Taishang, thus chose the investment model of an enclave economy. With the help of local officials, Taishang used the "pseudo TVE (township and village enterprises), real FDI (foreign direct investment)" (*jiahezi* 假合資) model to isolate the OEM process from troublesome environments in the host country (L. Cheng 1999). The spatial concentration of Taiwanese factories was an expected outcome. When visiting a large Taiwanese shoemaker in Dongguan in 2004, I noticed a row of light orange buildings surrounding the factory. Later, I realized that these buildings were parts makers and processing makers who were suppliers and subcontractors for the factory. All of them were from the same ethnic background. The reason for this spatial concentration was that they could help each other if one of the factories had trouble with local officials. Taishang also socialized after work at Taiwanese-financed restaurants, karaoke bars, and golf clubs to overcome feelings of homesickness. The unfamiliar and unstable environment in China accounted for the close and trusting relationship among Taishang. This made it difficult for local factories to enter the production network of Taishang at that time (C. Cheng 2014, 48).

The situation changed in 2008 when Taishang began to incorporate local factories into their production networks. The incorporating strategies were subcontracting and insourcing (*changnei chengbao* 场内承包).[5] Although recruiting new partners from different ethnic backgrounds could cause numerous technical and cultural problems, the Taishang could transfer the cost of the Labor Contract Law to local factories using these two strategies. One of the Taiwanese managers explained the reasons for this:

> Insourcing not only solves the problem of unstable orders, but also maintains the control of critical production activities inside the factory. Furthermore, this strategy also reduces the huge labor cost caused by the Labor Contract Law, international buyer audits, and deficit labor supply in China. Most important of all, emerging local factories incorporated by Taiwanese export-led manufacturing industry through insourcing are able to cope with the requirements from the central government, moving toward a well-off society (*benxiang xiaokang shehui* 奔向小康社会).[6] In recent years, local governments are also trying hard to promote their dominant areas toward moderate prosperity (interview, November 28, 2011).[7]

Subcontracting is a strategy used to spread risk among economic actors. It can help Taishang avoid accusations of running sweatshops. What is important in this respect is how local factories unfamiliar with the OEM could pass the audit of international buyers. As subcontractors, Taishang played a crucial role in helping their contractors satisfy the requirements of buyers. For example, it would preaudit local partners according to the buyers' corporate code of conduct on labor standards. They asked their partners to pay attention to child labor and social insurance, which were the focus of a recent audit. They asked their partners to allow child laborers to take a week off work during the audit and prepare the "correct" social insurance documents. Local factories usually bribed workers with material rewards in exchange for their "correct" answers regarding social insurance coverage. A manager from a local factory I interviewed on July 10, 2012 said that he used many methods to solve the problem of social insurance coverage, such as building a factory in a smaller area with a labor-check holiday.

International buyers knew what Taishang did with its local factories, but they feigned ignorance. Furthermore, different kinds of international buyers applied different human rights standards. Because of the procurement price, branded companies, such as Nike, Adidas, and Nine West, enforced the audit on manufacturers more strictly than did retailers, such as Wal-Mart, Target, and J.C. Penney. It seems that local governments did the same by paying more attention in terms of a labor check to Taishang and other foreign-owned factories than they did local factories. Using this subcontracting strategy, Taishang companies, which had been transforming themselves from manufacturers to trading companies, could satisfy the Labor Contract Law. In conclusion, Taishang, local officials, and international buyers together led to the underregulation of the Labor Contract Law. The capacity of the central government to enforce the law was limited at this stage.

What was the situation for workers during this stage? On the basis of the findings of my field study, most rural migrant workers, the expected beneficiaries of the social insurance system, did not want to buy pension insurance even though employers asked them to do so. Although the central government had been reforming this system by creating personal accounts, provincial differences in regulations for pension insurance rendered the transfer of personal accounts problematic. Workers did not trust the local government, who manages the social insurance funds, to not steal their money. Moreover, the next employer might not be so willing to purchase insurance. Consequently, most of the rural migrant workers preferred to keep their salary in their pockets, rather than joining the social insurance system.

Stage III: Impact of the 2014 Yue Yuen Shoe Factory Strike on the Labor Contract Law

Before investing in the Pearl River Delta in 1988, the Pou Chen Group, founded in 1969, was the parent company of the Yue Yuen Group. It was a Taiwanese shoe company with more than 1,000 workers at that time. Because of China's cheap labor and land, Pou Chen, which was listed on the Taiwan Stock Exchange in 1990, had grown to become the largest shoemaker in the world. Yue Yuen, its subsidiary, was listed on the Hong Kong Stock Exchange in 1992. In 2014, the number of Pou Chen employees reached approximately 400,000 worldwide, and its total revenue was NTD244 billion. Meanwhile, it produced 307 million pairs of shoes, accounting for 20 percent of global athletic and athletic-inspired shoe markets. Its major buyers are Nike, Adidas, Reebok, Asics, New Balance, Puma, Converse, Salomon, and Timberland. Pou Chen's production bases include China, Vietnam, and Indonesia, although China's status as a leader has been diminishing since 2008, particularly following the 2014 strike at Yue Yuen.

Why did the 2014 strike prove to be so crucial? Given that labor unions at the national and local levels are weak in fighting for workers' rights, strikes have been the main strategy of Chinese rural migrant workers to express their grievances in the workplace. What made the Yue Yuen strike unique was the target of its protest because it was the first large-scale strike to target the social insurance and housing provident fund (*zhufang gongji jin* 住房公积金) in China (fig. 8.2).[8] More than 40,000 workers joined this strike, which lasted nearly a month, from April 5 to April 26, 2014. It was regarded as one of the largest strikes in China in recent years. After the Yue Yuen strike, other Taishang factories in the Pearl River Delta held similar strikes, including the Stella shoe factory, which produces high-end and fashionable women's shoes for well-known international brands. In the global footwear industry, Stella is known as the queen of shoes, a direct comparison with Yue Yuen's status as the king of shoes.

During the strike, workers argued that Yue Yuen did not buy social insurance for them or, if they did, they bought it using a payment base lower than their real wages. This was particularly the case for pension insurance. For a long time, Yue Yuen had been making pension contribu-

FIGURE 8.2 Strike at the Yue Yuen shoe factory in Dongguan. The banner reads, "I want my social insurance and housing provident fund back! Shame on Yue Yuen." *Source:* boxun.com, April 15, 2014, https://boxun.com/news/gb/china/2014/04/201404150033.shtml.

tions for workers on the basis of the city's average monthly wage. The real wages of Yue Yuen's workers were often higher than the average monthly wage. Other Taishang factories did the same, and some used the minimum wage as the payment base for workers' pension insurance. The key point is that most Taishang factories did not buy social insurance for workers until implementation of the Labor Contract Law. The local governments looked the other way on this issue. Pension insurance coverage in Dongguan ranged between 30 and 40 percent from 2008 to 2014. In addition, Yue Yuen did not provide the housing provident fund for most workers. Although the State Council announced its Regulations on Management of Housing Provident Fund (*zhufang gongzhi jin guanli tiaoli* 住房公积金管理条例) in 2002, local officials applied their own interpretations to explain and enforce this regulation. They paid less attention to the housing provident fund than they did to social insurance. These circumstances all led to the strike at Yue Yuen, but they do not explain why the strike occurred at Yue Yuen rather than in other Taishang factories nor how such a large-scale strike could last for three weeks. Two likely explanations are as follows.

First, for the previous 10 years, senior workers made up the largest group at Yue Yuen. More than 50 percent of employees had worked in the Yue Yuen factory for more than 10 years, and some had worked there for nearly 20 years. This is quite different from most Taishang factories, where the workers are younger and there is greater turnover. According to the Social Insurance Law, workers can acquire a pension if they have been paying insurance for more than 15 years. This means that many workers in the Yue Yuen factory would qualify for their pension in a few years. They were much more concerned with pension insurance than were their counterparts in coastal China.

Second, Yue Yuen, as the largest shoe manufacturer in the world, has been a role model for the Dongguan city government. At the outset of the strike, Yue Yuen was negotiating with the city government over how to respond to workers' demands (C. Chen 2015). Yue Yuen, under pressure from international buyers, was inclined to accept workers' demands to adopt real wages as the basis of pension insurance and provide 100 percent social insurance coverage. However, the Dongguan city government did not agree with Yue Yuen's proposal. Local officials worried that it would have a substantial impact on other foreign factories. This disagreement extended the strike for a few more days.

Once this local strike had escalated into a national and international labor dispute following news coverage by the Xinhua News Agency and the BBC, the Dongguan city government changed its attitude toward the proposed solution. Local officials started to become involved in actively handling the strike from April 19 onward. Most important, the central state asked Dongguan city government and Yue Yuen to resolve the strike as quickly as possible. When a spokesman from the Ministry of Human Resources and Social Security said in a news conference on April 25 that Yue Yuen had indeed engaged in illegal behavior regarding social insurance, it was clear the strike was approaching its end. The Ministry of Human Resources and Social Security also asked Yue Yuen to satisfy the request for 100 percent social insurance coverage and provide compensation for the social insurance and housing provident fund if workers file an application. Ultimately, the issue at stake for the Dongguan city government had transformed from one of class conflict to maintaining stability (*weiwen* 维稳). After the strike, the city government enacted a new policy on social insurance. This required the amount of pension insurance to be equivalent to that of work-related injury insurance, which had the highest coverage of all types of social insurance. Effectively, the Dongguan city government increased social insurance coverage in response to the central government's requirements regarding the Labor Contract Law and Social Insurance Law.

The Yue Yuen strike had an impact on local labor policy governance. Yue Yuen and its suppliers, as well as other large foreign factories, were now required by the Dongguan city government to enforce the Labor Contract Law in its entirety, including 100 percent labor contract and social insurance coverage. They had to provide the housing provident fund to workers. During my visit to Dongguan for a field study on July 10, 2015, one of Yue Yuen's suppliers complained that the local officials checked the labor conditions in his factory more often than before and without notification. Other Yue Yuen suppliers faced a similar situation. This meant that there was no excuse for these Taishang factories. Having favorable *guanxi* (social relations) with local officials would no longer work for them. In recent years, local governments have begun to pay more attention to maintaining stability than to capitalist interests, especially regarding large-scale social protests. Furthermore, the source of local governments' revenue has increasingly switched from enterprises to real estate (Hsing 2010). Some local officials even asked enterprises to leave so they could acquire land. This demonstrates that capitalist interests are no longer the top priority for local governments.

In general, rural migrant workers were more interested in receiving the housing provident fund than in having pension insurance. In the case of Yue Yuen, only 777 workers filed an application to buy back pension insurance after the strike, which constituted a small proportion of the total workforce. This outcome was expected because workers had to pay their own share and this would have cost them a lot of money. Moreover, workers could not draw a pension until their retirement, and they need to wait at least 15 years to do this. By contrast, they can use the housing provident fund to build, buy, and repair homes at any time. One of Yue Yuen's suppliers stated that the number of rural migrant workers filing an application for housing provident fund compensation in his factory was higher than the number filing for pension insurance compensation.

Yue Yuen's strike also influenced other Taishang factories in the Pearl River Delta. Initially, Taishang factories increased social insurance coverage from 30–40 percent to 50–60 percent, which was requested by local officials in the second half of 2014. These local officials also announced to Taishang that social insurance coverage should reach 100 percent by the beginning of the following year. However, local officials did not take any further action until 2017. When I visited Dongguan on July 13, 2017, one of the Taishang interviewees explained, "All of the computer systems in the departments of Dongguan city government have eventually been unified into one. There are no more gray areas for Taishang in the coverage of social insurance." Taishang are now required to purchase social insurance for each new employee.[9] Local enterprises who serve as Taishang subcontractors in Dongguan still enjoy labor-check holidays from the Dongguan city government and international buyers. Factories located in inland areas get the same treatment. This shows that labor policy governance in China is differential. I call it the dual-track system of the labor regime (*shuang guizhi* 双轨制). This system exists not just between foreign and local factories but also between coastal and inland areas. The system directly strengthens the competitiveness of local factories and forces Taishang to move toward the west.

Conclusion: The Evolution of Policy Coalitions

Following implementation of the Labor Contract Law, two policy coalitions emerged. The first comprises Taishang and local governments, and the second comprises rural migrant workers and the central government. The long-term partnership between Taishang and local governments that existed since the 1990s directly undermined the effectiveness of the Labor Law before 2008 and accounted for underregulation of the Labor Contract Law between 2008 and 2014. International buyers also acquiesced in this situation. The Yue Yuen strike marks a critical juncture that changed the status quo. Workers and the central government worked together to improve the outcomes of the Labor Contract Law. Even so, this coalition makes strange bedfellows because each side had its own goal. For the workers, the Labor Contract Law finally started to function better than the Labor Law of 1995. The central government increased the legitimacy of its regime. It behaved differently from the Dongguan city government on this issue. The Labor Contract Law may simply serve as a means for the central government, rather than an end. To a certain degree, it attempted to use the strike to reclaim its power in the first coalition and facilitate moving foreign investors inland. This resonates with the findings in chapter 9. Consequently, the Labor Contract Law forms one part of the 11th Five-Year Plan or *tenglong huanniao* policy applied by the central government to manage capital. The dual-track system of the labor regime provides the evidence for this.

This study shows that China's state–society interactions in the arena of labor policy governance are complex. "The state" in research on state–society relations usually refers to the central government (Evans 1995; Evans, Rueschemeyer, and Skocpol 1985; Skocpol 1979; Tarrow 2011). Since the socialist period, local governments have also been major players in China. As mentioned previously, financial decentralization after the economic reforms of 1978 further empowered local governments to become relatively autonomous agents. A decentralized political system is therefore a distinguishing feature in the Chinese authoritarian regime. This characteristic of the regime would certainly affect labor policy governance. Without any knowledge of this context, it would be impossible to understand why and how the coalition of local states and Taishang compromised implementation of the Labor Law and the Chinese Labor Contract Law.

Although the decentralized political system reduced the infrastructural power of the CCP,[10] it paradoxically created a protective umbrella for them in terms of localizing social protests. In the case of the Yue Yuen strike, Taishang and the Dongguan city government implemented the Labor Contract Law and Regulations on Management of Housing Provident Fund incompletely; thus, they, rather than the central government, were the primary targets of rural migrant workers' protests. The role of the central government became that of an arbiter between rural migrant workers and the first coalition, even though it was responsible for enacting these policies. This division of labor between the central and local governments in policy governance helps explain regime stability under the CCP (C. Lee 2007; Tang 2016). Cai's (2010) analysis of why social protests succeed or fail in China further shows that the opportunities for collective resistance often arise from divisions between state authorities at different levels. The Yue Yuen strike provides support for this rationale. Collective action by disadvantaged rural migrant workers led to pressure from above being exerted on the Dongguan city government's implementation of the Labor Contract Law in Taishang factories. Moreover, the power that local governments had to explain and execute national policies flexibly would be restricted by the central government once they were deemed incapable of handling local social protests. Thus, collective resistance plays a crucial role in shaping Chinese state–society relations because it can "invite" intervention from the central government. Most important, this study highlights the role played by the coalition between Taishang and local governments as an intermediary in the demonstration of state–society interactions. In addition, the potential for mutual dependence between rural migrant workers and the central government is borne out in this study.

What is next for state–capital–labor interactions under a decentralized and differential labor regime? Taishang and other foreign capitalists are leaving China because of the Labor Contract Law and the labor regime characterized by the dual-track system. In terms of the proportion of production at Yue Yuen in 2018, Vietnam has now become the leader (45 percent), with Indonesia in the second position (37 percent) and China in the third position (18 percent) (Pan 2019). The coalition between Taishang and local governments in coastal areas was not dismantled, but it became increasingly unstable. Ultimately, foreign investors did not move westbound as the central government expected. The central government is aware of the situation. On February 28, 2018, the Taiwan Affairs Office of the State Council launched "31 incentives" (*huitai 31 xiang zhengce* 惠台 31 項政策) to reattract Taiwanese investment; however, the effect was not significant (Lin, Shen, and Cheng 2019). Moreover, the US–China trade war and spread of COVID-19 accelerated the withdrawal of Taiwanese and foreign capital from China. Stemming the flight of foreign capital from manufacturing sectors poses a dilemma during China's "new normal" phase of more moderate growth rates.

Notes

1. Since the 1990s, Taishang have been ranked as one of the top five investors of FDI in China. Although Hong Kong is always ranked at the top in terms of FDI, part of its capital derives from reinvestment originating from Taiwan (C. Cheng and Lin 2017).

2. According to Burawoy (1979), whose research focused on the labor process under monopoly capitalism, there are two types of labor regimes; one is despotic and based on coercion, and the other is hegemonic and based on consent. Most studies focusing on China's labor regime argue that foreign factories in China are despotic, an exception being Thomas Peng's (2007) research.

3. This law was applied to foreign-invested factories in 1997.

4. The stratified medical insurance system was canceled at the end of 2013. However, if workers in foreign, private, and town-owned enterprises want to join a higher level of medical insurance, they still need approval from the enterprises. This entitles enterprises to make the final decision for its workers.

5. In contrast to popular outsourcing (i.e., contracting work to an outside supplier), insourcing refers to hiring an entire team from outside to work in the factory.

6. The 11th and 12th Five-Year Plans are the guidelines used by the central government to progress toward a prosperous society.

7. This interview text has been addressed in another book chapter (C. Cheng 2014, 53).

8. In China, the five types of social insurance and the housing provident fund are called the "five insurances and one fund" (*wuxian yijin* 五险一金).

9. There is still a gray area regarding local labor policy governance of the housing provident fund. The Dongguan city government keeps "one eye open with another one closed" on this issue.

10. Infrastructural power is the term Michael Mann (1984) uses to describe the state's capacity to penetrate civil society and implement political decisions without resistance from below.

References

APICCAPS (Portuguese Footwear, Components and Leather Goods Manufacturers' Association). 2018. *World Footwear Yearbook*. Porto: Portuguese Footwear, Components and Leather Goods Manufacturers' Association.

Baum, Richard, and Alexei Shevchenko. 1999. "The 'State of the State.'" In *The Paradox of China's Post-Mao Reforms*, edited by Merle Goldman and Roderick MacFarquhar, 333–60. Cambridge, MA: Harvard University Press.

Burawoy, Michael. 1979. *Manufacturing Consent: Changes in the Labor Process under Monopoly Capitalism*. Chicago: University of Chicago Press.

Cai, Yongshun. 2010. *Collective Resistance in China: Why Popular Protests Succeed or Fail*. Stanford, CA: Stanford University Press.

Chan, Anita. 2001. *China's Workers Under Assault: The Exploitation of Labor in A Globalizing Economy*. Armonk: M. E. Sharpe.

Chen, Chih-Jou Jay. 2015. "Popular Protest in an Authoritarian Regime: A Wildcat Strike in Southern China." *Taiwanese Sociology* 30: 1–53.

———. 2017. "Policing Protest in China: Findings from Newspaper Date." *Taiwanese Sociology* 33: 113–64.

Cheng, Chih-peng. 2008. "Markets as Politics: The Formation and Transformation of the Chinese Export-Led Footwear Industry." *Taiwanese Sociology* 15: 109–63.

———. 2014. "Embedded Trust and Beyond: The Organizational Network Transformation of *Taishang*'s Shoe Industry in China." In *Border Crossing in Greater China: Production, Community and Identity*, edited by Jenn-Hwan Wang, 40–60. London: Routledge.

———. 2016. "Chinese Capitalism from Outside: The Case Study of the Emergence of Chinese Private Enterprises in the Pearl River Delta." *Taiwanese Sociology* 31: 141–91.

Cheng, Chih-peng, and Thung-hong Lin. 2017. "The Limitations of Embeddedness: An Analysis of the 'Transnational Field of Capital Accumulation' about Taiwanese Enterprises in China." In *Unfinished Miracle: Taiwan's Economy and Society in Transition*, edited by Zong-rong Lee and Thung-hong Lin, 612–44. Taipei: Academia Sinica Press.

Cheng, Lu-lin. 1999. "The Invisible Elbow: Semi-periphery and the Restructuring of the International Footwear Market." *Taiwan: A Radical Quarterly in Social Studies* 35: 1–46.

Duckett, Jane. 1997. "China's Social Welfare Reforms for a Market Economy: Problems and Prospects." In *The China Handbook*, edited by Christopher Hudson, 262–75. Chicago: Fitzroy Dearborn.

Esping-Anderson, Gosta. 1990. *The Three Worlds of Welfare Capitalism*. Princeton, NJ: Princeton University Press.

Evans, Peter. 1995. *Embedded Autonomy: States and Industrial Transformation*. Princeton, NJ: Princeton University Press.

Evans, Peter, Dietrich Rueschemeyer, and Theda Skcopol, eds. 1985. *Bringing the State Back In*. Cambridge: Cambridge University Press.

Gallagher, Mary, John Giles, Albert Park, and Meiyan Wang. 2015. "China's 2008 Labor Contract Law: Implementation and Implications for China's Workers." *Human Relations* 68.2: 197–235.

Guan, Xinping. 2005. "China's Social Policy: Reform and Development in the Context of Marketization and Globalization." In *Transforming the Developmental Welfare State in East Asia*, edited by Huck-ju Kwon, 231–56. New York: Palgrave Macmillan.

Haggard, Stephan, and Robert R. Kaufman. 2008. *Development, Democracy, and Welfare States: Latin American, East Asia, and Eastern Europe*. Princeton, NJ: Princeton University Press.

Holliday, Ian. 2000. "Productivist Welfare Capitalism: Social Policy in East Asia." *Political Studies* 48: 706–23.

Howell, Jude. 2007. "Civil Society in China: Chipping Away at the Edges." *Development* 50.3: 17–23.

Hsiao, Sheng-Hung. 2007. "Labor Costs Will Increase by 50%, and Terry Guo Is Anxious to See Yi Wu." *Taiwan Business Weekly* 1035: 62–63.

Hsing, You-Tien. 1996. "Blood, Thicker than Water: Interpersonal Relations and Taiwanese Investment in Southern China." *Environment and Planning A* 28: 2241–61.

———. 2010. *The Great Urban Transformation: Politics of Land and Property in China*. Oxford: Oxford University Press.

Lee, Ching-kwan. 1998. *Gender and the South China Miracle: Two Worlds of Factory Women*. Berkeley: University of California Press.

———. 2007. *Against the Law: Labor Protests in China's Rustbelt and Sunbelt*. Berkeley: University of California Press.

Lee, Ching-kwan, and Yonghong Zhang. 2013. "The Power of Instability: Unraveling the Microfoundations of Bargained Authoritarianism in China." *American Journal of Sociology* 118.6: 1475–508.

Lee, Yih-jiunn, and Yeun-wen Gu. 2003. "Another Welfare World? A Preliminary Examination of the Developmental Welfare Regime in East Asia." *Taiwanese Journal of Sociology* 31: 189–241.

Lieberthal, Kenneth G., and David M. Lampton, eds. 1992. *Bureaucracy, Politics, and Decision Making in Post-Mao China.* Berkeley: University of California Press.

Lin, Thung-hong. 2013. *Research on China's Social Security System and its Transformation.* Taipei: Mainland Affairs Council, ROC.

Lin, Thung-hong, Yi-ling Lin, and Wei-Lin Tseng. 2016. "Manufacturing Suicide: The Politics of a World Factory." *Chinese Sociological Review* 48.1: 1–32.

Lin, Thung-hong, Hsiu-hua Shen, and Chih-peng Cheng. 2019. *China's Promotion of 31 Incentives against Taiwan and the Impact of Specific Education-Related Measures on Taiwan.* Taipei: Mainland Affairs Council, ROC.

Liu, Yia-Ling. 2010. "The Making of a Chinese Semi-Planned Administration: Soft Budget Constraints and Local Transition from Entrepreneur to Rentier." *Taiwanese Journal of Sociology* 45: 163–212.

———. 2017. *Reform from Below: The Divergences in the Path of China's Local Economic Development.* Taipei: Liwen Publishing Group.

Lu, Kuo-Chen, and Tzu-Yen Yu. 2008. "China Has Changed and the Big Escape of Taishang." *Taiwan Business Weekly* 1071: 140–47.

Mann, Michael. 1984. "The Autonomous Power of the State: Its Origins, Mechanisms and Results." *European Journal of Sociology* 25.2: 185–213.

Mertha, Andrew. 2009. "'Fragmented Authoritarianism 2.0': Political Pluralization in the Chinese Policy Process." *China Quarterly* 200: 995–1012.

National Bureau of Statistics of China. 2018. *China Statistical Yearbook 2002–2018.* Beijing: China Statistics Press.

Oi, Jean. 1989. *State and Peasant in Contemporary China: The Political Economy of Village Government.* Berkeley: University of California Press.

———. 1992. "Fiscal Reform and the Economic Foundations of Local State Corporatism in China." *World Politics* 45: 99–126.

———. 1999. *Rural China Takes Off: Institutional Foundations of Economic Reform.* Berkeley: University of California Press.

Pan, Yi-jing. 2019. "Patty Tsai, the President of the Pou Chen Group, Warned: Vietnam Has No Cheap Labor!" *Wealth Magazine* 583: 92–94.

Peng, Thomas. 2007. "Hourly Wages, Hard Workers, and a Hegemonic Regime: The Factory Regime of a Taiwanese-invested Factory in South China." *Taiwanese Sociology* 14: 51–100.

Peng, Yusheng. 2001. "Chinese Villages and Townships as Industrial Corporations: Ownership, Governance, and Market Discipline." *American Journal of Sociology* 106.5: 1338–70.

Pun, Ngai. 2005. *Made in China: Women Factory Workers in a Global Workplace.* Durham, NC: Duke University Press.

Saich, Anthony. 2000. "Negotiating the State: The Development of Social Organization in China." *China Quarterly* 161: 124–41.

Saunders, Peter, and Xiaoyuan Shang. 2001. "Social Security Reform in China's Transition to a Market Economy." *Social Policy and Administration* 35.3: 274–89.

Shi, Shih-jiunn. 2009. "Sub-Nationalization of Social Protection: The Spatial-Politics Transformation of Social Citizenship in China." *Taiwanese Sociology* 18: 43–93.

Skocpol, Theda. 1979. *States and Social Revolutions: A Comparative Analysis of France, Russia and China*. Cambridge: Cambridge University Press.

———. 1992. *Protecting Soldiers and Mothers: The Political Origins of Social Policy in the United States*. Cambridge, MA: Harvard University Press.

Solinger, Dorothy J. 1999. *Contesting Citizenship in Urban China: Peasant Migrants, the State, and the Logic of the Market*. Berkeley: University of California Press.

Spires, Anthony J. 2011. "Contingent Symbiosis and Civil Society in an Authoritarian State: Understanding the Survival of China's Grassroots NGOs." *American Journal of Sociology* 117.1: 1–45.

State Council, PRC. 2004. "China's Social Security and Its Policies." http://www.gov .cn/gongbao/content/2004/content_62994.htm.

Tang, Wenfang. 2016. *Populist Authoritarianism: Chinese Political Culture and Regime Sustainability*. New York: Oxford University Press.

Tarrow, Sidney G. 2011. *Power in Movement: Social Movements and Contentious Politics*, 3rd ed. Cambridge: Cambridge University Press.

Thornton, Patricia M. 2013. "The Advance of the Party: Transformation or Takeover of Urban Grassroots Society?" *China Quarterly* 213: 1–18.

Unger, Jonathan, and Anita Chan. 2008. "Association in a Bind: The Emergence of Political Corporatism." In *Associations and the Chinese State: Contested Spaces*, edited by Jonathan Unger, 48–69. Armonk, NY: M. E. Sharpe.

Walder, Andrew G. 1995. "Local Government as Industrial Firms." *American Journal of Sociology* 101: 263–301.

Wank, David. 1999. *Commodifying Communism: Business, Trust, and Politics in a Chinese City*. Cambridge: Cambridge University Press.

Wu, Jieh-min. 1997. "Strange Bedfellows: Dynamics of Government-Business Relations between Chinese Local Authorities and Taiwanese Investors." *Journal of Contemporary China* 6: 319–46.

———. 2011. "Strangers Forever? Differential Citizenship and China's Rural Migrant Workers." *Taiwanese Sociology* 21: 51–99.

———. 2019. *Rent-Seeking Developmental State in China: Taishang, Guangdong Model and Global Capitalism*. Taipei: National Taiwan University Press.

CHAPTER 9

Governing Foreign Capitalists in the Name of Workers

Policy Shifts Following Worker Suicides at Foxconn

THUNG-HONG LIN

Foxconn's experience in China provides insight into how different levels of government in an authoritarian regime may use labor unrest to discipline foreign capital and serve national developmental priorities. When there are labor incidents, suicides, or protests at a leading foreign company, the central and local governments seize the opportunity to publicize labor issues in the name of defending domestic workers. This takes the form of party-state agencies communicating changes in industrial labor policies to the management of foreign-invested firms. When management complies with labor regulations, central and local governments may support the company by downplaying the issue or suppressing protesters. Other foreign firms, particularly those in the same province, are informed of the policy. According to the China Credit Information Service Mainland China Research Database, which includes firm-level information of the top 1,000 Taiwanese business groups, promoting industrial policy in the name of workers appears successful. However, evolutionary interactions among different levels of government, foreign investors, and domestic workers have yielded unanticipated responses, including increasing labor unrest and capital flight. Rather than demonstrating authoritarian resilience, the case of suicides by Foxconn workers shows that the Chinese government tends to punish both sides of the industrial relationship for its own interests, instead of defending the interests of either foreign capital or domestic labor.

In May 2010, news about a series of migrant worker suicides in Shenzhen broadcast by CCTV4 (an official Chinese news outlet) shocked the public.

Throughout the year, Chinese and foreign mass media explored at least 24 cases of suicide of Foxconn workers. Foxconn belongs to Hon Hai, a Taiwanese business group that is the largest privately owned manufacturer in the world by employment and owns the major factories producing the iPhone and iPad for Apple (Kraemer, Linden, and Dedrick 2011). The news triggered more worker suicides and widespread criticism of Foxconn's management and labor rights in China. These reactions led official state media to block information about new suicide cases after June 2010 (Lin, Lin, and Tseng 2016).

In the summer that the Chinese media first exposed and attempted to downplay the issue of Foxconn worker suicides, faculty and students from 20 universities in China, Hong Kong, and Taiwan organized a research group to investigate labor abuse on the shop floor (Ngai, Chan, and Selden 2013). The author of this chapter was also involved in the research program. Despite the general concern about labor conditions, the Taiwanese research team used personal networks to approach Foxconn's management and examine the insider perspectives (Lin, Lin, and Tseng 2016).

During interviews, Foxconn's Taiwanese managers generally defended themselves by suggesting a conspiracy that the Chinese government intended to disclose the worker suicide events as political punishment for the company. Since 2008, the new leadership of Guangdong province had requested industrial upgrading and increased the minimum wage, both of which pressured Foxconn to improve labor conditions. Subverting the expectations of the Guangdong government, the chairman of Hon Hai, Terry Gou, openly criticized local policy and showed his friendship with Bo Xilai, the Chongqing party secretary who was later punished by the Chinese Communist Party (CCP) for a scandal (Tseng 2012). Interviews with high-level managers revealed that they believed Foxconn was framed by the state-controlled media. Some argued that the suicide rate at Foxconn might not be higher than at other factories, but the events were disclosed mainly because of Foxconn's "wrong" political affiliation (Lin, Lin, and Tseng 2016).

The conspiracy argument does not address the issue of managerial accountability related to the Foxconn worker suicide events, however. Research suggests that organizational issues inside the company were responsible for the tragedies (Lin, Lin, and Tseng 2016). In addition, the company was always welcomed by most local governments in the process of moving to inland provinces; this cannot be explained by incorrect political affiliation. However, the Foxconn case study and in-depth interviews provide clues to how the Chinese government disciplines foreign companies to adhere to industrial policies and how companies respond to these policies. This case study indicates that to regulate foreign-owned factories according to industrial policy, the government uses the strategy of punishing companies in the name of workers, yet labor rights hardly improved after the disputes. The experiences of Foxconn management and workers before and after the events provide an informative example for studying the interaction among the state, foreign capital, and the working class in China.

A New Perspective on the Foxconn Study

The Foxconn worker suicides inspired academic and public interest in the labor conditions in China's world factories. Existing literature has analyzed the Foxconn suicide incidents from three perspectives: Durkheimian, Marxist, and state–society relations. From the Durkheimian perspective, studies have pointed to the Foxconn workers' psychological alienation, absence of social supports, and emotional exhaustion. The difficulties of developing social capital has been used to explain the psychological alienation of the Foxconn workers, who tend to develop depression and even commit suicide (Z. Li, Lin, and Fang 2010; Yang 2014b). From a Marxist perspective, the despotic management and terrible working and living conditions have been reported as reasons for the suicides and worker resistance (Lee 1998; Ngai and Chan 2012; Ngai and Lu 2010; Selden and Wu 2010; Smith and Ngai 2006; So 2003). A recent study implied that the fragmented and despotic production regimes introduced by global brands were responsible for worker suicides. Marxist approaches might interpret the suicides as an indicator of rising class consciousness among Chinese workers. However, Foxconn workers were mobilized by networks of activists and exhibited greater empowerment through increased protest after the suicides rather than before them (Lin, Lin, and Tseng 2016). Other studies have focused on the roles of intellectuals and non-governmental organizations (NGOs) participating in the Foxconn investigation projects and related protests (Cairns and Elfstrom 2014; Hao 2014; He and Huang 2014), and the spread of other protests against global brand companies (Chunyun Li and Liu 2018). In evidence that competes with the sanguine stance of China's labor movement, NGOs and left-wing student activists have encountered intensified repression by the party-state in recent years (J. Chan 2019). The literature (hereafter, Foxconn studies) reflects similar concerns about growing labor protests in China (Lin, Lin, and Tseng 2016).

Emphasizing concern about labor conditions, Foxconn studies have mostly neglected the ambiguous role of the party-state and the responses of the local governments during and after the suicides. Despite avoiding blame, the conspiracy of the Foxconn managers shows the reality of the Chinese government's changing industrial policies as seen in the attitude of the official media. Jumping incidents had occurred at Foxconn before 2010, but these had not attracted media interest. Moreover, the party-state allowed the media to stimulate public concern for three weeks and then helped the company downplay the issue, demonstrating contradictory roles of the party-state (Tseng 2012). As Chih-peng Cheng similarly observes in chapter 8, central and local governments formed different policy coalitions with labor and Taiwanese investors in the context of China's labor laws.

This chapter analyzes the experience of Foxconn after the suicides from an alternative perspective to investigate the puzzling role of the authoritarian regime. Studies of the CCP's authoritarian rule have found that the central and local governments learned from the experience of other developmental states and applied policies as leverage to reward foreign capital for industrial investment (Bolesta 2012; Knight 2014; Nee, Opper, and Wong 2007). Scholars have observed that local governments typically use tax breaks, cheap land expropriated from peasants, and a supply of low-wage labor partially brokered by official human resource agencies as policy tools or personal favors when bargaining with foreign investors (Landry 2008; Naughton 1995, 2007). However, most of these studies have neglected the possibility that the Chinese government's policy tools may have punitive effects on foreign investors. When central and local governments pursue industrial upgrading and geographic realloca-tion of industries, what can they do if the policy rewards are constrained or insufficient?

The study of Foxconn and other Taiwanese business groups provides insight into how authoritarian governments (central or local) punish for-eign capital by regulating but not diminishing it. The Foxconn case shows that the discipline may follow sequential patterns. First, when labor inci-dents, suicides, or protests arise at a leading foreign company, central and local governments want to seize the opportunity to publicize labor dis-putes in the name of workers. Second, party-state agencies inform the company management of industrial policy changes. When management reluctantly or voluntarily follows industrial policy, the central and local governments may sustain the company by downplaying the issue or sup-pressing the protesters. A Chinese proverb says, "Kill the chicken [e.g., Foxconn] to threaten the monkeys [e.g., Taiwanese companies]." Other foreign-owned firms, particularly those in the same province, are then informed of the policy. In turn, other foreign enterprises may follow the leading company to change their investment decisions in the direction suggested by the regime. Thus, the CCP may use labor issues as political leverage to govern foreign capital in a way that promotes its developmen-tal objectives. A similar scenario was observed in the strike of Yue Yuen shoe factory (chapter 8) and protests of Wal-Mart workers (J. Chan 2019). This chapter shows the evolution of how labor issues can become a pol-icy tool to regulate foreign investment and evaluates the relative effec-tiveness of such a strategy.

From 2010 to 2014, my research team interviewed more than 40 workers and managers who worked for Foxconn at all levels of the com-pany hierarchy. The employees included Chinese, Taiwanese, and US citi-zens, and most worked at the plants located in Shenzhen and Chengdu. At least one-third of them were interviewed more than twice in different years (Lin, Lin, and Tseng 2016). Furthermore, data were collected from the China Credit Information Service (CCIS) Mainland China Research Database, which includes firm-level information of the top 1,000 Taiwan-ese business groups, to trace the investment of Foxconn and other Tai-wanese business groups in China before and after the Foxconn worker suicides (CCIS 2019). According to fieldwork and firm-level data, Foxconn and other Taiwanese business groups followed industrial policy, suggesting

efforts at improving governance of industrial relations during the Hu-
Wen era (2002–2012).

Although industrial policy in the name of workers appeared successful, from an evolutionary perspective, the interaction among the (central
and local) states, capital, and labor led to unintended consequences, including increased worker protests and capital flight. Under Xi Jinping's
rule, the party-state has turned to suppressing activist labor NGOs and
labor disputes in southern China (Franceschini and Lin 2019; Kuruvilla
2018). Following China's economic depression in 2013 and the beginning
of the iPhone 6 production cycle, Foxconn and Apple withdrew from
China, shifting their investments to Japan and Southeast Asia (Lin and
Hu 2019), and showcasing Apple's return to the United States (BBC News
2017).

Rather than demonstrating authoritarian resilience, a case study of
the Foxconn labor issue revealed that the CCP had not successfully coordinated the interests of capital and labor (Cheng Li 2012), but showed
stronger autonomy and capacity to punish both sides of the industrial relationship. However, the stronger state also faced higher risks of capital
flight and labor protests, which might have led to greater political instability. In contrast to the rational-choice theory of dictatorship associated
with the expectation of deliberate and resilient authoritarianism in China
(Bueno de Mesquita et al. 2003; B. He and Warren 2011; Mertha 2009;
Nathan 2003), a diachronic historical-institutionalist perspective considering that the intention of political elites and the unintended consequences
of institutional change may be more suitable for explaining the evolutionary and interactive labor policies of the central and local Chinese governments and the responses of capital and labor (Lieberthal and Oksenberg
1988; Tsai 2006).

Shaping Foxconn Investment in the Name of Workers

The worker suicides of Foxconn were exposed in the unique context of
the Chinese government's developmental policies since the early 2000s.
To balance the uneven development of coastal and inland China, the Chi-

nese government promoted several developmental projects, such as the Great Western Development Strategy and the Rise of the Central China Plan in 2002 (Goodman 2004). The effectiveness of these projects was dubious. Before the mid-2000s, foreign investment in certain inland provinces, such as Guizhou, Guangxi, and Ningxia, declined in competition with coastal provinces. Studies have argued that the decline of foreign investment in western regions was a consequence of Beijing's attempt to recentralize the province's economy with mega-projects such as Guizhou's west–east electricity transfer project. Strengthening the central control over the economy eroded the trust of foreign investors (Oakes 2004).

In 2007, the Chinese government reiterated industrial upgrading of the coastal provinces and a developmental project for the western provinces in the 11th Five-Year Plan (National Development and Reform Commission 2007). In January 2008, the central government enforced a new taxation law, increasing the income tax from 17 to 25 percent for foreign companies, and reducing it from 33 to 25 percent for local companies. The reformed taxation system was intended to provide local companies with an equal chance to compete with foreign ones. The Labor Contract Law was introduced in 2008, followed by the Social Insurance Law (January 2010), which the Chinese central government implemented to increase domestic demand by improving wage and labor conditions (see chapter 10 in this volume and Chih-peng Cheng 2014). The Chinese economy was soon damaged by the depression of exports triggered by the global financial crisis. To sustain rapid economic growth, the Chinese government declared plans to expand domestic demand through increasing consumption and public investment in urban infrastructure in November 2008 (Pei 2011).

The economic crisis inspired some local governments to promote policy experiments. The most famous experiment was to "empty the cage to change the birds," a propaganda slogan popularized in March 2008 by Wang Yang, party secretary of Guangdong province at that time. The official policy was written in a document titled "A Decision about Industrial Transfer and Workforce Transfer," which refers to a series of new local regulations promoting industrial upgrading and expelling labor-intensive and high-pollution factories from the Pearl River Delta (Jacobs 2012). The plan, however, did not offer sufficient incentive for foreign investors and lower-level local cadres at the beginning. Terry Gou, who led the largest foreign company in Guangdong, openly doubted its practicability and lobbied others to pressure Wang Yang to revise or postpone the plan (*Apple Daily* 2008). To fulfill the major orders of iPhones and iPads from Apple, Foxconn did not follow the policy to empty its cage; instead, it increased employment in Shenzhen from 2008 to 2010 (Tseng 2012).

As mentioned previously, most Foxconn managerial interviewees claimed that the exposure of the worker suicides was Wang Yang's political revenge, and he openly urged the company to reform its management style when the incidents occurred. Although confirming the conspiracy is difficult, the interviewees reported their bargaining process with local governments after the suicides. A manager mentioned, "The investigators from the Shenzhen city government said that we can keep some revenue here (referring to Shenzhen, where most suicides occurred), but told us not to keep so many production lines. After the suicide issue, what will people think if you still keep your assembly lines in Shenzhen?" (fieldnote C6).

Following suggestions from the investigation team sent by the central and local governments, Foxconn relocated its factories to inland China starting in June 2010. Some special projects (SPs), such as the Henan and Chengdu SPs, named according to the new locations of Foxconn's plants, were promoted by the management and the local governments. The SPs were plans to establish new factories in approximately 100 days to fulfill the production capacity that was moved out of Shenzhen, and they mostly matched the requirements and deadlines of Apple's products (the iPhone 5 and 5S at that time). During the most difficult time for Foxconn, Bo Xilai, a rising politician governing Chongqing, openly supported the company and promised to offer land and workforce for the Chongqing SP in July 2010.

In the factional struggles of the CCP before Xi gained power, Wang and Bo represented the polarized factions of neoliberal versus leftist economic ideology and the Youth League versus "princelings" political factions, respectively. Before stepping down as party secretary in Chongqing, Bo initiated a movement against organized crime, increased public spending on expanded welfare programs, maintained GDP growth, and campaigned to revive Cultural Revolution values. Bo's advertising of egalitarian values and his Chongqing model made him the forerunner of the New Left in China, a group of intellectuals and policy elites disenchanted with market-oriented economic reforms and increasing social inequality (Jacobs 2012). By contrast, Bo welcomed Foxconn, a foreign company notorious for its sweatshop issues, to invest in his city. This favor was viewed as compensation for the punishment Wang imposed on the company in the name of protecting labor rights.

Bo was not the only local leader who accepted Foxconn's investment. The Henan SP in Zhengzhou, the first new Foxconn factory producing iPhones and iPads, was opened in August 2010. The employment of Henan SP increased to 140,000 workers in the following year. Chengdu SP, another major Foxconn investment project in Sichuan province, hired more than 160,000 workers through 2012 (Tseng 2012). Local cadres of Chengdu's urban development and labor bureaus, who were interviewed in 2011, reported that following the promises of the city government, they exhausted their organizational capacity to efficiently offer land and workforce to fulfill the needs for the new Foxconn factories. With the local cadre's efforts and migrant workers' illegal overtime labor, Foxconn successfully recovered from the scandal of the suicides. Its production capacity matched the increasing demand for iPhones and retained its primary client, Apple (Mishkin 2013).

Although Terry Gou openly met and supported Bo in early February 2012 (*Apple Daily* 2012) just before Bo was dismissed from public office, this questionable political decision did not hinder new Foxconn investment in China. The changing location of Foxconn's net sales (revenue) could be a useful indicator of the new dispersal of investment in production lines. Using the CCIS (2019) database of top 1,000 Taiwanese firms in China, this study traced the changing net sales of the Foxconn group in different provinces from 2009 to 2015. As figure 9.1 shows, the net sales of the Foxconn group were mainly concentrated in Guangdong province before 2009. From the 2010 suicide events to 2013, as figure 9.2 shows, the group's revenue spread from Guangdong to western and central China, including Henan, Sichuan, Chongqing, Hubei, Guangxi, and Shanxi. The locations, range, and speed of Foxconn's new investment cannot be explained by the competition between Bo and Wang or their associated conspiracies. The exposure and censorship of

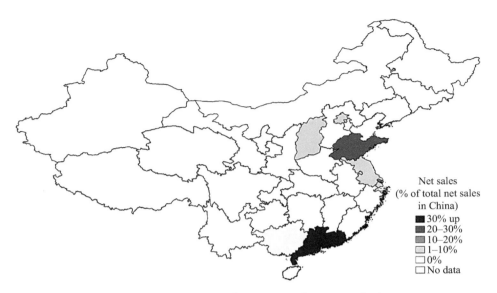

FIGURE 9.1 Geographical distribution of net revenue of Foxconn subsidiaries, 2009
Source: CCIS (2019).

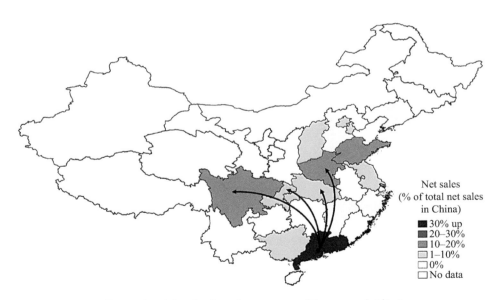

FIGURE 9.2 Geographical distribution of net revenue of Foxconn subsidiaries, 2013
Source: CCIS (2019).

the suicides and the national-scale factory reallocation could not have happened without the tacit consent of the central government.

Foxconn adjusted its internal division of labor for reallocating factories (Lin, Lin, and Tseng 2016). An engineer who worked for Apple reported,

> Our Foxconn team primarily co-worked with engineers in the US, and brought back the prototype as well as all the codes of conduct, built the pilot production line in Longhua (Shenzhen), and ensured that the line was stable and the quality of the product was satisfactory. Because of the increasing wages and cost in Shenzhen, the team reallocated the mass production line to Chengdu SP from October 2010. Still, a few products and some crucial parts are assembled in Longhua. (fieldnote A1)

The industrial clusters around the new factories indicate that Foxconn redistributed its production lines to match local suppliers on the basis of the cost-down strategy without considering worker conditions. For instance, Foxconn decided to produce motherboards in Chengdu, because some suppliers were there (Lin, Lin, and Tseng 2016).

However, management encountered difficulty in moving employees on the same line as a whole from Shenzhen to other provinces. Most migrant workers were reluctant to move to less developed inland areas, which were similar to the villages they came from. The company tried to reallocate workers on the basis of the new factories' distance from their original hometowns. For example, migrant workers from Hubei were persuaded to migrate to the new production lines at the Wuhan SP in Hubei (Lin, Lin, and Tseng 2016). Those who had work experience in Shenzhen might be promoted to foreperson or supervisor at the new line to lead newcomers recruited from local labor brokerage agencies. These strategies could not immediately solve the labor shortage at the new plants. Through the brokerage of local governments, the company cooperated with some vocational high schools and brought thousands of student workers into the factories (Chan 2013). Sustained by local governments, Foxconn effectively overcame the labor shortage and increased its employment of Chinese workers to 1.29 million in 2012.

Taiwanese Capital Flows under Changing Industrial Policy

The jumping suicide incidents elicited criticism on the Internet and mass media of the military-style Taiwanese management, not only at Foxconn but at most Taiwanese-owned factories. Subsequent developmental and labor policies shocked other Taiwanese business groups. First, Foxconn's responses, which included increasing basic salaries and social insurance coverage, changed the labor market and worker expectations of wage and working conditions, particularly in the Pearl River Delta. Second, the rearrangement of Foxconn factories resulted in reallocating supply chains in the electronics industry in China. Third, new industrial and labor policies in coastal China caused other Taiwanese business groups to follow Foxconn inland.

In addition to the Foxconn incident serving as an example for other Taiwanese companies, the differential legal minimum wages across provinces was a source of leverage for the Chinese government. As figure 9.3 shows, the increasing official minimum wages were usually higher in the eastern areas (especially Shenzhen) than in western regions. Shenzhen and Dongguan started to improve their minimum wages in 2008, but the minimum wages in Suzhou and the western provinces remained unchanged until 2010. Therefore, the wage gap between the eastern and western areas widened before 2010. This wage gap strongly affected the incentives of Taiwanese groups, whose labor-intensive, subcontracted manufacturers depended on low-wage migrant workers. When Taiwanese investment moved to inland China, the minimum wages of these provinces began to catch up with those of coastal China in 2013.

Some evidence shows that Foxconn's punishment and changing state policies effectively reshaped Taiwanese investment. This study used the CCIS (2019) database, from which each firm's time-series data between 2004 and 2017 were downloaded, to trace the capital flow of Taiwanese business groups. The net sales and employment numbers from the top 1,000 firms each year were aggregated according to province of registration, and the provinces were then pooled into six major areas following the official Chinese geographic categorization: north, northeast, east, central, south, and west. Therefore, the results shown in figures 9.3 and 9.4

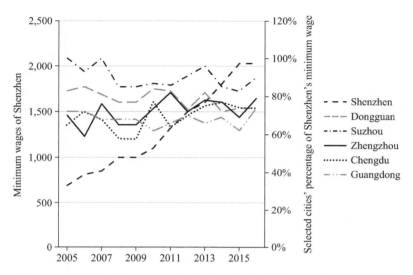

FIGURE 9.3 Official minimum wages of selected major Taiwanese investment destinations in China and the percentage of Shenzhen's minimum wage, 2005–2016
Source: The Announcement of Adjustment of Minimum Wages Standard from each province in China, 2005–2016.

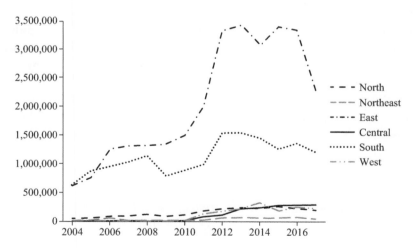

FIGURE 9.4 Number of employees in the top 1,000 Taiwanese companies in China
Source: CCIS database, 2019. The numbers are aggregated from the top 1,000 firms of each year. Aggregate numbers of firms are separated by province and then pooled into six major areas following the official Chinese geographic areas: North, Northeast, East, Central, South, and West.

can be used to analyze the reallocation of Taiwanese business groups as a whole.

Figure 9.3 shows the changing net sales of the top 1,000 Taiwanese firms in six major areas and shows that net sales increased until 2012. From 2010 to 2012, although businesses in eastern and southern China were developing continuously, net sales increased, especially in the central, northern, and western provinces. This indicates the reallocation of Taiwanese business groups. As official data revealed, Chinese economic growth slowed, which affected net sales of Taiwanese companies from 2012 to 2013 but gradually recovered and stagnated over 2014–2017.

Figure 9.4 shows changing regional patterns of employment, which may be a more useful indicator of the reallocation of factories owned by the top 1,000 Taiwanese firms in the six major areas. The employment of Taiwanese-owned businesses rapidly increased, especially in eastern China, which surpassed southern China in 2005. The data show that the employment of Taiwanese business groups was redistributed among six localities, such that approximately 300,000 workers were relocated from southern China after 2008. Affected by the economic depression in 2012, Taiwanese firms removed approximately 150,000 workers from the eastern provinces. By contrast, after the Foxconn suicides, Taiwanese firms—including Foxconn—moved to the central, northern, and western provinces and employed approximately 400,000 additional workers from 2010 to 2013. The Taiwanese business groups were highly affected by the Chinese economic downturn and increasing wages. Except in the western provinces, their employment in China has stagnated since 2013. In 2016–2017, the aggregate number of workers employed by Taiwanese business groups rapidly declined, which indicates the trend of Taiwanese capital flight from China.

Unintended Consequences: Worker Protests and Capital Flight

Although the Foxconn case and labor policies have affected Taiwanese investment since 2010, industrial policies in the name of the workers led to unintended consequences. Facing public criticism, Taiwanese companies immediately applied several strategies to prevent workers from committing suicide, such as limiting overtime hours (particularly for Apple's production lines), forbidding forepersons from using inappropriate language on the shop floor, and constructing safety nets around the factory and dormitory buildings to prevent death by jumping. Moreover, Foxconn increased the base salaries of rank-and-file workers to slightly higher than the legal minimum wages mandated by local governments. For example, the basic salary of Foxconn workers in Shenzhen gradually increased from ¥900 to ¥1,200 and then to ¥2,000 from 2010 to 2012. To maintain revenue, most production lines replaced rewards for engineers with rewards for operators. Low-ranking Chinese engineers, supervisors, and forepersons often complained about their reduced wages after the suicides.

The public did not know about the Foxconn labor union, established in March 2007, of which the chair was Terry Gou's executive assistant, until the exposure of the jumping suicides (Ngai and Chan 2012). After the incidents, the union announced a phone number for workers to call to express their discontent. My interviewees reported that some workers expressed problems about dormitory conditions, which led to improvements. Others who expressed concerns regarding line management were fired (fieldnotes C21 and C22). In the Chengdu SP, the local government helped the union establish some "youth apartment" models with gyms, swimming pools, and internet bars to show their concern for improving labor conditions, but workers complained that they did not have time to enjoy the facilities after long work hours. Excluding some progress in Chengdu SP, reports showed that the working and living conditions of migrant workers were similar to those under management in Shenzhen (Chan, Pun, and Seldon 2020). Evaluating improvements in labor conditions was difficult. Nevertheless, new state policies challenged Foxconn's managerial authority. This was a political opportunity for discontented workers, who had been suppressed by management for years (Elfstrom and Kuruvilla 2014).

Following reduction in overtime hours and the increase in the basic salary, production line workers expressed more grievances and organized more wildcat strikes and riots. As some studies on the Chinese "insurgency trap" have argued (Friedman 2014; Gallagher 2014), the characteristics of such collective resistance departed from institutionalized labor movements. First, they were typically led by Chinese forepersons and low-rank engineers because their income and rewards were reduced by the overtime restrictions. Second, some disputes clearly occurred because of long-distance reallocation of the labor force for Apple's urgent production orders (Lin, Lin, and Tseng 2016). Furthermore, the exposure of the suicides showed not only the changing industrial policy of the Chinese government but also the weakness (at least temporarily) of managerial authority without the political support of the central and local governments. Learning from the suicide events, some Foxconn workers realized how to involve mass media and apply the labor regulations against management (Elfstrom 2019). Because of the rapid reallocation of production lines and skilled workers by Foxconn, workers' collective actions were diffused by experienced leaders from the eastern to western provinces (Zhang 2015).

This study obtained and analyzed information from 19 cases regarding collective worker actions that occurred between 2010 and 2016 from media news and websites (extended from Lin, Lin, and Tseng 2016). The disputes were mostly stimulated by the reduction of income resulting from overtime restrictions, large-scale reallocation of migrant workers from higher minimum wage coastal provinces to lower minimum wage inland provinces, or conflicts between migrant workers and local security in the new factories. For example, in January 2012, 300 indignant workers in Hubei threatened suicide after being rejected for pay raises and compensation (Fu 2017). One of these was an interviewee in Shenzhen: he was transferred back to Hubei, and his basic salary was reduced accordingly. In June 2012 in Chengdu, some employees with grudges prevented security from catching a thief who came from their hometown, leading to a riot, followed by some workers burning the factory buildings. In Taiyuan in late September 2012, 1,000 workers rioted because the migrant workers, mostly from Hunan, opposed the local security's gangster-style management. In September 2013, a similar violent riot occurred in Yantai.

Gou showed his support to Bo in early 2012, but Foxconn managers reported that their chairman bet wrong when Xi secured the helm of the CCP's top leadership and violently purged Bo's faction in the name of anticorruption over the next two years. From late 2013, the company silently moved production capacity from Chongqing to other newly invested provinces. The changing strategy reduced revenue as well as the wage and overtime payment of employees, particularly those of low-ranking Chinese engineers and forepersons at the Chongqing SP. Several wildcat strikes took place because the plant ended assembly lines and reduced overtime hours.

The number and scale of the protests peaked in 2013 after the first-wave reallocation of Foxconn's production lines (see Appendix Table 9.1 at the end of the chapter). Earlier Foxconn studies explored the role of intellectuals and NGOs in the investigation and improvement of labor rights in China, but these intellectuals and NGOs did not openly condone the Foxconn worker strikes and riots. They maintained cautious distance from the protests for their own survival. Since 2013, official media has blocked most of the news about the aftermath of this series of collective action and suicides, which the company also tried to conceal. However, Foxconn worker problems were already mostly exposed on the internet and overseas media. Similar wildcat strikes and labor disputes organized by workers against foreign companies (e.g., Japan's Honda and Taiwan's Yue Yuen) spread and increased in frequency and location (C. Chan 2010, 2012; C. Chan and Hui 2012; Chen 2015).

The political turmoil of the CCP's factional struggles and the high transportation cost to inland provinces might have shaped a new wave of factory reallocation, which did not follow state directions. Foxconn's changing revenues and worker protests showed that a second wave of factory reallocation began in 2013. As shown in figure 9.5, in 2015, Foxconn

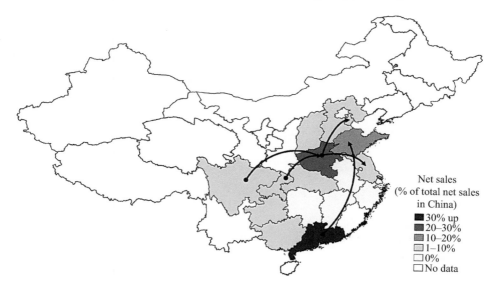

Net sales
(% of total net sales
in China)
■ 30% up
■ 20–30%
■ 10–20%
□ 1–10%
□ 0%
□ No data

FIGURE 9.5 Net revenue of Foxconn subsidiaries in 2017
Note: Arrows indicate the second wave of reallocation, beginning in 2013 reported in news.
Source: CCIS (2019).

covertly and frequently invested in Zhengzhou, Shandong, Jiangsu, and Guangdong bases, rather than in Guangxi, Chongqing, or Chengdu. This reversed the distribution of the group's revenue from the western provinces to the eastern coastal provinces. In addition, changing state policies and labor protests shocked Taiwanese investors, who considered leaving China.

Some news reported that because of increased expenses, at least one-third of Taiwanese factories were bankrupt, and most owners chose to flee China (Cheng 2014). For example, with Apple's consent, Foxconn accelerated its investment project in Maharashtra, India, which is expected to create a million new jobs. In 2015 Foxconn announced the acquisition of Sharp Corporation, the 10th largest television manufacturer in the world and the third largest cellphone producer in Japan, to access advanced panel technology. Fearing Foxconn's capital flight, in May 2017 Chinese Prime Minister Li Keqiang met Gou in the Zhengzhou factory to ask for Foxconn's commitment to the continuity of the manufacturing sector in China.

On July 27, 2017, US President Donald Trump, together with Gou, announced a plan to invest US$10 billion in a new factory in Wisconsin. This factory is expected to employ 3,000 people initially. Trump claimed credit for Foxconn's "incredible investment" to follow his rhetoric about reviving the US manufacturing sector and "making America great again" (BBC News 2017). The dramatic announcement of Foxconn's investment in the United States reflected not only the return of factories to the United States but also general capital flight of the global electronics supply chain from China. The new wave of Foxconn's large-scale investment in Japan, India, and the United States shows declining confidence of its management in China's business and political future.

Discussion and Conclusion

For years, China's central government and some local governments have indicated pursuit of industrial upgrading on the east coast and reallocation of labor-intensive industries to inland areas, but the policy impact has been mixed. Some prominent foreign capitalists, such as Gou, have openly challenged such developmental projects. What can an authoritarian regime do to secure the cooperation of foreign capitalists who do not depend on state-owned finance and the domestic market? The central and local governments exposed labor disputes and improved enforcement of labor regulations probably because of the labor shortage, increasing labor protests, and the need to reshape the incentives of foreign investors.

This chapter used the case study of Foxconn to show the unexpected impact of the party-state's industrial policies over time. After the policy changes in 2008, Foxconn management initially hesitated to follow Guangdong's industrial upgrading plan and the labor regulations established by provincial leader Wang Yang. In 2010, the scandal of Foxconn workers' jumping suicides was exposed by CCTV, a mass media platform controlled by the central government. The event sent a strong policy signal to Foxconn's top managers, who decided to invest in the western provinces, especially Chongqing and Sichuan. These were led by Bo Xilai, a major factional figure competing against Wang.

In contrast to the open condemnation and state intervention in the labor issues in Guangdong, Foxconn was welcomed in the western provinces, where local governments voluntarily became brokers for land and labor. Although Foxconn initially sided with the wrong political side, the company was not significantly affected in the end. Western provinces welcomed its investments and Foxconn retained its major customer.

According to interviewees, improvements occurred in Foxconn working and living conditions at a few major factories. It is difficult to argue that the suicides and increasing strikes forced the Chinese authoritarian regime to allow workers' collective actions and improve labor rights. Accordingly, this case study suggests that exposing the Foxconn suicides was a political strategy to incentivize cooperation with the party-state's developmental project. The same pattern can be found in other large-scale labor disputes of leading foreign companies; it is inappropriate to view the resolution of these labor disputes as indicating substantive improvements in labor rights conditions in China. Instead, they should be viewed as a signal of industrial policy changes by the party-state in the name of Chinese workers.

The Foxconn worker suicides could be regarded as a successful tool by "killing the chicken" (Foxconn) to "threaten the monkeys" (other Taiwanese businesses). The increasing wage level and social insurance coverage in the eastern provinces, and the relatively low wage level and active local state labor brokerage in the western provinces contributed to the push and pull of foreign capital. The contradictory labor policies of the eastern and western provincial governments were allowed by the tacit consent of the central government. As a result, the statistics show that other major Taiwanese companies followed the developmental project to invest in central and western China, particularly after the suicides in 2010. The strategy for regulating Taiwanese capital seemed effective.

In this volume's theoretical framework, the evolutionary interaction between the state and foreign capital illustrates the advantage of arbitrary state autonomy and capacity. Changing labor policies led to some unintended consequences for governments, however. After the worker suicides, Foxconn continuously improved its wage level and labor conditions, but the workers became more active in wildcat strikes and labor disputes as they diffused from the eastern to western provinces. Active labor protests alarmed the central and local governments, which suppressed labor NGOs and strikes. After the business cycle reached production of the iPhone 6, Foxconn accelerated its investment projects in India, Japan, and the United States. Taiwanese capital flight from China accelerated following the outbreak of the US–China trade war, and revenues of the entire electronics industry began to decline in 2018. Although the punitive state policy of disciplining capital and labor seemed effective in the short term, the rigidities of CCP authoritarianism are now challenged by risks of economic slowdown, increasing capital flight, and labor disputes.

How will the world's factory secure investment when the CCP regime is becoming riskier and perhaps less resilient? Foxconn has suffered from the US–China trade war through increasing tariffs and other measures since December 2018. In spring 2019, Guo resigned as Foxconn's chair and announced his campaign for Taiwan's presidential race. As Foxconn's biggest shareholder, his family retains control of the company's board. The dramatic strategy did not attract enough Taiwanese voters, who suspected that his motivation for pursuing power was to protect his own assets in China. During the campaign, Guo was criticized by NGO activists and Taiwanese mass media for the Foxconn suicides. Although Guo lost the presidential nomination bid in the Kuomintang's primary election, he demonstrated to Beijing his political influence in Taiwan and the United States. As the earlier stage of disciplining foreign capitalists in the name of workers has displayed, Foxconn's dramatic story showed

Appendix Table 9.1

News events of Foxconn workers' collective action, 2010–2016

Date	Location	No. of People	Event
November 2010	Foshan	6,000–7,000	Foxconn workers protested their low wages and opposed the factory's plan to move the plants to inner provinces in China. They claimed that they had asked high-level administrators to raise their wages but were threatened with dismissal. One anonymous worker stated that a notice warned employees not to go on strike or they would lose their jobs. Another worker said that their monthly salary was lower than promised.
January 2012	Wuhan	150	Foxconn workers threatened mass suicide; one of them was an interviewee. The workers were eventually coaxed down by Foxconn managers and local CCP officials after two days on the roof of their three-floor plant in Wuhan. The latest protest began on January 2 after managers reassigned about 600 workers to a new production line that produced computer cases for Acer, a Taiwanese computer company.
January 2012	Yantai	1,000+	Foxconn Yantai workers went on strike because of the disparity in salary among workers. A high-level executive explained that this was a new rule. The factory administrators separated workers to disperse the mob. A worker stated that all workers were to receive a raise in salary to ¥1,750 in September. Although all of the workers were promoted to E1 (the lowest level of Foxconn official employees), they did not receive the commensurate salary.
January 2012	Jiangxi	1,000+	On January 11, approximately 1,000 workers staged a protest. They went on strike in the factory on January 10 to protest low wages, unbalanced pay raises, terrible food, and rigid management. Some workers were reportedly arrested during the demonstration. One worker said that everyone was required to deduct ¥9 from their food stipends and ¥80 from their wages.

(continued)

Appendix Table 9.1 (*continued*)

Date	Location	No. of People	Event
March 2012	Shanxi, Taiyuan	Hundreds	Workers at the A9 plant in Taiyuan, Shanxi, went on strike because of the wage adjustment. Some of the workers stated that the wage adjustment was not for everyone, but only for administrators and technicians. E1 workers in particular did not benefit from the wage adjustment.
April 2012	Wuhan	100+	To protest low wages, approximately 100 workers gathered on a roof and threatened to jump from the building. According to an anonymous worker, these workers were working at DT2 Personal Computer Enclosure Group. After combining the DT2 plants from Shenzhen and Yantai, the Wuhan administration began to regulate additional overtime hours while demanding that employees increase production. Thus, the income was reduced.
June 2012	Chengdu	1,000+	As two security guards were pursuing a thief and shouting for help, some workers who resented the guards gathered to interfere. Approximately 1,000 workers threw trash bins, stools, wash basins, firecrackers, and beer cans from the dormitories, destroying facilities and causing chaos. The factory managers called the police, and some workers were arrested.

September 2012	Shanxi, Taiyuan	2,000+	In a riot in Taiyuan, Shanxi, thousands of workers destroyed various items and even set fire to cars. Local police officers suppressed the riot; reportedly, at least 10 people were killed. An anonymous source stated that the riot was caused by workers who were dissatisfied with the adjustment of overtime regulations. Foxconn workers from various provinces were assembled in Taiyuan to meet the production deadline of the iPhone 5 release. The riot originated from a fight between Hunan workers and security guards. The Hunan workers were beaten severely and later started the riot. After drinking alcohol, the Hunan workers quarreled with the security guards. Other workers heard the noise and then joined, smashing all the safety facilities in the plant and igniting the security guards' electric bikes. At 2 a.m., local and antiriot police arrived to beat and detain workers. The severity of the riot prompted Foxconn to close the plant for one day, and traffic was controlled within 2 km of the plant.
October 2012	Zhengzhou	3,000–4,000	China Labor Watch reported that the riot at Foxconn Zhengzhou occurred due to excessively strict quality inspections. Workers from the production lines went on strike to protest the unreasonable quality inspections. Workers and inspectors had quarrels and fistfights during the strike. Because some iPhone 5 users complained that the paint was peeling off the outer shell, Apple directed Foxconn to address the matter. Thus, Foxconn adopted a considerably more rigid quality inspection of the outer shells. Another possible factor contributing to the riot was the requirement to work on holidays.
November 2012	Shenzhen	5,000	Liberty Times Net reported that a riot occurred in Shenzhen Longhua, in which approximately 5,000 workers gathered to protest the bullying from security guards. However, Foxconn announced that the conflict was not a riot but a personal gambling quarrel.

(continued)

Appendix Table 9.1 (*continued*)

Date	Location	No. of People	Event
January 2013	Beijing	1,000+	Approximately 1,000 workers gathered in a restaurant demanding that high-level executives respond to the arrears of year-end bonuses. Because the factory did not answer the questions clearly and directly, the workers went on strike until midnight. The local government enlisted the police to control the situation.
June 2013	Longhua, Shenzhen	3,400+	Innolux Display Group shut down in May for one month. According to informed sources, at least 3,000 workers were relocated; however, they rejected reassignment to different plants. Instead, the employees requested that the company lay off the staff to allow them to gain compensation.
July 2013	Shenzhen	200	Although a Foxconn spokesperson denied the strike, 200 Consumer and Computer Products Business Group workers did not show up for work. They walked directly to the headquarters of the labor union shouting, "Raise our wages!" A participant said to a reporter that Foxconn raised the wages by 20% for technicians in a specific department, but that others did not receive equal raises. Moreover, the annual bonus was not paid on time. Working overtime was another factor that contributed to the strike. Foxconn limited overtime hours; however, they reduced total wages.
July 2013	Foshan	1,500+	Approximately 1,000 workers gathered in the halls and refused to work, stating that Foxconn did not follow the original contract and continued to postpone the end of the workday.

September 2013	Yantai	300–400	A massive fight occurred at Foxconn's Yantai factory during the Mid-Autumn Festival. More than 200 workers from Guizhou beat workers from Shandong. Although the military police were called to quell the riot, another violent outbreak occurred the next day. Reports claimed that the riot led to three deaths, injured at least 20 workers, and resulted in hundreds of arrests. The riot was reportedly caused by a quarrel in an internet café between two female workers.
December 2013	Chongqing	100	Nearly 100 Chongqing Foxconn workers went on strike because of low wages. The two-day strike occurred because of a dispute over pay and uneven raises.
March 2014	Tianjin	1,000+	Some Foxconn production lines and workers moved from Zhengzhou to Tianjin, but the salary and benefits promised by the management were unfulfilled. More than 1,000 workers that migrated from Zhengzhou went on strike but were beaten by local security agents. The strike ended two days later once management fulfilled the promises of salary and benefits.
June 2014	Chongqing	800+	More than 800 Chongqing Foxconn workers were involved in a dispute over severance pay. The plant planned to terminate notebook assembly. However, sources reported that operators did not receive adequate severance pay, whereas engineers did.
September 2015	Longhua	50	Approximately 50 Longhua Foxconn workers organized a rally with banners claiming that management had paid bribes with their housing provident fund, but 16 activists of the protest were soon fired.

SOURCE: Extended from Lin, Lin, and Tseng (2016), appendix table 9.1.

the rising economic uncertainty and political dynamics of foreign investment in the evolution toward a less resilient authoritarian regime.

References

Apple Daily. 2008. "Terry Gou Met Chiang Pin-kung and Petition for the Taiwanese Businesses." *Apple Daily*, April 28. http://www.appledaily.com.tw/appledaily/article/headline/20080428/30495032.

———. 2012. "Bo Xilai Met Terry Gou in a High Profile." *Apple Daily*, February 26. http://hk.apple.nextmedia.com/international/art/20120226/16103459.

BBC News. 2017. "Trump takes credit for Foxconn's 'incredible investment.'" BBC News, July 27. http://www.bbc.com/news/business-40732035.

Bolesta, Andrzej. 2012. "China as a Post-Socialist Developmental State: Explaining Chinese Development Trajectory." PhD diss., London School of Economics and Political Science.

Bueno de Mesquita, Bruce, Alastair Smith, Randolph M. Siverson, and James D. Morrow. 2003. *The Logic of Political Survival*. Cambridge, MA: MIT Press.

Cairns, Christopher, and M. Elfstrom. 2014. "Strikes, Social Media and the Press: Why Chinese Authorities Allow or Suppress New and Old Media Coverage of Labor Disputes." Paper presented at the American Political Science Association of the 2014 Annual Meeting, Washington, DC. August 28–31.

Chan, Chris King-Chi. 2010. "Class Struggle in China: Case Studies of Migrant Worker Strikes in the Pearl River Delta." *South African Review of Sociology* 41.3: 61–80.

———. 2012. "Class or Citizenship? Debating Workplace Conflict in China." *Journal of Contemporary Asia* 42.2: 308–27.

———. 2013. "Contesting Class Organization: Migrant Workers' Strikes in China's Pearl River Delta, 1978–2010." *International Labor and Working Class History* 83 (Spring): 112–36.

Chan, Chris King-Chi, and E. S. I. Hui. 2012. "The Dynamics and Dilemma of Workplace Trade Union Reform in China: The Case of Honda Workers' Strike." *Journal of Industrial Relations* 54.4: 653–68.

Chan, Jenny. 2019. "State and Labor in China, 1978–2018." *Labor and Society* 22: 461–75.

Chan, Jenny, Mark Selden, and Pun Ngai. 2020. *Dying for an iPhone: Apple, Foxconn, and the Lives of China's Workers*. Chicago: Haymarket Books.

Chen, Chih-Jou Jay. 2015. "Taiwanese Business in China: Encountering and Coping with Risks." アジア研究 (*Asian Studies*) 60.3: 31–47.

Cheng, Chih-peng. 2014. "Embedded Trust and Beyond: The Organizational Network Transformation of Taishang's Shoe Industry in China." In *Border Crossing in Greater China: Production, Community and Identity*, edited by Jenn-Hwan Wang, 40–60. London: Routledge.

China Credit Information Service (CCIS). 2019. "Databases Online." CCIS. http://www.credit.com.tw/creditonline/en/service3.asp.

Elfstrom, Manfred. 2019. "A Tale of Two Deltas: Labour Politics in Jiangsu and Guang-dong." *British Journal of Industrial Relations* 57: 247–74.

Elfstrom, Manfred, and Sarosh Kuruvilla. 2014. "The Changing Nature of Labor Un-rest in China." *ILR Review* 67.2: 453–80.

Franceschini, Ivan, and Kevin Lin. 2019. "Labour NGOs in China: From Legal Mo-bilisation to Collective Struggle (and Back?)." *China Perspectives* 1.3: 75–84.

Friedman, Eli. 2014. *Insurgency Trap: Labor Politics in Postsocialist China.* Ithaca, NY: ILR Press.

Fu, Diana. 2017. "Disguised Collective Action in China." *Comparative Political Studies* 50.4: 499–527.

Gallagher, Mary E. 2014. "China's Workers Movement and the End of the Rapid-Growth Era." *Daedalus* 143.2: 81–95.

Goodman, David S. G., ed. 2004. *China's Campaign to "Open Up the West": National, Provincial-level and Local Perspectives.* Cambridge: Cambridge University Press.

Hao, Zhidong. 2014. "The Role of Intellectuals in Contemporary China's Labor Move-ment: A Preliminary Exploration." *International Perspectives on Social Policy, Admin-istration, and Practice* 1: 239–53.

He, Alex Jingwei, and Genghua Huang. 2014. "Fighting for Migrant Labor Rights in the World's Factory: Legitimacy, Resource Constraints and Strategies of Grassroots Migrant Labor NGOs in South China." *Journal of Contemporary China* 24.93: 471–92.

He, Baogang, and Mark E. Warren. 2011. "Authoritarian Deliberation: The Delibera-tive Turn in Chinese Political Development." *Perspectives on Politics* 9.2: 269–89.

Jacobs, Andrew. 2012. "As China Awaits New Leadership, Liberals Look to a Provincial Party Chief." *New York Times*, November 5. http://www.nytimes.com/2012/11/06 /world/asia/liberals-in-china-look-to-guangdongs-party-chief.html?_r=1.

Knight, John B. 2014. "China as a Developmental State." *World Economy* 37.10: 1335–47.

Kraemer, Kenneth L., Greg Linden, and Jason Dedrick. 2011. "Capturing Value in Global Networks: Apple's iPad and iPhone." UC Irvine Working Paper. http://economia deservicos.com/wp-content/uploads/2017/04/value_ipad_iphone.pdf.

Kuruvilla, Sarosh. 2018. "Editorial Essay: From Cautious Optimism to Renewed Pes-simism: Labor Voice and Labor Scholarship in China." *ILR Review* 71.5: 1013–28.

Landry, Pierre F. 2008. *Decentralized Authoritarianism in China: The Communist Party's Control of Local Elites in the Post-Mao Era.* Cambridge: Cambridge University Press.

Lee, Ching Kwan. 1998. *Gender and the South China Miracle: Two Worlds of Factory Women.* Berkeley: University of California Press.

Li, Cheng. 2012. "The End of the CCP's Resilient Authoritarianism? A Tripartite As-sessment of Shifting Power in China." *China Quarterly* 211: 595–623.

Li, Chunyun, and Mingwei Liu. 2018. "Overcoming Collective Action Problems Fac-ing Chinese Workers: Lessons from Four Protests against Walmart." *ILR Review* 71.5: 1078–105.

Li, Zhang, Zhang Lin, and Wan Fang. 2010. "Study on the Effect of Job Insecurity on Emotional Exhaustion: An Example of Foxconn Jumping Incidents." Paper presented at the 2010 International Conference on Management Science and Engineering (ICMSE), Melbourne, Australia, November 24–26.

Lieberthal, Kenneth, and Michel Oksenberg. 1988. *Policy Making in China: Leaders, Structures, and Processes.* Princeton, NJ: Princeton University Press.

Lin, Thung-Hong, Yi-ling Lin, and Wei-Lin Tseng. 2016. "Manufacturing Suicide: The Politics of a World Factory." *Chinese Sociological Review* 48.1:1–32.

Lin, Thung-Hong, and Bowei Hu. 2019. "Subcontractors' Dilemma: The Expansion of Taiwanese Firms 2002–2015." *International Journal of Taiwanese Studies* 2.2: 199–229.

Mertha, Andrew. 2009. "'Fragmented Authoritarianism 2.0': Political Pluralization in the Chinese Policy Process." *China Quarterly* 200: 995–1012.

Mishkin, Sarah. 2013. "Apple Builds Relations beyond Foxconn." *Financial Times,* May 14. http://www.ft.com/cms/s/0/b3ef10b4-bca1-11e2-9519-00144feab7de.html.

National Development and Reform Commission of the People's Republic of China (NDRC). "Great Western Development Strategy for the Eleventh Five-Year Plan." NDRC. http://www.sdpc.gov.cn/fzgggz/fzgh/ghwb/gjjgh/200709/P020150630514150488919.pdf.

Nathan, Andrew. 2003. "Authoritarian Resilience." *Journal of Democracy* 14.1: 6–17.

Naughton, Barry. 1995. *Growing Out of the Plan: Chinese Economic Reform, 1978–1993.* Cambridge: Cambridge University Press.

———. 2007. *The Chinese Economy: Transitions and Growth.* Cambridge, MA: MIT Press.

Nee, Victor, Sonja Opper, and Sonia Wong. 2007. "Developmental State and Corporate Governance in China." *Management and Organization Review* 3.1: 19–53.

Ngai, Pun, and Jenny Chan. 2012. "Global Capital, the State, and Chinese Workers: The Foxconn Experience." *Modern China* 38.4: 384–410.

Ngai, Pun, Jenny Chan, and Mark Selden. 2013. "The Politics of Global Production: Apple, Foxconn and a New Generation of Chinese Workers." *New Technology, Work and Employment* 28.2: 100–115.

Ngai, Pun, and Huilin Lu. 2010. "Unfinished Proletarianization: Self, Anger, and Class Action among the Second Generation of Peasant-Workers in Present-Day China." *Modern China* 36.5: 493–519.

Oakes, Tim. 2004. "Building a Southern Dynamo: Guizhou and State Power." In *China's Campaign to "Open Up the West": National, Provincial-Level and Local Perspectives,* edited by David S. G. Goodman, 153–73. Cambridge: Cambridge University Press.

Pei, Minxin. 2011. "China's Ticking Debt Bomb." *Diplomat,* July 5. http://thediplomat.com/2011/07/chinas-ticking-debt-bomb/.

Selden, Mark, and Jieh-min Wu. 2010. "The Chinese State, Suppressed Consumption and Structures of Inequality in Two Epochs." Paper presented at the conference Authoritarianism in East Asia. Southeast Asia Research Centre, City University of Hong Kong.

Smith, Chris, and Ngai Pun. 2006. "The Dormitory Labour Regime in China as a Site for Control and Resistance." *International Journal of Human Resource Management* 17.8: 1456–70.

So, Alvin Y. 2003. "The Changing Pattern of Classes and Class Conflict in China." *Journal of Contemporary Asia* 33.3: 363–76.

Tsai, Kellee. 2006. "Adaptive Informal Institutions and Endogenous Institutional Change in China." *World Politics* 5.9: 116–41.

Tseng, Wei-Lin. 2012. "Governing a World Factory: The Case Study of Foxconn." Master's thesis, National Taipei University.

Yang, Daniel You-ren. 2014a. "A Tale of Foxconn City: Urban Village, Migrant Workers and Alienated Urbanism." In *Villages in Urban China: Migrants and Urbanized Villages in Chinese Cities,* edited by Fulong Wu, Fangzhu Zhang, and Chris Webster, 143–63. London: Routledge.

————. 2014b. "Social Alienation and Labor Regime: A Primary Exploration of the New-generation Migrant Workers' Urbanism in Shenzhen's Foxconn City." *Taiwan: A Radical Quarterly in Social Studies* 95: 57–108.

Zhang, Wu. 2015. "Protest Leadership and State Boundaries: Protest Diffusion in Contemporary China." *China Quarterly* 222: 360–79.

CHAPTER 10

Unintended Consequences of Enhanced Labor Legislation in Reform-Era China

CHRISTINA CHEN

*T*he Chinese central state has become increasingly responsive to workers' needs for better legal rights and protections, yet workers have become more contentious during the reform era. Evolutionary analysis of China's labor policy reveals that enhanced legal institutionalization of workers' rights has unexpectedly triggered more conflict. The party-state has become more responsive to workers' demands for legal protections, but workers lacking access to the political process have found the state's implementation of new laws to be inadequate. The case of Guangdong demonstrates that even though their acts were localized and often uncoordinated, workers' protests have succeeded in pushing the local state to pass labor legislation. This finding reflects the volume's theme that the state–society relationship is interactive and demonstrates the circumstances under which politically weak societal actors may exert meaningful influence on the party-state.*

This chapter examines the evolving relationship between the Chinese state and workers and its implications for authoritarian governance. Since China started marketizing its economy in the early 1980s, hundreds of millions of people have moved from the countryside to work in the cities' nascent factories and industries, thereby contributing to the rapid economic growth of urban areas. Such large internal migration contributed an estimated 15–20 percent to China's GDP growth between 1978 and the mid-1990s; the combination of labor input, human capital accumulation, and labor reallocation has made up nearly 70 percent of GDP growth since the outset of economic reforms (Cai and Wang 2008).

Throughout the post-Mao era, the Chinese government has become increasingly responsive to workers' demands and needs. In 1994, the Standing Committee of the National People's Congress (NPC) passed the Labor Law, which was the nation's first comprehensive law addressing workplace issues. In June 2007, the NPC passed the Labor Contract Law (LCL) and two related laws. At the same time, the Chinese Communist Party (CCP) established an improved system for labor dispute resolution. Observers such as the *Washington Post* viewed the LCL as a landmark law, representing a major victory for Chinese workers (Cha 2008). Taken together, these laws seemed to transform the formal employer–worker relationship in China to reach standards comparable to those of many advanced industrialized European countries (Allard and Garot 2010).

A closer examination of these laws shows that the actual influence of Chinese workers on the country's labor policy remains minimal. Legislators and labor activists lobbied for additional regulation after the passing of the first Labor Law in 1994. It took the NPC another decade to pass the LCL and two other labor laws. The legislative process has been dominated by the NPC, Ministry of Labor, official union organizations (the All-China Federation of Trade Unions, ACFTU), and labor scholars. Workers' opinions were solicited after the first draft of the LCL, but there is no evidence that their input shaped the final version (Chou 2011). Meanwhile, the number of labor disputes and strikes has increased continually since the mid-1990s, indicating a working environment that has become more complex and contentious. Overall, the state–worker relationship since the initiation of market reforms has been characterized by the state's soft strategy of legislation and the workers' hard strategy of protests. Industrial relations have become more contentious over time, which has enhanced the state's responsiveness to workers, but legal developments have fomented further discontent among the workers, who have continued to exert limited power over the country's labor policy process. Given that the CCP claims to be the true representative of the proletariat, it is ironic that such a pattern of minimal political interaction between the state and labor characterizes workplace relations in contemporary China.

Much research has sought to explain the various patterns of labor conflict in the Chinese workplace. Some scholars have investigated workplace-related factors that induce workers to participate in labor protests (Chen 2002; Hurst 2012), whereas others have argued that state institutions are the cause of industrial conflict (Gallagher 2003; Lee 2003). Studies focusing on labor conflict at the micro-level—in individual cases or through regional comparisons—have concluded that collective action on the part of workers has yet to instigate major political or economic changes (i.e., political liberalization). This chapter adopts the volume's analytic premise that the state–society relationship is interactive and observes that society can influence state policy even if some societal actors appear weak politically because they are marginalized and exert minimal influence. To be sure, the state's overall developmental priority is the primary force that shapes labor policy. As shown in chapters 8 and 9 of this volume, labor policy in the early 2000s acted as the state's front for forcing foreign-invested enterprises to relocate inland. But examination of labor–state relations shows that workers' actions also matter. Labor activism, even when uncoordinated, has induced state responses and policy changes. Existing studies share an underlying consensus that the Chinese state is adept at preventing rising labor unrest from disrupting its rule and will respond through proactive or reactive means—including strategic inaction—as appropriate to the situation. As Lee and Zhang (2013) assert, the state relies on legal-bureaucratic institutions such as labor dispute arbitration committees to absorb and atomize labor unrest, and workers "played by the legal-bureaucratic rules" to gain both material and symbolic concessions. This chapter shows that although the state has withstood labor unrest thus far, the institutions established to thwart labor initiatives have unexpectedly augmented labor grievances and conflict.

This chapter presents an evolutionary account of state–worker relations since market reforms to show that the state responds to workers' demands despite the latter exerting limited influence on labor policies. The first argument is that the incentives and organizational capacity of workers affects their strategy for acting against the state. These factors channel the means through which they express their grievances and from whom they demand redress. Then the chapter argues that labor legislation has occurred in several phases. The phases resulted in passage of labor legislation, but the rationale for the state's legislative activities has varied.

Irrespective of the state's motives, which typically seek to prevent labor unrest, workers have responded to legislation with further contentious action. Finally, this chapter highlights the case of Guangdong to show how labor unrest was an important factor driving the Guangdong provincial government to adopt ameliorative labor legislation between 2000 and 2010. The interaction between the two sides of this struggle illustrates the peculiar way Chinese labor policy has developed and the ongoing reality that workers lack meaningful channels for political participation.

Chinese Workers: Characteristics, Expressions of Grievance, and Influence on State–Worker Relations

Chinese labor is fragmented. Compared with other workers, the migrant workforce faces unique issues that affect how it expresses its grievances and from whom they seek redress. In China's context, the term "labor" encompasses workers, trade unions, and nongovernmental organizations (NGOs). These groups often exhibit divergent and even conflicting interests. Furthermore, independent unions are not permitted in the country. All trade unions belong to the ACFTU, an official union organization tightly controlled by the CCP. The ACFTU and its subordinate branches are frequently criticized for representing the interests of the party rather than those of workers. Labor NGOs have been active in some parts of China (e.g., Beijing and Guangdong), and their labor rights advocacy has prompted some state actors to incorporate these NGOs into policy discussions to subdue tensions. For example, since 2012 Guangdong province has passed a series of regulations to promote the development of civil society. These measures include simplifying registration, NGO capacity building, and subcontracting social services to labor and other types of grassroots NGOs (Guangzhou Municipal Committee on Social Work 2013). Since the early 1990s, an increasing number of people have left their rural hometowns to work in China's flourishing cities. These migrant workers are often mobile and do not hold urban residence permits, which prevent them and their children from accessing crucial health and social services.

Migrant workers thus find themselves in a more precarious position than urban workers or those laid off from state-owned enterprises (SOEs). Migrant workers rarely have the support of trade unions and lack access to the political process. In addition, the rootlessness of these workers prevents them from establishing close bonds with labor NGOs and other fellow workers, which are crucial for collective action (interview with labor NGO representative, Shenzhen, April 10, 2013). The characteristics of migrant workers and the lack of support they receive from other actors partially explains why their grievances mostly manifest in spontaneous, scattered protest activities with material-based (e.g., wages, social insurance) rather than rights-based claims (e.g., the right to form independent unions) (Lee 2003).

In such a context, the state must respond to contentious worker actions, even when they are uncoordinated, because individual expressions of grievance could influence other workers and cause a spillover effect (e.g., suicides at Foxconn's factories discussed in chapter 9). Worker conflict has rarely blossomed into persistent, transregional, mass protests, but the disruption it causes affects social and economic stability in the long run. This in turn challenges the party-state's rule. Thus, even if the threat of regime change is not imminent, the state responds to workers' grievances. Indeed, it is precisely because the threat is not imminent that the state responds to labor grievances and unrest with ad hoc and piecemeal policies that do not prevent violations of workplace rights. A reform-minded union official described state policy with an analogy: "We are aware of the rising trend of labor conflicts and that workers need to have better protection of their legal rights. We want to be the fire alarms that can inform law enforcers of workplace violations and worker discontent, but so far the party has only allowed us to act as firefighters" (interview with union official, Hangzhou, January 27, 2010).

Motivations for China's Turn to the Law in Labor Politics

The evolution of China's labor policy can be separated into several phases. The overall goal of the CCP has been to maintain control over the workplace (Gallagher 2003), but the precise rationale guiding the state's turn to law has varied during these phases. The following section describes the actors involved, the strategies used, and the resulting interactions.

PHASE I: WITHDRAWAL OF STATE PRESENCE
FROM WORKPLACE AFFAIRS AND ALIENATION
OF WORKERS

China's economic reforms and subsequent development have dramatically transformed labor relations. To foster a market economy, the government opened China to foreign investment, privatized SOEs, and loosened restrictions on population mobility. These policies resulted in privatization of the labor market. Rather than assigning individuals to jobs and setting their wages, the state allowed employers and workers to negotiate employment terms. The CCP introduced and promoted the labor contract system, and employers gained autonomy over workplace practices. Conversely, workers, once the recipients of guaranteed lifelong employment and workplace benefits, saw their bargaining power in relation to the employers decline (Gallagher 2003). However, the state has not relinquished total control over labor. Trade unions in China remain dependent on the CCP. Because of these developments, workers have acquired de jure individual rights, but their collective rights remain substantially repressed. To use the framework introduced in this volume, the Chinese state's overall approach to labor includes a mix of hard and soft strategies, including preemption (union control and repression of collective rights) and policy absorption (provision of de jure individual rights through the law and dispute resolution), to maintain its control over labor.

PHASE II: WEAK IMPLEMENTATION OF THE
LABOR LAW BY LOCAL GOVERNMENTS

Local governments are responsible for state policy implementation, but their focus on economic development often discourages them from complying fully with central policies intended to safeguard worker interests. During the early reform period, China underwent fiscal decentralization, and the central government gave localities greater fiscal authority through delegation of budgetary control and various revenue-sharing contracts with local governments (Shirk 1993). These institutional reforms incentivized local governments to develop their economies. Granted authority over the allocation and retention of fiscal budgets, local governments pursued economic growth to increase their revenue (Montinola, Qian, and Weingast 1996; Oi 1992; Zhuravskaya 2000). In addition, political centralization—the tightening of central appointment of local officials—motivated local government officials with career aspirations and stimulated their desire to develop their local economies to meet the state's demand for growth (Blanchard and Shleifer 2001; Zhou 2004). External investment and industrialization were identified as the keys to development, and local governments rushed to satisfy demand from business owners for a cheap and flexible workforce under managerial control (Cooney 2007; Ngok and Zhuang 2009). Trade unions remained marginalized during this time, particularly when the CCP permitted greater privatization of SOEs. Unions had little influence on the welfare of workers, and a majority of the union branches at the enterprise level often sided with management when disputes arose. Moreover, the state's control of the population and organized labor through the household registration (*hukou* 户口) system—which was partially relaxed to create surplus labor from rural areas to support industrializing coastal regions—perpetuated the problems of weak labor protection and social inequality. Migrant workers lived and worked in cities where they lacked residence permits, rendering them ineligible for social services and vulnerable to eviction (*China Labour Bulletin* 2013). Local governments intentionally sacrificed the rights and interests of workers for rapid economic growth, leading to substantial social inequality (P. Huang 2011). As a result, it was common to find local officials tacitly allowing businesses to disregard labor laws and standards (see chapter 8 in this volume).

PHASE III: INCREASING WORKER GRIEVANCES
AND LABOR CONFLICT

The absence of de facto individual and collective rights resulted in many violations of workers' rights in the workplace. Many of these workers relied on illegal and legal means to express their grievances. Strikes, street protests, and other violent outbursts by workers were less common in an atmosphere that discouraged collective action through suppression, but workers nevertheless engaged in militant actions (Chan 2001). Some workers engaged in illegal activities, such as forming underground unions and gangs. Because the risks of engaging in these activities are higher in China than in democratic contexts, their appearance is a powerful signal of collective worker discontent with the government in China, especially with local governments that are believed to have the power and responsibility to address workers' demands (Y. Cai 2003). Alternatively, workers could choose to appeal to local governments through the dispute settlement mechanism, which was instituted in 1993. This mechanism was separated into a three-step process: firm-level mediation, local-level arbitration, and civil court litigation. Labor bureaus replaced enterprise-level CCP leadership to mediate or arbitrate disputes, and unions took the role of putative worker advocate. Before 1993, only SOEs implemented the dispute resolution mechanism, but after that point, the mechanism was applied to private and foreign-owned enterprises (Gallagher 2003; Guo and Li 1994). For workers, a legal mechanism constituted a less costly form of grievance expression: the need to organize collective action and the risk of suppression were substantially reduced. Nevertheless, the cost of arbitration remained high for most workers. The presence and growth of legal labor dispute mechanisms credibly signaled an increase in the collective discontent of workers toward management and local governments.

The number of labor disputes and labor conflicts increased during this time, indicating that the labor dispute mechanism failed to adequately address and resolve workers' grievances. As figure 10.1 shows, in 2001 approximately 150,000 cases were settled by local labor bureaucracies, called labor dispute arbitration committees (LDACs). Six years later, the number increased to approximately 350,000. Popular protests known as "mass incidents" also increased during the 2000s. The Chinese Academy of Social Sciences reported that over 60,000 mass incidents occurred in 2006, and more than 80,000 occurred in 2007.[1] The workers' responses represented a hard strategy; the prevalence of labor rights violations and the lack of adequate channels through which to resolve their grievances prompted workers to take initiative and protest on the streets to declare their rights.

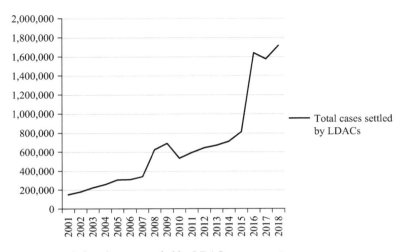

FIGURE 10.1 Labor disputes settled by LDACs, 2001–2018
Source: China Labor Statistical Yearbook, various years.

PHASE IV: SECOND WAVE OF LEGISLATION

The workers' responses, which included mass incidents and protest on the streets as described in the previous section, contributed to a second wave of labor legislation. Even though these labor incidents remained localized, the experiences of some East European nations whose communist regimes were overthrown by labor movements reminded the party of the potential for labor unrest to challenge the regime's control. This partially contributed to the party leadership's change of policy. When Hu Jintao took office, the slogans, "harmonious society" and "people-oriented, comprehensive, balanced, and sustainable development," were introduced into party documents, thereby signifying the shift of emphasis from complete prioritization of GDP growth to economic development balanced by some concern for social issues (PRC Central Committee 2003, 2006). The phrase "balanced, sustainable development" also reflected the party's intention to achieve industrial upgrading, particularly by moving labor-intensive enterprises from coastal to inland provinces, as well as ending the preferential treatment that foreign-invested enterprises had been receiving since economic reform (see chapter 8). The change of policy emphasis enabled unions to expand their influence in workplace affairs.

Beginning in the early 2000s, the NPC passed laws to strengthen the individual rights of workers and simplify the dispute resolution process. The widely debated LCL amended the 1994 Labor Law in several major ways. First, it required that a written labor contract be executed at the commencement of a labor relationship. The LCL provided that an employer who fails to sign a written contract within one year of beginning the labor relationship shall be deemed to have entered into a non–fixed-duration contract with the employee and must pay double the agreed-on wage (PRC Labor Contract Law, art. 14, 82). Second, the law prohibited an employer from terminating contracts with employees who work continuously for 15 years for that employer and who will reach the legal retirement age in less than 5 years (PRC Labor Contract Law, art. 41–42). Trade unions gained consultative authority in workplace matters with the new law. Any management decision regarding the establishment or modification of remuneration, work time, holidays and vacations, safety conditions, insurance and benefits, training, discipline, or any other conditions of employment must first be negotiated with the union or worker representatives (PRC Labor Contract Law, art. 4). The Law on Mediation and Arbitration of Labor Disputes deemed mediation a crucial step in the dispute resolution process and provided detailed regulations on the mediation process. If a labor dispute arises within an enterprise, either the employer or employee may request mediation assistance. Mediation services can be provided by any designated labor dispute mediation committee in the enterprise or by certain governmental or quasi-governmental organizations (PRC Law on Mediation and Arbitration of Labor Disputes, art. 10).

The legislative responses of the CCP in this phase reflected the party's intent to thwart labor conflicts. The LCL contained several prolabor clauses that reduced employers' flexibility in hiring and managing workers, but the law only provided trade unions with consultative authority in workplace matters, not authority to compel employer compliance (interview with ACTFU official, Beijing, November 20, 2009).[2] The Law on Mediation and Arbitration gave trade unions the tasks of providing legal aid consultation to workers and participating in the dispute resolution process as mediator or arbitrator, but not the task of advocating solely on behalf of an aggrieved worker, implying that unions would still be asked to balance the interests of employers and employees. The law continued to weakly permit or outright ban commonly recognized core functions of labor unions: collective bargaining and the right to strike. The nature and scope of the party's legislative agenda suggest that the party-state instituted a dispute resolution regime to prevent large-scale labor unrest from disrupting workplace productivity and challenging local governments. Specifically, the party-state directed worker grievances into a dispute resolution mechanism to appease and atomize labor, rather than protect and represent it. In this stage, the CCP implemented a soft strategy of political absorption and exhaustion to subdue labor conflicts.

PHASE V: INADEQUATE LOCAL IMPLEMENTATION OF NEW LABOR LAWS

Despite the passage of new labor laws that reduced the barriers workers confront when pursuing labor dispute resolution, the system still has several problems. First, it is highly bureaucratic. The process of dispute resolution, particularly labor arbitration, is dominated by the labor bureaucracy. The committees are within the local labor bureaus, and the chairs are representatives from labor bureaus. LDACs are nominally independent, but in reality, the committees are highly dependent on labor bureaus for administrative work. Furthermore, LDACs cannot control their financial operations and pay wages to arbitrators. Hence, LDACs are highly dependent on local governments for resources (Cooney 2007).

Resource constraints are another problem in the system. In 1995, arbitration committees had 11,292 arbitrators; this number has increased to 23,000 in 2006. The number of cases, however, grew dramatically over the period, from 34,159 in 1996 to 502,048 in 2006 (Chen 2020). A former arbitrator in Hangzhou's municipal labor department complained, "The LDACs in Hangzhou, even the ones at the county level, are understaffed. We tried to hire many part-time arbitrators, but we are still short on personnel" (interview with labor department official, Hangzhou, September 8, 2009). Numerous LDACs lack funding to obtain office space and equipment to handle dispute resolution.

The system's lack of independence and resources puts workers at a major disadvantage. Because of the lack of resources and a desire to reduce their workload, LDACs and arbitration committees have the tendency to use various excuses to reject cases. Cases are rejected if workers cannot provide an identifiable employer, which usually happens when no written contract exists, when workers are from restructured or privatized SOEs, or when their cases exceed the 60-day filing limit (Cooney 2007). In her book, *Factory Girls*, Leslie Chang describes the protagonist experiencing the labor dispute resolution process. The protagonist's experience illustrates the obstacles that workers in China face when seeking help through dispute resolution. She visited the Guangdong provincial labor bureau and faced a long queue in which every labor bureau staffer was surrounded by at least six workers. To get a company document, the labor case first had to be accepted by the labor bureau. Thus, the protagonist visited municipal and county labor bureaus and discovered that every bureau gave inconsistent information and instructions. When she finally gathered all the necessary documents, she found the arbitration form too complicated and gave up (Chang 2008). This story effectively demonstrates how the system avoids handling numerous complaints by workers.

Workers continue to experience difficulties even after their cases are accepted by LDACs. LDAC arbitrators have a strong incentive to be biased against employees because LDACs are dependent on local governments for funding and other support. Concerned about maintaining economic growth, many local governments are more interested in meeting the business demands for a flexible and loosely regulated labor market than protecting worker rights. As a result, they avoid taking actions that would benefit workers but might alienate employers. Figure 10.2 shows that the percentage of labor disputes in which a worker received a favorable ruling declined after 2008 in major coastal regions. Figures 10.1 and 10.2 together illustrate a trend in which the Chinese local states turned to dispute resolution, which increased the number of workers seeking dispute resolution, but fewer cases resulted in proworker rulings. In addition to this probusiness bias, the structure of the system puts workers at a disadvantage. The dispute resolution process is slow, requiring at least a year for a case to proceed from arbitration to litigation (Chen 2020). Workers must invest their time, effort, and money to collect evidence and attend the proceedings; yet if an employer loses a case, it can appeal the verdict to delay payment or remove its assets from the jurisdiction (Cooney, Biddulph, and Zhu 2013). As a result of this structural bias, workers who

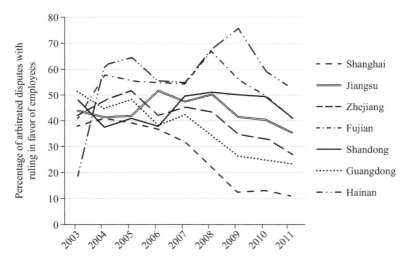

FIGURE 10.2 Proworker dispute outcomes in selected coastal regions, 2003–2011
Source: China Labor Statistical Yearbook, various years.

rely on the dispute resolution process tend to be skilled workers with more resources than unskilled workers (Thireau and Hua 2005). The system thus excludes unskilled migrant workers who cannot afford the process. A negative feedback loop evolved in this system: the rapid increase in labor disputes increased the burden on the system and the potential for large-scale labor conflicts because labor bureaus failed to resolve disputes adequately.

PHASE VI: LABOR CONFLICTS INCREASE AS AN UNINTENDED CONSEQUENCE OF LABOR LEGISLATION

Legislation of labor relations was intended to weaken rather than strengthen the overall power of labor, but the resulting laws and institutions inadvertently fomented more labor conflict. The number of labor disputes, indicated by the number of cases settled by LDACs, surged between 2001 and 2016. Although the number declined after 2010, it rose again after 2011 (see fig. 10.1). Workers expressed their grievances through the dispute resolution mechanism and expressed them in the streets. In June 2010, workers at Honda's Nanhai plant in Guangzhou engaged in a large-scale strike demanding higher wages. This action triggered similar activities across the country. Strikes or "work stoppages" (*tinggong* 停工), as the Chinese media called them, became even more common after Nanhai. According to *China Labour Bulletin*, there were 235 strike incidents in July 2014: 49 percent more than the same period of the previous year (2013), which had 158 incidents, and 180 percent more than the second quarter of 2012, which had 84 incidents (*China Labour Bulletin* 2014).

Labor legislation possibly contributed to the spike in labor conflicts. The overall economic slowdown, migrant labor shortage, rising wages, and other economic factors may have increased grievances and encouraged workers to engage in protests (P. Cai 2014; *The Economist* 2015). At the same time, the new laws simplified the dispute resolution process, which encouraged more workers to seek dispute resolution. The active promotion of the 2007 labor laws, particularly the LCL, before and immediately after their passage by labor NGOs, labor bureaucracies, and trade unions raised workers' awareness of their legal rights, thereby causing workers to be more likely to pursue dispute resolution and engage in strike activities.[3]

PHASE VII: LEGISLATING STATE REASSERTION AND CONTROL, DEEPENING LABOR CONFLICTS

The party-state's approach toward civil society took a dramatic turn after 2014. While legislation established during this period addressed civil society as a whole, it also had an impact on labor. Between 2014 and 2016, the state passed a series of security-related laws that tightened control over foreign NGOs (ChinaFile 2017). The 2016 Charity Law clarifies the framework on the regulation of domestic Chinese NGOs, and the 2016 Law on the Management of Foreign Non-Governmental Organizations' Activities requires foreign NGOs to register with a public security unit and an officially approved "Chinese partner." Passage of the 2016 laws were seen as further blows to NGOs, as they put an end to the legal ambiguity that provided NGOs with gray areas to maneuver in and made it difficult for foreign organizations to operate legally in China (Hsieh 2017; Kaja and Stratford 2016, 2). Local governments became more repressive toward labor as well. Throughout 2015, many NGOs across the country were closed down; in December, several labor NGOs in Guangdong were raided by public security units. NGO staff members were even arrested and charged with embezzlement or other crimes (Chan 2018, 8; Franceschini and Nesossi 2018, 122; Lee 2017). In effect, the Chinese state has adopted a two-pronged strategy for maintaining state-controlled institutions (LDACs, trade unions) while marginalizing civil society actors. The state's overall approach during this stage constitutes a mix of hard (against NGOs and labor activists) and soft (vis-à-vis workers) strategies. The goal was to enhance social (and therefore political) stability by further atomizing the labor movement and channeling worker grievances to state-controlled mechanisms.

Similar to the previous phase, legislation and local government actions that sought to weaken labor actually incited more conflict. As figure 10.1 shows, the number of labor disputes rose sharply from 2015 to 2018. Furthermore, the number of strike incidents decreased dramatically in 2016 and 2017, but rebounded again in 2018 (table 10.1). Indeed, the number of strikes in 2018 exceeded that between 2011 and 2014. Labor legislation partially contributed to the bifurcated pattern of increase in labor disputes but temporary decline in strikes after 2015. China's economic downturn persisted after 2015, which has had negative effects on employment and worker compensation, thereby contributing to more labor grievances and workers turning to LDACs to seek compensation. The repressive legislation may have succeeded in curbing strikes for a while, but they increased again in 2018. This suggests that, facing very limited channels to express their grievances, workers were pressed to use

Table 10.1
Strike incidents in China, 2011–2018

	Number of strikes	% Difference from previous year
2011	184	
2012	382	107.61
2013	645	68.85
2014	1,358	110.54
2015	6,675	391.53
2016	2,664	−60.09
2017	1,258	−52.78
2018	1,702	35.29

SOURCE: China Labour Bulletin Strike Map.

more extreme ways to air their frustration and extract concessions. Second, even though the number of strike incidents decreased between 2015 and 2017, *China Labour Bulletin* observes that strikes have become more "sophisticated"—they have become better organized, more purposeful, utilize the latest social media and telecommunications technology, and last longer to exert greater pressure on business and local officials (*China Labour Bulletin* 2018a). These developments suggest that legislation passed in this period inadvertently triggered more effective collective action. It is unlikely that labor conflicts will decline in the near future. In December 2019, a novel coronavirus was detected in the city of Wuhan, Hubei province, which subsequently infected tens of thousands of Chinese citizens and spread to many other countries in early 2020. The pandemic caused a major shutdown of the Chinese economy, and some analysts believed the outbreak may force companies and investors to move their production out of China (Bremmer 2020; E. Huang 2020). If widespread unemployment results—and civil society and official trade unions remain marginalized—then workers have no ways other than protests to express their discontent, thereby posing more challenges to the CCP's rule.

THE CASE OF GUANGDONG: 1990–2018

The state rarely issues policy responses in the face of individual, uncoordinated labor actions, but it becomes more responsive once a pattern of unrest emerges that disrupts social stability and affects workplace productivity. The case of Guangdong illustrates the effects of uncoordinated labor uprising.

Guangdong has long been known as the hot spot of labor unrest in China. It was one of the first provinces to experience increasingly complex and contentious labor relations. In 1995, Guangdong had 3,200 disputes, the second highest number of disputes of any province. In 1997, the number rose to 24,704 in Guangdong, whereas the other experimental areas for market reform, Jiangsu and Zhejiang, recorded only 2,493 and 2,496, respectively. In 1998, the number of disputes in Guangdong reached 28,813, while Jiangsu and Zhejiang had 8,413 and 3,536, respectively. Although systematic reports on labor protests are lacking, media reports provide a glimpse into the scale of protests in these regions. *China Labour Bulletin*, an NGO based in Hong Kong, compiled a list of 100 labor protests and related actions covered by the Chinese and foreign media from 2007 to 2008: 26 of the 100 protest incidents occurred in Guangdong (*China Labour Bulletin* 2009).

Since the early 2000s, protecting the rights and welfare of workers has been one of the major policy emphases of Guangdong's leadership. In its 10th Five-Year Plan, the Guangdong government listed unemployment as a key obstacle to stable social development and proposed the promotion of employment and social security services to solve the problem. Three more goals were also described in the plan: improvement of regulatory mechanisms (labor legislation and implementation, particularly enforcing and supervising labor regulations), improvement of the labor contract system, and improvement of the dispute settlement mechanism (Guangdong Provincial Government 2001). The provincial party leadership announced the "Opinion on the Establishment of Stable Guangdong" in 2005 and "Opinion on the Implementing 'Decision on the Establishment of Socialist Stable Society by the CCP'" a year later. In these documents, the Guangdong government named the "floating population" of rural migrants as one of the issues affecting social stability and identified improving dispute resolution as a key objective for the provincial government. Improving the implementation of labor laws and regulatory mechanisms, particularly adding staff and procuring other resources for labor inspections and dispute settlement teams, was seen as a major objective. In addition, more unionization—establishing enterprise-based union branches and recruiting union members—was set as another goal that if achieved would improve the protection of workers (Guangdong Provincial Government 2005).

Guangdong is known not only as a hot spot of labor conflicts but also as a pioneer of labor legislation. Local governments in Guangdong have used labor legislation as the primary method to deal with changes in labor relations, and many local regulations initiated in Guangdong province were later adopted by governments in other localities (interview with union official, Shenzhen, June 15, 2009). Two pieces of legislation established the model for other provinces: Regulations on Enterprise Collective Contracts, Guangdong Province (*Guangdongsheng qiye jiti hetong tiaoli* 广东省企业集体合同条例) in 1996 and Regulations on Union Labor Supervision, Guangdong Province (*Guangdongsheng gonghui laodong jiandu tiaoli* 广东省工会劳动监督条例) in 2001. Local governments in Guangdong also passed several innovative labor laws. For example, the

Shenzhen Federation of Trade Unions was involved in drafting the Implementing Regulation on the Trade Union Law of PRC, Shenzhen City (*Shenzhenshi shishi Zhonghua renmin gongheguo gonghuifa banfa* 深圳市实施中华人民共和国工会法办法), amended and passed in 2008. This labor legislation not only used the words "collective bargaining" instead of "collective consultation," it contained a unique "public censure" clause. Article 51 of the implementing regulation states that if an enterprise does not correct its behavior after receiving warnings from the labor department, then higher-level union branches can publicly censure the company for violating the legal rights of its employees or for violating the Trade Union Law and its implementing regulations (along with several other conditions) (Shenzhen Prefecture-level Government 2008). After 2008, however, local governments in Guangdong appeared to have less interest in protecting worker rights and welfare. There were few significant regulations that advanced the rights of workers. Moreover, workers faced greater obstacles when they attempted to secure their legal rights. In May 2018, workers in Jasic Technology of Shenzhen established an enterprise-level trade union in response to deteriorating working conditions. Even though workers are legally entitled to establish and participate in enterprise unions, those at Jasic faced official scorn, police detention, and other repressive measures by the authorities (Hui and Friedman 2018). Furthermore, labor NGOs became the scapegoats of this incident. The state-controlled Xinhua News Agency claimed that a Shenzhen NGO and a Hong Kong–based civil organization were culprits behind the Jasic incident (Pringle and Chan 2018). The Jasic incident is a further testament to the two-pronged strategy of the state in recent years—the hard strategy of marginalizing NGOs and other labor activists (in this case, even official trade unions were prohibited from playing their legal role), which left workers with little choice but to rely on institutional channels of LDACs or turn to extreme measures of strikes/labor protests.

Analysis

During the reform period, a pattern of state policy changes and establishment of institutions evolved in response to labor unrest. During the 1990s, the government used the strategy of dispute resolution (receiving worker complaints and mediating or arbitrating disputes) to regulate workplace relations. This strategy constituted a soft method to "absorb" or "incorporate" workers (*rouxing xina* 柔性吸納). However, the workers responded with strikes and other collective actions, which constituted a hard strategy of resistance. The workers' response compelled the state to respond with a new set of labor laws and an improved dispute resolution system. The state attempted to incorporate workers, but labor unrest persisted, as seen in a rising number of disputes and protests. In other words, despite the state's reliance on a soft strategy of incorporation, workers responded with a hard strategy of protest and other forms of labor conflict. Legislation appears as the dominant strategy for the state, and conflict appears as the dominant strategy for the workers.

An examination of the Chinese state offers insight into why incorporation is its dominant strategy. The CCP is an authoritarian regime that lacks legitimacy and trust from society, and it must respond to an increasingly complex and diverse society. The state has relaxed its control of the country's economy, thereby permitting some degree of autonomy to members of society, but it has continued to refuse to permit those members to have more political representation and has continually attempted to reassert its control (Linz 2000). In the case of labor, legislation and the resultant expansion of de jure individual rights reflected CCP attempts to subdue labor unrest. Because trade unions remain strictly controlled by the CCP, workers continue to have few collective rights that could be leveraged to gain political representation and access to the policymaking process. The party's responses to social pressure remain limited because the CCP ultimately does not intend to fully incorporate society into the governance system.

Policy implementation at the local level has affected the CCP's incorporation of workers. Labor stability in China has been affected by the fragmentation of the party-state because Beijing's interests have diverged from that of local states in some respects. As a result, the state has often been driven to act inconsistently and in a contradictory manner. Although the Labor Law provides for comprehensive protection of workers' individual rights, it has not been adequately enforced because local governments benefit from allowing low wages to attract business interests.

The divergent interests of different levels of government persisted and affected policy implementation in the 2000s. Despite passage of three major labor laws and improvements in the dispute resolution system, local governments continued to prioritize economic interests over those of workers. Consequently, workers continued to have difficulty expressing their grievances and receiving fair compensation through the labor dispute resolution system. Nonetheless, local governments started to address workers' demands, albeit infrequently. Local governments were multitasked agents that juggled the objectives of economic growth and social stability, so local governments would be driven to protect labor interests if acts by workers affected social stability. Guangdong between the 1990s and early 2000s illustrates the positive effects of labor conflicts on legislative developments.

The findings of this chapter have implications for the CCP. Successful incorporation of workers will require the party to grant workers the right to participate in policymaking. As an authoritarian regime, however, the state remains disinclined to grant workers political representation and is incapable of pressuring local states to comply strictly with its policies. Thus, the party is limited to ad hoc policy responses that increase workers' influence in social governance and grant workers channels for pressuring the state to address their grievances. In the absence of political power, however, workers cannot lobby local governments to enforce the labor laws, and local governments will continue to rely on a mix of hard and soft strategies toward workers and labor organizations. This strategic approach allows local governments to balance the policy priorities of economic growth and social stability. Lacking adequate access to political representation and finding their channels for expressing grievances even more limited after 2015, workers became more distrustful of the state and even more resolute to rely on themselves to secure material and symbolic concessions. Hence, they must rely on labor uprisings to express their grievances. With experience, workers have organized more effective protest activities, such as strikes. In this context, the adversarial dynamics of state–labor relations are unlikely to change despite the apparently favorable evolution in labor legislation.

Notes

1. Unfortunately, the number of labor protests before the late 2000s was not available—no official resources have ever reported it, while news stories about labor protests were scattered and thus difficult to analyze. "Mass incidents" constitute the next best alternative

as many protest incidents were sparked by labor disputes. See CASS (2009) and Hou (2014).

2. In the first draft of the LCL, trade unions and employee representative congresses had veto power over work rules. Such a proposal was changed in later drafts due to opposition from the business community and some lawmakers from the labor ministry and National People's Congress. Interview with ACFTU official, Beijing, November 20, 2009.

3. Several government and nongovernmental bodies have used playing cards to promote the LCL. They would distribute the cards (each card has a common question and answer, pictures and other useful information) to migrant workers on the street or during workshops they sponsored. Playing cards are useful tools to promote the law because many migrant workers have little time to read the actual law and play cards regularly. "Shiming lushi xianchang jieshi laodong hetong fa 十名律师现场解释劳动合同法" (Ten lawyers explain the Labor Contract Law), http://wznews.66wz.com/system/2007/12/02/100452271.shtml.

References

Allard, Gayle, and Marie-Jose Garot. 2010. "The Impact of the New Labor Law in China: New Hiring Strategies for Foreign Firms?" *Revista Direito GV* 6.2: 527–40.

Blanchard, Olivier, and Andrei Shleifer. 2001. "Federalism with and without Political Centralization: China versus Russia." *IMF Staff Papers* 48: 171–79.

Bremmer, Ian. 2020. "How the Coronavirus Epidemic Could Upend the Global Economy." *Time*, February 6. https://time.com/5778995/coronavirus-china-global-economy/.

Cai, Fang, and Dewen Wang. 2008. "Impacts of Internal Migration on Economic Growth and Urban Development in China." In *Migration and Development across Borders: Research and Policy Perspectives on Internal and International Migration*, edited by Josh DeWind and Jennifer Holdaway, 247–73. New York: IOM International Organization for Migration and the Social Science Research Council. http://essays.ssrc.org/acrossborders/wp-content/uploads/2009/08/ch11.pdf.

Cai, Peter. 2014. "Is a Labour Shortage Looming in China?" *China Spectator*, February 21.

Cai, Yongshun. 2003. "Collective Ownership or Cadres' Ownership? The Nonagricultural Use of Farmland in China." *China Quarterly* 175: 662–80.

Cha, Ariana Eunjung. 2008. "New Law Gives Chinese Workers Power, Gives Businesses Nightmares." *Washington Post*, April 14. http://www.washingtonpost.com/wp-dyn/content/article/2008/04/13/AR2008041302214.html.

Chan, Anita. 2001. *China's Workers under Assault: The Exploitation of Labor in a Globalizing Economy*. Armonk, NY: M. E. Sharpe.

———. 2018. "The Relationship between Labour NGOs and Chinese Workers in an Authoritarian Regime." *Global Labour Journal* 9.1: 1–32.

Chang, Leslie. 2008. *Factory Girls: From Village to City in a Changing China*. New York: Spiegel & Grau.

Chen, Feng. 2002. "Subsistence Crisis, Managerial Corruption and Labour Protest in China." *China Journal* 44: 41–63.

———. 2020. *The State and Labor in Contemporary China: Institution, Conflict and Change*. Hong Kong: Chinese University of Hong Kong Press.

ChinaFile. 2017. "Fact Sheet on China's Foreign NGO Law. The China NGO Project." ChinaFile. http://www.chinafile.com/ngo/latest/fact-sheet-chinas-foreign-ngo-law.

China Labour Bulletin. 2009. "Going it Alone: The Workers Movement in China (2007–2008)." *China Labour Bulletin*. http://www.china-labour.org.hk/en/files/share/File/research_reports/workers_movement_07-08_print_final.pdf.

———. 2013. "A Decade for Change: The Workers' Movement in China, 2000–2010." *China Labour Bulletin*. http://www.clb.org.hk/en/sites/default/files/File/research_reports/Decade%20of%20the%20Workers%20Movement%20final_0.pdf.

———. 2014. "Strikes and Worker Protests Gain Momentum in China as Economy Stutters." *China Labour Bulletin*. http://www.clb.org.hk/en/content/strikes-and-worker-protests-gain-momentum-china-economy-stutters.

———. 2018a. "The Workers' Movement in China: 2015–2017." *China Labour Bulletin*. https://clb.org.hk/sites/default/files/Workers%20Movement%202015-17%20full%20text.pdf.

———. 2018b. "Labour Relations in China: Some Frequently Asked Questions." *China Labour Bulletin*. https://clb.org.hk/content/labour-relations-china-some-frequently-asked-questions.

———. 2019. "Strike Map." *China Labour Bulletin*. https://maps.clb.org.hk/strikes/en.

Chinese Academy of Social Sciences (CASS). 2009. "Analysis and Forecast of China's Social Trends in 2008–2009." In *Zhongguo shehui xingshi fenxi yu yuce* (2009: analysis and forecast of China's social trends), edited by Ru Xin, Lu Xueyi, and Li Peilin, 1–14. Beijing: Social Sciences Academic Press.

Chou, Chelsea Chia-chen. 2011. "When Does an Autocrat Compromise with Social Forces? The Politics of Labor Policy Reform in China, 1978–2009." Ph.D. diss., Cornell University.

Cooney, Sean. 2007. "China's Labour Law, Compliance and Flaws in Implementing Institutions." *Journal of Industrial Relations* 49: 673–86.

Cooney, Sean, Sarah Biddulph, and Ying Zhu. 2013. *Law and Fair Work in China*. London: Routledge.

The Economist. 2015. "Out Brothers, Out!" *The Economist*, January 31. http://www.economist.com/news/china/21641275-guangdong-province-pioneers-new-approach-keeping-workers-happy-out-brothers-out.

Franceschini, Ivan, and Elisa Nesossi. 2018. "State Repression of Chinese Labor NGOs: A Chilling Effect?" *China Journal* 80: 111–29.

Gallagher, Mary E. 2003. *Contagious Capitalism: Globalization and the Politics of Labor in China*. Princeton, NJ: Princeton University Press.

Guangdong Provincial Government. 2001. "Tenth Five Year Social and Economic Development Plan of the Guangdong Province" (*Guangdongsheng guomin jingji he shehuifazhan di shiwunian jihua gongyao*). http://www.foshan.gov.cn/zwgk/fzgh /hggh/201009/t20100927_1854655.html.

———. 2005. "Opinion by the CCP Guangdong Provincial Party Committee, Guang-dong People's Government on the Establishment of Stable Guangdong" (*Zhonggong Guangdong shengwei Guangdong renmin zhengfu guanyu goujia hexie Guangdong de ruogan yijian*). http://www.gd.gov.cn/gdgk/sqwx/200709/t20070928_21542.htm.

Guangzhou Municipal Committee on Social Work. 2013. "Scheme on Further Devel-oping and Regulating Social Organizations of Guangdong Province" (*Guangdong sheng guan yu jinyibu peiyu fazhan he guifan guanli shehui zuzhi de fangan*). http://m .dayoo.com/127909/128979/201306/12879_3125570.htm.

Guo, Jun, and Wenhua Li, eds. 1994. *Laodongfa yu laodong zhengyi shiyong shouce* (Man-ual on the labor law and labor disputes). Beijing: China Procuratorial Publishing House.

Hou, Liqiang. 2014. "Report Identifies Sources of Mass Protests." *China Daily*, April 9. http://www.chinadaily.com.cn/china/2014-04/09/content_17415767.htm.

Hsieh, Shawn. 2017. "Putting the Overseas NGO Law in Perspective." NGOs in China, March 12. http://ngochina.blogspot.tw/2017/03/.

Huang, Elaine. 2020. "Apple Supply Chain Disrupted by Novel Coronavirus, Expedit-ing the Flight of Foreign Investment from China." *CommonWealth Magazine*, Febru-ary 11. https://english.cw.com.tw/article/article.action?id=2655.

Huang, Philip C. C. 2011. "China's Neglected Informal Economy: Reality and Theory." *Modern China* 35.4: 11–12.

Hui, Elaine, and Eli Friedman. 2018. "The Communist Party vs. China's Labor Law." *Jacobin*, October 2. https://www.jacobinmag.com/2018/10/china-communist-party -labor-law-jasic.

Hurst, William. 2012. *The Chinese Workers after Socialism*. Cambridge: Cambridge Uni-versity Press.

Kaja, Ashwin, and Timothy P. Stratford. 2016. "China Implements New Charity Law." *Covington: Global Policy Watch*, November 1. https://www.globalpolicywatch.com /2016/11/china-implements-new-charity-law/.

Lee, Ching Kwan. 2003. "Pathway of Labor Insurgency." In *Chinese Society: Change, Con-flict, and Resistance*, 2nd ed., edited by Elizabeth J. Perry and Mark Selden, 73–95. London: Routledge.

———. 2017. "After the Miracle: Labor Politics under China's New Normal." *Catalyst* 1.3: 92–115.

Lee, Ching Kwan, and Yonghong Zhang. 2013. "The Power of Instability: Unraveling the Microfoundations of Bargained Authoritarianism in China." *American Journal of Sociology* 118.6: 1475–508.

Linz, Juan J. 2000. *Totalitarianism and Authoritarian Regimes*. Boulder, CO: Lynne Rienner.

Ministry of Human Resources and Social Security of the People's Republic of China. 2002–2019. *China Labor Statistical Yearbook (2001–2018)*. Beijing: China Statistical Press.

Montinola, Gabriella, Yingyi Qian, and Barry Weingast. 1996. "Federalism, Chinese Style: The Political Basis for Economic Success in China." *World Politics* 48.1: 50–81.

Ngok, Kinglun, and Wenjia Zhuang. 2009. "Labor Inspectorate Regime in Transition in Contemporary China: An Integrated Research from the Perspective of Governance." *Journal of Public Administration* 5.

Oi, Jean C. 1992. "Fiscal Reform and the Economic Foundations of Local Corporatism in China." *World Politics* 45.1: 99–126.

PRC Central Committee. 2003. "Zhonggong zhongyang guanyu wanshan shehui zhuyi shichang jingji tizhi fuogan wenti de jueding" (The decision on several issues in perfecting the socialist market economy). http://www.gov.cn/gongbao/content/2003/content_62494.htm.

———. 2006. "Zhongyang zhonggong guanyu guojian shehui zhuyi hexie shehui ruogan zhongda wenti de jueding" (Resolution on the major issues regarding building a harmonious socialist society). http://big5.www.gov.cn/gate/big5/www.gov.cn/gongbao/content/2006/content_453176.htm.

Pringle, Tim, and Anita Chan. 2018. "China's Labour Relations Have Entered a Dangerous New Phase, as Shown by Attacks on Jasic Workers and Activists." *South China Morning Post*, September 19. https://www.scmp.com/comment/insight-opinion/article/2164817/chinas-labour-relations-have-entered-dangerous-new-phase.

Shenzhen Prefecture-level Government. 2008. "Implementing Regulation for the Trade Union Law of PRC, Shenzhen City" (*Shenzhenshi shishi Zhonghua renmin gongheguo gonghuifa banfa*). http://law-star.com/cacnew/200807/180020962.htm.

Shirk, Susan. 1993. *The Political Logic of Economic Reform in China*. Berkeley: University of California Press.

Thireau, Isabelle, and Linshan Hua. 2005. "One Law, Two Interpretations: Mobilizing the Labor Law in Arbitration Committees and in Letters and Visits Office." In *Engaging the Law in China: State, Society, and Possibilities for Justice*, edited by Neil J. Diamant, Stanley B. Lubman, and Kevin J. O'Brien. Stanford, CA: Stanford University Press.

Zhou, Li-An. 2004. "The Incentive and Cooperation of Government Officials in the Political Tournaments: An Interpretation of the Prolonged Local Protectionism and Duplicative Investments in China." *Jingji yanjiu* (Economic Research Journal) 6: 33–40.

Zhuravskaya, Ekaterina V. 2000. "Incentives to Provide Local Public Goods: Fiscal Federalism, Russian Style." *Journal of Public Economics* 76: 337–68.

PART V

Social and Religious Governance

CHAPTER 11

State–Society Interactions in the Campaign against Domestic Violence in China

WEITING WU

This chapter examines how self-organizing women's groups have expanded their political space by strategically interacting with the state and campaigning against domestic violence from 1988 to the present. Diachronic process-tracing reveals that feminist activists have continuously pressed and negotiated with government entities for their survival and learned from adaptive responses of the party-state. This evolutionary and interactive process has provided feminist activists with the opportunity to deepen their involvement in shaping legal reform and implementing new legal protections by local governments. Partnership between feminist cadres at the central and local levels of governments facilitated the remarkable progress of feminist activists compared with other social groups. Their political lobbying has yielded meaningful legal reforms despite concurrent harassment of women's groups by the party-state.

In March 2003, 30 representatives of the National People's Congress (NPC) introduced the Domestic Violence Prevention and Intervention Law. This marked a unique moment in China's legislative history because it was the first national legislative proposal prepared by nongovernmental organizations (NGOs), marking a potentially new relationship between the state and social groups. At the same time, women's groups involved in this campaign experienced harassment from the party-state.

In the campaign against domestic violence, the Maple Center, the Peking Women's Law Center, and Common Language chose different strategies to expand their political space for advocacy work. Each group's strategy reflected the organizers' assessment of how to best achieve and leverage their relationships with the central government. The Maple Center opted for a cooperative strategy, whereas the Peking Women's Law Center pursued a much more confrontational approach. Common Language joined the campaign against domestic violence to capitalize on an opening in the political opportunity structure and develop its organizational capabilities.

The organizers' efforts to expand their boundaries vis-à-vis the central authorities represent a process of interactive political liberalization. In particular, the organizers' expectations concerning possible reactions from the central government to their boundary-expanding efforts are a major determinant of each group's selected strategy. Consequently, an adaptive government is crucial in changing the relationship between the state and societal actors. In addition to strategically anticipating the government's response to policy and action, other reasons for adopting their selected strategies indicate different stages of development of the organizations, as well as learning from the experiences of one another.

This chapter starts by briefly summarizing the development of the campaign against domestic violence and identifies the UN Fourth World Conference on Women in 1995 as creating the main political opening for the emergence of this campaign. This political opportunity bridged the gap between the international community and Chinese women's groups. Since then, phrases originating in the West, such as "domestic violence," "gender equity," and NGOs, as well as activism-related resources, have been incorporated by Chinese women's groups. Chronological analysis of the selected strategy of each organization is presented in the next part of the chapter, focusing on the resultant political opportunity or constraint. Two main factors affect the available strategies of activists: the organization's developmental stage and the activists' anticipated response from the government. Analysis of these organizational approaches reveals that some strategies create both political opportunities and constraints. Meanwhile, examination of the strategies selected by the three women's groups in the campaign against domestic violence confirms my contention that a cooperative strategy may result in a relatively high degree of organizational autonomy, whereas a confrontational strategy leads to a relatively high degree of empowerment. Ultimately, breaking down the public–private distinction regarding domestic violence contributed to the success of the campaign against domestic violence.

Brief Introduction of the Women's Groups

The three gender-based advocacy groups that were studied in this research are the Maple Center, the Peking Women's Law Center, and Common Language. The Maple Center was established by Wang Xinjuan and others in 1988 (see fig. 11.1). Its mission is to provide psychological counseling and social services to women, children, and families in urban and rural areas. In addition, the organizers perform gender-centered research and policy advocacy work. The Maple Center was the first grassroots women's group established in China.

The Peking Women's Law Center was established by Guo Jianmei and others in 1995 and has lawyers fighting pro bono for the legal rights

FIGURE 11.1 Founder of the Maple Center
Source: Photo by author.

of disadvantaged women. The center has three major missions: providing legal aid, protecting women's rights, and promoting gender equality. It was the first public-interest organization in China specializing in legal aid for women, and it has represented thousands of cases in 26 provinces, several of which were cases against the state.

Common Language was established by Xu Bin in 2005, and despite being a relatively young group, it is China's leading lesbian, gay, bisexual, and transgender (LGBT) rights organization. According to its website, Tongyulala.org, "Through community mobilization, public education, and legal advocacy, Common Language is dedicated to raising public awareness of the issues of gender and sexual diversity, combating violence and discrimination against LGBT persons, and advocating for equal rights." As an LGBT group centered in Beijing, Common Language has encountered marginalization since its establishment because the stigma of homosexuality is still pervasive in Chinese society, and many still associate homosexuality with HIV/AIDS. Institutional repression has reinforced the stigma of homosexuality.

Most activists working at Common Language are in their early 20s. During our interviews, I could strongly feel their enthusiasm for the LGBT movement, even though they had been unaware of the idea of a social movement before joining Common Language. Because most of the activists are students, they spend their leisure time working for and participating in Common Language's activities. Unlike the older generation, most of them openly identify as LGBT and believe they should have the same civil rights as heterosexual people.

Phase 1 (1988–2000): Society Acts First and Sets the Agenda

This section presents three stages of state–social group relations. The stages are identified according to changes in the organizational capabilities of the women's groups. Furthermore, "the state" refers to different governmental institutions, including the All China Women's Federation (ACWF), the juridical department of the central government, local women's federations, and local governments.

In the first stage, societal actors took initiative and set the agenda. This chapter identifies 1988 to 2000 as the first phase because Maple Center was established in 1988 and the Anti-Domestic Violence Network of the China Law Society was established in 2000. Maple Center created the first nationwide women's hotline in 1992 in response to inquiries concerning domestic violence incidents. However, the center did not set up a task force to address the issues of domestic violence at the beginning of its existence. During this time, society still viewed domestic violence as a family matter, and governmental institutions had not yet turned their attention to the issue.

Wang Xingjuan recalled that a phone call she received one night in 1994 awakened her to the seriousness of the situation of domestic violence victims. A staff person of a government unit called Wang to ask if Maple Center could shelter a woman who had just run away from her family and visited the unit to complain about her husband's physical abuse. "Maple Center failed to give a hand to this woman," Wang said in a repentant tone (interview, March 18, 2013). At that time, no shelters for victims of domestic violence were available in China. This failure compelled Wang to start working on domestic violence issues. Maple Center began to fight against domestic violence by researching the various contexts in which domestic violence occurs.

1992: THE FIRST PUBLIC DISCUSSION CONCERNING DOMESTIC VIOLENCE

It was not until 1992 that the first news reports regarding domestic violence appeared in the media. A female lawyer, Pi Xiaoming, wrote "A White Paper on Domestic Violence." After several failed attempts, the magazine *Chinese Women* finally agreed to publish Pi's paper. In the same year, the Maple Center established the first women's hotline and began to receive inquiries regarding domestic violence issues.

When the NPC passed the Law of the People's Republic of China on the Protection of Rights and Interests of Women (*funü quanli baozhang fa* 妇女权益保障法) on October 1, 1992, the law neither mentioned domestic violence nor included a provision for protective orders to restrain abusers from contacting their victims. During this period, the efforts of women's groups, both national and international, raised awareness of the severity of the domestic violence problem, resulting in some progress. However, it was the 1995 UN Conference on Women that first created the political opportunity for women's groups to learn about and initiate campaigns against domestic violence.

THE POLITICAL OPPORTUNITY: THE 1995 UN CONFERENCE ON WOMEN

Most researchers have contended that the UN Fourth World Conference on Women in Beijing was a critical event that stimulated the initiative and ability to organize Chinese women's groups (e.g., Judd 2002). The conference and the accompanying Nongovernmental Organization Forum introduced the Western phrase "nongovernmental organization" to contemporary Chinese discourse.[1] At the same time, it brought women's groups in China to the attention of international donors.

It was not until this conference that the Chinese government agreed to recognize the Beijing Declaration and Platform for Action (BPFA), which was passed at the conclusion of the conference. The BPFA brought the issue of domestic violence to the attention of the government and the media. Preventing violence against women is one of the 12 agenda items of the BPFA.

Based on interviews and field observations, I found that the Conference on Women created a political opportunity for activists to organize against domestic violence because it not only turned government's attention to the issue, it also brought in resources from the international community. The Ford Foundation is among the many international donors that shifted their sponsorships to women's groups, and it has played a major role in the campaign against domestic violence.

THE FORMATION OF THE ANTI-DOMESTIC VIOLENCE NETWORK

Wang Xingjuan, who is now in her 80s and has fought for women's rights for more than 20 years, recalled the reason she and Guo Jianmei formed the network:

Guo Jianmei and I have often teamed up. At that time, we found that many organizations worked on domestic violence issues, but they did not work cooperatively with each other. Therefore, we suggested the formation of an alliance. We invited Chen Mingxia (who later became the founder of the Network) to join us because we knew the Network would need someone to help with registration, and we wanted to unite more people in this campaign against domestic violence. (interview, July 16, 2012)

Concerning the cooperation between women's groups, Wang further explained,

We have been working together on domestic violence issues since the 1995 UN women's conference. Guo Jianmei, Xie Lihua [the founder of Rural Women Knowing All], and I formed a task force on domestic violence issues. We included contributions of NGOs and the government . . . but in fact, it is mainly the NGOs that have been working on domestic violence issues. (interview, July 16, 2012)

The formation of the Anti-Domestic Violence Network relied on financial support from the international community, including the UN Development Programme, the Swedish International Development Cooperation Agency, and Oxfam Novib (the Dutch Organization for International Development Cooperation).

THE ROLE OF THE INTERNATIONAL COMMUNITY

The most crucial development for Chinese women's organizations to fight domestic violence was the formation of the Anti-Domestic Violence Network. In 1998, the Ford Foundation sponsored four activists, including Wang Xingjuan, to attend a conference in India. This conference gathered representatives from women's NGOs throughout Asia to discuss gender-based violence. Before the trip, the Ford Foundation reminded the participants that they would be expected to work on this issue after returning home.

Two of the main founders of the Anti-Domestic Violence Network, Chen Mingxia and Ge Yongli, shared that they had discussed a possible work plan to fight gender-based violence during the conference. They decided to focus on domestic violence issues, and thus, the Anti-Domestic Violence Network was established in June 2000.[2] Wang Xingjuan and Guo Jianmei were also founders of this network.

STATE–SOCIETY SEQUENCE AT THIS STAGE

During this stage, society set the agenda to address domestic violence. Women's groups applied various strategies to awaken the state and wider society to the problem, including providing social services, conducting research, and most significantly, forming an alliance. With the support of the international community, women's groups slowly began to get the state's attention. At this stage, the major state actor was the ACWF.

THE STATE REACTS: THE ACWF

The ACWF was established in 1957. Prior to 1949, the CCP had set up the All-China Democratic Women's Federation to oversee women's mobilization. The task of the ACWF is to represent the CCP and perform the party's policies at each level of the bureaucratic system. This means that the main mission of the ACWF is to help the party maintain social stability rather than respond to the interests of women.

The interaction between women's groups and the ACWF in this stage could be described as follows. Maple Center's efforts gained the attention of the international women's groups, and it was agreed that the center would host a workshop on domestic violence at the Conference on Women. However, representatives from the ACWF refused to attend this workshop and accused Maple Center of damaging the country's image. ACWF officers told Wang Xingjuan and representatives of international women's groups, "There are no domestic violence incidents in China" (interview, March 18, 2013).

Phase 2 (2000–2009): Society Made Significant Progress and Local Governments Joined the Effort of Implementation

The second phase in the campaign against domestic violence spans from 2000 to 2009. In this stage, societal actors were proactive, as seen in the advocacy work of women's groups and cooperation with local government. Most important, women's groups made significant progress in the legislative process. In March 2003, 30 NPC representatives introduced the Domestic Violence Prevention and Intervention Law. This was the first time an initiative of the NPC was submitted by an NGO.

In fact, women's groups had put efforts into the lawmaking process for a long time. Before the 2003 law, one sign of progress was revision of the family law. On April 28, 2001, the Standing Committee of the NPC announced that domestic violence was prohibited and that a victim of domestic violence would be granted a divorce. However, "domestic violence" was not defined, and no punishment was indicated for violation of the law. In addition to promoting the anti–domestic violence law, women's groups tried to develop a cooperative relationship with local governments and implement their ideal model for preventing domestic violence. The following sections analyze each actor's strategies during this second phase.

THE MAPLE CENTER

During this stage, the Maple Center applied three strategies: forming an alliance, providing social services, and working with local governments. The Maple Center, along with the Peking Women's Law Center, China Women's University, and the Shaanxi Research Association for Women and Family, formed the Chinese Against Domestic Violence Task Force in 2000 in preparation for Beijing+5, which was a UN conference that would review progress made since the 1995 conference.

In addition to working with other women's groups, the Maple Center provided social services to domestic violence victims. On March 8, 2004, the Maple Center opened its first hotline for preventing domestic violence. The center worked with the Peking Women's Law Center, the legal department of the ACWF, and the Anti-Domestic Violence Network to provide assistance to victims of domestic violence.

At this stage, the key strategy of the Maple Center was to build co-operative relationships with local governments. In 2001, the center worked with the Tianjin Women's Federation to conduct an experimental project titled Community Intervention in Family Problems in a Tianjin Municipal Community. For this project, the Maple Center developed the following three programs to serve local women: a women's hotline, the Half-Sky Homeland (a project to build up a zero-domestic-violence-incident community), and a women's legal service station.

The cooperative relationship between the Maple Center and the Tianjin Women's Federation is not exceptional. Women's groups have tried to implement their ideal model to combat domestic violence in as many provinces as possible. The cooperative strategy has resulted in political opportunities and constraints for the Maple Center. For example, although this project provided an opportunity to increase the Maple Center's relative empowerment, the Tianjin Women's Federation's decision to end this project in 2006 caused a relative decline in the Maple Center's degree of autonomy.

THE PEKING WOMEN'S LAW CENTER

Litigating symbolic cases and awakening the legal system to domestic violence were two major strategies of the Peking Women's Law Center during this stage. The Law Center shifted its organizational approach in 2002, choosing to litigate cases that are considered representative of serious social problems. Litigating these symbolic cases and building alliances have been the two major strategies that enabled the Peking Women's Law Center to create political opportunity and expand its political space for advocacy work.

Litigating symbolic cases has created political opportunities for the Law Center. Lawyers introduced the Western emphasis on protecting domestic violence victims to the Chinese judicial system (*Renmin Wang* 2003) and have used important cases to highlight the severity of the domestic violence problem. The Tong Shenshen incident is an example of this process.[3]

Tong Shenshen suffered domestic violence even before marrying her abusive husband. She sought help from the police on multiple occasions and managed to run away from home. However, she was beaten to death by her husband, who was sentenced to prison for only six years and six months at the first trial for this crime. Most media reports expressed anger at the light sentence, and the newspaper of the juridical system even published a special report on this incident, arguing that reluctance to enforce existing laws was the major cause of this tragedy.[4] A lawyer from the Peking Women's Law Center represented this case. During my interview with her, she recalled that the Law Center used this case to alert judges and experts to the insufficient protection that the legal system offers to domestic violence victims (interview, July 18, 2012).

The Peking Women's Law Center provides training sessions for members of the legal system to increase their sensitivity to domestic violence victims. Furthermore, the Law Center holds these training programs in collaboration with local women's federations to recruit help for enforcing the monitoring requirements of the existing laws on domestic violence. As the director of a local women's federation told me, "When Guo Jianmei held a training program for our legal system, I helped her to invite all the leaders of the public security divisions, prosecutorial divisions, and the people's courts" (interview, April 7, 2017).

COMMON LANGUAGE

During this stage, an additional societal actor emerged, Common Language, which was established in 2005. Compared with the Maple Center and the Peking Women's Law Center, Common Language is a relatively young organization and has fewer social connections. At this stage, training organizers and building connections with women's groups and the state were its major strategies.

After the Anti-Domestic Violence Network was established, it developed a strategy to involve more organizations in the campaign against domestic violence, mainly giving grant funding to other groups that would work on this issue. Common Language applied for this funding in 2007, proposing that it would conduct research into incidents of domestic violence among lesbians. To implement the project, Common Language set up a website to recruit interviewees. It also cataloged the legal actions used to prevent and punish acts of domestic violence in Taiwan, the United States, and Canada. Common Language introduced legislative policies and processes concerning domestic violence in the lesbian population.

According to the founder of Common Language, Xu Bin, and other organizers, the project was intended to increase the awareness of women's activists to the situation of lesbians. Xu, who has influenced many lesbian organizers in China, stated: "In China, the campaign against domestic violence is organized by social groups. However, most experts of domestic violence issues are not familiar with queer issues. Only a few individuals within this campaign will express their personal support toward lesbian situations" (interview, May 17, 2016).

Xu further emphasized the role of Common Language in participating in the campaign against domestic violence: "I think this project [on lesbian victims of domestic violence] is an important task. This is the first time that we have had the chance to discuss a common issue with other women's groups. Furthermore, we can introduce lesbian situations to all the discussions. These experts are willing to listen because they are concerned about violence against women" (interview, May 17, 2016).

In interviews with the organizers of lesbian groups and women's groups, most indicated that they were not familiar with the issues of each other's campaigns. Many women's groups have not discussed issues relating to the LGBT population, and many young activists in lesbian groups have not paid attention to gender issues. My research will further examine Common Language's strategy of building a communication bridge between women's groups and lesbian groups in the following section.

THE STATE'S REACTION

The campaign against domestic violence worked with the ACWF and local women's federations. In some areas, new institutions to prevent domestic violence depended on efforts by local women's federations.

The ACWF In addition to progress in the lawmaking process, the ACWF's attitude changed at this stage. The ACWF is a government-organized NGO and is the mass organization for women. Women's groups and the Anti-Domestic Violence Network have long tried to recruit ACWF's participation in the campaign against domestic violence with different strategies. For example, women's organizations invited high-ranking ACWF officers to advise their task forces and organized several training programs on domestic violence issues with local women's federations.

The director of a provincial women's federation shared her learning experiences concerning domestic violence: "Of course I had heard about the issue of domestic violence because I have some legal background. But I learned the whole picture of domestic violence incidents when I participated in the training program provided by the Anti-Domestic Violence Network" (interview, November 7, 2018). After completing this training program, the director designed more training that invited experts on women's issues to talk to the leaders of local governments in her province.

During a news interview in 2008, an ACWF department director stated that the ACWF will make a concerted effort to prevent domestic violence and, in addition to public education, will begin the lawmaking process for the Domestic Violence Prevention Act (All-China Women's Federation 2008). In April 2009, the ACWF released a survey showing that 30 percent of families in China suffer from domestic violence.[5] In this news release, the ACWF vowed to work to prevent domestic violence.

The Tianjin Women's Federation The Tianjin Women's Federation accepted the Maple Center's offer to implement a model for preventing incidents of domestic violence. This cooperative model created a political opportunity for the Maple Center to implement its ideal model for preventing domestic violence in the community and enhance its reputation for influencing public policy nationwide.

However, this collaboration politically constrained Maple Center. In February 2006, the Tianjin Women's Federation decided to end its collaboration and continue the project on its own. In 2007, the federation decided to implement the model designed by the Maple Center in every community in Tianjin. During the opening ceremony of the citywide Half-Sky Homeland, the chairperson of the ACWF, Gu Xiulian, praised the project as "the outstanding product of the Women's Federation's service."

In this last statement, Xiulian failed to acknowledge the Maple Center's role in initiating and designing the project. The Maple Center organizers chose not to release a clarifying statement. Since 2007, whenever a news report has mentioned the Half-Sky Homeland, it has been presented as a project of the Tianjin Women's Federation.

During our interviews, Wang Xingjuan shared her evaluation of this project: "You can witness how we practice our mission of influencing the lives of others by contributing our own lives to the Tianjin project. Tianjin is a municipal city, but they were willing to carry out our project citywide" (interview, August 15, 2011). Although the leading role of Maple Center in this collaborative project was obscured through government interference, Wang nevertheless felt satisfied because the center had the chance to implement an effective model for helping victims of domestic violence.

Phase 3 (2009–2013): Expanding Political Space for Advocacy Work

State and society were both active during this phase of interaction. The three women's groups continued putting their efforts into advocacy work, social services, and public education, while the state focused on the legislative process. The women's groups' strategies are discussed in the next section.

During this phase, the Maple Center chose cooperative strategies, and the Peking Women's Law Center chose a much more confrontational strategy. Common Language joined the campaign against domestic violence to take advantage of the political opportunity to develop its organizational capabilities.

THE MAPLE CENTER

The Maple Center continued its various tactics in fighting domestic violence, namely, by providing social services to victims of domestic violence, participating in the lawmaking process, and working with local governments. One significant incident occurred in September 2012. Li Yang, the founder of Crazy English and a public figure,[6] was involved in a domestic violence incident. This incident turned people's attention to the issue of domestic violence nationwide (Osnos 2011). The media heavily reported on this incident, and in an interview with *China Daily*, Li Yang said, "I hit her [his wife] sometimes, but I never thought she would make it public since it's not a Chinese tradition to expose family conflicts to outsiders" (*China Daily* 2011a).

Kim Lee, Li's wife, posted photos of her injuries on her blog, but the actions of the organizers in the campaign against domestic violence brought her experience of abuse to the attention of the public and the media. The Maple Center offered individual and marital counseling to Kim and Li, but Li only showed up once for marital counseling. Wang Xingjuan was interviewed by the national and international media, and an introduction to the Maple Center was included in most news reports. This was another opportunity the Maple Center capitalized on to enhance its national reputation.

In addition to its advocacy work, the founders and organizers of the Maple Center adopted the strategy of becoming a part of the auxiliary mechanism through which central authorities provide public goods. The center thereby won recognition from the central authorities. Simultaneously, by receiving media attention, the Maple Center gradually established its reputation in society, which is a challenge, considering the size of China's population and geographic scale.

THE PEKING WOMEN'S LAW CENTER

During this stage, the Peking Women's Law Center continued its efforts of litigating symbolic cases and working with local governments. It also became involved in the Li Yang incident. In reaction to this notorious case, the Law Center chose to work with the Maple Center and introduced legal and counseling procedures for domestic violence victims and the whole society (Wang and Zhang 2011). This action was reported widely by the news media, which helped domestic violence victims understand the complexity of the legal system.

The Peking Women's Law Center continued its cooperation with local governments. I interviewed several local officials and learned that the specific reason that local governments sought collaboration with the Law Center was to avoid the occurrence of any egregious incidents in their jurisdictions—such as Tong Shenshen's case—that might leave them with a poor reputation. Working with local women's federations also helped the Law Center enhance its reputation for capably influencing public policy.

Another strategy of the Peking Women's Law Center was to litigate symbolic cases. This led the organization to adopt another strategy: submitting recommendations for new legislation that related to the plans of the central authorities. Reforms adopted by the NPC created a political opportunity for social groups to participate in the lawmaking process.

Compared with the strategy of litigating symbolic cases, submitting expert recommendations has been better received by central authorities. This alternative strategy helped the Peking Women's Law Center enhance its professional reputation among government institutions, as seen by the increasing number of invitations to attend legislative workshop conferences, especially those concerning domestic violence.

COMMON LANGUAGE

During this stage, Common Language's main focus was to cultivate a working relationship with the state, including central and local governments. The ACWF was the major target. According to Xu Bin,

> Compared with male gay groups, the lesbian population with AIDS is much smaller. Therefore, no government organization will communicate with us directly. The ACWF is the only government mechanism that Common Language can relate to [because lesbians are included in the women's population]. We have tried very hard to build our connections with local women's federations, but it was not until we joined the Anti-Domestic Violence Network that we made significant progress. (interview, August 12, 2011)

Another organizer from Common Language shared Xu's point of view:

> Compared with other government organizations, the ACWF is not powerful. However, it is still a part of the governing system; therefore, it has channels for working within the established political system. Take the Domestic Violence Prevention Act as an example: it was the ACWF that pushed this Act to be included in the government's legislative process. (interview, August 13, 2011)

This statement reveals the organizers' evaluation of Common Language's relationship with the ACWF. In addition to building connections with women's groups and local women's federations, a third political opportunity was created through Common Language's research into incidents of domestic violence among lesbians. Their research findings garnered media attention to the status of China's lesbian population.

One example is a news report published on January 11, 2010, in *Legal Daily* that covered several key findings from Common Language's investigation and included an interview of Xu and the formal director of the Anti-Domestic Violence Network. The reporter wrote that the incidents of domestic violence among the lesbian population were neglected, even by the staff of the ACWF, which was the state major organization given the task of preventing domestic violence. The report argued that cases of lesbian domestic violence deserve the attention of the government during the process of drafting the Domestic Violence Prevention Act (Du 2010).

STATE RESPONSES

During this stage, different parts of the state responded to the domestic violence issue, namely, the legal system, legislature, ACWF, and local women's federations. Significantly, changes in the legal system and the lawmaking process may be regarded as evidence for the creation of a new public sphere for discussing domestic violence issues.

The Legal System Beginning in 2008 and continuing until 2013, 10 of the Basic People's Courts voluntarily joined the effort of the China Institute of Applied Jurisprudence of the Supreme People's Court of China and applied the Trial Guide for Cases that Involve Domestic Violence and Marriage to strongly intervene in domestic violence incidents. According to the government document, nine district courts were chosen to be experimental courts that can issue protective orders for domestic violence victims.[7] By the end of 2011, more than 100 Basic People's Courts had applied to be experimental courts for domestic violence trials, and more than 200 protective orders had been granted. These statistics reveal a crucial change in the legal system. In the course of my field research, I found that the legal system has represented the general conservatism of society where women's issues are concerned. Thus, any breakthrough in the legal system can be considered a major achievement.

One lawyer from the Peking Women's Law Center shared her experiences in court. On several occasions, when a husband admitted to abusing his wife physically, the judge declined to include domestic violence as a reason for divorce. The lawyer remembered one case where the judge kept asking her to explain how the husband could have beaten his wife to death because the husband looked, quoting the judge, "so in love with his wife" (interview, August 17, 2011).

Guo Jianmei pointed out that based on her observations, in China there are only three legal experts with the ability to discuss legal issues from a gender perspective. The ignorance of gender issues among law enforcement agents is so prevalent that the director of a local women's federation in charge of its lawmaking process stated, "I did not support the enactment of any legislation for preventing domestic violence because I believed this action was useless. From my point of view, I would rather spend time educating our prosecutors and judges about gender issues" (interview, August 18, 2011).

These quotations demonstrate how difficult it is for women's organizations to create a public space for domestic violence issues and advocate for transforming the legal system. Few legal experts may be actively engaged in work on women's rights, but the Peking Women's Law Center and other women's groups continue to work to raise awareness of gender issues among experts and recruit them to join in the fight against domestic violence. The China Institute of Applied Jurisprudence of the Supreme People's Court of China has been a key partner for women's groups in their efforts to alter the prevailing attitude of the legal system.

The Lawmaking Process During this stage, both the central and local governments responded to the anti–domestic violence campaign through the legislative process. The legislative lobby of women's groups gained momentum in 2012 when the NPC announced its decision to include an anti–domestic violence law on its legislative agenda. Furthermore, illustrating the progress at the local government level, 28 provinces had passed domestic violence prevention acts by April 28, 2013 (*China Daily* 2011b).

The ACWF The lawmaking process for the Domestic Violence Prevention Act was in its final stage before being introduced to the NPC. The

ACWF had played a major role in this process and since 2009 had sought cooperation with other parts of the central government to promote the Anti-Domestic Violence Act. Reports at the time included the following: "As the Law against Domestic Violence has entered the legislative phase of soliciting public opinion, the ACWF has called on women's organizations and Chinese women to take an active role in expressing their opinions to help produce an optimal domestic violence law" (Wu 2014) and "the All China Women's Federation (ACWF) and the National Working Committee on Children and Women under the State Council jointly held a seminar on November 25, 2013 to discuss anti–domestic violence legislation" (Liu 2013).

Local Governments In this stage, many local governments cooperated with women's groups. Partnering with local governments helped women's groups reach out to marginalized women. An activist from a remote area of China explained the importance of working with local women's federations: "We chose to work with women's federations because their unit exists at the lowest level of governance organs. There is a contact person of the women's federation in each village" (interview, July 25, 2012).

Local governments included women's groups in their tasks to establish or enhance their own reputation for good governance or to avoid possible criticism. As one director of a local women's federation stated, "These [women's] groups are doing the women's federations' jobs. Hence, I always tell my staff that we need to learn from the women's groups" (interview, July 26, 2012).

Phase 4 (2013–2018): The Closing Down of Space for Civil Society

The relationship between the state and social groups became strained during this time, and Xi Jinping began recentralization to consolidate power. Since then, the central–local governments' relationship and state–society relations have been altered. Kostka and Nahm (2017, 568) describe that Xi "removed powers and discretion from local governments." As for the state–society relation, Elfstrom (2019) concluded that the central government has changed the balance between responsiveness and repression and shifted toward repression when facing protest from society.

Regarding the main theme of this chapter, the state engaged in contradictory actions concerning domestic violence, opposing activism but passing anti–domestic violence legislation. In an act of repression, the state launched the first mass arrest of organizers of the gender equality movement. On the eve of International Women's Day in 2015, five women activists were detained under suspicion that they were planning protests to highlight the problem of sexual harassment in China. The detainees were known for their work on women's and LGBT rights, including a campaign in 2012 to "occupy" men's toilets in an effort to highlight the shortage of women's restrooms.

This incident received much attention from the international community, and these activists were dubbed the Feminist Five. The campaign to free them applied various strategies, especially the use of news media, which had proven to be helpful for raising awareness of LGBT and domestic violence issues. The Feminist Five were freed under conditional release on April 13, 2015. This incident demonstrates the changing dynamics of the relationship between the state and gender groups. This was the first time the state launched a serious attack on these groups, which was viewed as a case of insensitivity by most scholars. However, on December 27, 2015, the government passed the Anti-Domestic Violence Law, which had been initiated and promoted by women's grassroots groups for decades.

These two significant events in 2015 exemplified the adaptive strategies that the state uses for controlling social groups, and the passage of the Law on the Administration of Activities of Overseas Non-Governmental Organizations within the Territory of China on April 28, 2016, represents another state governance strategy.

This section focuses on the strategies of both the state and the gender groups in the campaign against domestic violence.

COMMON LANGUAGE

Compared with other women's groups, Common Language made several significant moves in this period to capture people's attention about the situation of the lesbian population facing domestic violence issues. Two efforts were most significant.

At the end of 2015, Common Language announced the first national report concerning domestic violence in China. This report was conducted online and compiled 3,334 responses, including those from 877 heterosexual people. The key finding of this report was that compared with heterosexual and homosexual people, bisexual people suffered the most severe psychological violence. The report also documented domestic violence incidents among homosexual couples.

The second significant effort of Common Language was the establishment of the Rainbow Anti-Gender-Based Violence Service Center for LGBTI People. This marked the first ever publicly announced shelter for LGBTI people, and was also the first such shelter that had the cooperation of local women's federations and experts in social work.

STATE ACTORS

The Central Government The central government demonstrated its adaptive and rapid governance strategies in this period. Passage of the Anti-Domestic Violence Law and the Law on the Administration of Activities of International Non-Governmental Organizations within the Territory of China (INGO Act) signaled that the central government would regulate gender groups' activities in the campaign against domestic violence.

Women's groups now had access to shape public policy regarding domestic violence issues. However, the campaign against domestic violence depended on major support from international donors. Passage of the INGO Act immediately affected the operations of gender groups. This new act made two significant changes in the relationship between the state and groups in the campaign against domestic violence. First, it regulated the activity of INGOs, which meant that they were required to register with the government and indicate which issues they worked on. As of the end of 2018, no INGO had identified domestic violence as its primary issue. Second, if gender groups could no longer rely on the support of international donors, they could only rely on domestic sources. Doing so would result in more changes in the relationship between the state and gender groups.

Local Governments Because the Anti-Domestic Violence Act was included in the national lawmaking agenda in 2013, local governments were very active in responding to this new situation. Several significant moves ensued to shift the relationship between the state and gender groups.

First, several local women's federations, including those of Shanghai, Zhejiang, and Guangdong, commenced governmental purchase of services for domestic violence prevention. Second, Hunan province launched a cross-departmental cooperation initiative to prevent domestic violence in 2013. Hunan modeled its program on that of Taiwan and included the police department, judicial system, medical department, educational department, and bureau of civil administration. Because of this initiative, the Hunan bureau of police announced its principles for handling domestic violence incidents on April 9, 2013 and became the first police department in the nation to do so.

Third, similar to Hunan province, several local governments launched pioneer projects to prevent domestic violence incidents. For example, in 2014, the judicial system of Jiangsu province established its first shelter, which is run by the court. Jiangsu was also the first local government to set up a system to admonish domestic abusers.

The Anti-Domestic Violence Law was implemented in March 2016. We have observed many more news reports about local governments' enforcement efforts, such as restraining orders issued by Chengdu city against live-in perpetrators of domestic violence and the censure system launched by Nanning City of Guangxi province. A Gansu province campaign was held in Lanzhou, Gansu's capital, co-organized by ACWF and UN Women for the second phase of a UN program to end domestic violence. The objective was to promote in the entire province an exemplary mechanism—the Jingyuan model—that has successfully linked multiple agencies at the province, city, and county levels to deter domestic violence (Equality 2017).

The Judicial System In this stage, the judicial system played a vital role before the passage of and during the implementation of the Anti-Domestic Violence Act. On March 2, 2015, the Supreme People's Court coordinated with the Supreme People's Procuratorate, the Ministry of Public Security, and the Ministry of Justice to announce the Opinion on Handling Criminal Cases of Domestic Violence in Accordance with Law. This marked the first judicial document regarding criminal procedure for domestic violence cases. From the implementation of the Anti-Domestic

Violence Act on March 1, 2016, until the end of that year, media reports indicated that courts issued 680 restraining orders nationwide.

Conclusion: Evaluation of Women's Groups' Strategies

This chapter's analysis of the campaign against domestic violence identified five major actors that affected the strategies selected and used by campaigning groups: central authorities, societal organizers, local governments, the international community, and the media. In the face of challenges posed by China's system of governance, organizers chose to ally with different actors to transform these challenges into political opportunities. Sometimes organizers chose a strategy that unintentionally led to political constraints. Nevertheless, the three organizations detailed herein achieved the following substantive outcomes: social empowerment, policy formation, and a relatively high degree of political mobilization.

First, the successful introduction of the draft law to the NPC blurred the strict distinction between the public and private spheres and challenged the long-held view that domestic violence is a family matter. In addition to efforts to create a new public sphere for discussing domestic violence, the campaign against domestic violence also succeeded in making the government and society aware of individual rights.

According to lawyers affiliated with the Peking Women's Law Center, the number of domestic violence victims who sought legal help increased dramatically after 2002. Furthermore, 2002 was also when lawyers received the most requests for help since the establishment of the Law Center in 1995. The increasing number of women seeking legal counsel for domestic violence incidents demonstrates burgeoning respect for the concept of rights in Chinese society. This is a major victory for women's groups and may have contributed to the advancement of civil society, if not political mobilization in China. Historically, people in China have been accustomed to obeying rulers. According to Kevin J. O'Brien, "There is little evidence that villagers consider rights to be inherent, natural, or inalienable; nor do most claimants break with the common Chinese practice of viewing rights as granted by the state mainly for societal purposes rather than to protect an individual's autonomous being" (2001, 426).

In such a cultural context, it was more challenging for domestic violence victims to claim their own rights, especially when most of society viewed domestic violence as a dishonorable family matter. Lawyers at the Peking Women's Law Center have observed that domestic violence victims have become more willing to reveal the "dirty laundry" of their households and fight for their rights, demonstrating a new awareness and appreciation of rights.

The situation of the lesbian population has also gained visibility. In addition to increasing the media's awareness, Common Language successfully developed connections with women's groups, and lawyers from the Peking Women's Law Center began to represent lesbians in court. In addition to transforming the engagement of societal actors, the strategies each group selected and implemented affected their organizational development. Common Language strategically chose to join the campaign against domestic violence to achieve the recognition of lesbian groups in society. By participating in this campaign, its degree of autonomy and empowerment increased. Organizers at Common Language continue to fight for the lesbian population to be included in legal provisions that protect domestic violence victims. Whether their efforts succeed will be a crucial evaluative criterion for judging its strategies. The Maple Center chose a cooperative strategy, and the outstanding question for them is whether the strategy reduced its degree of autonomy in exchange for a gain in its degree of empowerment. The Peking Women's Law Center pursued a much more confrontational strategy; as a result, organizers have faced the most interference from the government. To counteract government interference, the Law Center has chosen to cooperate with the media. However, it is an open question whether the media would continue their support if the government decided to intervene and repress media reporting.

In conclusion, this research agrees with Feng Yuan's evaluation of the contributions of Maple Center, the Peking Women's Law Center, and Common Language in the campaign against domestic violence. Feng is a founder and a three-term director of the Anti-Domestic Violence Network. She stated, "Maple Center provided the fundamental research data for the campaign against domestic violence. Its analyses of one hundred cases provided a better understanding of domestic violence incidents. The Maple Center's research helps both prevention work and policy advocacy to move forward" (interview, May 22, 2016).

With respect to the Peking Women's Law Center and Common Language, Feng commented,

> The Peking Women's Law Center plays a critical role in reforming the legal system. Without the understanding of domestic violence issues and without the gender perspectives [contributed by the center], law enforcement could cause more harm to abused victims. As for Common Language, it is Common Language's report on lesbian domestic violence victims that supplements our shortage of prevention work. Further, Common Language's research provides most people in China with their first opportunity to learn more about sexual minorities. (interview, May 22, 2016)

Each organization chose a distinct strategy on the basis of its developmental stage and in anticipation of governmental response. According to my field research, the Peking Women's Law Center, which opted for a confrontational strategy, increased its degree of autonomy; and Maple Center, which chose a cooperative strategy, increased its degree of empowerment. Common Language, a relatively young group, leveraged the opportunity to join the campaign against domestic violence to increase its degree of autonomy and degree of empowerment (see fig. 11.2).

I conclude that the following three lessons are significant in expanding organizational space for advocacy work. First, these three organizations successfully established their professional image. This is crucial when an organization hopes to be included in the policymaking process. Second, these three organizations successfully built their coalitions with cross-issue groups. The Maple Center teamed up with mental health groups, and Common Language has cooperated with women's groups. Third, these groups have successfully made connections with governmental officials. These connections help when these groups try to be included in the policymaking process.

In addition to changes in the relative autonomy, empowerment, and organizational capabilities for the social groups, China's system of governance coevolved. This chapter identified the following changes in the governance system toward domestic violence: local governments engaged in

FIGURE 11.2 Map of universities showing where Common Language has delivered lectures
Source: Photo by author.

cooperative projects with women's groups to eradicate domestic violence, the ACWF turned its attention to domestic violence issues, the NPC undertook the Anti-Domestic Violence Act in its legislative agenda, and China's judicial system improved its capacity to handle domestic violence cases fairly and thoroughly.

These changes in state–society relations reflect the contraction of governmental boundaries to allow for social organizing and demonstrate the emergence of a public sphere for open discussion of the problem of domestic violence. More broadly, these developments indicate that adaptive dynamics in governance can create pockets of political liberalization when the issue does not threaten regime legitimacy.

Looking Forward: Will Women's Groups Survive the Closing Space of Civil Society?

Since 2018, the relationship between the state and social organizations has shifted dramatically. Implementation of the INGO Act led to the departure of many foreign NGOs from China. The 2019 Hong Kong protests (also known as the Anti–Extradition Law Amendment Bill movement), deepened the central government's anxiety about the influence of foreign NGOs.

On November 26, 2019, a Ministry of Foreign Affairs spokesperson pointed out that Asia Catalyst was operating illegally in China and was punished by the government. On December 2, 2019, the ministry accused five US NGOs of fomenting Hong Kong's protests, including the National Endowment of Democracy, National Democratic Institute, International Republican Institute, Human Rights Watch, and Freedom House. Asia Catalyst and these five NGOs have supported women's and gender groups in the past, including capacity building, agenda setting, and training programs. Organizers of women's and gender groups have survived severe challenges from the state. The recent government strategy is to break the alliance between global civil society and domestic social groups. It remains to be seen whether the organizers will evolve and continue their work.

Notes

1. This statement does not mean that social organizing did not exist before the conference. Instead, this statement emphasized that the term "NGO," similar to many other Western terms regarding social organizing and gender issues, was introduced to Chinese women's groups at this conference.

2. Growing Stronger Along with the Network for Combating Domestic Violence, 8. The website of the Anti-Domestic Violence Network no longer exists.

3. Tong Shenshen was 26 years old at her death. She and her family reported domestic violence incidents eight times within several months. But the police were unable to provide much assistance. Tong tried to run away and lived by herself, but she was unable to escape her husband. Her husband stated in court that he could not remember how many times he kicked her and that he just kept kicking her during the last violent incident. The court only accused him of an abusive crime.

4. See http://news.eastday.com/s/20100809/u1a5381742.html.

5. See "Should the Victims of Domestic Violence Publicly Forgive the Abusers?," December 4, 2019, http://yn.people.com.cn/BIG5/n2/2019/1204/c361322-33602174.html, translation mine.

6. Crazy English (*fengkuang yingyu* 疯狂英语) is a brand name for a nontraditional method of teaching English in China conceived by Li Yang. See http://en.wikipedia.org /wiki/Crazy_English.

7. See "Protection Order: Makes the Anti-Domestic Violence Act Grow 'Teeth,'" http://www.npc.gov.cn/npc/c16115/201510/113bebebf93b4492976d95293d1f3117.shtml (accessed on June 20, 2020), translation mine.

References

Caixin. 2018. "Almost 70% of Sexual Minorities Experienced Domestic Violence. Their Human Rights are Ignored." *Caixin*, November 30. http://china.caixin.com/2018-11 -30/101353715.html

China Daily. 2011a. "Renowned Teacher Admits Abusing His U.S. Wife." *China Daily*, September 13. http://usa.chinadaily.com.cn/us/2011-09/13/content_13671481.htm.

———. 2011b. "Multiple Reasons that Lead to China's Frequent Domestic Violence Cases. There Is an Urgent Need to Legitimize Anti-Domestic Violence." *China Daily*, November 24. http://www.chinadaily.com.cn/dfpd/shehui/2011-11/24/content_14157866 .htm.

Elfstrom, Manfred. 2019. "Two Steps Forward, One Step Back: Chinese State Reactions to Labor Unrest." *China Quarterly* 240: 855–79.

Equality. 2017. "The First Year Report on the Observations and Suggestions after the Passage of the Anti-Domestic Violence Act." *Equality*, March 2. http://www.equality -beijing.org/newinfo.aspx?id=24.

Judd, Ellen R. 2002. *The Chinese Women's Movement between State and Market*. Stanford, CA: Stanford University Press.

Kostka, Genia, and Jonas Nahm. 2017. "Central-Local Relations: Recentralization and Environmental Governance in China." *China Quarterly* 231: 567–82.

Liu, Yunting. 2013. "ACWF, NWCCW Hold Anti-Domestic Violence Legislation Seminar." Women of China, November 27. http://www.womenofchina.cn/womenofchina /html1/news/leaders/16/7609-1.htm.

O'Brien, Kevin J. 2001. "Villagers, Elections, and Citizenship in Contemporary China." *Modern China* 27.4: 407–35.

———. 2009. "Rural Protest." *Journal of Democracy* 20.3: 25–28.

Osnos, Evan. 2011. "'Crazy English' Teacher Admits to Domestic Violence." *New Yorker*, September 13. http://www.newyorker.com/online/blogs/evanosnos/2011/09/crazy -english-teacher-admits-to-domestic-violence.html.

Renmin Wang. 2013. "There Are Ways to Constrain Domestic Violence" (*Jiating baoli youren guanle*). *People's Daily*, January 22. http://www.people.com.cn/BIG5/paper68 /8314/783228.html.

Wang, Kala, and Gailun Zhang. 2011. "Liyang's Wife: Do Not Be Silent When You En-counter Domestic Violence." *Xin Jing Bao*, November 25.

Wu, Amanda. 2014. "China Issues Anti-Domestic Violence Law Draft." Women of China, December 26. Available at: http://www.womenofchina.cn/womenofchina /html1/special/1412/1715-1.htm.

CHAPTER 12

Local Strategies of Engaging the State

The Cultural Legitimation and Heritagization of Mazu Belief

Ming-chun Ku

*T*his chapter analyzes the cultural legitimation of Mazu belief, a popular religion in southeastern China, through three decades of state–society interactions. During the Mao era, the party-state banned Mazu belief because it was regarded as a feudalistic superstition. Starting in the late 1970s, Mazu believers in Fujian rebuilt a temple in her honor and resumed traditional worshiping practices and rituals. Through extensive engagement between religious community leaders and various state actors, leaders of Mazu belief communities eventually succeeded in persuading the state to acknowledge the indigenous cultural value of Mazu; in 2009, Mazu belief was added to UNESCO's Representative List of the Intangible Cultural Heritage of Humanity. As a case study in the evolution of religious governance and the politics of recognition, the chapter demonstrates that both state and societal actors reached mutually beneficial outcomes. By reframing religious practices as cultural heritage worthy of preservation, community leaders partnered with select governmental entities to promote the legitimation of a local folk religion in a state-sponsored cultural framework. In addition, the state was able to leverage officially recognized and regulated religious activities to achieve other governmental goals, such as united front outreach to Taiwanese religious communities. These empirical observations are based on field research conducted between 2011 and 2015.

Scholarship on China's religious revival since the late 1970s reveals a complex relationship between religion and the party-state. Some case studies have focused on the coercive reach of the authoritarian state. Others have highlighted bargaining or cooperation between the local government and popular religious communities. The revival of popular religions may be supported by the local governments because of the commercial benefits of tourism (Chan and Lang 2015; Koesel 2014, 106–16) and ritual economies (Siu 1989, 1990; Yang 2007). Furthermore, popular religious communities may pursue alliances and cooperate with local officials in exchange for material or nonmaterial resources (Chau 2006; Ku 2018). These case studies have illustrated the variation in governance tools adopted by the local state, from repression to collaboration with various forms of partnership.

To understand this variation, the uncertain status of popular religions in existing modes of governance in China must be considered. The term "religion" emerged in the process of modernization and state formation during the early twentieth century in China (Goossaert and Palmer 2011, 43–63). The categorization of religions was institutionalized in the Chinese Communist Party (CCP)'s policy on religion, which limited legal religious activities to five faiths: Buddhism, Taoism, Islam, Protestantism, and Catholicism. The CCP's mode of religious governance is state corporatist such that the state has created patriotic associations to supervise these religions (Goossaert and Palmer 2011, 139–65; Marsh 2011). It retains control over their classification as "legal religions" versus "diversified religious activities." Because the popular religions are not officially considered "religions," the conventional approaches and institutional mechanisms of religious governance in China do not apply to them.

This raises practical problems for local and central governance with the variety and mushrooming of popular religions. For once-repressed popular religious groups, their revival and development confront different types of local regimes, which may be constituted by social networks of traditional solidary groups (Tsai 2007) or may modify their governance in various forms of "authoritarianism with adjectives," as summarized in this book's introductory chapter. Most case studies have contributed to the understanding of the local variety of state–religion relations. A gap remains in the existing literature concerning the adaptation and institutionalization of local changes in the evolution of the state governance of popular religions, particularly those ideologically labeled by the CCP as feudal superstitions that hinder the progress of socialist modernity in society (Goossaert and Palmer 2011, 140–52).

Mazu belief offers an empirical entry to filling this gap. Along with other popular religions, the legend and worship of the sea goddess Mazu was forbidden in the Mao era. During the Cultural Revolution, temples honoring Mazu and other popular spiritual icons were destroyed and traditional ceremonies were halted because they were denounced for being "feudal" and "superstitious" (Z.-M. Zheng 2010). In 2009, the United Nations Educational, Scientific and Cultural Organization (UNESCO) inscribed Mazu belief and customs on to its Representative List of the Intangible Cultural Heritage of Humanity (ICH). This was the first UNESCO ICH designation of a popular religion in China. Inscription as ICH items on the list is an indicator of "heritagization," a social and cultural process that institutionalizes specific cultural values as official "heritage" and legitimates particular ideas and norms regarding "heritage practices" (Harrison 2013, 43–56; Smith 2006, 21–24). Most accounts of heritagization in China from the 1980s have been state-centric in highlighting the intentions of official heritage projects (Silverman and Blumenfield 2013). Local initiatives are neglected or considered passive responses to state policies and narratives in the trajectory of heritagization (Zhu and Li 2013). However, this top-down approach cannot explain why the party-state has selected certain "feudal and superstitious" practices as national cultural values for preservation and safeguarding in state-led heritagization. By contrast, this study presents the ICH inscription of Mazu belief as a path-dependent result of three decades of interaction between various state actors and religious community leaders in the religious revival in China's reform era. Over the course of such interaction, Mazu belief gradually evolved in the state's governance framework from being a local folk cult to a collateralized and culturified official instrument.

In the following section, this chapter illustrates the strategic actions of religious community leaders of Mazu belief in Meizhou Island, Fujian, and includes four rounds of interactions with the local and central state: (1) building temples in the late 1970s, (2) resuming traditional ceremonies in the early 1980s, (3) being mobilized through the provincial- and national-level ICH listing process in 2005, and (4) proactively applying for national nomination for UNESCO ICH inscription in 2008. In each phase, community leaders secured the support of some state actors when experiencing opposition or potential repression from other state actors. Community leaders started by emphasizing the cultural legitimacy of the Mazu belief to deal with the ambiguous reaction of the state toward its revival. Over time, culturification gradually became a strategy for community leaders to claim material and nonmaterial resources in a changing opportunity structure. The eventual success in securing the ICH status for Mazu belief represented the culmination of this creatively pragmatic strategy.

Phase 1: Rebuilding Temples (1978–1980s)

As with other once-forbidden popular religions in China, Mazu belief was revived in the changing political climate of the late 1970s, and some followers in southeastern China endeavored to reconstruct destroyed temples despite the political risks. Leaders of the Meizhou Mazu Ancestral Temple were among these pioneers. In 1969, the Meizhou Mazu Ancestral Temple was destroyed by the Revolutionary Committee of the People's Commune of Meizhou Island (Jiang and Zhu 2011, 555). During the late 1970s,[1] a charismatic elderly woman of the Lin lineage, Mrs. Lin Ah-be, organized an informal group of followers to begin the reconstruction of the Meizhou Mazu Ancestral Temple (fig. 12.1), initially with their own money and tools (Jiang and Zhu 2011, 556; Z.-M. Zheng 2010, 127–28). Donations began arriving from abroad during the 1980s when Mazu followers in Taiwan and other parts of Asia learned about the construction effort.

From inception, the temple building effort evoked opposition from the People's Liberation Army on Meizhou Island because the temple was located in the military garrison area (Z.-M. Zheng 2010, 128). The military's objections were rational from a bureaucratic perspective because the rebuilt temple could increase the number of illegal Taiwanese pilgrims to the island, thereby increasing their responsibilities in ensuring national security (An 2014). The military ordered demolition if the believers proceeded with rebuilding the temple. Facing military repression, religious community leaders on Meizhou Island did not react confrontationally. Instead, they mobilized personal connections to access various state actors

FIGURE 12.1 Worshipers at Meizhou Mazu ancestral temple

Source: Photo by Ying-fa Hong.

that might be more supportive. For community leaders, the state was perceived as a complex with various types of power holders and full of ambiguous possibilities. Drawing initially on lineage connections and then reaching out indirectly to provincial officials and cadres, community leaders gradually accumulated support from sympathetic state actors and nonstate policy entrepreneurs, including the chair of the Chinese People's Consultative Committees at the city and provincial levels and local officials in charge of Taiwanese affairs (Chang 2014, 144; Z.-M. Zheng 2010, 128). These efforts helped postpone the military's threat of demolishing the temple. Meanwhile, changing cross-strait relations in the early 1980s also reduced the military's influence on local affairs. Demilitarization of Meizhou Island was symbolized by abolishing the military garrison area in 1983, and the island was officially considered a key location for managing Taiwan affairs in Fujian province (Putian Foreign Trade and Economic Commission 1995, 20). In the same year, the Fujian party secretary wrote an official comment "suspending temple demolishment," which offered greater security for the community leaders and their rebuilt temple (Chang 2014, 144; Z.-M. Zheng 2010, 128).

During the temple building process, religious community leaders discovered a tactic to avoid potential military repression. When the community leaders and their followers retrieved an old main beam from the previous temple, which had been (secretly) preserved in the commune's storage facility, they noted a calligraphy inscription on the beam listing the names of Lin lineage gentry as the major donors. They were also aware that the chair of the Chinese People's Consultative Committee in Putian was a descendant of this clan. This old main beam was perceived by the religious community leaders as a Lin lineage relic, an item embodying a historic representation that links the honorable status of someone in the past with someone in a power position in the present. This relic helped these leaders enlist certain state actors for support. The value of historic artifacts was implicitly or explicitly recognized by the community leaders for linking the symbolic power of relics and social capital in the local power structure. To gain legitimacy, community leaders attempted to have the temple and its artifacts listed as historic relics with an official status. Assisted by local cultural experts, it took several years of application to obtain the relic status of historical and cultural relics protected at the provincial level in Fujian. Official recognition as a relic item may not necessarily prevent demolition elsewhere in China; in this case, the status of a provincial-level relic perhaps was not as powerful as the support by key state-affiliated actors. During the temple rebuilding, community leaders reached out to cultural experts for sympathy and support. These connections were mobilized repeatedly in sequential rounds of engaging the state, and a coherent strategy for action gradually emerged among community leaders to legitimate their religious practices—the culturification of Mazu belief.

Phase 2: Restarting Grand Ceremonies (1983–1994)

When the construction of the main hall of the Meizhou Mazu Ancestral Temple was completed, religious community leaders reintroduced elaborate ceremonies in the spring and autumn that had been forbidden for decades. The religious tone of these ceremonies caused controversy in 1983, and provincial cadres and officials were unable to reach consensus about their status (Jiang and Zhu 2011, 556). Thus, the leaders again searched for support from previously established connections. They also adopted a new strategy to gain legitimacy: enhancing connections with overseas Mazu worshipers, including Taiwanese, who contributed financially during the temple construction (Ku and Hong 2017). Such connections were instrumentally cultivated for several reasons. In addition to maintaining friendship and collaboration in the revival of the Mazu belief, as the leaders claimed, other reasons may have included the following. First, because there were still other halls of Meizhou Mazu Ancestral Temple under construction, local religious leaders expected to need overseas donations. Second, the Taiwanese connection had a powerful role in changing cross-strait relations in the late 1980s. To attract overseas pilgrims, a lavish ceremony was held in 1987 commemorating 1,000 years since the ascension of sea goddess Mazu (Ku and Hong 2017). Leading up to this ceremony, a board of trustees for the temple was established in 1986 to coordinate among governmental actors, the local religious community, and overseas groups. The Meizhou Mazu Ancestral Temple leadership was reconstituted by the official assignment of the head of the board committee in 1986 to someone trusted by the local party-state and accepted by the religious community—the aforementioned Lin lineage descendant and chair of Chinese People's Consultative Committees in Putian (Chang 2014, 144). Mrs. Lin Ah-be, the charismatic religious leader, was assigned as the deputy (Lin and Chen 2012), which was still a position of power over financial donations (Dean 1998, 264) and decision-making in temple affairs (Zhu 2012). The assignment was both symbolic and functional. It symbolized the submission of the religious community leadership to the authority of the local state. It was functional because the assigned chair created a channel of communication between the governmental sectors and the religious community.

In preparation for the ceremony, the board of trustees sent numerous invitations to overseas temple organizations. More than 10,000 visitors attended the event, including guests from Taiwan, Hong Kong, Singapore, Japan, and other Southeast Asian countries. Since then, the board of trustees has maintained its legitimate status by playing two key roles in local governance. First, the trustees facilitate cross-strait relations by working with the officials in charge of Taiwanese affairs at provincial and city levels to deal with pilgrims from Taiwan. Second, the trustees manage the Meizhou Mazu Ancestral Temple as a pilgrimage tourist attraction.

Currently, two festive revival ceremonies of the Mazu belief are organized annually on Meizhou Island. The spring ceremony is held on Mazu's birthday on the 23rd day of the 3rd month of the lunar year, and the fall ceremony is dedicated to Mazu's ascension, on the 9th day of the 9th month of the lunar year (fig. 12.2). The board of trustees intentionally enlarged the scale of the ceremonies and included formal etiquette. This was not only a symbolic gesture of religious revival but also a strategy to increase the prominence of the Meizhou Mazu Ancestral Temple among religious communities overseas. In the early 1980s, it was challenging to restart something that had been halted for decades. Rather than reviving the ceremony based solely on local social memory, the trustees asked for assistance from historians and folklorists to reinvent the traditional ceremonies. The formality, rather than the authenticity, of the ceremonies was the main concern of the trustees.

In 1994, the Mazu ceremony was officially chosen as a major tourist attraction in the inaugural Mazu Cultural Tourism Festival organized by the Putian city government. With the approval of the local government,

FIGURE 12.2 Grand Ceremony at Meizhou Mazu Ancestral Temple

Source: Photo by Ying-fa Hong.

the trustees organized a team to visit Shandong province and learn about the Grand Ceremony Dedicated to Confucius. Emulating the Confucius ceremony, the spring ceremony on Mazu's birthday has become standardized and formalized since the 1994 tourism festival (Lin 2017). Religious rituals and practices were reintroduced to the public in the name of Mazu culture. In addition to using the religious ceremonies as tourist attractions and events associated with Taiwan affairs, the trustees sponsored several conferences related to Mazu culture that were presided over by local officials and attended by cultural experts and scholars domestically and from abroad. The strategy of culturification was applied frequently in the 1990s and 2000s, not just by the board of trustees but also by local cadres to receive symbolic or financial support from the local and central governments. For example, the deputy of the Administration Committee of Meizhou Island proposed to extend the plaza in front of the Meizhou Mazu Ancestral Temple in 2000 to provide a venue for ritual performances for honored guests, pilgrims, and journalists visiting during the ceremonies. The construction was approved by the governor of Fujian province, Xi Jinping, and funded by the provincial government (Y. Zheng 2012).

Phase 3: Mobilized in Provincial and National ICH Listing (2005)

Since the People's Republic of China became a signatory to international conventions for heritage, such as the World Heritage Convention in 1985 and the Convention for the Safeguarding of the Intangible Cultural Heritage (ICH Convention) in 2004, there has been a paradigm shift in China's official heritage discourse that facilitated the emergence of new types of heritage, including ICH. In the early 2000s, some local literati in Putian advocated the promotion of Mazu belief as World Heritage. According to my interviews with a trustee of the Meizhou Mazu Ancestral Temple and staff in the semi-official organization Chinese Mazu Cultural Exchange Association, none of the locals in Meizhou were aware of the difference between World Heritage and ICH (interviews, April 2012). Moreover, even though its supporters believed that the status of Mazu should be internationally recognized, they had no idea about how to proceed.

In 2005, after the Chinese government signed the ICH Convention, the central state launched the first provincial and national ICH listings. A cultural expert from the Putian Mass Art Center, a city cultural institute, was officially assigned to prepare the inventory and documents for the provincial listing; he had previously been assigned to collect folk literature and songs in the 1980s.

The board of trustees was informed by the cultural expert and other provincial officials to prepare for ICH listing. From their perspective, ICH was an honorable title comparable to National Relics and World Heritage, which symbolized official recognition and brought resources and opportunities. With approval from provincial leadership to list Mazu-related items on this inventory, the cultural expert mobilized the trustees of Meizhou Mazu Ancestral Temple and two other well-known Mazu temples to file related materials.

In response to the cultural expert's request, the trustees proposed that 18 items be listed. One of the concerns of this cultural expert was fairness for different Mazu believer communities in Putian (interview with a local cultural expert, April 2012). To manage local politics, he included items from three major local Mazu temples when preparing the inventory for ICH candidacy. The cultural expert eventually persuaded the trustees to reduce the list to one major item that best represented the Meizhou Mazu Ancestral Temple—the Mazu ceremony. As such, the inventory still had space for items representing the two other temples.

The other concern regarded the criteria of Mazu-related practices as ICH items. The cultural expert from Putian Mass Art Center had been working on folk art collecting since the 1980s and was well aware of the ideological concerns and the importance of interpretation in official cultural works. Before his work on ICH inventory preparation, he was assigned to attend intensive classes on ICH organized by the provincial cultural bureau. Using his formal knowledge of ICH discourse and requirements and tacit knowledge of the ideological concerns in cultural works, he identified the value of the potential ICH items and interpreted that value according to ICH criteria. To reformulate Mazu-related practice into ICH items properly, he consulted other cultural experts within and outside the subcommittee under the provincial cultural bureau and gradually concluded that the discursive framework of Mazu-related items as ICH should not fall into the category of popular religion, which lacked official legitimacy. Because provincial leaders supported the listing of Mazu-related items in the ICH inventory, the cultural expert mentioned in my interview that the first priority was to reduce the degree of uncertainty in the listing process (interview, April 2012). While he worked on the application document, he consciously framed the value of the Mazu-related items in terms of "traditional culture" and "customs." By doing so, he pointed out that when the application document was submitted to the provincial and national levels, it was still "exclusively at the hands of the cultural bureau and cultural experts" and the opinions from other departments, such as the religious bureau, may not be involved in the process.

The item representing Meizhou Mazu Ancestral Temple in the inventory submitted to the provincial and national committees was the Mazu ceremony. During my interview, the cultural expert emphasized that "the item is under the category of rituals and ceremonies, not religion" (interview, April 2012). When the application material of the Mazu ceremony was submitted to the provincial committee, some cultural experts criticized that the ceremony emulated the Confucius ceremony and was not authentic, and they vetoed the application. The cultural expert from the Putian Mass Art Center was commanded by provincial officials to write and submit supplementary materials for the case. The provincial culture bureau reorganized the committee to reevaluate the application materials. With these efforts, the Mazu ceremony was finally approved as a provincial ICH item. Its candidacy was later reviewed and approved by the national committee. This item was officially approved as a provincial and national ICH item in 2006.

In the application process for provincial and national ICH status, major efforts were made by state actors, including the cultural expert and the officials in the provincial cultural bureau. In addition to administratively facilitating the application, their efforts were mainly for discursive justification, including preparing application materials submitted to the provincial and national committees. Local religious community leaders were mobilized by these state actors, and they were responsive and cooperative toward the state-launched ICH. Their cooperation with the state was facilitated by the cultural expert, who mediated between state and religious communities, as well as a cultural translator, who reframed the religious practices as an ideologically risk-free cultural custom.

Phase 4: Applying for UNESCO ICH Inscription (2008)

Although passively mobilized in 2005, the Meizhou Mazu Ancestral Temple Board of Trustees played a different role in 2008 on learning about the opportunity to compete for national nomination as China's representative ICH on the UNESCO list. The board of trustees in 2008 was a complex mix of religious leaders, cultural entrepreneurs, and local cadres (Ku and Hong 2017), compared with its predecessor, an informal group organized during the temple building in the late 1970s and early 1980s. After the previous chair and deputy stepped down from 10 years of leadership, the new chair was assigned in 1997 to a township cadre. The authority of this new chair rested on a traditional base because he was a Lin lineage descendant and the eldest son of Mrs. Lin Ah-be. Equally important is the fact that his position as the chair of the board was assigned by the party secretary of Meizhou Island with approval from the city party secretary (Zhu 2012). By 2008, the new chairman had served three terms and developed a religious tourism business complex under the administration of the Board of Trustees (Ku and Hong 2017; Zhou 2012). He had been aware of the opportunities and resources under the label of "Mazu." From his perspective, the inscription of the Mazu ceremony as a national ICH in 2006 heralded different opportunities and resources.

To improve coordination with local officials, the deputy of the board of trustees was assigned in 2008 to a capable local cadre, the deputy of the Administration Committee of Meizhou Island (Chinese Mazu 2008). This cadre had previously requested official financial support for the temple plaza extension in 2000 and participated in the founding and registration of the Chinese Mazu Cultural Exchange Association, a government-organized nongovernmental organization (GONGO) on Meizhou Island (Y. Zheng 2012). In 2008, the deputy of the Administration Committee of Meizhou Island heard the unofficial news that because of the renewal of the Intergovernmental Committee for Safeguarding Intangible Cultural Heritage at UNESCO, an opportunity had emerged to increase the number of China's representative elements on the UNESCO ICH list. However, he was also told that other applicants had been preparing for years to compete for this national nomination. He contacted the board chair, and they decided to enter the domestic competition. A team was organized for the application, of which three major players were board members. They included the temple's chair of the board, the deputy of the Administration Committee of the island, and a local Lin lineage literati in the Chinese Mazu Cultural Exchange Association. A college student was officially assigned to this team for assistance. In fact, the three major players in this team—a political cadre, religious leader, and lineage literati—were typical village elites who held political or traditional authority in the daily life of the village.

The team quickly realized that the situation was different from the previous application for the status of provincial and national ICH. In 2005, the official assignment from the state caused local officials and state-patronized cultural experts to work on the project. Now there were other competitors who had been working on the nomination with official assistance for submission. The team noted the passive attitude of the provincial officials, whose major concerns included the limited timeframe for preparing the nomination and negotiating with different temples. The team thus decided to proceed on their own. The main problem they faced was in preparing the nomination. After consulting several cultural experts, the team realized that the previous materials could not be used because they did not fulfill the submission requirements for UNESCO ICH inscription. In addition, the materials covered Mazu-related practices representing three different major Mazu temples in Putian, while the team members opted to focus on what was relevant to Meizhou Mazu Ancestral Temple, the Mazu ceremony. Narratives on the Mazu ceremony in those materials, however, had to be rewritten to elaborate on its significance and influence to satisfy the UNESCO ICH inscription domains and criteria. The submission guidelines also requested other supplementary materials, such as videos with relevant information and letters of commitment from communities participating in the safeguarding.

None of the team members were cultural officials or cultural experts in the subcommittee of the provincial or national cultural bureaus. As a result, they felt they lacked the discursive capacity to culturally translate the belief and practices into heritage elements that would meet the

UNESCO ICH criteria. To solve this problem, the team sought the assistance of state-patronized cultural authorities, such as cultural experts and university scholars. It was typical for these cultural authorities to be mobilized during the ICH application and nomination process to assist local communities in writing the texts and preparing the required materials for the nomination. In some cases, local governments assigned cultural experts to work on the nomination, and in other cases (such as this one), local communities hired cultural experts or scholars as consultants. The Mazu team contracted a local prestigious scholar to write the text for national nomination. After filing their application, they were informed by provincial officials that the ICH experts and cultural officials in Beijing considered the nomination materials to be inadequate.

Although the team lacked the capacity for discursive production, they clearly understood that the opinion of national cultural authorities outweighed that of local scholars and experts. However, national cultural authorities were too eminent to hire as writers. Because the deadline was approaching, they had no other choice but to revise the nomination themselves, which they did while attending a conference and a referee meeting convened by the subcommittee of cultural heritage under the Bureau of Cultural Heritage in the Ministry of Culture. According to my interviewee (interview with a team member, April 2012), the team attended the referee meeting during the day to learn from the other candidates' presentations and consult cultural experts they could reach in Beijing. They spent the night revising the text and putting together the required materials. Within a few days of the meeting, the revision of the application documents and all the required materials, including videos and letters of commitment, were complete. The case won the support of the cultural expert referees at the national meeting and was nominated by the state as China's element submitted for UNESCO ICH inscription, which was eventually accepted by UNESCO.

The revision of the text and materials in the nomination is worthy of discussion in terms of the learning process of the team and their acquired capacity. In their previous rounds of actions engaging the state, they usually mobilized social connections (*guanxi* 关系) and sought the support of local state actors. In the 2005 provincial and national ICH listing, the community leaders' engagement with the state's agenda was mainly institutionally mediated by a state-assigned local cultural expert. Even though the strategy of action under the name of religious culture had been formulated during these three rounds, the community leaders still had to rely on cultural experts' assistance on the discursive content of religious culture. This time, with minimal assistance from provincial officials and cultural experts, the team chose to seize the opportunity of inscription. The team members regarded the conference and referee meeting in Beijing as a free lesson in obtaining the requisite skills and knowledge. Most important, they learned to reorient the discursive framework and choose rhetoric with a finer-tuned sense of political judgment. One of the national cultural experts I interviewed explained to me that at the time, the uncertain status of popular religion in official ideology was still a concern of the committee (interview, May 2013). Therefore, he and other sympathetic cultural experts suggested that the application "downplay the religious dimension and emphasize the dimensions of folks and customs, so that the application would not be jeopardized by the uncertainty in the attitude of other authorities and religious departments." The advice was well received by the team members. They realized that their earliest version included inappropriate words, such as "Cultural Revolution" and "religion." They also invoked the official rhetoric such as "belief and customs" and "community participation in safeguarding heritage" (interview with a team member, April 2012). The revision was reframed to highlight "cultural tradition" and "heritage protection" instead of "popular religion" and "revival." Community leaders learned from cultural experts who had mastered the discursive vocabulary of cultural translation and knowledge of applying for ICH status.

The success of this case benefited local communities and leaders in several ways. First, the inscription of the Mazu belief and customs on the UNESCO ICH list recategorized superstitious belief activities as heritage with official status, thereby providing Mazu belief communities with cultural legitimacy in their rituals and ceremonial practices. In addition, the nomination for the UNESCO inscription identified that the core of this belief and these customs was located in Meizhou Island, and the major group for safeguarding ICH was the Meizhou Mazu Ancestral Temple Board of Trustees.[2] Not only did the symbolic status of Meizhou Mazu Ancestral Temple increase, the effects of branding following the UNESCO inscription brought new resources and opportunities to Meizhou Island.

Individual actors involved in the application were rewarded. The chair of the board of the Meizhou Mazu Ancestral Temple was lauded as an

"ICH transmitter," an honorable title that comes with a state stipend. The deputy of the Administration Committee of Meizhou Island was promoted to the director of that committee. The success of this milestone case had broader cultural implications beyond the local level. The UNESCO inscription of Mazu belief and customs was adopted as a legitimate ICH category in China and paved the way for other folk belief groups in China to apply for ICH status under the same criteria. Culturification of religion in the name of ICH has since been recognized as an effective strategy for community leaders pursuing cultural legitimacy, official recognition, and potential material resources.

Conclusion

The revival of Mazu belief created new forms of state–society interactions in the asymmetrical power between the state and popular religious communities. Although the state power manifests itself in various forms, including coercive and administrative power, the power asymmetry between popular religions and the state ultimately concerns the politics of recognition and cultural legitimacy. Because of the cultural legitimacy of popular religions, renovated governance initially emerged at local religion–state engagement and later evolved and became institutionalized by the central state.

As detailed here, local community leaders engaged the state in four rounds of interaction over three decades of religious revival to achieve formal cultural recognition of Mazu belief. In each phase, local actors strategically sought assistance and support from selected state actors to overcome opposition from other state actors. This study observes two expressions of path dependency during this process. First, local community actors tended to strengthen their alliance with specific state actors who exhibited sympathy or support in previous interactions. In particular, local officials responsible for Taiwanese affairs, cultural experts, and officials in the local cultural bureau became increasingly reliable partners of community leaders pressing for Mazu recognition. Second, as certain framing tactics gained traction, local community leaders reinforced those frames in later actions. In the case of Mazu, local community leaders developed the "culturification of religion" strategy to increase the legitimacy of their actions.

The leadership of the local religious community was restructured in the process of engaging the state. In the late 1970s and early 1980s, the Mazu initiative was led by a charismatic leader supported by devoted followers working mainly on temple affairs. While furthering their efforts in the religious revival of Mazu and increasing their interaction with the local state in the second round, the religious leadership became institutionalized through the establishment of a board of trustees. This new organizational body enabled religious leaders to bestow honorable titles or positions with partial authority to sympathetic local state actors, while the local party-state also assigned a trusted representative to serve on the board. In 1997, the chair of the board was mutually appointed by the local party-state and the religious leader. As of this writing, the board of trustees includes a local cadre and the director of the Taiwan Affairs Office on the island of Meizhou. Concurrently, the chair also serves as a deputy in a national-level GONGO, Chinese Mazu Cultural Exchange Association. The leadership of temple affairs is now intertwined with local administration, Mazu-related cultural exchanges, Taiwan affairs, and tourism development.

The phrase "community leader" rather than "religious leader" was used in this study when the leadership of such an actor is emphasized for their role in local community affairs rather than their influence on believers. In traditional China, popular religions constituted the cultural and social fabric of local society. In contemporary China, some cases of popular religious revival, such as Mazu belief, are intertwined with local development and social changes. Actors devoted to temple-related affairs have the opportunity to participate in local political or economic affairs, which dilutes the overtly religious component of their leadership in community affairs. In this case, the cultural legitimation of popular religion enhanced the board chair's influence on local development because "Mazu culture" rather than "cult-like religious worship" mobilized material and nonmaterial resources from the government and abroad that substantially enhanced the development of Meizhou Island and its residents.

Overall, "culturification of religion" is a framing strategy that downplays religious implications and highlights the cultural dimensions of folk symbols and ceremonies. This strategy can be observed in other parts of China, particularly in ethnic minority areas, as a means to reduce the political sensitivity of legitimating local beliefs and rituals (e.g., Nagatani 2010; Sutton and Kang 2010). In the case of Mazu belief, a popular Han religion in an area remote from central power achieved legitimacy with this strategy. During the first two rounds of interaction between local actors and the state, however, community leaders depended on cultural experts or cultural officials for discursive framing. By the fourth round, community leaders had matured in their framing capacity to the point that they translated their religious practice into the official cultural discourse of the UNESCO ICH. The political opportunity structure for alternative cultural framings expanded in the context of the legitimacy crisis of Marxist-Leninist-Maoist thought in the 1980s. Ambitious community leaders such as those in Meizhou were able to leverage this opportunity to achieve cultural legitimacy of a local belief while also promoting local development through heritage-based tourism.

Ultimately, ICH inscription of popular religions should not be depicted as a top-down process whereby society passively responds to state actors. Beijing's adoption of the international convention created a platform for local actors to engage with the state through the culturification of religion. The application for ICH listing of Mazu belief resulted from the entrepreneurialism of local actors who recognized the opportunity provided by a newly emerging state-sanctioned heritage discourse. The evolution of heritage affairs in China's reform era has involved government-led initiatives and highly motivated local actors seeking status and resources following ICH inscription. At the same time, the heritagization of Mazu belief was more complicated than a linear narrative about the triumph of local activism. The multiple rounds of interaction and the evolutionary governance of popular religion revealed that local yearnings for cultural legitimacy must still be articulated in the parameters of party-state consent and ideological conformity.

The state's governance capacity in this case is reflected through the incorporation of societal initiatives in the changing politics of recognition by reshaping leadership in a local religious community and endowing legitimate status to specific religious communities in a state-sponsored cultural framework. By redefining specific popular religious activities as "religious culture" (culturification) and ICH (heritagization), the state has endowed legitimate status to specific types of popular religions, such as

Mazu belief. This coevolutionary process has enabled the party-state to regulate legitimated religious activities with the cooperation of religious community leaders. Under these circumstances, officially recognized religious activities can contribute to other governmental goals, including nationalism, mobilization, and United Front Work propaganda (Ku 2019). During Xi Jinping's administration, the heritagized Mazu belief has been shaped into an official instrument of China's offshore influences. In 2016, the phrase "Mazu culture" appeared in the outline of the 13th Five-Year Plan; it is expected to play a positive role in folk cultural exchanges in the Belt-and-Road initiative.

Notes

1. There are different versions regarding the beginning year of the construction of Meizhou Mazu Ancestral Temple. According to the officially published local gazetteer, *Meizhou Mazu Zhi* 湄洲妈祖志 (*Literary Collection of Meizhou Mazu*), edited by two scholars sponsored by the trustee board of Meizhou Mazu Ancestral Temple, the construction started in 1978 (Jiang and Zhu 2011, 556). In Zhen-Man Zheng's research (2010), Mrs. Lin organized volunteers during the construction in 1981 based on her reputation that she had built two other local temples since 1978. I choose to ignore the inconsistency between these two versions and simply acknowledge that Mrs. Lin had been devoted to revival popular religion by building temples since the late 1970s.

2. It was translated as "the board of the First Mazu Temple" in the nomination form.

References

An, Ge. 2014. "Ange zhuanlan: dao Meizhoudao qing Mazudan" (An Ge's column: Going to Meizhou Island to celebrate Mazu's Birthday). Southern Metropolis Daily, May 29. https://kknews.cc/zh-tw/news/jv89nnp.html.

Chan, Selina Ching, and Graeme Lang. 2015. *Building Temples in China: Memories, Tourism, and Identities*. New York: Routledge.

Chang, Hsun. 2014. "Zhongguo dalu minjian xinyang de bianqian yu zhuanxing: yi Mazu xinyang weili" (The transition and transformation of folk beliefs in mainland China: Mazu belief as an example). *Humanities and Social Sciences Newsletter Quarterly* 15.2: 142–49.

Chau, Adam Yuet. 2006. *Miraculous Response: Doing Popular Religion in Contemporary China*. Stanford, CA: Stanford University Press.

Chinese Mazu. 2008. "Meizhou Mazu zumiao disanjie dongjianshi chengyuan" (Members of the third board of trustees of the Meizhou Mazu Ancestral Temple). Chinese Mazu. http://big5.xinhuanet.com/gate/big5/www.fj.xinhua.org/mazu/wh_zmdsh.htm.

Dean, Kenneth. 1998. *Lord of the Three in One: The Spread of a Cult in South-East China.* Princeton, NJ: Princeton University Press.

Goossaert, Vincent, and David A. Palmer. 2011. *The Religious Question in Modern China.* Chicago: University of Chicago Press.

Harrison, Rodney 2013. *Heritage: Critical Approaches.* London: Routledge.

Jiang, Wei-tan, and He-pu Zhu. 2011. *Literary Collection of Meizhou Mazu (Meizhou Mazu zhi).* Beijing: Publishing House of Local Records.

Koesel, Karrie J. 2014. *Religion and Authoritarianism: Cooperation, Conflict, and the Consequences.* Cambridge: Cambridge University Press.

Ku, Ming-chun. 2018. "ICH-ization of Popular Religions and the Politics of Recognition in China." In *Safeguarding Intangible Heritage: Practices and Politics,* edited by Natsuko Akagawa and Laurajane Smith, 187–99. London: Routledge.

———. 2019. "Mazu Culture: An Instrument of the Chinese Communist Party Expanding Offshore Influences." *Mainland China Studies* 62.4: 103–32.

Ku, Ming-Chun, and Ying-Fa Hong. 2017. "Mazu xinyang de kuahai xia liyi" (Dividends of cross-strait Mazu belief). In *Anaconda in the Chandelier: Mechanisms of Influence and Resistance in the China Factor,* edited by J.-M. Wu, H.-J. Tsai, and T.-B. Cheng, 289–324. New Taipei City: Rive Gauche.

Lin, Chengbin. 2017. "Meizhou Mazu zumiao jidian" (Rituals and festival in the Meizhou Mazu Ancestral Temple). List of Intangible Cultural Heritage, Putian Mass Art Center. http://www.ptsqzysg.com/ptsfwzwhycbh/fymldg/20171122/151122.shtml.

Lin, Yuan-bo, and Chong-zhang Chen. 2012. "Lin, Wen-hao xiansheng de Mazu yuan" (Mr. Lin, Wen-hao's Mazu Yuan). Putian Culture Network. http://www.ptwhw.com/?post=4911.

Marsh, Christopher. 2011. *Religion and the State in Russia and China: Suppression, Survival, and Revival.* New York: Continuum.

Nagatani, Chiyoko. 2010. "The Appearance of 'Religious Culture': From the Viewpoint of Tourism and Everyday Life in Dehong, Yunnan." *Senri Ethnological Studies* 76: 39–54.

Putian Foreign Trade and Economic Commission. 1995. *Local Gazetteer of Putian City Foreign Trade and Economy.* Beijing: Publishing House of Local Records.

Silverman, Helaine, and Tami Blumenfield. 2013. "Cultural Heritage Politics in China: An Introduction." In *Cultural Heritage Politics in China,* edited by Tami Blumenfield and Helaine Silverman, 3–22. New York: Springer.

Siu, Helen F. 1989. "Recycling Rituals: Politics and Popular Culture in Contemporary Rural China." In *Unofficial China: Popular Culture and Thought in the People's Republic,* edited by Perry Link, Richard Madsen, and Paul Pickowicz, 121–37. Boulder, CO: Westview Press.

———. 1990. "Recycling Tradition: Culture, History, and Political Economy in the Chrysanthemum Festivals of South China." *Comparative Studies in Society and History* 32.4: 765–94.

Smith, Laurajane. 2006. *Uses of Heritage*. New York: Routledge.

Sutton, Donald S., and Xiaofei Kang. 2010. "Making Tourists and Remaking Locals: Religion, Ethnicity, and Patriotism on Display in Northern Sichuan." In *Faiths on Display: Religion, Tourism, and the Chinese State*, edited by Tim Oakes and Donald S. Sutton, 103–28. Lanham, MD: Rowman and Littlefield.

Tsai, Lily L. 2007. *Accountability without Democracy: Solidary Groups and Public Goods Provision in Rural China*. Cambridge: Cambridge University Press.

Yang, Mayfair Mei-hui. 2007. "Ritual Economy and Rural Capitalism with Chinese Characteristics." In *Cultural Politics in a Global Age: Uncertainty, Solidarity and Innovation*, edited by Henrietta L. Moore and David Held, 226–32. Oxford: Oneworld Publications.

Zheng, Yujun. 2012. "Mazu xinsu shenyi xiaozu zuzhang Tangbingchun: yipian danxin xie chuanqi" (Team leader Tang Bingchun in the ICH inscription of Mazu belief and customs). Putian Culture Network. http://www.ptwhw.com/?post=4731.

Zheng, Zhen-Man. 2010. "Meizhou Ancestral Mazu Temple and the Dragon Well Temple of Duwei: The Construction of the Cult of Mazu in the Xinghua Region." *Journal of Chinese Ritual, Theatre and Folklore* 167: 123–50.

Zhou, Jin-yan. 2012. "Mazu gongmiao guanli moshi tanlun" (Exploring the management model of Mazu temples)." *Journal of Putian University* 19.4: 6–11.

Zhu, Hepu. 2012. "Nanwei Mazu chuanchengren" (The difficulties as a Mazu heritage transmitter). Putian Culture Network. http://www.ptwhw.com/?post=4728.

Zhu, Yujie, and Na Li. 2013. "Groping for Stones to Cross the River: Governing Heritage in Emei." In *Cultural Heritage Politics in China*, edited by Tami Blumenfield and Helaine Silverman, 51–71. New York: Springer.

CHAPTER 13

Governing an "Undesirable" Religion

Shifting Christian Church–State Interactions in Post-Mao China

KE-HSIEN HUANG

This chapter traces the evolution of the interactions between the state and Christian churches over four phases during China's reform era: (1) restoring "normal" religious activities after the Cultural Revolution; (2) intensifying the institutionalization of religion for better governance since the early 1990s; (3) reshaping religion for a harmonious, socialist society in the 2000s; and (4) opposing undesirable religions during the Xi administration. Three main conclusions are derived from this temporal perspective into the church–state interactions. First, church–state relations have become increasingly institutionalized. Interactions between the state and many Christian churches—both registered and unregistered—are more likely to take the form of negotiations, rather than the previous pattern of conflict. Second, the state's religious policy remains tightly controlled by the central government, which can easily overturn locally established practices in state–religion interactions. This is particularly evident during politically sensitive moments, such as a transition in central party leadership or regime-threatening events. Because many churches have been institutionalized as part of the state apparatus, Christian leaders now face considerable pressure to align their religious activities in accordance with the party-state's expectations. Third, the Chinese Communist Party categorizes each religion as either undesirable or desirable. Based on a religion's organizational features and its perceived ideological stance, this evaluation mediates the nature of state interactions with religious communities. The nationalist vision of "the China Dream" promoted under Xi Jinping has rendered Christianity even more undesirable in the eyes of the government.

In China today, religion–state relations seem to have moved away from mutual hostility, with state leaders pragmatically prioritizing economic development and overlooking ideological issues. Observers differ on describing the current nature of these relations and their future. Some contend that China's officially atheist state is inherently suspicious of religious activities and seeks opportunities to suppress freedom of religion (Laliberté 2011; F. Yang 2013). Others observe that officials have forged successful partnerships with religious groups in the interest of constructing a harmonious society and promoting a thriving local economy (Cao 2007; Qu 2011). I have argued elsewhere (K. Huang 2014) that whether the religion–state relationship in China has been harmonious or antagonistic strongly depends on micro-level processes of pragmatic negotiation between local bureaucrats and religious leaders—both of whom face constant pressure from hardliners and must keep a shifting distance from one another to maintain legitimacy in their respective organizations. In this chapter, I further analyze state–religion relations in China by situating these micro-level dynamics in the evolutionary context of broader political dynamics during the reform era. This process-tracing approach elucidates how communist governmental concerns and policy orientations at the central level frame the micro-level dynamics of state–religion relations in China.

To illustrate evolutionary shifts in Christian church–state relations, I divide the post-Mao era into four stages: (1) restoring "normal" religious activities after the Cultural Revolution; (2) intensifying the institutionalization of religion for better governance since the early 1990s; (3) reshaping religion for a harmonious, socialist society in the 2000s; and (4) rhetorically opposing undesirable religion during the Xi administration. Through temporal analysis, I develop three key arguments for a better understanding of how Chinese religion–state relations have evolved under communist rule. First, state–religion interactions have been successfully institutionalized as part of governance during this period. One of the most obvious policy trends across these stages is the gradual consolidation of state corporatism. The state's apparatus for soft governance of religions has been successfully established. Thus, the current interactions between the state and many churches—both registered and unregistered—have been much more common than before, characterized by negotiation, rather than an earlier pattern of conflict. The second is that the state's religious policy remains tightly controlled by the central government, which can easily overturn locally established practices in state–religion interactions. This can be illustrated clearly in significant cases of policy change, which were stimulated by either a transition in the central power of the Chinese Communist Party (CCP) or regime-threatening events. As many churches have been institutionalized as part of the state apparatus, Christian leaders now face considerable pressure to adapt their religious practices in accordance with the state's purpose. Third, different religions can be categorized as either undesirable (e.g., Christianity, this chapter) or desirable (e.g., Mazu beliefs, chapter 12) in the mind-set of the CCP. This (un)desirability, based on a combination of a religion's organizational features and its ideological tendencies, substantially influences how the state interacts with particular religions, even though every recognized religion in China is governed under nominally similar regulations. The nationalist vision of the "China Dream" promoted by the Xi administration has rendered Christianity even more undesirable from the government's perspective. The arguments presented here are based on extensive fieldwork conducted across 17 provinces since 2010, including interviews in more than 100 churches with 48 religious leaders and half a dozen religious affairs officers. A combination of government documents, newspaper reports, and external secondary source policy analyses provide additional context.

Stage 1: Restoring "Normal" Religious Activities (1978–1991)

Since the CCP was founded in 1921, the party debated how to interpret religion and deal with the "religion problem." Fundamentally, there have been two camps of atheism among party leaders—militant and enlightenment atheists—who hold radically different views toward religion. Militant atheists treat religion as a dangerous "opium" that serves the interest of the antirevolutionary and dominant class; they believe the CCP must control and eliminate religion. By contrast, enlightenment atheists regard religion as illusory, nonscientific, and backward but hope for a decline in religion through scientific development, mass education, and propaganda. For national development, political stability, and positive international relations, the CCP must recognize the long-term persistence of religion, allow its reasonable presence, and unite religious people (F. Yang 2012, 45–48). While militant atheism gained prominence beginning in 1958 and reached its political peak during the Cultural Revolution, 1978 marked a momentous shift in the CCP from "distorted religious policy" (Xiao 2004, 57) to enlightened atheism. The party-state has reportedly reverted to permitting "legal" religious activities; however, militant viewpoints still gain sporadic support, particularly in CCP-run schools and among Marxist academics. In the first stage of the church–state relationship in contemporary China, the state attempted to "dispel chaos and restore righteousness" (*boluan fanzheng* 拨乱反正) by reinstating religious venues, allowing the resumption of religious activities, and readdressing the state's "mistaken treatment of" religious leaders, previously deemed to be antirevolutionary.

In the national meeting of the central United Front Work Department (UFWD) in 1979, it was announced that the CCP had to assist religious organizations and patriotic organizations to resume activities and to exercise their active functions" (F. Yang 2012, 74–75). The central UFWD further took the actions of (1) surveying religious clergy and returning them from prison to religious venues as soon as possible; (2) correcting wrongdoing against crucial religious figures and restoring their political status; (3) ensuring important religious figures' jobs were secure and their needs met; and (4) ensuring that these crucial religious figures' children would not be discriminated against when applying for jobs, schools, or CCP membership. Orchestrated by the central UFWD, in 1982 the central party issued a circular titled "The Basic Viewpoint and Policy on Religious Affairs during the Socialist Period of Our Country." Often referred to as Document no. 19 and considered the basis for religious policy in post-Mao China, the circular embodies the CCP's intentions to correct far-leftist errors and rally patriotic religious members for national economic development. Accordingly, the Religious Affairs Bureau (RAB; *zongjiao shiwu ju* 宗教事务局) was officially established in

1954, annexed to the UFWD in 1961, deactivated in 1975, and resumed operations in 1979 at the central and local levels. RAB has worked alongside the UFWD to tackle "normal religious affairs," meaning officially recognized religious groups conducting state-sanctioned activities in registered religious venues. In practice, the church–state relationship is still dominated by the political-legal sector and the Public Security Bureau (PSB). In particular, the political-legal sector has the authority to determine which activities are antisocial, illegal, or antigovernmental, operating under the cover of religion. Such activities fall under the jurisdiction of the PSB in what I consider to be the rigid suppression apparatuses of China's religion-regulating regime. As for the RAB and UFWD, soft governance apparatuses in this stage were marginalized and served more as simply a symbol of the party-state's resumed openness to religion.

My informants, senior police officers and experienced religious leaders, confirmed this fact. In their memories, local governments and religious groups were either unfamiliar with the new religious policy announced by the central government or skeptical of the CCP's true intentions during the 1980s. Director Lee, currently a senior leader in a division of the county PSB in Anhui, served as a local police officer during the 1980s. He remembered how the police perceived religious people as problematic and potentially criminal, and thus often persecuted them through violence. Lee's superior at the time, whom he described as farsighted about the CCP's orientation, suggested, "We should not view religious people as troublemakers and always harass them and their temples" (interview, February 17, 2015). Lee's veneration of his superior provides a personal reflection on the ignorance of local officers regarding religious policy and the pervasiveness of religious persecution at that time.

Several Christian leaders of house churches recalled how they were arrested simply because their gatherings were perceived as antigovernmental riots or feudal superstitions in the eyes of bureaucrats. They were usually released after the police were updated on new religious policies by communications with the local RAB. For most religious leaders, the party-state, represented by local police officers, was still hostile toward religion; hence, the optimal policy in their approach to the state was to maintain a safe distance. Nevertheless, some religious leaders endured these arrests due to bureaucratic misconduct and used them as examples of religious persecution from an "anti-Christ" state. In turn, such arrests may have enhanced the symbolic capital of their leadership; thus, these leaders could use the story of being arrested by the state as part of "mnemonic practice" (see K. Huang 2018) to attract more believers.

According to some sources, in their "the last stop before retirement," local RAB officers would rather be "passive and stay out of troublesome matters." Several Christian leaders in their 60s remembered how they were arrested for merely gathering families together for Bible study. They were usually released after a couple of days. A senior deacon in Fujian, who has had substantial experience in negotiating with local officers since the late 1970s, commented, "The stance of the RAB was the worst. It was the one with little power and much obedience to the political-legal sector, and the one to which the least capable cadres with little chance of promotion in the bureaucracy were usually assigned" (interview, February 15, 2015).

During this stage, central state authorities took the initiative to "renormalize" the religion–state relationship by moderating excessively antireligious policies of the past. This was largely a symbolic act and required more time and effort to trickle down in practice, particularly to those at the grassroots level. Christians tended to avoid interacting with the state as much as possible. Once they were forced to do so, the rigid suppression apparatuses—rather than soft governance tools—were the institutions they were required to fight against or negotiate with. In general, church–state interactions at this time were unsustainable and often confrontational, if they existed at all.

Stage 2: Intensifying Institutionalization for Better Governance (1991–2000)

Around the end of the 1980s and the beginning of the 1990s, the church–state relationship entered a new phase because of significant political events that made the CCP take heed. After their aspirations for political reforms that would have established harmonious secular society were broken, many disappointed Chinese citizens gravitated to religion, particularly forms of Christianity imbued with a modern character, for new hope or salvation (Wielander 2009; F. Yang 2014, 8–10). In addition, Christian churches played a decisive role in the disintegration of communist regimes in Eastern Europe by the end of the 1980s, which served as an example to Chinese communists. With international and domestic crises threatening political stability, the central state government became aware of the importance of religious regulation and started to seriously consider the administrative and legal construction of religious regulations. In 1990, Chen Yun, a second-in-command in Deng Xiaoping's era, wrote a letter to remind Jiang Zemin, an upcoming successor to Deng, of the seriousness of religious infiltration from domestic and international enemies and of how important it was that the CCP tackle this "critical matter" of religious affairs for the sake of national stability (Leung 2005, 905). In 1993, the first year of the post-Deng period, Jiang announced more attention on the party's ethnic and religious issues, asserting the governmental principle that "as for religious affairs, they are never trivial at all" (*zongjiao wu xiaoshi* 宗教无小事).[1]

Instead of returning to the far-left position of attempting to eliminate religion or continuing to loosen controls on religion, the party-state chose to govern religion more efficiently and effectively with an institutionally inclusive approach. The soft governance apparatuses were thus equipped with an unprecedented level of resources. Since its resumption, the RAB of the State Council (*guowuyuan zongjao shiwuju* 国务院宗教事务局), as a symbolic institution, had received little attention. However, the RAB's administrative structure was expanded, followed by significant increases in the number of religious affairs cadres in 1988 and 1994. In 1998, the RAB of the State Council was further elevated when it was renamed the State Administration of Religious Affairs (SARA; *guojia zongjiao shiwuju* 国家宗教事务局) and bestowed with increased administrative powers within the central government (K. Yang 2012, 79).

The most fundamental undertaking of the central religious regulatory unit was to realize what Jiang announced in 1993 as the key goal of religious affairs under his rule: "intensifying the management of religious affairs according to laws" (*yifa jiaqiang zongjiao shiwu de guanli* 依法加强宗教事务的管理). To manage religion according to laws, the RAB of the State Council and later SARA strove to release many legal documents on religious regulation in the 1990s, including two state-level decrees in 1994: Provisions on the Administration of Religious Activities of Aliens within the Territory of the People's Republic of China and Regulations on the Administration of Sites for Religious Activities. Several supplementary provisions were issued thereafter, including Procedures on the Registration of Venues for Religious Activity (1994), Procedures for the Annual Inspection of Venues for Religious Activity (1996), and Specific Rules for Implementing Regulations on Managing the Religious Activities of Foreigners in China (2000). Eventually, the Religious Affairs Provisions (2005) replaced these ordinances and took effect as the most recent comprehensive document on religious affairs, serving as the overall guidelines for the local governance of religions (Qu 2011, 443–44).

At the local level, the RAB was granted more resources, discretion, and power in dealing with religious affairs. To implement the slogan regarding the phase of "rallying with patriotic religious people" (that is, forming a united front), the RAB endeavored to include as many religious groups as possible into the state-sanctioned patriotic structure. The guiding principle was managing religious groups through inclusion and treating them in different ways depending on how well the groups fit into state perceptions of socialism, a judgment made by local bureaucrats who understood CCP policy but implemented it on the basis of their own discretion and interests. Thus, while some Christian groups chose to be registered or incorporated with existing legal ones, others remained unregistered and were deemed to be illegal organizations by the police and other government offices (K. Yang 2012). I discovered that new generations of Christian leaders that emerged in the 1990s became much more pragmatic and adept at engaging in beneficial relations with the state after the political socialization they experienced during the collectivization era. With the capacity to navigate the complex bureaucratic system of the party-state and tactfully use political rhetoric in communication with religious cadres, they became ready to form positive church–state relationships to gain more resources for their religious activities, as well as a favorable legal status to facilitate further church development (K. Huang 2014, 713).

As more and more churches were constructing stable relationships with governments in this phase, one can see how local bureaucrats and religious leaders developed mutual agreements (possibly tacitly) on practices that might violate government regulations on religions but could be tolerated in exchange for a continued harmonious church–state relationship. Although these adaptive informal practices (Tsai 2007) were

FIGURE 13.1 Clergy conducting water baptism rite in northern China
Source: Photo by author.

sometimes temporarily suspended because of pressure from the hard-line central government or fundamentalist religious grassroots organizations (K. Huang 2014), local officials and religious leaders usually resumed these informal practices when possible. Religious leaders might seek to continue certain illegal religious activities or conventions practiced long before joining the Three-Self Patriotic Movement (TSPM, a state-sanctioned Protestant organization; *sanzi aiguo yundonghui* 三自爱国运动会) structure. Adding a denominational sign on a chapel, for example, could violate the policy in the sense of eliminating "the imperial legacy of denominational differences," and replacing it with Christian unity under Chinese patriotism. Some local officials tolerated such signs as long as no complaints were filed. If this occurred, the official could provide an excuse that it was a mere expression of religious members who "have freedom to choose a particular denomination," as stipulated in Document no. 19 (K. Huang 2014, 717). In some cases, to prevent potential difficulties or political inconvenience caused by strictly observing administrative procedures, religious leaders relied on tacit agreement or assistance from friendly officials, such as inviting Taiwanese missionaries to visit without reporting it to the RAB. Officials considered it necessary to do simple favors for religious leaders by overlooking minor infractions that would not cause any damage to their careers to maintain the delicate positive relationship that had been established. Some local grassroots officials overlooked cross-regional and international interactions among religious groups that central religious ordinances and repeated announcements asserted were forbidden without prior official approval (following a long and complicated bureaucratic process). Some UFWD staff members even encouraged trusted religious leaders to engage in interactions with Taiwanese churches, which might serve to "enhance cross-strait interflow for unification of the nation" (interview, April 5, 2011).

Stage 3: Reshaping Religion for a Harmonious, Socialist Society (2000–2012)

Once the regulatory infrastructure for religion was established, the state took more steps in religious governance. This phase occurred under the Hu Jintao administration, which proposed the ideal of constructing a harmonious, socialist society. The central government attempted to use cooperative alliances with religious leaders to actively reshape religion into forms the CCP anticipated would be beneficial. In early 1993, when Jiang had just assumed power, he stipulated that the party-state would strive for religion's "adaption to socialism," a phrase that has become a staple of the rhetoric that religious officials at all levels have tried to implement since 2000. With the now robust soft governance apparatuses of the RAB and UFWD, which had constructed relatively stable relationships with religious groups, the state was more capable of cooperating with patriotic organizations of different religions to interpret religious doctrines in ways that corresponded with the requirement for religious groups to contribute toward building a harmonious society and resisting "illegal activities against the socialist homeland and people's interest" (interview, February 20, 2015). During this stage, the official perception of Christianity as an "undesirable" religion with connections to Western imperialism intensified. Religious leaders in the TSPM, a bridge between the atheist state and lay Christians, were drawn into conflict between these groups more seriously than before. They acquired some religious freedoms, but at the same time they damaged their reputations by being labeled "faith betrayers" or the "state's servant." For many unregistered churches, the state's intention to reshape Christianity was considered a political infiltration of their faith, and they reacted by trying to distance themselves from the state to a greater extent. Their registered counterparts, already deeply embedded in the institutional environment of resources and relationships, had no choice but to implement the policy of adapting Christianity to socialism. Two measures were typically undertaken: cooperating in constructing either a vigorous local economy or a harmonious society. Difficulties ensued in both endeavors, revealing how Christianity is not easily restructured to suit the CCP's requirements.

Specific faith-based groups peacefully manage their venues or activities as profit-making enterprises that fulfill mutual interests embedded in an increasingly liberalized economy. Officials, following the policy guidance that "culture builds the stage and the economy performs" (*wenhua datai, jingji changxi* 文化搭台, 经济唱戏), gladly hold mass religious gatherings disguised as cultural activities to achieve two goals: generating income and accumulating the bureaucratic merits of successful governance (Ji 2015). For example, studies on the revival of Daoist temples (Fan 2012; Lang, Chan, and Ragvald 2005) and Buddhist monasteries (Borchert 2005) have illustrated that local governments felt pressured to demonstrate their capacity to generate revenue and improve local finances in the era of market liberalization. Meanwhile, ambitious temple managers tended to revolutionize the historical legacy of rituals and practices. The revival of such facilities ultimately elicited considerable revenues from patrons and believers, and the government shared in the economic benefits of a considerable increase in tourism. In addition to the economic concerns, the state promoted certain "Chinese" religions to serve as contemporary protectors of the cultural orthodoxy, allowing it to establish legitimacy in ruling the Middle Kingdom (Madsen 2014).

The premise for implementing the policy "culture builds the stage and the economy performs" is that the culture or religion being promoted must be attuned with "the main melody" (*zhuxian lu* 主旋律) promulgated by the party-state. The dominant refrain of Chinese nationalism heralds the CCP as leading the nation to become a significant global power. The soft power of Chinese culture is intended to be a means for realizing the China Dream. Christianity encountered difficulty in associating itself with official discourse on Chinese culture because it is still perceived as foreign and alien by Chinese officials and scholars. The TSPM, an organization comprising Christian leaders, felt increasing pressure to mirror Jiang's calls for religious adaption to socialism and the Sinicization of Christianity. In 1996 its chair, Bishop Ding Guangxun (丁光训), stated, "We Chinese believers should think about how not to be left behind, how to catch up with the trend of adapting to socialism . . . and speed up to move forward . . . this is the victory of the party's united front, and the consequence of religious people being willing to get reformed" (Chang 2004, 37). Since 1998, the TSPM has undertaken a comprehensive campaign known as Theological Thought Construction (*shenxue sixiang jianshe* 神学思想建设), highlighting the ethics and morality within religion regarded as facilitating a harmonious society and downplaying Christian ideas that might be considered mysterious, transcendent, or against governmental policy. For example, the TSPM preferred to interpret Jesus as a moral crusader and humanistic liberator of the disadvantaged, rather than the son of God, a deliverer of other-world salvation, or a miracle performer. In addition, the core Christian belief of justification by faith was replaced with the gospel of love. In sermons, mentioning the distinctions between those believing and not believing in Jesus was discouraged, while discussing reconciliation of Christians with non-Christians was encouraged strongly (Chang 2004, 39–46).

The dichotomy between the state's requirement of Sinicization and Christians' reluctance to pursue it remains evident. At the end of 2011, the party-state issued a document titled The CCP's Decision on Deepening Reforms of Cultural Systems (*zhonggong zhongyang guanyu shenhua wenhua tizhi gaige de jueding* 中共中央关于深化文化体制改革的决定), calling for "religious personnel and believers to exercise positive functions in promoting the development of cultural prosperity" (Sina.com.cn 2011). In response to this, Christian leaders and scholars proposed their opinions in annual meetings of the government-sanctioned Christian organizations in early 2012. Notably, they were not discussing how Christianity could promote cultural prosperity but reflecting on how Christianity should be Sinicized, a controversial theme that has long concerned Chinese Christians and communists. The chair of the national TSPM urged that Chinese Christianity should accommodate itself to Chinese culture by absorbing the great elements in Chinese culture.

However, state officials and scholars did not seem to appreciate the degree of Christian leaders' anxiety and efforts at responding to the state's declaration. Several months after the release of the 2011 document, top-tier universities and academic institutions held a conference about studies on Christian Sinification, which included prominent scholars of Chinese religions. The attendees expressed pessimism. One scholar lamented, "To become Sinicized, Christianity has walked a zigzag path, but it has not been able to shed being labeled a 'foreign religion'" (*Tianfeng* Editor 2012, 36). Another attendee stated more bluntly, "The question of Sinicizing Christianity is a political problem worthy of concern, a scholarly issue worthy of discussion, and a problem for religious groups to struggle with" (*Tianfeng* Editor 2012, 36). At the local level, Christian leaders similarly complained about the difficulties of obtaining funding to support activities intended to increase the social influence of their group. "RAB officials would rather give money to idol-worshipping temples . . . they thought what they did was culture. We Christians belong to no Chinese culture at all" (interview, April 16, 2011).

Even among religious populations, Christian leaders in patriotic associations faced continuous blame and hostility. The Theological Thought Construction campaign provoked criticism from grassroots Christians, whether lay or clergy (Huang and Yang 2005; Vala 2009). As Bishop Ding and other key figures of the campaign were decried as renegades or "party-state servants" at local churches, many pastors, even in officially registered groups, tended not to implement the recommendations of the Theological Thought Construction campaign in their chapels and only advocated it during TSPM meetings or conversations with RAB officials. At the grassroots level, many Christians informed me that the TSPM church was "not a church, but a propaganda machine that speaks for the party . . . a lot of Christians who want to seek the truth cannot tolerate the TSPM. They defect to true churches" (interview, June 2, 2011). In addition, among the laity, the situation in which "we Christians belong to no Chinese culture at all" is proudly embraced. I asked interviewees about the idea of religion as part of culture, and almost all respondents refuted this equation, which they considered blasphemous. A college-graduate lay speaker stated in a Saturday morning sermon, "Currently, society treats faith as a kind of culture, a spiritual civilization . . . this is secularization . . . my highly educated friends discuss the Bible as if it is a book full of secular knowledge. Such an approach undermines faith by portraying it as intellectual capital. Such an understanding will decay faith" (sermon transcript, July 30, 2011).

It seemed that the effort during the previous phase of constructing and strengthening mutual institutional ties between Christian leaders and the state led intermediary brokers to experience backlash from both sides. However, the platform constructed mainly by RAB and patriotic religious associations produced a condition in which religious freedom was favored: the creation of a strong sympathizer with religion within an atheist state. Through more interactions with religious people, SARA staff developed a keen awareness of how Christian clergy and laypersons dislike the infiltration of political propaganda into interpretations of religious material. They tended to permit a greater degree of religious autonomy among clergy and had more respect for religious orthodoxy.

This is elucidated in Kuo's research (2011) on the work (since 2002) of editing new textbooks on religious patriotism to be used in seminaries and by clergy, a project administered by SARA. When beginning this ambitious initiative, officials in charge demonstrated their sensibility as a political entrepreneur and decided against inviting atheist researchers specializing in Marxism and Leninism to assist in formulating the text as before. Instead, they approached respected scholars recommended by patriotic religious associations. Before the manuscript went to print, the official sought comments from religious leaders and theologians, which eventually resulted in adding two new chapters. When the new textbooks were released, teachers and clergy were more willing to adopt them than they had previous publications because they were the most liberal version of textbooks on religious patriotism at that time and included more biblical theologians' commentaries on the topic than ever before. I witnessed registered church leaders asserting that their evangelical constituents liked to distribute religious pamphlets in public venues such as parks, beaches, and shopping malls, which violated the regulation on religious activities. Although the police would have arrested transgressors in the past, during this stage, they simply maintained a record and reported the incident to TSPM to resolve it. At the TSPM meeting, these church leaders, with networks and an opportunity to explain the situation, would have a more favorable chance of avoiding punishment.

Stage 4: Opposing Undesirable Religion Symbolically (2012–)

The Christian church–state relationship entered a new stage after Xi Jinping's assumption of power in 2012. Xi's new nationalist vision of the China Dream (*zhongguo meng* 中国梦) seemed incongruous with "Western-influenced" Christianity. To realize the China Dream in the realm of religion, the state launched a series of reforms against Christianity, particularly in areas of strategic necessity for the CCP to reassert its ideological dominance. At the local level, the restrictive atmosphere was ascribed to local governments attempting to hamper often-tolerated Christian practices in places where religious freedom had been taken for granted. With mutual embeddedness built in the last two stages, the state acquired more efficient means to achieve its goals in governing Christians. Some informal adaptive practices agreed to by local bureaucrats were discontinued. Some have been treated as transgressions that officials immediately and strictly enforce based on relevant regulations. Others are no longer tolerated but are dealt with by jurisdiction. Despite the continued existence of gray areas, symbolic communist gestures aimed at containing Christianity are undoubtedly felt. At the grassroots level, one can discern suppressing transgressions has become increasingly effective because of the institutionalization of church–state relations established in previous phases.

Notably, Xi's speeches and activities after 2012 repeatedly alluded to the affinity between Confucianism, previously dismissed as a "feudal poison" by the CCP, and the current development of the CCP-led country. The rapid expansion of Confucius Institute, a state-affiliated institution that promotes Chinese language and culture internationally, embodies the constitution of ancient indigenous thought as part of Chinese soft power. By the end of 2017, there were more than 1,600 facilities in 146 countries. In terms of domestic governance, Confucianism, which extols the virtues of Chinese civilization, harmonious society without protest, and enlightened dictatorship, also serves as a tool for Xi to rule an enormous country experiencing a stagnating economy and an increase in collective riots, which the CCP conveniently blames on foreign interference and the negative influence of Western thought. By contrast, the "undesirable" religion of Christianity has reportedly faced the most severe persecution in over a decade. The China Aid Association announced a report stating that 1,274 Christians were sentenced to prison in 2014, 10 times more than that in 2013, whereas the number of reported cases of religious persecution in 2014 was triple of that in 2013 (Unruh 2015). Among those involved were influential Christian figures, such as Zhang Shaojie (张少杰), a human rights advocate and TSPM pastor in Henan province; the leaders of Shouwang Church (*Shouwang jiaohui* 守望教会); and Peter Hahn, a Korean American aid worker (Long 2015).

These severe actions targeting Christianity represent the party-state's response to the growing number of Christians in China, which in 2014 was forecast to be the country with the most Christians in the world by 2030 (F. Yang 2014). Some hard-line, high-ranking communists have been eager to declare a new type of "mind-protecting" war against Christianity, whose believers have surpassed the number of Chinese communists. Those on the front line include Chinese universities and the party-state itself. Numerous Chinese research papers have tackled the questions of how popular religious faiths (particularly Christianity) are among college students, why these highly educated people with a firm grasp of scientific knowledge and Marxist atheism turn to religion, and how this "problem" can be fixed. The CCP's branches in universities are especially vigilant of possible infiltration by foreign Christian missionaries, particularly those from countries with plans to systematically transform China into a Christian nation, such as Korea and the United States. As such, campus fellowships are forced to disband once they are discovered by authorities.

This campaign against Christianity across college campuses has occurred for many years and intensified due to Xi's call for greater "ideological guidance" at China's universities, which "shoulder the burden of learning and researching the dissemination of Marxism . . . and practicing the core values of socialism" (Reuters 2014). Around Christmas time in 2014, Northwest University in Xi'an complied with tightened ideological control in higher education by erecting banners stating, "Endeavor to be excellent Chinese sons and daughters! Protest against kitsch foreign celebrations!" At night, the university organized students to watch old-fashioned propaganda films instead of engaging in Christmas-oriented activities (BBC 2014).

Although CCP members all swear personal allegiance to Marxist atheism, many cadres are religious. At my field site, several Christian college students who joined the CCP informed me that the pledge is simply a formality and the CCP is unconcerned about whether new recruits are religious. However, the ban on believers joining the CCP has been reiterated in Zhejiang province, where prescreening of aspiring party members' atheism is intended to be strictly implemented, according to the CCP-owned media, the *Global Times* (Kaiman 2015). In early 2015, the chair of the Chinese People's Political Consultative Conference, Yu Zhengsheng (俞正声), emphasized the importance of ensuring that Catholic patriotic associations "be controlled firmly by patriots," reminding intermediary religious leaders that their foremost duty is loyalty to the CCP, rather than the Vatican (BBC 2015).

In addition to reasserting ideological orthodoxy at critical front lines of the battle, there has been a noticeable campaign against Christianity in China's so-called Jerusalem, Wenzhou, in Zhejiang province. Wenzhou has one of the wealthiest and most influential concentrations of Christians. In October 2013, the provincial government commenced a campaign called Three Rectifications and One Demolition (*sangai yichai* 三改一拆) with the reported aim of demolishing illegal structures that violate land management and planning laws. The governmental document directing how the campaign should be implemented indicated that it was meant to "correct the local situation of excessively rapid religious development, too many (religious) venues and overly intense (religious) activities" (*New York Times* 2014). In the instructions, Christian crosses were the only religious symbols specified, with action required if they were "hung too high," "equipped with light," or "visible from highways and other main arteries." According to Christian Solidarity Worldwide, more than 500 crosses have been removed, demolished, modified, or covered up since October 2013, with 37 churches' architecture wholly or partially demolished, and more than 100 people arrested, detained, or summoned in 2014 in connection with these events (CSW 2019). Despite considerable international attention and local resistance among Christians, this campaign has persisted for several years.

Many of the officers who have proposed or executed this campaign have been promoted, and other ensuing orders from the Zhejiang government have echoed these anti-Christian measures. For example, local schools are forbidden from celebrating Christmas, and believers in Wenzhou are required to "relearn" political propaganda. Wenzhou authorities have asked party members to sign a guarantee called the Communist Commitment of No Allegiance to Religion. Three local officials in charge of religion-related affairs were found to be religious and thus transferred (Jiang 2015). The provincial government issued draft legislation aiming to reduce the appearance of Christian crosses by strictly regulating the form, color, and size of Christian buildings. Christian leaders appealed for reconsideration of the legislation, which they argued would harm the rights of religious people and violate religious freedoms. Later in July 2015, the Christian Council of Zhejiang issued a public letter to the government, asserting that the demolition campaign "had hurt the feelings of over 2 million Christians," and that the function of the council being a bridge between Christian populations and the government had ceased to exist. In January 2016, the chair of the council was arrested due to "misappropriation of public funds," as the government claimed; for many observers and local Christians, this was apparently in retaliation for the council's earlier letter.

It is still too early to conclude that the overall tone of the Chinese church–state relationship in general has substantially changed from mutual adaption to confrontation. The cross removal campaign was limited to Zhejiang. Nonetheless, policy restrictions on controversial issues and the stronger ideological control under the Xi administration have translated into the termination of some informal adaptive practices mutually agreed to by the dyadic nexus of religious leaders and officers at the local level. In my field research, it is common to observe churches or affiliated structures constructed without proper government-issued licenses or approval. Christian leaders may spend time and money striving to file applications for their churches; local officials tend to slow down, impede, or even refuse bureaucratic processing of these applications, simply because of bureaucratic inaction or their superiors favoring the reduction of registered Christians and venues. Thus, a more favorable approach is to "build first and then you would get registered more easily . . . officials want no trouble and they understand that tearing down chapels constructed already

FIGURE 13.2 Chapel in rural southeastern China
Source: Photo by author.

would make believers very angry," as a pastor in Guangzhou informed me (interview, July 14, 2011). In general, local officials turn a blind eye to these buildings lacking proper approval. The magnificent, castle-like cathedral of the Sang-Jiang (*sanjiang* 三江) church (fig. 13.2) was even called "the city's model construction" (*quanshi yangban gongcheng* 全市样板工程) by the Wenzhou government months before it was demolished during the hard-line activities in April 2014. Other informal adaptive practices have suddenly been terminated. The churches I observed in Fujian have engaged in continuous exchanges with overseas counterparts (K. Huang 2014, 716–77). In 2011, church elders were encouraged by the UFWD to take the initiative to visit Taiwan to "promote the great work of the motherland's unification" (*cujin zuguo tongyi daye* 促进祖国统一大业) (interview, April 3, 2011). However, in 2014, the same official seemingly advised against such interactions. In 2015, he directly requested that the church should "immediately stop any sensitive activity" (interview, February 8, 2015).

The Xi Jinping administration has taken an even harder stance against unsanctioned "house" churches. The newly revised Regulation on Religious Affairs, which was issued in 2017 and took effect in early 2018, puts more restrictions on religious groups, particularly in terms of religious locations. Reports of church closures, demolition of worship sites, and imprisonment of believers have become more frequent since 2014. The persecution of the influential Early Rain Covenant Church in Chengdu, which was raided and closed just before Christmas 2018, further raises the alarm that Chinese church–state relations have come to a crossroads.

Conclusion: What Is Changing? What Has Remained Unchanged?

Madsen (2009) discussed how the Chinese state regulates religion. In the wake of the post-Mao era, the CCP attempted to resume its initial religious policy in the 1950s by correcting "hard-left" Maoist policies/decisions. A centrally controlled approach with a locally adapted strategy has been used: using soft governance apparatuses to unify the CCP with "normal" religions, while attacking "abnormal" religions through rigid suppression apparatuses. The central authority draws the line between normal and abnormal and maintains the optimal balance between soft and rigid apparatuses. Central decisionmakers shift their religious policy according to international relations and the domestic stability of religious ethnicity.

Meanwhile, the position of China in the world arena envisioned by the CCP's foremost leaders changed how the state treats religion. In the 1950s, China allied closely with the Soviet Union to promote communist ideals against Western enemies. Since the collapse of the communist bloc and its embrace of capitalism, China has had to reconsider its sources of legitimacy. The West and its encounters with China in modern history evoke painful humiliation for many Chinese people and is a substantial threat to the Chinese path to becoming a superpower. Thus, cultural nationalism has become a convenient option for the CCP to unite the nation and legitimate its leadership. Religion is a fundamental source energizing Chinese cultural nationalism. This new function creates a division rendering some faiths desirable and others undesirable in the eyes of the CCP. Confucianism is appealing to today's communist leaders because it is world-oriented, emphasizes social harmony, and supports enlightened dictatorship. Folk beliefs, Buddhism, and Daoism seem to fit and fuse well with capitalist characteristics of the tourism industry (Borchert 2005; Fan 2012; Lang, Chan, and Ragvald 200). By contrast, the party-state has consistently perceived Christianity as deriving from Western plots to subvert the Chinese state, and thus must be contained and even eliminated.

At first glance, the undesirability of Christianity in China to the state seems to reflect ideological conflict between China and the West. However, the key to the state's hostility toward Christianity is rooted in this religion's organizational features and mobilizing capacity. Followers of Chinese religions generally worship deities privately at home or separately at public religious occasions. By contrast, Christians come together—whether secretly in someone's home or at a public chapel—to form well-organized congregations. These groups share transcendent (especially nation-transcending) beliefs, which politically ambitious religious leaders may use to protest against secular authorities. In addition, the beliefs are universalized rather than localized. Effective organizational infrastructures with attractive religious interpellations have demonstrated potential for establishing political subversion in Western and Chinese history. Historical affinity with the West has further deepened the concern of communists that this machine could be easily used by their imperialist enemies, particularly the Americans. Thus, to many Chinese authorities, Christianity in China must be contained, suppressed, and terminated when the time comes. For them, the mission of Sinicizing Chinese Christianity entails three practices: (1) severing all its connections with the West, (2) making it stand firmly with the state ideologically, and (3) keeping its organizations under the close, watchful eye of the state. This policy has not changed since 1990, despite shifts in emphasis during different administrative phases.

Among the aforementioned practices, the state has made the greatest progress in the third. The state has been lessening the threat of the organizational and mobilizing capacity of Christians by facilitating state corporatism with religious groups. In the beginning, many Christian leaders may have welcomed it, since they may have gained some advantages, perhaps not for the overall Chinese Christian population but for themselves and their individual groups. This mutual incorporation transformed the nature of church–state relations in China. It created sympathizers toward religion in the party-state, which facilitated believers' struggle for religious freedoms. While opinions from religious people can be channeled to change religious policies, mutually agreed on informal adaptive practices often emerge while the formal regulations remain intact.

During the process of consultative political liberalization under Hu Jintao's rule, religious groups undertook considerable risk in cooperating with the state. Registered Christian leaders had to compromise by adapting to the state requirement of reshaping Christianity based on a nationalist ideology. This in turn evoked doubt and opposition from grassroots Christians toward its leadership. When the central government tightened its religious policy and local authorities suspended informal adaptive practices, the responses that religious leaders adopted became even more disciplined than before. Nevertheless, some leaders have not been willing to tolerate the state's interference and thus left the government-sanctioned structure. However, they are a minority. For the majority, either relinquishing institutional support or confronting organizational inertia is difficult. Institutionalization subdues most religious populations, leading them to use approaches to their problems that the state prefers.

Although Christian leaders and local officers maintain long-term, trustful relationships through which informal adaptive practices flourish, these practices have not been consolidated into stable institutions (formal or informal) over time, unlike the consolidation that Tsai (2002, 2007) demonstrated in her studies of private entrepreneurs. By contrast, in the sphere of religious regulation, leaders from the central government and the politico-legal sector dominate policy orientations and how policies are executed at the grassroots level, regardless of long-term conventions that have been mutually constructed by local officials and religious leaders. The removal of crosses from churches in Wenzhou is a testament to this. Because of the government's unexpectedly willful attacks against Christianity, the suspicions and hostility of many believers toward the party-state have deepened. Many Christian groups resist joining patriotic associations and building relationships with governments because remaining unregistered provides an optimal degree of religious freedom. The dynamics of the church–state relationship are complicated. Currently, what the Xi administration actively attempts to undertake and passively allows seems to be changing the dynamics from previous phases. Whether the church–state relationship in China evolves into a new pattern remains to be seen.

Note

1. See the document online at the CCP Important News and Archive database, http://cpc.people.com.cn/BIG5/64184/64186/66685/4494217.html (accessed May 9, 2015). No longer active ("403 Forbidden") as of December 2, 2019.

References

BBC. 2014. "Chinese Religion Chief Says to Resist Christianity Infiltration into China." BBC, December 25. https://www.bbc.com/zhongwen/trad/china/2014/12/141225 _china_christmas_ban.

———. 2015. "Yu Zhengsheng: Ensuring Leadership for Patriotism and Patriotic People." BBC, January 31. https://www.bbc.com/zhongwen/trad/china/2015/01/150131 _china_church_policy.

Borchert, Thomas. 2005. "Of Temples and Tourists: The Effects of the Tourist Political Economy on a Minority Buddhist Community in Southwest China." In State, Market and Religions in Chinese Societies, edited by F. Yang and J. Tamney, 87–112. Boston: Brill.

Cao, Nanlai. 2007. "Christian Entrepreneurs and the Post-Mao State: An Ethnographic Account of Church–State Relations in China's Economic Transition." Sociology of Religion 68.1: 45–66.

Chang, Yi-zhen. 2004. "Seeking the Common Ground: A Study of 'Theology and Thought Construction Movement' of China Three-Self Church." MA thesis, Chinese Evangelical Seminary.

Christian Solidarity Worldwide (CSW). 2019. "Zhejiang Church Demolitions: Timeline of Events." CSW. http://www.csw.org.uk/zhejiangtimeline.

Fan, Guangchun. 2012. "Urban Daoism, Commodity Markets, and Tourism: The Restoration of the Xi'an City God Temple." In Daoism in the Twentieth Century, edited by D. Palmer and X. Liu, 108–20. Berkeley: University of California Press.

Huang, Jianbo, and Fenggang Yang. 2005. "The Cross Faces the Loudspeakers: A Village Church Preserves under the State Power." In State, Market and Religions in Chinese Societies, edited by F. Yang and J. Tamney, 41–62. Boston: Brill.

Huang, Ke-hsien. 2014. "Dyadic Nexus Fighting Two-Front Battles: A Study of the Micro-Level Process of Religion–State Relations in Contemporary China." Journal for the Scientific Study of Religion 53.4: 706–21.

———. 2018. "Restoring Religion through Collective Memory: How Chinese Pentecostals Engage in Mnemonic Practices after the Cultural Revolution." *Social Compass* 65.1: 79–96.

Ji, Zhe. 2015. "Secularization without Secularism: The Political-Religious Configuration of Post-89 China." In *Atheist Secularism and Its Discontents: A Comparative Study of Religion and Communism in Eurasia*, edited by Tam T. T. Ngo and Justine Buck Quijada, 92–111. New York: Palgrave Macmillan.

Jiang, Yennan. 2015. "Zhejiang chai shizijia fengbao buxi" (The storm of tearing down crosses has not ceased). *Yazhou Zhoukan* 29.7. http://www.yzzk.com/cfm/blogger3.cfm ?id=1423109005147&author=%E6%B1%9F%E9%9B%81%E5%8D%97.

Kaiman, Jonathan. 2015. "Communist Party Bans Believers in Province of 'China's Jerusalem.'" *Guardian*, February 2. https://www.theguardian.com/world/2015/feb/02 /chinese-communist-party-officials-crack-down-believers.

Kuo, Cheng-tian. 2011. "Chinese Religious Reform." *Asian Survey* 51.6: 1042–64.

Laliberté, A. 2011. "Religion and the State in China: The Limits of Institutionalization." *Journal of Current Chinese Affairs* 40.2: 3–15.

Lang, Graeme, Selina Chan, and Lars Ragvald. 2005. "Temples and the Religious Economy." In *State, Market and Religions in Chinese Societies*, edited by F. Yang and J. Tamney, 149–80. Boston: Brill.

Leung, Beatrice. 2005. "China's Religious Freedom Policy: The Art of Managing Religious Activity." *China Quarterly* 184: 894–913.

Long, Dan. 2015. "2014 Saw Worst Persecution of Chinese Christians in a Generation." *La Croix International*, January 6. https://international.la-croix.com/news/2014-saw -worst-persecution-of-chinese-christians-in-a-generation/573#.

Madsen, Richard. 2009. "Back to the Future: Pre-Modern Religious Policy in Post-Secular China." Foreign Policy Research Institute. http://www.fpri.org/articles/2009 /03/back-future-pre-modern-religious-policy-post-secular-china.

———. 2014. "From Socialist Ideology to Cultural Heritage: The Changing Basis of Legitimacy in the People's Republic of China." *Anthropology and Medicine* 21.1: 58–70.

New York Times. 2014. "'Three Reforms and One Demolition' Implementation Plan for Disposal of Religious Illegal Buildings 2013." *New York Times*, May 30. https://cn .nytimes.com/china/20140530/cc30document/zh-hant/.

Qu, Hong. 2011. "Religious Policy in the People's Republic of China: An Alternative Perspective." *Journal of Contemporary China* 20.70: 433–48.

Reuters. 2014. "China's Xi Calls for Tighter Ideological Control in Universities." Reuters, December 29. https://www.reuters.com/article/us-china-universities/chinas-xi-calls -for-tighter-ideological-control-in-universities-idUSKBN0K70TI20141229.

Sina.com.cn. 2011. "Zhonggong zhongyang guanyu shenhua wenhua tizhi gaige de jueding" (Decision of the CCP Central Committee on deepening reform of the cultural system). Sina.com.cn, October 26. http://news.sina.com.cn/c/2011-10-26/001923361344.shtml.

Tianfeng Editor. 2012. "Zhuanjia xuezhe tantao 'jidujiao zhongguohua'" (Experts and scholars discussing "Sinicization of Christianity"). *Tianfeng yuekan* (Tianfeng Monthly Magazine), June: 36–37.

Tsai, Kellee S. 2002. *Back-Alley Banking: Private Entrepreneurs in China.* Ithaca, NY: Cornell University Press.

————. 2007. *Capitalism without Democracy: The Private Sector in Contemporary China*. Ithaca, NY: Cornell University Press.

Unruh, Bob. 2015. "Sentencing of Christians Explodes 10,000% in China." *WND*, April 25. https://www.wnd.com/2015/04/sentencing-of-christians-explodes-10000-in -china/.

Vala, Carsten T. 2009. "Pathways to the Pulpit: Leadership Training in 'Patriotic' and Unregistered Chinese Protestant Churches." In *Making Religion, Making the State*, edited by Y. Ashiwa and D. Wank, 96–125. Stanford, CA: Stanford University Press.

Wielander, Gerda. 2009. "Protestant and Online: The Case of Aiyan." *China Quarterly* 197: 165–82.

Xiao, Hong. 2004. "Ruhe zhengque kandai zhongguo de zongjiao zhengce" (How are Chinese religious policies understood correctly?). *Zhongguo zongjiao* (Religion in China) 5: 57–59.

Yang, Fenggang. 2012. *Religion in China: Survival and Revival under Communist Rule*. Oxford: Oxford University Press.

————. 2013. "Research Agenda on Religious Freedom in China." *Review of Faith and International Affairs* 11.2: 6–17.

————. 2014. "What about China? Religious Vitality in the Most Secular and Rapidly Modernizing Society." *Sociology of Religion* 75.4: 564–78. doi:10.1093/socrel/sru062.

Yang, Kaile. 2012. "Basic Principles for Managing Privately Set-up Christian Meeting Sites." *Chinese Law and Religion Monitor* 8.1: 77–95.

EPILOGUE

China's (R)evolutionary Governance and the COVID-19 Crisis

Elizabeth J. Perry

The COVID-19 pandemic underscores the urgency of an informed inquiry into Chinese governance practices. Although it is too soon to reach a definitive conclusion on China's handling of the crisis, initial contradictory assessments indicate the high stakes—political and academic—riding on the issue. Detractors chastise the PRC for a lack of government transparency and accountability that allowed a local contagion to escalate into a global pandemic (Jaros 2020). Defenders commend the government for imposing the largest and longest quarantine lockdown in history, a show of strength that slowed the spread of the virus and bought valuable time for the rest of the world (Joseph and Theilking 2020). These competing portraits are both grounded in fact, but they neglect key elements of China's authoritarian governance.

As the illuminating chapters in this volume make clear, a complete account of governance in the People's Republic must include a crucial role for society. This insight is in line with recent comparative theory, prompted by an awareness that policy formulation and implementation often occur outside the formal chain of government institutions. The *Handbook on Theories of Governance* defines governance as "the interactive processes through which society and the economy are steered toward collectively negotiated objectives" (Ansell and Torfing 2016, 4). The emphasis on state–society interaction may seem obvious enough in the case of democracies, where the roles of civil society and civic engagement in "making democracy work" have been recognized for some time (Putnam 1993). As this volume points out, societal participation and pressure are also central to governance practices in authoritarian systems such as China. In the case of COVID-19, information suppression by authorities in Wuhan and Beijing would probably never have come to light without the courageous revelations of Dr. Li Wenliang and his followers on social media. At the same time, the impressive lockdown of an entire metropolis (and the surrounding province) could not have been accomplished without the cooperation of millions of ordinary citizens. In other words, Chinese society plays a major part in subverting and sustaining the state's authoritarian governance.

Another contribution of this volume is its insistence that neither state nor society remains constant or consistent in its objectives or operations. Attitudes and actions by citizens and officials alike are subject to dramatic change in reaction to each other as well as in response to new circumstances. A Chinese public that was initially angered by the state's cover-up attempts and alienated by its heavy-handed quarantine restrictions could turn sympathetic and supportive once the strong-arm approach seemed to be working to control the epidemic. The shift in domestic public opinion was helped by the swiftly moving international scene, as Western populations from Italy to the United States succumbed to the deadly virus. Increased citizen cooperation in turn allowed the Chinese state to relax some of its more draconian measures in favor of greater reliance on voluntary compliance. A crisis that had once looked like China's "Chernobyl moment" now seemed as likely to contribute to regime legitimacy as to regime collapse (Rithmire and Han 2020).

Terrible though it is, the challenge that COVID-19 has posed to all countries—authoritarian and democratic alike—offers an unusually illuminating natural experiment for investigating the sources of effective governance. Standard political science explanations focused on regime type offer limited insight for this critical investigation (Duara and Perry 2018). Although some of the most impressive national responses have come from democracies (e.g., New Zealand, Germany, South Korea, and Taiwan), the world's flagship democracies—the United States and the United Kingdom—have fallen tragically short. Among authoritarian regimes, the record is decidedly mixed. Vietnam seems to have done a remarkable job of containing the virus, whereas Russia presents a much bleaker picture—although the final prognosis for any individual country remains to be seen. Future waves of contagion loom on the horizon, and the long-term impact on gross domestic product and unemployment will become evident over time. But indications are that regime type provides minimal leverage in accounting for the variation in epidemiological and economic outcomes. As noted in the introductory chapter, numerous adjectives have been coined to qualify the nature of authoritarianism and democracy because of the bluntness of these dichotomous concepts.

More revealing than regime type as an explanation for varying responses to COVID-19 is a factor that has fallen out of favor among political scientists in recent decades: political leadership, a key variable in the perception and execution of state strategies. Countries whose national leaders managed to convey a consistently reassuring sense of resolution, compassion, and need for public cooperation in the face of crisis fared better than those whose leaders withdrew, vacillated, or downplayed the seriousness of the emergency. Leaders who prioritized the advice of public health experts inside and outside of the government performed better than those who privileged political or economic calculations. Gender may have helped shape such differences in leadership style, with countries led by women—Angela Merkel in Germany, Jacinda Ardern in New Zealand, and Tsai Ing-wen in Taiwan—experiencing unusually positive outcomes. Countries led by "macho" populists hostile to scientific authority—Donald Trump in the United States, Boris Johnson in the United Kingdom, Vladimir Putin in Russia, and Jair Bolsonaro in Brazil—delivered dismal results.

In China, Xi Jinping's initial reaction did not inspire confidence. As public anxiety mounted in the wake of the Wuhan outbreak, President Xi remained conspicuously quiet, deputizing Premier Li Keqiang to take responsibility for the crisis response. When popular dismay at Xi's absence exploded on social media, he obviously realized that a more visible and forceful presence would be required. Referencing the legacy of the Chinese Communist Revolution, Xi proclaimed a "people's war" against the virus in which he assumed the prominent role of commander. Once the situation on the ground was under control, Xi made a well-publicized inspection tour to the "front line of battle" to offer personal condolences to the people of Wuhan. The radical makeover of leadership style—from reticent onlooker to revolutionary battle commander—was apparently welcomed by many citizens willing to forgive initial missteps in exchange for clear and forceful top-down direction (Huang 2020). In the language of this volume's analytical framework, an initially "hard" state strategy of denial followed by nearly total lockdown gradually softened, encouraging society to become more accommodating in return. This dynamic of (reflexive) state repression yielding to episodes of engagement with society is illustrated in preceding chapters in the cases of the "rights defense" (*weiquan* 维权) movement (chapter 5), HIV/AIDS governance (chapter 6), anti-incineration protests (chapter 7), women and LGBT rights activists (chapter 11), and legitimation of Mazu belief (chapter 12). At the central or local levels, political leadership was pivotal for responding to societal demands.

Attention to leadership, while undertheorized in the political science literature, is a well-recognized feature of China's authoritarian governance. To that end, the Central Organization Department of the Communist Party has developed detailed metrics and procedures for annual performance reviews of cadres at all levels (Ang 2016, 105–25; Edin 2003). Officials under consideration for transfer or promotion are subject to more comprehensive evaluations that include annual performance results and an assessment of underlying leadership style, gleaned from interviews with colleagues, public opinion polls, and even psychological tests (Jiang and Luo 2019). Latent keyword analysis of internal leadership evaluations has identified two distinct yet complementary styles—which one could characterize as "hard" and "soft"—among those selected for top party posts. On one hand is "an assertive, autocratic style that focuses on centralized decision-making and efficient execution"; and on the other hand is "a collegial, democratic style that respects dissent and fosters intra-elite collaboration" (Jiang and Luo 2019, 2). In 2007, when Xi Jinping was appointed Party Secretary of Shanghai, his work style was deemed to be "pragmatic, cautious, low-key and collegial," traits that would help him rise to the pinnacle of the Party hierarchy (Jiang and Luo 2019, 12). Once in command as General Secretary, Xi showed himself capable of pivoting to a more muscular, dictatorial approach when the situation seemed to demand it.

In using martial rhetoric drawn from the Chinese revolution, Xi's belated "hard" line signaled that henceforth the fight against COVID-19 would be conducted as a "mass campaign" (*qunzhong yundong* 群众运动)

in the Maoist tradition of governance (Rithmire and Han 2020). The mass campaigns for which Mao's China was famed—stretching from Land Reform and Thought Reform through the Great Leap Forward and the Cultural Revolution—had their historical origins in the Chinese Communist Revolution that predated the founding of the People's Republic (Bennett 1976; Cell 1977; Kelkar 1978). Over the ensuing decades, this revolutionary mode of governance was repurposed to serve a wide range of developmental and disciplinary goals. Although campaigns could be credited with impressive achievements in areas such as water conservancy, mass literacy, and public health, they also incurred substantial costs in terms of quality, legality, and sustainability (Oksenberg 1973).

The inherently coercive and disruptive nature of mass campaigns led Deng Xiaoping to declare an end to them soon after Mao's death; in fact, however, campaign-style governance (in a somewhat modified form) remained a distinguishing feature of policy implementation in the PRC (Perry 2011). In the 1980s and 1990s, for example, the one-child policy was implemented in campaign fashion (White 2006). In the 2000s, the New Socialist Countryside continued the pattern (Looney 2020, 117–54). More recently, Xi Jinping's signature initiatives—anticorruption and precision poverty alleviation—have also been conducted as state-mobilized campaigns, complete with work teams and inspection teams dispatched by higher levels of party and government to the grassroots to ignite mass activism and enlist mass supervision. Campaigns targeting "evil cults" and "undesirable religion" (including Christianity) followed similar suit in various localities, as discussed in chapter 13.

In framing the response to COVID-19 as a "people's war," Xi perpetuates a familiar pattern of public health campaigns that can be traced back to the earliest years of the People's Republic (Huang 2013, chap. 2). In 1952, at the height of the Korean War, China launched the first in what became a continuing series of so-called Patriotic Health Campaigns (*aiguo weisheng yundong* 爱国卫生运动). Conducted as battles to immunize the body politic against disease, these mass campaigns were generated by international and internal concerns. In the 1952 campaign, nearly five million Chinese were inoculated with antiplague vaccine within two weeks in response to what the government claimed were strange insects being dropped over Chinese territory by US warplanes (Endicott 1998). Soon the campaign expanded into a comprehensive public health effort that mobilized ordinary citizens to improve personal hygiene, eliminate rodents and other pests, and sanitize community facilities (Rogaski 2002). In the city of Nanjing, for example, the 1952 mass movement was carried out by a combination of youth health shock brigades (*qingnian weisheng tujidui* 青年卫生突击队) organized by factories; mosquito and housefly catching teams (*buwenbuyingdui* 捕蚊捕蝇队) dispatched by neighborhoods; and disease prevention teams (*fangyidui* 防疫队) from hospitals (Nanjing Bureau of Public Health 1991). In subsequent years, Patriotic Health Campaigns occurred frequently in response to chronic and critical public health challenges. In spring 1989, the State Council designated April as "Patriotic Health Month." For more than thirty years since, every April has seen the unfolding of a large-scale state-sponsored mass effort to improve national health and hygiene. This annual event provides a mundane mobilization infrastructure that can be readily activated and expanded at moments of crisis.

In May 2003, the SARS epidemic prompted the Hu Jintao–Wen Jiabao regime to declare all-out "people's war" on the SARS virus as an extension of the previous month's Patriotic Health Campaign. As Patricia Thornton observes, China's response to SARS replicated a Maoist pattern of revolutionary campaign governance that worked to centralize political power while targeting certain elements of society for heightened surveillance and control. "Campaign-style grassroots mobilization combined with increased application of coercive measures against target populations defined the 'people's war against SARS' in a manner that the Great Helmsman himself would have found familiar" (Thornton 2009, 48). In Mao's day, the designated victims of mass campaigns had been "class enemies," such as landlords, capitalists, and "rightists," but in the people's wars against SARS and COVID-19, the targets have included not only the disease but also those blamed for its transmission. The harsh treatment experienced in 2020 by the citizens of Wuhan, and the even harsher treatment suffered by those of African ancestry living in Guangzhou, are symptomatic of the iron-fisted mechanisms that remain integral to this revolutionary mode of governance. Despite the introduction of cutting-edge technologies (e.g., contact tracing by QR codes on cell phones) that were beyond imagination in Mao's day, the revolutionary roots of Xi's people's war on COVID-19 remain clearly visible.

As Kellee Tsai notes in her comprehensive introduction to this volume, analysts of politics in post-Mao China have spawned a vibrant cottage industry of "authoritarianism with adjectives." Seeking to take account of the bewildering complexity and dynamism of state–society relations in the era of "reform and opening," scholars have turned to models of evolution and coevolution to emphasize that governance in contemporary China, in Yuen Yuen Ang's words, is composed of "many moving parts that interact with one another and change together, triggering outcomes that cannot be precisely controlled or predicted in advance" (Ang 2016, 10). Or, as Vivienne Shue and Patricia Thornton (2017, 13–14) put it, "We require a new metaphor, or frame for analysis capable of capturing incremental factors and processes . . . an interlaced modeling of the multiple directions of flow in patterns of political evolution over long periods of time."

The chapters gathered here graphically illustrate how governance practices in contemporary China are indeed connected, contingent, cumulative, yet changeable. Moreover, the post-Mao era has been marked by the entrance of a multitude of new actors to the policy process: nongovernmental organizations, investigative journalists, netizens, business lobbies, and more (Kennedy 2008; Mertha 2008; Yang 2011). But in labeling this development an *evolutionary* process, we should not lose sight of the fact that baked into the Chinese Communist Party's DNA is its *revolutionary* heritage. No less an authority than Xi Jinping has argued forcefully against dividing the history of the PRC into Mao and post-Mao periods (MacFarquhar 2018). Enjoining his comrades never to forget the party's original mission (*buwang chuxin, laoji shiming* 不忘初心，牢记使命), Xi repeatedly returns to the revolutionary past to legitimate current operations. To be sure, the CCP from revolutionary days to the present has shown remarkable flexibility with respect to a wide array of ever-changing challenges (Heilmann and Perry 2011). Yet this adaptability should not be taken to mean that the PRC has gradually evolved into a new, advanced species of authoritarianism that is no longer recognizable as a Leninist party-state.

Policy flux attributable to the intertwined hard and soft strategies of Chinese state and society recalls the cycle of *fang-shou* (放收) that Mao invoked in describing the shift from the "loosening" of the Hundred Flowers Movement to the "tightening" of the Anti-Rightist Campaign in 1956–57 (Baum 1994, 5–12; Shambaugh 2018, 98–99). Drawing the comparison between then and now by no means denies that governance practices have changed profoundly since Mao's day. Rather, it reminds us that "evolutionary" governance in reform-era China still bears the (often painful) stigmata of its revolutionary progenitor. The influence of this complicated ancestry may not always be obvious in the quotidian state–society interactions that animate the very informative case studies in this volume. As these cases convincingly demonstrate, patterns of governance in issue areas such as home ownership, environmental pollution, labor rights, domestic violence, and religious observance have evolved over decades of sometimes contentious and sometimes cooperative collective action. Yet at moments of perceived regime crisis (the Tiananmen uprising in 1989, the SARS epidemic in 2003, and the COVID-19 pandemic in 2020), the PRC falls back on Mao's revolutionary playbook for strategic guidance. Whether we judge China's response to this latest crisis in a more favorable or unfavorable light, it cannot be gainsaid that the continuing hold of revolutionary modes of governance must figure in our assessment.

References

Ang, Yuen Yuen. 2016. *How China Escaped the Poverty Trap*. Ithaca, NY: Cornell University Press.

Ansell, Christopher, and Jacob Torfing. 2016. "Introduction." In *Handbook on Theories of Governance*, edited by Christopher Ansell and Jacob Torfing, 1–16. Cheltenham: Edward Elgar.

Baum, Richard. 1994. *Burying Mao: Chinese Politics in the Age of Deng Xiaoping*. Princeton, NJ: Princeton University Press.

Bennett, Gordon. 1976. *Yundong: Mass Campaigns in Chinese Communist Leadership*. Berkeley: Center for Chinese Studies, University of California.

Cell, Charles P. 1977. *Revolution at Work: Mobilization Campaigns in China*. New York: Academic Press.

Duara, Prasenjit, and Elizabeth J. Perry, eds. 2018. *Beyond Regimes: China and India Compared*. Cambridge, MA: Harvard University Press.

Edin, Maria. 2003. "State Capacity and Local Agent Control in China." *China Quarterly* 173: 35–52.

Endicott, Stephen Lyon. 1998. *The United States and Biological Warfare: Secrets from the Early Cold War and Korea*. Bloomington: Indiana University Press.

Heilmann, Sebastian, and Elizabeth J. Perry. 2011. "Embracing Uncertainty: Guerrilla Policy Style and Adaptive Governance in China." In *Mao's Invisible Hand: Political Foundations of Adaptive Governance in China*, edited by Sebastian Heilmann and Elizabeth J. Perry, 1–29. Cambridge, MA: Harvard University Press.

Huang, Yanzhong. 2013. *Governing Health in Contemporary China*. New York: Routledge.

———. 2020. "Xi Jinping Won the Coronavirus Crisis: How China Made the Most of the Pandemic it Unleashed." *Foreign Affairs* (May/June), https://www.foreignaffairs.com/articles/china/2020-04-13/xi-jinping-won-coronavirus-crisis.

Jaros, Kyle. 2020. "China's Early COVID-19 Missteps Have an All-Too-Mundane Explanation: How Intergovernmental Dynamics Influenced the Coronavirus Outbreak in China." *Diplomat*, April 9.

Jiang, Junyan, and Zhaotian Luo. 2019. "Leadership Styles and Political Survival of Chinese Communist Party Elites." Available at SSRN, https://papers.ssrn.com/sol3/papers.cfm?abstract_id=3329665.

Joseph, Andrew, and Megan Thielking. 2020. "WHO Praises China's Response to Coronavirus." *STAT*, January 29.

Kelkar, Govind S. 1978. "The Chinese Experience of Political Campaigns and Mass Mobilization." *Social Scientist* 7.5: 45–57.

Kennedy, Scott. 2008. *The Business of Lobbying in China*. Cambridge, MA: Harvard University Press.

Looney, Kristen E. 2020. *Mobilizing for Development: The Modernization of Rural East Asia*. Ithaca, NY: Cornell University Press.

MacFarquhar, Roderick. 2018. "Does Mao Still Matter?" In *The China Questions: Critical Insights into a Rising Power*, edited by Jennifer Rudolph and Michael Szonyi, 26–32. Cambridge, MA: Harvard University Press.

Mertha, Andrew. 2008. *China's Water Warriors: Citizen Activism and Policy Change*. Ithaca, NY: Cornell University Press.

Nanjing Bureau of Public Health, ed. 1991. [Nanjing Patriotic Health Campaign Gazetteer] 南京爱国卫生运动志. Beijing: China Medical Science and Technology Press.

Oksenberg, Michel, ed. 1973. *China's Developmental Experience*. New York: Praeger.

Perry, Elizabeth J. 2011. "From Mass Campaigns to Managed Campaigns: 'Constructing a New Socialist Countryside.'" In *Mao's Invisible Hand: Political Foundations of Adaptive Governance in China*, edited by Sebastian Heilmann and Elizabeth J. Perry, 30–61. Cambridge, MA: Harvard University Press.

Putnam, Robert D. 1993. *Making Democracy Work: Civic Traditions in Modern Italy*. Princeton, NJ: Princeton University Press.

Rithmire, Meg, and Courtney Han. 2020. *China's Management of COVID-19: People's War or Chernobyl Moment?* Harvard Business School, Case Study no. 720-035.

Rogaski, Ruth. 2002. "Nature, Annihilation and Modernity: China's Korean War Germ-Warfare Experience Reconsidered." *Journal of Asian Studies* 61.2: 381–415.

Shambaugh, David. 2018. *China's Future*. Cambridge: Polity Press.

Shue, Vivienne, and Patricia M. Thornton. 2017. "Introduction: Beyond Implicit Dichotomies and Limited Models of Change in China." In *To Govern China: Evolving*

Practices of Power, edited by Vivienne Shue and Patricia M. Thornton, 1–26. Cambridge: Cambridge University Press.

Thornton, Patricia M. 2009. "Crisis and Governance: SARS and the Resilience of the Chinese Body Politic." *China Journal* 61: 24–48.

White, Tyrene. 2006. *China's Longest Campaign: Birth Planning in the People's Republic, 1949–2005*. Ithaca, NY: Cornell University Press.

Yang, Guobin. 2011. *The Power of the Internet in China: Citizen Activism Online*. New York: Columbia University Press.

Harvard Contemporary China Series
(*out-of-print)